Praise fc

M000267864

Engaging Extremists
Trade-Offs, Timing, and Diplomacy

"Negotiating with terrorists is not for the faint-hearted. States face political and practical risks in engaging with extremists whose aims may be quite incompatible with the interests of the larger society and its government. The "bad guys" also risk delegitimizing their cause. Even the mediators face dangers in facilitating negotiations. But many intractable conflicts have ended only when parties overcame their mistrust (if not disgust). I. William Zartman and Guy Olivier Faure have assembled a fine group of scholars to parse the when, how, and why of engaging with terrorists. They deepen our understanding of what conditions need to be present for such a process to be productive—such as when the "absoluteness" of the terrorists' position begins to give way to a more moderate approach, when states are willing to acknowledge underlying causes of the grievance or prepare to offer something in return for such moderation. This is a serious and useful collection of great value to diplomats and scholars and another important contribution to the study of peace by USIP."

—Ellen Laipson, The Henry L. Stimson Center

"Bill Zartman and Guy Faure have done a great service by producing this long-needed study. Whether one agrees with the analysis or not, the authors raise issues which policymakers ought to consider if we are to succeed in combating terrorism."

—Andrew S. Natsios, Georgetown University

"*Engaging Extremists* is an excellent application of theory and historical experience to a topic that has received insufficient attention. Dealing with extremist groups is too often oversimplified as a task of stamping out incorrigibles. This volume explores the actual complexity of the subject with clarity and empirical richness. It is an outstanding guide for policymakers in deciding when and how to use engagement effectively while avoiding the pitfalls."

—Paul R. Pillar, Georgetown University

"This is a fine scholarly study on an important issue of our time. This well-written volume examines negotiation and engagement between states and terrorist organizations, and underscores well the difficulties of mediation in cases of insurgency."

—Bruce Riedel, senior fellow in the Saban Center at
   the Brookings Institution

Engaging Extremists

Engaging Extremists

Trade-Offs, Timing, and Diplomacy

I. William Zartman and

Guy Olivier Faure,

editors

UNITED STATES INSTITUTE OF PEACE PRESS

Washington, D.C.

The views expressed in this book are those of the authors alone. They do not necessarily reflect views of the United States Institute of Peace.

UNITED STATES INSTITUTE OF PEACE
2301 Constitution Ave., NW
Washington, DC 20037
www.usip.org

First published 2011.

To request permission to photocopy or reprint materials for course use, contact the Copyright Clearance Center at www.copyright.com. For print, electronic media, and all other subsidiary rights, e-mail permissions@usip.org.

Printed in the United States of America.

The paper used in this publication meets the minimum requirements of American National Standards for Information Science—Permanence of Paper for Printed Library Materials, ANSI Z39.48-1984.

Library of Congress Cataloging-in-Publication Data

Engaging extremists : trade-offs, timing, and diplomacy / I. William Zartman and Guy Olivier Faure, editors.
    p. cm.
  Includes index.
  ISBN 978-1-60127-074-0 (pbk. : alk. paper)
  1. Terrorism—Government policy.   2. Negotiation.   3. Crisis management.
I. Zartman, I. William.   II. Faure, Guy Olivier.
  HV6431.E5465 2011
  363.325'16—dc22

                                        2010052949

To Martti Ahtisaari,
master mediator,
who brought extremists back to normal politics

Contents

PART III: CONCLUSION

Acknowledgments

We are grateful for the support of the United States Institute of Peace and the Smith Richardson Foundation for this project of the Processes of International Negotiation (PIN) Program. We are also grateful to Isabelle Talpain-Long for carefully monitoring the manuscript and to Michael Carr for his meticulous and diplomatic editing.

Introduction
Why Engage, and Why Not?

I. William Zartman and Guy Olivier Faure

Fuad Ali Saleh, a radical Islamist head of a terrorist network, is about to be judged. Victims who have survived his bomb attacks are present, among them a woman on a wheelchair and another with her face horribly distorted by an explosion. The presiding judge begins the hearing by verifying the identity of the accused.
"Your name is Fuad Ali Saleh?"
"My name is 'Death to the West!'"
(Paris: Jan. 29, 1990, the Law Court. *Le Monde 1998*)

Contrary to popular notions, negotiating with terrorist organizations is not talking with the devil. It is not soul-selling or evil pacting, nor does it require a surrender of goals and values that the parties have held dear. Rather, the challenge is one of making extremist movements negotiable. This means inducing moderation and flexibility in their demands, reshaping their ends into attainable reforms, and forcing an end to their violent means of protest while, at the same time, opening the political process to broader participation and more effective policies on the deeper problems of society and governance that underlie extremist organizations' protests. Without such movement on *both* sides, the horror of terrorism will stay with us.

But there is more. Unless the extremist movement's tactics are shown to be counterproductive, it will not abandon them. Dealing with terrorism, therefore, means keeping its violent means in check, transforming its ends from destruction to participation, and undercutting the grievances

1

on which it rides. These three elements are the ingredients of a policy of engagement. Thus, confrontation and engagement are not just polar opposites; they are the two ends of a continuum, and the elements in a causal relationship. Engagement may appear to constitute a sharp change from a policy of confrontation, but containment and isolation are the means of causing the moderation that makes the extremists engageable. Engaging extremists, as the following chapters show, works as part of a broad policy that is complex in tactics, deliberate in balance, and, ultimately, indispensable.

This policy, like any other, does not always succeed, and there are terrorist organizations beyond even its reach. These are absolute terrorist organizations (Zartman 2003). As long as the organization's ends are millennialist dreams, globalist transformations, and activated worldviews that require terrorist means, there is no point in negotiating and no hope in engaging. Such groups require contact and surveillance to detect changes in ends, means, and personnel, for the category "absolute" is an attribute, not a permanent condition. However, for an organization to become engageable, its ends as well as means—and probably its personnel—must be changeable. To cite names, this means that al-Qaeda is not considered here to be engageable, whereas Hamas is, with the more complex Taliban located somewhere in between. Others, such the Revolutionary Armed Forces of Colombia (FARC) and National Liberation Army (ELN) in Colombia, the Liberation Tigers of Tamil Eelam (LTTE) in Sri Lanka, the Coalition for the Defence of the Republic (CDR) in Rwanda, and Hezbollah in Lebanon—all identified more fully in the following chapters—may be difficult to engage but are not absolutes or intrinsically unengageable. Several chapters below deal with ways of separating engageable (contingent) terrorists from al-Qaeda absolutes, and the volume's conclusion will discuss development of criteria that help sort out possibilities in such cases.

This book concerns engagement and negotiation with political terrorist organizations, not just isolated hostage takers (Faure and Zartman 2010). Such groups include nationalist terrorist organizations, which use terrorist methods to gain self-determination and independence for their territorial claims, revolutionary terrorist organizations, which seek a change in government to accomplish deep-seated social changes, and also religious or millennialist organizations belonging to the fourth wave of modern terrorism, which seek to overthrow and replace a government they see as impious and unjust (Rapoport 2006).

Although these same organizations are also sometimes called "freedom fighters," "resistants," "national liberation movements," "holy warriors," or "martyrs," the important distinction is not whether the observer favors their cause but whether they use violent methods directly against noncombatant civilian populations for the purpose of influencing policy—essentially the U.S. and UN definition of terrorism (UNSC 2001; U.S. Code 2001). The U.S. administration currently tends to avoid the term "terrorist" and prefers "extremist." How synonymous the two terms are is a matter for a not-too-interesting debate, and they will be used more or less synonymously here. However, for the purposes of analyzing state decisions, the term "terrorist" must be accepted as meaning "any movement termed 'terrorist' by the state," since it is that designation that underlies the state's problem with engagement. Similarly, "engagement" and "negotiation" here are also used almost synonymously, although the latter refers to engagement undertaken specifically to reach an agreement.

It is more useful to see terrorism as a phase in a conflict waged by ethnic, religious, ideological, and other groups than as a distinctly separate phenomenon with no background, antecedents, or resemblances to other types and stages of identity conflicts (Zartman 2010; Anstey, Meerts, and Zartman 2011). This underlying assumption permits investigation of ends as well as means—a major theme of this book. Few terrorist conflicts start out as such. They begin with "lesser" means to the disaffected group's ends and escalate into terrorism when those earlier means do not produce progress toward the group's goals. This understanding allows the analysis to include relevant material from current understanding of other conflicts *before* they have reached the terrorist phase.

Negotiation and the broader policy of engagement, while ultimately necessary in the absence of one side's clear victory, run through enormous associated difficulties and paradoxes and depend much on timing and diplomatic skills. Engagement has its risk for both sides, which explains their reluctance to engage. Before deciding the question of *how* to engage, we must grapple with the questions that precede them: Why engage? And why not? Both sides need to weigh carefully the benefits of engagement and its possible outcomes, as well as its dangers and obstacles, against the benefits and perils of continued confrontation and isolation. The first challenge is to clarify the risks and opportunities, in order to develop guidelines for the inevitable policy choices. If engagement were an obviously good thing, there would be no need to ask why, and we could immediately jump to *how*. But engagement is a risky choice, for both sides, which explains their reluctance to engage. There are many arguments against negotiating with extremists, and many of the same arguments the state makes, the extremists can also make against negotiating with the state—a parallel that is important to understand from the state side, as Camille Pecastaing's chapter points out. That is why much of the analysis is relevant to both sides (even though readers on the state side are likely to be more numerous than those on the terrorist side). This is not to suggest that the two sides are mirror images, only that questions of engagement that are often regarded from one side only are, in fact, posed to both parties.

Thereafter, the questions of *when* and *how* come to the fore. If engagement is inevitable, why not do it early and save all those lives, including those of the many innocent civilian bystanders? Part of the answer certainly comes from the difficulty of reversing a policy commitment to confrontation, but another part comes from the need to await or create appropriate conditions for a policy shift to engagement. When these conditions, including the possibility of conducting a policy reversal, are assembled, the final issue is *how* to engage. This introduction discusses why and why not engage. *When* and *how* to engage, and the consequences, are the questions the rest of this work addresses.

Obstacles to Engagement

Just as politics is the art of the possible, negotiation is the art of compromise. The basic question, therefore, is, what does engagement between states and extremist organizations seek to obtain, and what are the chances of obtaining it? Negotiations with terrorists to end hostage crises seek, above all, to save lives, both those of the hostages and those subject to the future hostage crises that negotiation might encourage (Faure and Zartman 2010). The negotiations occur between two parties that have something to trade—hostages in exchange for something else (demands, publicity, safety)—and who are looking for a deal. Negotiations with political terrorist organizations are much broader in scope. They involve national, not just personal, security, and the fate of friends as well as enemies. Unlike negotiations with hostage takers, they do not involve parties looking for a deal, who try to define a zone of possible agreement and find appropriate terms of trade. Negotiations with political terrorist organizations seek to change the means that terrorists use but also, to some degree, the ends they pursue. If the terrorists' ends were immediately acceptable, the extreme means (terrorism) would not be necessary.

Both the state and the extremist organization face these questions. Generally, the few works on terrorist negotiations examine the state's choices, as if to assume that the terrorists are ready to negotiate if only the state will (Rubin 1990; Hughes 1990; Beyer and Bauer 2009). While this may be true for terrorists as hostage takers, it is not true at all for terrorist political organizations, which often face the same sorts of questions as do states—a point of departure for William Donohue and Moty Cristal's chapter, and of analysis for Aldo Civico's. In fact, the terrorist political organization lies midway on a continuum between the state at one end and looser rebellions and individuals such as hostage takers at the other. It usually develops an institutionalized structure, including a military and a political wing, a tax and service system, foreign diplomacy, and, often, actual territorial control (even if only at night), as well as a complex belief system. All these properties can combine to make the terrorist political organization a sort of pro-tostate, lacking only state status, as seen with FARC, the Afghan Taliban, and LTTE. "You are not dealing with a political party," declared LTTE's chief negotiator. "We have a judicial system, various structures where civilians are participating. So you have to take us seriously" (Sivaram 2006, 178). Yet the relative clarity of state-to-state negotiations, even with all the two-level international and domestic complexity that it might cover, is absent (Evans, Jacobson, and Putnam 1993).

As a result, the process of arriving at an agreement is complex, time-consuming, and frustrating, and even when the parties get there, the result is unstable, unreliable, unencompassing, and unenforceable. Negotiations with terrorist organizations are notoriously difficult, as evidenced by the long negotiations with the LTTE, described in the chapters by Kristine Höglund and by Maria Groeneveld-Savisaar and Siniša Vuković; with Colombia's ELN, described in the chapter by Aldo Civico; and with the Free Aceh Movement (GAM), the National Union for the Total Liberation of Angola (UNITA), the Sudan People's Liberation Movement/Army (SPLM/A), and the various Darfur rebel groups, among others. Indeed, "organization" is usually a misnomer. Usually there are many organizations, of unclear structure, competing with one another, riddled with factions, torn over the tactical question of whether to talk or fight (Haass and O'Sullivan 2000; Zartman and Alfredson 2010). Over these "organizations," whether territorial or millennialist, often hangs a maximalist goal sanctified by an absolute, all-justifying religious or ideological mandate. And beneath the "organization" often lie substrata of tribal, ethnic, and traditional groups and allegiances, increasingly mingled with, or replaced by, criminal elements as time goes on. The ethos of both the state's and the terrorists' mandate permits temporary agreements and justifies their rupture.

To begin with, engagement and negotiation carry with them the recognition of the terrorist organization (and, for the terrorists, the recognition of the state). Recognition confers a degree of legitimacy and status, and an implication that the party speaks for the client population it claims to represent. For the state, engagement gives the terrorist organization legitimacy that overshadows its illegitimate tactics. For the terrorists, recognition of

negotiation = legitimacy = weakens state position.

the state weakens their own claim of exclusive [1]   for the mediator, recognition of the terrorists weaken-   tions with
the terrorists' opponent (the state), a-   against
terrorist tactics. No side can expe-   goals
and claims of representation, v-   gotia-
tion. Regime change may c-   rorist
organization makes its deal wit-   derate,
but for the moment, the state m-   ...legal terrorist organization. And the mediator deal-   unsavory characters," in
President Jimmy Carter's characteris-   -ase. Since terrorist groups, like
any other rebel group, seek, above all, status and representational recognition, engagement carries them a long way toward their goal.

In sum, recognition weakens the state's position and strengthens the terrorist's—something the state does not engage in without some initial payment or expectations of a later one. Since reciprocity is the expectation, state engagement actually compromises the terrorist group as well, particularly if it has not actually beaten the state into submission. Thus, engaging extremists raises problematic implications, setting up precedents for future encounters, rewarding extremist methods, risking entrapment in a relationship that may elicit more and more concessions to reward the other side. The question of recognition of organizations termed "terrorist" paralyzed potential negotiations between the Algerian government and the Islamic Salvation Front in the early 1990s, as it had between the French government and the Algerian National Liberation Front, and also between Israel and the Palestine Liberation Organization (PLO) until 1993 and then in the next round between Israel and Hamas. Negotiations in Mozambique and South Africa in 1990–94, with the National Resistance Movement (Renamo) and the African National Congress respectively, were carried out not with the state but with the governing parties in order to avoid these problems, and led to serious regime changes.

Deeper than the problem of status is the way the two sides see each other. States (and their populations) and terrorist organizations tend to demonize the opponent (Spector 1998; Martin 2003; Faure 2007; Staub 2010). Demonization is the characterization of individuals, groups, or political bodies as evil, for purposes of justifying and making plausible an attack, whether in the form of assassination, legal action, circumscribing of political liberties, or warfare. The purpose is to facilitate killing or destroying the demonized group and to rally support for the demonizers. It is a double process, addressing first the psychological dimension, by building on the anxiety, and then the strategic dimension, by degrading the opponent to justify extreme policies against it.

Governments and media demonize the extremists by developing a Manichaean worldview with "us" facing the "Green Peril" (successor to the "Red Peril"), by defining the Quran as a "war plan against non-Muslims," by referring to Muslims as "Islamo-fascists," or, indeed, by loose use of the label "terrorist." Terrorist groups demonize their enemies in no less caricatural ways. The United States is the "Great Satan" to Iran and the "head of the snake" to al-Qaeda. Westerners are labeled *kuffar* (unbelievers, against whom strong action is encouraged), heads of moderate Arab countries such as Egypt or Jordan are "apostates," the world is in a state of *jahiliyya*, or pre-Islamic ignorance, and "unreformed" governments are "lackeys of the United States." The moral disqualification of the counterpart on both sides is used to authorize behaviors that otherwise would not be countenanced, such as terrorism and torture, or, in a negotiation, lying, tricking, manipulating, and deception. The role of a negotiator is then viewed as a way to distract the enemies while the state or organization is preparing to attack them.

Beyond their images of each other, states and terrorist organizations differ fundamentally on policy, and so engagement signals a policy compromise. Almost universally, when engagement is sought, it is the state that does the seeking and, thus, is the *demandeur*—the side with the weaker negotiating position. When the terrorist organization talks of negotiation, it means the state's surrender (sometimes total), as in Iranian president Ahmedinejad's 2005 letter to President Bush, or Osama bin Laden's 2003 offer to the United States. Terrorists are the weaker party in the conflict, who overcome their weakness with high-cost means—the use of violence against civilians—to gain a stronger position. They seek to buy compromise on policy and sometimes on the very existence of the state, using unconventional violence as currency. Thus, engagement with terrorists can be seen as both admitting compromise on policy (and on the state's existence) and accepting unconventional violence as terms of trade. Since the terrorists' goals are considered unacceptable, there is nothing to engage or negotiate.

Both sides are in the conflict to win, and attempts at conciliatory policy undermine the commitment to that effort. Even when victory is not imminent, part of a winning strategy is simply to hold out until the effects of failure sink in on the other side. Very often, victory is achieved not by a single salient battle but by showing the opponents that their tactics are unavailing. To sue for peace is to destroy this effect.

Thus, dealing with terrorists demands a major policy shift, from total confrontation to a position admitting that the terrorists are at least engageable and that there is something in their position that can serve as the basis for a negotiated compromise. They are no longer the devil, with whom one should not shake hands, or the enemy, against whom one wages a total confrontation. The same is true on the extremists' side. Of course, tactical shifts are part of any conflict, but potential damage to one's political support and career is a strong inhibitor of shifts too radical. President George W. Bush was criticized by his own supporters for his engagement, in his second term, with North Korea, a state classified as a supporter of terrorism, as President Ronald Reagan also was criticized for his constructive engagement with Angola and South Africa over Namibia. A shift to engagement may gain new allies, but it will certainly lose old support and credibility. It rarely occurs without an important change in leadership. Policy changes toward dealings with terrorists after the elections of Charles de Gaulle in France (1958), Alfredo Christiani in El Salvador (1989), and Barack Obama in the United States (2008) are examples of the latter effect.

In any case, engagement may be rejected, leaving the engaging party with a hand extended into the void, and weakened by the attempt. In fact, engagement is quite likely to be rejected initially, so the initiator will have to persist and insist, accentuating its position as the weaker *demandeur*. There are many reasons why the attempt to engage may face rejection, at least initially and possibly for a while: misperception, reactive devaluation, or issues of credibility, justice, or obligation, to name a few.[1] The party being petitioned may find it hard to believe the policy change and may suspect the change as a trick to disarm it and rearm the initiator. The new signals may be misperceived, particularly because of contradictory noise or old signals coming at the same time. The opening may be dismissed as a sign that the initiators are suffering, so why not make them suffer more? Or it may be seen as something the initiators should be doing anyhow, so let them continue to move toward surrender. Finally, there is the known psychological reaction that devalues what the other part offers, and overvalues what the perceiver offers, making satisfactory reciprocation difficult (McDermott 2009). Iran's, North Korea's, Cuba's, and Venezuela's reactions to President Obama's extended hand in 2009 are cases in point. All these are common reactions to a conciliatory move by one party in a conflict, and stand in the way of a mutually beneficial engagement and negotiation.

Nonetheless, the state, as a legally responsible organization, engages itself in a long-term contract. For many, terrorism is an economic issue, if not over a penury of resources then over control of resources: desperate at not finding satisfactory conditions for themselves, their families, and their community, terrorists take refuge in extremist demands and millennialist goals, as explored in the chapters by Zartman and Khan, Lambert, and

Donohue and Cristal. To undercut these aspirations, the engaging state must provide measures to assure a better life, lest the terrorists return to their old ways. If territorial demands are involved, the states must provide development aid and call donors' conferences to underwrite the results of the negotiations. Engagement in Palestine, Kosovo, and Mozambique, to name a few conflicts labeled "terrorist," has been expensive and not particularly satisfying to donors and recipients. Engaging terrorists is ultimately as costly as fighting them, although in different terms. If the economic issue is control rather than supply of resources, satisfaction is available only through costly high-level negotiations, as seen in the oil crisis of the mid-1970s and the associated terrorism it unleashed.

On the moral level, the terrorists' choice of means—violence against civilians—makes engagement and negotiation unethical. The very act of dealing with terrorists, particularly given the status and equality that engagement and negotiation imply, tarnishes the state, since the state is supposed to represent the highest values of legality and legitimacy. No government wants to recognize a terrorist group of extortionists, civilian killers, and suicides as a legitimate counterpart. The terrorist organization's very tactics disqualify it from the recognition, status, and credibility that negotiation confers. Politics, as noted, demands compromises, procedural as well as substantive, but dealing with terrorist organizations compromises the very nature of the state—procedurally as well as substantively.

Beyond the unethicality of dealing with terrorists is the compounded moral problem that negotiation actually encourages terrorism. President Richard Nixon's statement on hostage negotiations that "saving one life endangers hundreds" can be expanded by orders of magnitude in regard to negotiations with political terrorist organizations. It is irresponsible to let terrorists shoot their way through civilian casualties into policy decisions; rewarding their blackmail only encourages others to do the same. Repeated negotiations with Charles Taylor's National Patriotic Front of Liberia spawned new rebel movements claiming a place at the table every time talks were revived, and negotiations in Darfur and northern Pakistan have had the same effect. Thus, engaging terrorists to bring terrorism to an end carries the moral hazard of doing the reverse (Kuperman 2006).

It is also a slap to one's allies, particularly those in the conflict area. Not only does a shift to engagement alienate former domestic support, it also leaps over moderates in the region to extend a hand to their radical rivals. Not only is undercutting the moderates politically incorrect, it also risks alienating significant parts of the population whose support the state seeks. Engagement with Hamas undercuts Fatah of the PLO; engagement with Hezbollah weakens the moderate parties in Lebanon; engagement with

Euskadi Ta Askatasuna (ETA) circumvents the democratic Basque parties in Spain. Thus, engagement tends to be counterproductive, in many ways undoing the very goals it purports to achieve.

The Benefits of Engaging Terrorist Organizations

The preceding risks and objections are logically tight and telling. Yet there must be another side to the question, since engagement does occur and would not if no benefits were forthcoming. Many of these benefits accrue to both sides, providing a positive-sum outcome for engagement that itself can be useful in moderating the terrorist organization. Others fall to one side or the other, so that they are of tactical use.

The least benefit of engagement is to gain information. Public statements by terrorists, usually for propaganda purposes, are an unreliable source about what they really want, think, believe, will accept, or seek to achieve. In fact, these ideas are often very unclear in their own minds, so that a chance to articulate them can lead to more reasonable formulations and more realistic thinking. It can also raise internal doubts about the validity of arguments and beliefs, as Zartman and Khan discuss and Lambert and Goerzig show (Staub 2010). Even before any negotiations are on the horizon, contacts and talks with terrorist organizations' representatives can elicit useful information. Such talks proved effective in successful cases such as Northern Ireland, Mozambique, and Kosovo, among others (Irwin 2005; Hume 1994; Judah 2008). They can also bring out differences of opinion among the representatives, preparing the ground for internal splits, promising contacts, and appropriate tactics, as occurred with LTTE in 2005 and with FARC in 1986. Incidentally, these benefits and effects may also come to light on the government's side, sometimes in response to clarifications and differences on the terrorists' side, feeding on each other and giving rise to improved government and terrorist policy. Thus, talks can provide useful inputs into intelligence and, eventually, policy, on both sides.

Moreover, communication is a potential path to influence (Fisher, Ury, and Patton 1991). Negotiation is a mechanism for influencing other parties' decisions, and given adverse or suboptimal circumstances, negotiation may be the best, if not the only, way of avoiding an undesirable outcome. The point, therefore, is not *whether* to negotiate but *how* to negotiate creatively (Zartman 2003). A decision to negotiate does not mean accepting the other side's behavior or values—means or ends. What one must accept is that the underlying humanity deserves due process and that the desire for recognition and dignity often lies at the bottom of terrorists' needs and drives.

At the other extreme, negotiation may be a necessity, the only alternative to defeat or endless, costly conflict. Holding out may be a way to avoid giving in, but the holdout must weigh the cost of such a policy. When a stalemate hurts, it is rational for the parties to come to terms; if both are caught in the impasse, the conditions are set for negotiations to provide a way out that benefits each (Zartman 2000). This situation does not guarantee a positive result, but it does provide the minimal conditions for one. Thus, the benefits of engagement are not fixed but depend on the conditions of the conflict.

The greatest benefit of engagement is to end the conflict or, at least, its terrorist form. If the terrorists can be pulled away from their violent methods, the state can meet them by getting off its nonengagement stance. This initial exchange is the beginning of the process of further exchanges. This brings up a previous objection: that negotiating with terrorists only encourages other terrorists. But it is not the act of negotiating that encourages or discourages further terrorist blackmail; it is the terms of the negotiated agreement (Zartman 2003). If the terrorists win their goals in the negotiation process and give the state little or nothing beyond the end of conflict in exchange, others will indeed be encouraged to follow the same course. Large-scale sociopolitical movements, such as the decolonization struggle, illustrate this effect, and the numerous recent secessionist movements (e.g., in Sudan, Eritrea, Casamance, Sri Lanka, Euskadi, Kosovo, Western Sahara, Tamil Eelam, and Aceh) involve a struggle over precedent as well as the individual secession cases. The normal "deal" is abandonment of terrorist means in exchange for entry into the competitive political system, with some moderation of ends as well. This is the basis of agreements with GAM in Aceh, the PLO in Palestine, Renamo in Mozambique, UNITA in Angola, the Macedonian National Liberation Army (NLA), reconciliation groups in Afghanistan, and the Sunni Awakening groups in Iraq.

Moreover, even considering engagement brings a salutary focus to the understanding of various national issues and conflicts. The end of the Cold War has made it possible for politicians and analysts alike to examine root causes of protest movements that use terrorist methods and to recognize that, unacceptable though the methods may be, they are a symptom that something is wrong. This is not to say that their cause, any more than their methods, is "right," but only that their actions are signs of a problem that needs—and indeed cries out—to be solved. Quite often, the extremists' protest echoes widespread public sentiment, even while at the same time eliciting strong disapproval of their methods. Research shows, strikingly, that every actual or threatened electoral or nonelectoral takeover by an Islamist movement—beginning with Iran in 1979 and continuing to Algeria in 1991, Afghanistan in 1997, Somalia in 2004, Palestine in 2006, and Egypt in the 2000s—was not the result of a mass religious revival movement but a protest vote against a corrupt and incompetent government. Thus, terrorist outbreaks are warning signals of a deeper problem, and a call for governments to pay attention before it is too late.

The broadest benefit of engagement is lowered tensions as a general tone in international relations. "Reach out and understand" replaces "combat and isolate." Concrete results may be slow in appearing, but the approach puts the state on the high moral ground, gives it a positive image among the undecided populace, and ultimately sends the message that "he who is not against us is with us," rather than the reverse. In so doing, an approach of engagement can reach out as well to other states supporting the terrorists for their own purposes. To conduct operations, terrorist groups have to rely on foreign sympathy, support, and asylum. When the terrorists' base lies within a host's territory, the group is subject to the host's authority. Thus, a host with sufficient political capacity may influence a group's behavior and ability to operate (Zartman 1995; O'Brien 1996). Countries hosting or supporting terrorist groups are often labeled "rogue states." According to U.S. intelligence, seven of them—Iran, Cuba, Iraq, Libya, North Korea, Sudan, and Syria—have recently been involved in state-sponsored terrorism, covering a wide range of actions including embassy bombings, suicide missions, and hostage taking. By controlling weapons supplies, funding, and political support, states such as Iran and Syria strongly influence terrorists' ability to operate (Ranstorp and Xhudo 1994).

Reducing tensions with sponsors also serves the secondary function of improving the terrorists' credibility in negotiation, thus enabling states to expect terrorists to implement an agreement once it is reached. The likelihood of negotiation increases if terrorists are constrained by a host state that has something to gain or lose (Zartman 1992). While unconstrained terrorists may defect from agreements without cost, constrained terrorists face punishment from host states that have an interest in pursuing a peaceful settlement. Since host states can also be punished for supporting terrorists, hosts have incentives to resolve terrorist events peacefully. Such is the hope, at least, in U.S. engagement with Syria regarding the actions of Hezbollah. Thus, engagement is aimed as much at third-party states and populations as at the terrorists themselves, and it can provide a ripple effect of benefits.

To begin and pursue engagement, third-party mediation is generally necessary. This also serves to improve relations between the necessary mediator and the parties—a theme examined in the chapters by Pettyjohn, Civico, and Groeneveld-Savisaar and Vuković (Zartman 1995; Greig

2005). The importance of relations with a mediator is not to be underestimated in international politics. Mediator pressure for negotiations was a decisive element in conflicts with terrorists in Kosovo, Indonesia, Macedonia, Angola, Sudan, Mozambique, and Palestine. Even if mediator pressure to pursue negotiations fails, as it did in Sri Lanka and Colombia, the state can at least point out that it tried before returning to the "tactical alternative"—the use of force.

Engagement also provides tactical benefits. Negotiations may split the terrorists' unity or facilitate divisions already latent (Cronin 2008, 2009). When moderates in the organization see that partial gains ("half a loaf") can be made or costs lowered by coming to terms, they are encouraged to reach out to the engaging hand. Engagement frees the moderates from the constraints of internal unity under which they operated and allows them to argue that the state will meet them halfway. Extremists will continue to operate, but they will be in the minority, sidelined by the engaging movement, and can be more easily controlled, as in the case of the Jund Ansar Allah in Gaza in 2009–10, Hamas in Palestine in 1993–96, and Front Nord in Casamance in 2000–2004. There will be internal conflicts as the moderates move to pull the mantle of the movement over themselves, but the need to cover the moderates will encourage the state to move further toward them. As in most instances of negotiation, these dynamics are reciprocal, even if not necessarily equally so, and each side's need for an agreement affects where "in the middle" the outcome will be.

Or the move can strengthen the formerly dominated moderates to the point where they can pull in the extremists and draw the mantle of unity over all the factions. Such was the effect of engagement with the NLA rebels in Macedonia, bringing both the Albanian parties and the National Liberation Army together around a common moderate platform at Prizren in 2001, and of engagement with GAM in Indonesia, uniting the factions around an agreeable "half loaf" in self-government. Properly presented, engagement can show that further confrontation is pointless and that the opponents can reach their goals by other means. Terrorism is, after all, the weapon of the weak and the tactic of desperation, in the absence of success with other tactics. When the weak see how weak they really are, how their tactics are only alienating both the state and the surrounding bystanders, and that alternative tactics are open to them, they can be brought to the engagement table. Thus, engagement can encourage and facilitate the evolution of the terrorist group.

Either way, negotiation is on the path to moderation, which is, in turn, the necessary condition for engagement. The circularity is obvious: moderation is both the result of, and the requisite for, negotiation and engagement. The terrorists' willingness to negotiate is a sign of the broadening or relaxing of their tactics, as it is for the state. But the state offers engagement and negotiation (since it usually is the initiator) only when it perceives enough relaxation of means—and, possibly, of ends—to indicate further movement in the same direction. The description makes clear the delicacy of the operation: the state has to elicit indications of moderation from the terrorists and encourage them in the same process—a complicated balance analyzed in Pettyjohn's chapter. Moderation is the goal of engagement, and the major benefit to be obtained from it. It aims at producing some agreement: the renunciation of terrorist means, in exchange for some concession that the state can provide, from either its own means or its ends.

When and How to Engage

The reasons against engagement outnumber the reasons for, but they do not outweigh them. Taken together, the reasons for and against indicate two things: that engagement and negotiation are difficult, risky challenges and that their opportuneness depends on evolving circumstances. The difficulty and the risk are clearly shown by the reasons not to engage and by the problems to surmount before negotiations can succeed. The evolving circumstances need further elaboration, for they indicate why negotiations are unlikely to be an opening strategy yet are bound to be a concluding strategy.

It is often true that the whole terrorist challenge might be prevented if original grievances had been handled by "normal politics" in the petition phase, although in many cases this is a frivolous suggestion: either the original grievances are beyond human capacity to meet (e.g., immediate economic development, total government benevolence, or restoration of the Golden Caliphate), or they are high goals, not to be met lightly and worth fighting for (e.g., independence or total revamping of the sociopolitical system). So the combat begins with the means at hand. Terrorism, like any other type of internal rebellion, works both to equalize power and to contest power, seeking desperately to overcome the power asymmetry enjoyed by the state. And so the fight goes, to victory/defeat, continued escalating confrontation, or stalemate—the only possible outcomes. In the absence of the first outcome, the two parties edge warily toward the realization that engagement is the only alternative, that there are other ways to achieve goals than by terrorism, that half a loaf now is indeed available.[2] There are ripe moments for engagement as for any other negotiatory path. The challenge is to sense them and seize them (Zartman and de Soto 2010).

In rational terms, the bargaining dynamics are simple and straightforward. The state wants the extremists to give up their terrorist means, but in exchange for what? Ultimately, for a better chance by using other, "lesser" means to get less of what they had hoped to get. Those terms are scarcely appealing *unless* a new condition is introduced: the impossibility of getting all they want by terrorist tactics. This means that the possibility for the extremists to achieve their current goals must be convincingly blocked, and also that the possibility of achieving at least something of those goals by alternative means must be convincingly open. Any other terms are of too little appeal to bring the parties to the table. Engagement and negotiation are about both means and ends and about impossibilities and possibilities. Civico and Groeneveld-Savisaar and Vuković lay out the drama and disappointments of this equation; Goerzig shows the effects of constrained options.

The following nine chapters address this challenge from various angles. They contain a mixture of conceptual discussions illustrated by case analyses. The cases have been chosen from salient conflicts of the moment, as particularly apt examples of points laid out in the conceptual discussions and as generators themselves of conceptual lessons and insights, on which original research could be conducted. The chapters are divided into questions of "when" and of "how." Admittedly, the two aspects are inherently inseparable and mutually dependent: "when" conditions "how," and "how" depends on "when" in the life of the terrorist phase of the conflict. So the distinction is a matter of emphasis. Logically, "when" comes first, in part I, as an important factor in conditioning appropriate ways of engagement. The first two chapters examine the life cycle of terrorism in order to identify times and tactics for engagement. The chapter by Zartman and Khan examines the life cycle of terrorists into an extremist group, evaluating ways that engagement and negotiation can be conducted at various moments—within the broad sociopolitical context, on the individual's path from context to group membership, with and within the group, and on the path to violence and beyond. To interrupt the cycle that leads to violence, there must be alternatives appropriate to the particular moment. The chapter by Donohue and Cristal views terrorism's life cycle as that of an organization, with openings for negotiation and engagement as the organization begins, matures, and declines. Again, from a different angle, it identifies appropriate times and tactics to take advantage of the terrorist organization's cycle.

The next two chapters illustrate some of these moments via two successful experiments in engaging potential terrorists and winning them away from tactics of violence. Robert Lambert describes the work of the Muslim Contact Unit in London, engaging the help of the Salafi community to counter recruiting tactics of extremists. By taking on existing groups and establishing a counterextremist presence, alternative teams were able to split al-Qaeda groups, win followers away from radical spiritual leaders, and delegitimize extremist means and, to some extent, extremist ends. Two other chapters, by Maria Groeneveld-Savisaar and Siniša Vuković and by Stacie Pettyjohn, examine attempts at engagement in Sri Lanka and in terrorist conflicts in the Middle East, South Africa, and Northern Ireland, to identify the conditions necessary for a powerful third party such as the United States to engage as a mediator in other states' terrorism problems. The Sri Lankan government and LTTE conducted on-again, off-again negotiations under international mediation, in which both sides underwent deep splits over the engagement issue. As a result, neither side was fully committed to the process, and the powerful mediator was not deeply enough engaged to press them to overcome their hesitations. When negotiations collapsed, the government dropped all pretense and wiped out the LTTE. On the other hand, at times when the third party felt its own interests in danger and a more moderate alternative to the terrorist organization was not available, engagement and mediation were pursued, often with positive results. The answer depends on the degree of vital interest by the third party, the degree of moderation shown by the terrorist organization, and the absence of more moderate alternatives, which in turn relates to the stage of organizational life, discussed in the Donohue-Cristal chapter.

Part II deals with the question of "how" in its own terms, independently of "when." Camille Pecastaing presents terrorism as a confrontation with the state over the grievances felt by the population, showing how a bottom-up strategy is best suited for bridging the gap, handling grievances, and reducing violent protest tactics. Two additional chapters examine ways of engaging extremists through delegitimization and suspension of violence and through isolation. Carolin Goerzig shows how the Islamic Society (Gama'a Islamiya) in Egypt examined its beliefs while in jail for terrorist assassinations (of tourists and President Sadat), to find that they did not justify killing in the name of Islam—a striking case of "burnout, . . . declining commitment [and] doctrinal debates" (Ross and Gurr 1989, 409). Kristine Höglund examines such measures as cease-fires as a step in incremental engagement, and banning as a way of isolating and weakening the extremists. She shows that both tactics can have positive effects on the process of engagement but can also make engagement more difficult. Finally, Aldo Civico illustrates the difficulties in pursuing a consistent policy of unmediated negotiation—in this case, the nation of Colombia and the terrorist organization ELN. During its four decades of protest and revolt, ELN, one of several revolutionary terrorist movements in Colombia, underwent a significant moderation, both in its terrorist means and in its process of engagement. But international politics over mediation, and the state's insistence on negotiating means only, without considering the protest's deeper causes, sank the negotiations.

The concluding chapter presents some remaining conundrums regarding talking versus negotiating, ends versus means, absolutes versus contingents, moderation as a process versus as a condition, and extremist divisions versus unity. It ends with some analytical insights into ways of moving the engagement process ahead. States and terrorists do negotiate and engage on occasion. Understanding the nature of those occasions can bring benefits that make the state more effective, and extremism and terrorism unnecessary.

Notes

1. I am grateful to Anthony Wanis-St. John for his suggestions.
2. It has been indicated elsewhere that there are two types of stalemate: the mutually hurting stalemate of ripeness and the S^5 (soft, stable, self-serving stalemate), also referred to as the mutually profitable stalemate (Zartman 1989, 2000, 2005; Wennmann 2011). The latter is not discussed here in detail.

References

Anstey, Mark, Paul Meerts, and I. William Zartman, eds. 2011. *To Block the Slippery Slope: Reducing Identity Conflicts and Preventing Genocide.* New York: Oxford University Press.

Beyer, Cornelia, and Michael Bauer. 2009. *Effectively Countering Terrorism.* Portland, OR: Sussex Academic Press.

Cronin, Audrey Kurth. 2008. *How Terrorism Ends: Understanding the Decline and Demise of Terrorist Campaigns.* Princeton, NJ: Princeton University Press.

———. 2009. "How Terrorist Campaigns End." In *Leaving Terrorism Behind,* ed. Tore Bjørgo and John Horgan. New York: Routledge.

Evans, Peter, Harold Jacobson, and Robert Putnam. 1993. *Double-Edged Diplomacy.* Berkeley and Los Angeles, CA: University of California Press.

Faure, Guy Olivier. 2007. "Demonization and Negotiation." *PIN Points* 28: 7–10. www.iiasa.ac.at/Research/PIN/PINPoints/pp28.pdf (accessed Nov. 10, 2010).

Faure, Guy Olivier, and I. William Zartman, eds. 2010. *Negotiating with Terrorists: Strategy, Tactics, and Politics.* London: Routledge.

Fisher, Roger, William Ury, and Bruce Patton. 1991. *Getting to Yes.* New York: Penguin.

Greig, J. Michael. 2005. "Stepping into the Fray: When Do Mediators Mediate?" *American Journal of Political Science* 49 (2): 249–66.

Haass, Richard, and Meghan O'Sullivan, eds. 2000. *Honey and Vinegar: Incentives, Sanctions, and Foreign Policy.* Washington, DC: Brookings Institution Press.

Hughes, Martin. 1990. "Terror and Negotiation." *Terrorism and Political Violence* 2 (1): 72–82.

Hume, Cameron. 1994. *Ending Mozambique's War.* Washington, DC: United States Institute of Peace Press.

Irwin, Colin. 2005. *The People's Peace Process in Northern Ireland.* Basingstoke, UK: Palgrave.

Judah, Tim. 2008. *Kosovo: War and Revenge.* New Haven, CT: Yale University Press.

Kuperman, Alan, ed. 2006. *Gambling on Humanitarian Intervention: Moral Hazard, Rebellion, and Civil War.* London: Routledge.

Le Monde. 1998. Statement from Fuad Ali Saleh, organizer of fifteen terrorist attacks reported by French media. *Le Monde,* Jan. 31.

Martin, Gus. 2003. *Understanding Terrorism: Challenges, Perspectives, and Issues.* London: Sage.

McDermott, Rose. 2009. "Prospect Theory and Negotiation." In *Negotiated Risks,* ed. Rudolf Avenhaus and Gunnar Sjöstedt. Berlin: Springer.

O'Brien, Sean P. 1996. "Foreign Policy Crises and the Resort to Terrorism: A Time-Series Analysis of Conflict Linkages." *Journal of Conflict Resolution* 40 (2): 320–35.

Ranstorp, Magnus, and Gus Xhudo. 1994. "A Threat to Europe? Middle East Ties with the Balkans and Their Impact on Terrorist Activity throughout the Region." *Terrorism and Political Violence* 6 (2): 196–223.

Rapoport, David. 2006. "Four Waves of Modern Terrorism." UCLA Burkle Center for International Relations. www.international.ucla.edu/burkle/article.asp?parentid=47153 (accessed Oct. 27, 2010).

Ross, Jeffrey Ian, and Ted Gurr. 1989. "Why Terrorism Subsides: A Comparative Study of Canada and the United States." *Comparative Politics* 21 (4): 405–26.

Rubin, Barry, ed. 1990. *The Politics of Counter-Terrorism: The Ordeal of Democratic States.* Washington, DC: Johns Hopkins University Foreign Policy Institute.

Sivaram, Dharmaratnam. 2006. "The Tamil Perspective." In *Negotiating Peace in Sri Lanka,* ed. Kumar Rupesinghe. Colombo: FCE.

Spector, Bertram I. 1998. "Deciding to Negotiate with Villains." *Negotiation Journal* 14 (1): 43–59.

Staub, Ervin. 2010. *Overcoming Evil: Genocide, Ethnic Conflict and Terrorism.* New York: Oxford University Press.

UNSC. 2001. Resolution 1373, "Threats to International Peace and Security Caused by Terrorist Acts." http://daccess-dds-ny.un.org/doc/UNDOC/GEN/N01/557/43/PDF/N0155743.pdf?OpenElement (accessed Oct. 27, 2010).

U.S. Code. 2001. *Definition of Terrorism under U.S. Law.* Title 22, US Code, §2656f(d). http://terrorism.about.com/od/whatisterroris1/ss/DefineTerrorism_5.htm (accessed Oct. 31, 2010).

Wennmann, Achim. 2011. *The Political Economy of Peacemaking.* London: Routledge.

Zartman, I. William. 1989. *Ripe for Resolution.* New York: Oxford University Press.

———. 1992. "Internationalization of Communal Strife: Temptations and Opportunities of Triangulation." In *The Internationalization of Communal Strife,* ed. Manus Midlarsky. London: Routledge.

———, ed. 1995. *Elusive Peace: Negotiating an End to Civil War.* Washington, DC: Brookings Institution Press.

———. 2000. "Beyond the Hurting Stalemate." In *International Conflict Resolution after the Cold War,* ed. Paul Stern and Daniel Druckman. Washington, DC: National Academy Press.

———. 2003. "Regional Conflict Resolution." In *International Negotiation: Analysis, Approach, Issues,* ed. Victor Kremenyuk, 348–61. San Francisco: Jossey-Bass.

———. 2005. *Cowardly Lions: Missed Opportunities to Prevent Deadly Conflicts and State Collapse.* Boulder, CO: Lynne Rienner.

———. 2010. *Preventing Identity Conflicts Leading to Genocide and Mass Killings.* New York: International Peace Institute.

Zartman, I. William, and Tanya Alfredson. 2010. "Negotiating with Terrorists and the Tactical Question." In *Coping with Terrorism: Origins, Escalation, Counter Strategies, and Responses,* ed. Rafael Reuveny and William Thompson. Albany, NY: SUNY Press.

Zartman, I. William, and Alvaro de Soto. 2010. "Timing Mediation Initiatives." United States Institute of Peace Peacemaker's Toolkit series. www.usip.org/files/resources/Timing%20Mediation%20Initiatives.pdf (accessed Oct. 28, 2010).

PART I

WHEN TO ENGAGE

Determining Strategic Moments

I. William Zartman and Guy Olivier Faure

Engaging depends on timing, with different strategies being more effective at some moments than at others. The "when" conditions the "how;" the context answers the "why." Timing—the "when"— can be defined both internally and externally. Internally, it involves understanding the evolution of the terrorist into someone who ultimately decides to turn to violent action. Part I presents two life cycles of terrorism: one focused on the individual within the group, the other on the mission within the organization. One of the case studies illustrates one such moment, identified differently in both life cycles. Externally, timing is defined by the conditions set by the mediator, whose services are almost always necessary to bring together the state and the terrorist organization. Two case studies illustrate these requirements.

The optimal time to handle any problem is, of course, before it happens. Any problem has its structural references and distant causes, so preventive action can target such conditions and causes to head off their effects. While such actions (if they can be identified and implemented) constitute an optimal response, their impact is often distant and delayed by their very nature. The next stage in dealing with the individual's or organization's movement toward terrorism is to identify moments of intervention as events head toward causes more proximate in time and more operational in form. Interventions that deal with potential or prospective actors before they turn to action can have important and at least middle-range, if not immediate, impacts. They involve contacts with groups and organizations as well as individuals. Such contacts seek to develop a deeper understanding of the problems that give rise to terrorism, and of the actors' perceptions of them. This understanding then serves as the basis of remedial measures and of tactics for dealing with those perceptions and reactions.

In attempting to deal with individuals on their way to becoming terrorists, these principles can serve as the basis of a careful, complex, and nuanced policy. They focus on means rather than ends, seeking to turn potential terrorists from expressing their aims and frustrations violently, without directly challenging their beliefs and perceptions of events. Such efforts begin with an empathetic analysis of the ambient conditions in the potential terrorists' upbringing, which work to shape their perception of events. Enrollment in a supporting in-group then hardens these perceptions and leads the individual toward violent action. But an understanding of this life cycle, as laid out in the chapter by Zartman and Khan, provides opportunities to break into it and engage individuals and even groups in a transformation of means and, eventually, ends. Both the broad sociopolitical and specific group contexts and the individual decision phases in joining a group and then turning to violence provide moments for appropriate engagement. The first entry point, as noted, is the apt occasion for efforts to change and remedy structural conditions. Failing this, a second-level effort can facilitate preemptively competing groups that turn common perceptions toward less violent interpretations and courses of action. A third-level effort, at a still later entry point, can provide individuals with exit options out of the extremist group.

The other life cycle examined in part I can be apprehended through understanding the evolution of terrorist organizations, from their incubation to a strategic, then to a political, and on to a transformational stage, as presented in Donohue and Cristal's chapter. This life cycle's first stage includes many of the activities portrayed in Zartman and Khan's earlier chapter on the life cycle of a terrorist, with negotiations that are largely preventive. The next two stages, however, involve internal consolidation and external confrontation respectively, using violence first to gather support and then to achieve goals. In the final stage, the organization begins to mainstream, trading its terrorist credentials for a role as a political party accepted and engaged in the political process. Negotiations become more and more likely as the organization proceeds through its stages. Negotiations disrupt the organization's purposes in the strategic phase, become part of the process in the political phase, and are the major activity in the transformational phase.

Such moments have been exploited in a number of important though generally unnoticed programs throughout the world. One of the most innovative of these is the Muslim Contact Unit, established by the British police to work with Muslims contacting fellow Muslims, to steer them from a path of violence. The idea is not to change the extremists' basic views, in particular toward the ends they desire, but merely to change their views about the appropriateness, availability, and effectiveness of violent means in accomplishing those ends. To do so, the intervenors engage the extremist group directly. Robert Lambert, one of the Muslim Contact Unit's originators, examines this project in chapter 3.

But direct contacts and negotiations between the extremists and the state are difficult by nature, even when engagement is considered as an option. For this reason, third-party assistance is usually required, with increasing involvement as the mediator moves from a role of communicator/facilitator to one of formulator and, eventually, manipulator (Touval and Zartman 2006). Moreover, since state efforts to stalemate the terrorists and bring them to accept engagement are often seen as running counter to efforts to engage, the two strategies, which depend on each other, can also *impede* each other, making third-party assistance even more crucial. Indeed, it is practically inherent in the notion of early contacts that an intermediary carry messages and open doors. Thereafter, when engagement reaches the stage of negotiations between the state and the terrorist organization, the mediator's service remains necessary. These elements are plumbed in the following chapters.

The last two chapters of part I turn to the required conditions for effective mediation by a powerful third party, as a different criterion of timing. The mediator has its conditions, and the conflict has its requirements, for effective mediation to occur. Using the case of negotiations between Sri Lanka and the Liberation Tigers of Tamil Eelam (LTTE) as an example, Maria Groeneveld-Savisaar and Siniša Vuković show the importance of engagement by committed mediators in a conflict. Negotiations ended with the defeat of the LTTE, at the cost of thousands of civilian lives—the very thing the fight against terrorism was designed to prevent. This occurred because the conflict was not important enough to powerful third parties to warrant the sustained pressure necessary and because weaker, even though dedicated, mediators simply did not have the combined interest and weight required to bring the two sides to an agreement. The final chapter of part I also examines the conditions required to engage the mediator's attention. Stacie Pettyjohn's analysis of experiences in Palestine, Northern Ireland, and South Africa show that the United States will engage political terrorist groups in negotiations when alternative and more moderate groups representing the same populations are not available and when the terrorists have shown their own willingness to negotiate and shift their means to political channels regardless of whether their ends have changed.

All these chapters serve to establish and then illustrate conditions of timing that govern the choice of methods in engaging states and terrorists in productive negotiations. The prime lesson of the chapters in this section is the focus on appropriate tactics for appropriate moments in demoting the choice of ends from violent to political, rather than in reorienting goals and belief systems. Engagement, rather than conversion, is the aim.

Reference

Touval, Saadia, and I. William Zartman. 2006. "International Mediation in the Post-Cold War Era." In *Turbulent Peace: The Challenges of Managing International Conflict*, ed. Chester A. Crocker, Fen Osler Hampson, and Pamela Aall, 427–43. Washington, DC: United States Institute of Peace Press.

1

Growing Up in Groups

I. William Zartman and Maha Khan

"The logic of faith is everlasting and eternal," said Fadil. "The Path is one at first, then it splits inevitably into two. One of these leads to love and obliteration of the self, the other to holy war. As for the people of obliteration of self, they are dedicated to themselves, and as for the people of holy war, they dedicate themselves to God's servants."

—Naguib Mahfouz, *Arabian Nights and Days*

The year 2007 saw 1,883 terrorist attacks worldwide, compared with 169 incidents a decade earlier (MIPT 2007). In light of this more than tenfold increase, it is important to understand the backgrounds, social environments, and beliefs that lead certain men and women to voluntarily perform politically motivated acts of violence. To develop effective policies to combat the problem, we must first understand the three levels of causation for terrorist acts: the individual, the group into which he or she is recruited, and the environmental and situational variables.

Terrorist movements do not arise out of nowhere. Since they are an ultimate phase of a larger sociopolitical movement, they arise because the previous means have proved ineffectual. Since terrorism is the weapon of the weak and a choice of desperation, all other choices having failed, the roots of the choice of violence go far back into the terrorists' life experiences (Brockett 1995; Tarrow 1996; McAdam 1996; Coser 2000; Pape

2003; Gunning 2009; Hoffman 2006). Even in a society inured to violence, terrorism is not the normal choice of everyday life (Staub 1989, 26).
Without indulging in infinite regress to Adam and Eve (she unnamed in
the Quran), the social context presents a useful starting place for examining the grievances it imposes on individual actors, hanging on a number of
turning points (della Porta and Rucht 1995; Moghaddam 2005; McCauley and Moskalenko 2008). If the roots of, or proneness to, the choice of
violent means of protest begin in the individual's context and experience,
the crucial node in that choice is the extremist group (Butler and Gates
2010). To begin the analysis of negotiation between states and terrorists,
this chapter builds a model of the paths individuals take to join a group
and then to choose violent action. The model is an ideal type that presents
pictures distilled from complex reality to bring out general characteristics
(Weber 1946, 292, 60). The life cycle model emphasizes the central place
and role of the group—the meso-social level that links the context and the
choice—to indicate where along that path different types of engagement
may be possible to deflect the course away from the choice of violence. The
following chapter, by Donohue and Cristal, also pursues this approach.

The grievances that mark this path come in several forms, producing
feelings of hurt and helplessness. Hurts are experiences that have left a
memory of deprivation and discrimination on the mind of the perceiver;
helplessness takes the form of anomie and alienation that leave a void in
the perceiver's mind. "You Israelis are Nazis in your souls and in your conduct. . . . Given that kind of conduct, there is no choice but to strike at
you without mercy in every possible way" (Post 2008). "It is a complicated
thing to want to kill yourself with your foes. You do that first to master
your own fear and rule yourself. To push the button becomes a form of personal revenge against humiliation. In one blow you kill the coward within
you, your impotence and the external threat" (Boustany 2005). These grievances can be either personal or collective, relating to incidents experienced
by the individual or conditions lived by the community (UNAMA 2007).
Jerrold Post quotes an Islamic terrorist: "My motivation in joining Fatah
was both ideological and personal. It was a question of self-fulfillment, of
honor, and a feeling of independence. . . . The goal of every young Palestinian was to be a fighter" (Post 2005). Collective grievances tend to have a
bigger impact than personal ones; they color personal perceptions of individual hurts and provide the setting for individual feelings of helplessness
that lead to violence.

This study proposes a model as a working hypothesis (fig. 1.1), combining the collective and personal dimensions that will later be refined by the
insertion of more details (fig. 1.2).

Figure 1.1. Analytical Model of Individual's Path to Terrorism

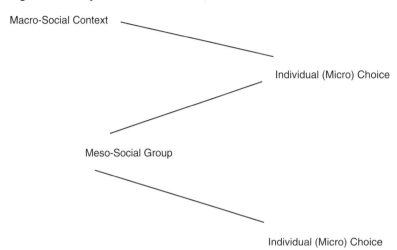

Macro-Social Context

Individual (Micro) Choice

Meso-Social Group

Individual (Micro) Choice

This discussion does not attempt to generalize or universalize the concept of a "terrorist." Rather, it looks at the common threads shared by men and women, young and old, who use violence against civilian targets to frighten civilians and demoralize government. Evidence from the collective interviews suggests that perceived grievances and ideology forming at a young age are the beginning of the common path that they all tread. These individuals perceive injustice, feel victimized by their circumstances, and find a group that shares and feeds into their grievances. What varies among the individuals is their specific trajectory and conversion to the in-group. Therefore, to understand their perceived victimization is to comprehend the frustration, anger, and shame evidently developing during their lives, and the organizations and communities that support them. It is on this basis that we use a terrorist's growing-up experience as a starting point.

The life cycle begins in the perception of grievances in society as the macro-social context (Gupta 2008). This perception needs to reach a point of anger, of "fed up" saturation, of frustration with an issue and the inadequacy of the means to resolve it, or the reverse: a point of hollowness, impotence, alienation, and anomie. The social context itself takes no action, but its collective exasperation or helplessness is necessary as a context for the individual, both as a supersaturated environment and as a support for action. The depiction then shifts to individuals—in the plural because it is the aggregate of single actors that the analysis addresses. As social movement theory holds, individuals react to the context—enough of them

Figure 1.2. Lilypond 1, Muslim Terrorist Trajectory: Islamic vs. Secular, Lower vs. Middle Class

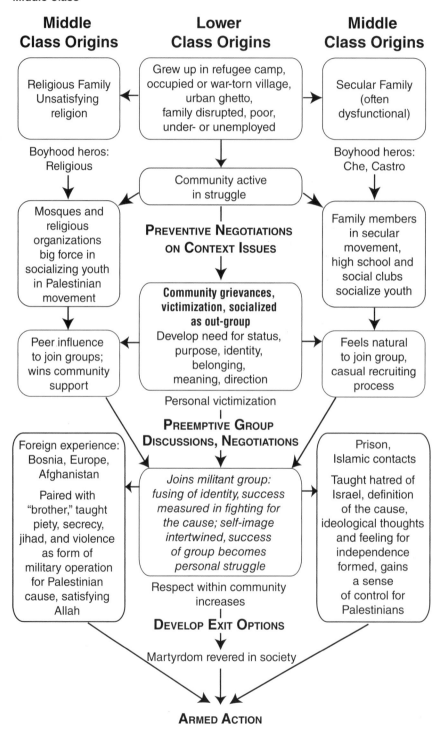

to constitute a movement (Laraña, Johnston, and Gusfield 1994; Jenkins and Klandermans 1995; Gunning 2009). The individuals break down into two subcategories: political entrepreneurs (PEs) and bystanders, arsonists and tinder, leaders and followers. These then constitute the second level of analysis: the micro-social. The group—the meso-social level—becomes the actor and the support for terrorist actions, and the focal point of the cursus. But not all group members go on to commit terrorist acts. The final step is the result of a combination of their own internal development and their selection by the PEs. What makes individuals in a social context join an action-oriented group? And then what takes certain individuals out of the group and leads them into action?

One advantage of this model is that it takes into account both the social, or collective, elements and the different types of individuals who constitute it, providing the macro-, micro-, and meso-levels of explanation (della Porta 1995; Horgan 2003; Wiktorowicz 2004). Individuals do not act without a supportive social context and group they are a part of. Or, if they do act in its absence, they become isolated instances, deranged cases—deranged by the very fact that they act alone without a group behind them. "The real transformation in individual motivations begins within the terrorist organizations" (della Porta 1992, 17).[1] The other advantage is that the model opens a window to research, in the accounts of individuals. It is hard to document a context and gain testimony from a group, but the individual accounts provide a perception of both the context (the perceived grievances, the first level of analysis) and the group actions (the third level). This research examines the publicly available accounts of terrorists to learn what it was in the context of perceived grievances that turned them to action, and then how their "conversion" from bystanders to agents took place in their minds and in their group behavior. The sources used are listed in the reference list appended; particularly illustrative quotes are cited, but the assemblage of sources is not referenced at each point.

Such material also allows a focus on the qualitative part of the explanation; that is, why did "location" on a moment—a particular pad on the pond— lead individuals to move on a path, to other pads on the pond, ending up in the group and then progressing to the decision to use violence? What follows is a synthesis of as many accounts of terrorists' life path to their terrorist action as we have been able to find. It does not stop, as many analyses do, at the discovery that the individuals involved are acting rationally (in the sense of "purposefully" [Weber's *Zweckrationalität*], not of "appropriately" [*Wertrationalität*]) (Weber 1946, 293). Rather, it seeks to go beyond that fact to identify typical paths to violent action, in order to find out when positive preventive measures can be employed through negotiation.

The results cannot be statistical, because there is no way of getting an appropriate population, either universe or sample. They can only be heuristic, indicating paths and nodes but never establishing the weight of any particular one. As one can imagine, finding failed suicide bombers or former terrorists willing to speak about their childhood experiences and beliefs is difficult (and finding successful suicide bombers much more so!). Fortunately, though, increased interest has led brave scholars to conduct such interviews, and our research draws heavily on these. This recognition has the advantage of permitting the aggregation of all sorts of testimonials, from individual cases (e.g., Ghannouchi) to large numbers, in which the smaller number of cases presumably gives the chance for greater depth of analysis (Tamimi 2001; Sageman 2004). The sources of these accounts, listed at the end of this chapter, form a thick empirical base on which the following discussion and analysis are grounded. Most of the accounts are by Muslims, notably Arabs, Afghans, and Pakistanis, but a few from Northern Irelanders, Tamils, and Colombians are included for comparison's sake.

In building this explanation, some key questions arise: What was it in the general perception of grievances that moved individuals from passive to active? How and why did they engage in the group? Did they become leaders (PEs)? Or how did PEs engage the followers into political action? How did this political action turn violent? What caused these individuals to actually carry out or direct a terrorist action? Since terrorism is an abnormal social activity, inertia, or gravity, makes the terrorists' climb to violence one that demands effort and commitment, which, when interrupted, causes them to fall back to normal or at least nonviolent life (Bjørgo and Horgan 2009; Hirschman 1982). Why do some hurt or alienated individuals turn to violence and others not? Why do people, once engaged, leave the terrorist path? Perhaps it is because they turn to personal over ideological concerns (e.g., save skin, save family), or because they see the possibility of achieving the same ends by other means (e.g., democratic elections). "Choosing to enter the Red Brigades—to become clandestine and therefore to break off relations with your family, with the world you've lived in till the day before—is a choice so total that it involves your entire life," a former member declared (Jamieson 1989). "In the long run you actually begin to feel different. Why? Because you are different. You become closed off, become sad, because a whole area of life is missing, because you are aware that life is more than politics" (Horgan 2005). Nationalist and religious groups work strenuously to fill this void, often successfully, but not always.

These questions underlie the second part of the chapter. The ultimate purpose of the study is to identify entry or turning points where dissuasive counteraction or negotiations are indicated. Is it indeed possible to stop or reverse the life cycle rising to terrorist acts? Are there points of return and no return, when it is possible and when it is no longer possible to cause disengagement? Are there appropriate tactics related to engagement that disengage the terrorist means from the ends, or do the radical ends inevitably carry the actor to the violent means? These two bundles of questions will guide the present inquiry into the terrorists' life cycle toward, and then away from, violence.

Growing Up Terrorist

Macro-Social Context

Support and recruitment into terrorist organizations tends to take place when a convergence of political, economic, and social trends results in lesser opportunities than what an individual expects and what other groups experience (Tilly 2003, 46-47; UNAMA 2007; Arena and Arrigo 2006). These two comparisons, referred to as *relative* and *comparative deprivations,* can generate social and individual frustration that terrorist groups can exploit (Davies 1962; Gurr 1970). Relative (intrapersonal) deprivation relates to the gap between rising expectations and worsening reality; comparative deprivation relates to a person's or group's fortunes compared to another person's or group's. Sometimes the relative frames appear rather distant, sometimes recent (Kahneman and Tversky 1979; Farnham 1994). Thus, the lack of an independence or decolonization dividend may take a generation or two to sink in, whereas the absence of expected job prospects may hit home in short order. Comparative deprivations particularly relevant to terrorism can be further separated into *personal deprivation,* in which an individual feels deprived of his or her own position within a group, and the more frequent *fraternal deprivation,* involving feelings that arise because of the position of an individual's group relative to that of other groups (Guimond and Dubé-Simard 1983; Gilbert, Fiske, and Lindzey 1998, 573, 610, 831). It is not hard for Palestinians to feel deprived compared with Israelis, Tamils compared with Sri Lankan Buddhists (particularly after the Tamil experience just before and after independence), Kosovar and Macedonian Albanians compared with Serbs and other Macedonians, or Casamançais compared with "Senegalese." Many also feel deprived when witnessing the fortunes and inefficacies of their own leadership, as shown by the Palestinian college student who blew herself up to point a finger at corrupt and ineffective PLO/PA figures.[2]

Among minorities, fraternal deprivation is more predictive of discontent than is personal deprivation (Moghaddam 2005). This is because terrorists who are more educated than their average community member and come from middle-class backgrounds tend not to be deprived in absolute terms within their communities but rather carry the burden of their community's deprivation in a larger context. Additionally, this effect may support the trend among some educated terrorists who view their opportunities as less attractive than their expectations and, hence, experience a life of frustration and banality. This makes the appeal of joining a solidarity group even greater.

It is thus important to get past the myth, popular among policymakers and society, that terrorists are mentally deranged or antisocial. The message should have gotten across by now that terrorists are rational, motivated (even if unconventional) individuals rather than crazies (Horgan 2005; Denoeux 2008; McCauley and Moskalenko 2008; Gunning 2009; *but* Miller 2008).[3] "I decided on jihad because I wanted to stop the occupation, not out of the love of blood," said a Lebanese suicide aspirant (MacFarquhar 2004). But some of the debate over rationality misses the point that a terrorist's rationality is not just a material cost-benefit calculation but is based on devotion, belief, salvation, and ideological ends (Atran 2003; Atran, Axelrod, and Davis 2007). As many analysts insist, terrorists live by a moral code supported by the group around them and, often, by the domestic context. But that provides a quite purposeful motivation, in terms of both their own future eschatological fate and the cause they proclaim. "I am not a murderer," said an Islamist terrorist commander. "A murderer is someone with a psychological problem; armed actions have a goal. Even if civilians are killed, it is not because we like it or are bloodthirsty. It is a fact of life in a people's struggle. The group doesn't kill because it wants to kill civilians, but because the struggle must go on" (Post, Sprinzak, and Denny 2003).

Terrorists work in well-organized groups with tight social cohesiveness (Atran 2004). "There was no room for questioning. The commander got his orders from his superior. You couldn't just take the initiative and carry out an armed attack without the commander's approval" (Post, Sprinzak, and Denny 2003). "The individual is not a monster as such but he becomes one when he is engaged in the mechanism of mass crime. It is through the group that the individual becomes a killer" (Semelin 2008). Both the moral justification and the authoritative command structure provide a key to why individuals find a group so appealing. A further reason why personal despair or mental instability may not be a significant factor in suicide terrorism is that the Middle Eastern, African, and Asian cultures where suicide terrorism is most frequently found tend to be less individualistic, more attuned to the environmental and organizational relationships that shape behavior, and less tolerant of individuals acting independently of the group

(Atran 2004). Terrorists in these societies also are more likely to be seeking a group, or collective, sense of belonging and justification for their actions.

Growing Up

Analysts have long considered whether those who eventually become terrorists come from humble, deprived origins (including refugee camps) or educated, middle-class professions. A raging debate then ensues between those who see terrorists as emerging from a deprived, uneducated, squalid background with nothing to lose and those who see them as educated middle-class individuals with everything to lose (Hewitt 2001; Krueger and Maleckova 2003; von Hippel 2002; Piazza 2006; Burgoon 2006; Krueger 2007; Denoeux 2008; Gambetta and Hertog 2007). A major contribution of the following analysis is that, as often happens in social science, it is the polarized debate that is wrong, because both explanations are factually correct. Terrorists come from both class sources, coming together from different backgrounds, by different paths, to find themselves in the action-oriented group (Victoroff 2005, 8). But it is not enough to recognize the fact; we must also examine it. First of all, the two claims are not opposites. One, that of impoverished origins, refers to family or even neighborhood conditions of early childhood; the other, of an educated middle-class, refers to later attainment. It is striking—and feeds into the earlier comments about relative deprivation—that a significant proportion of those who became educated and entered liberal professions came from humble origins that their families still occupy (Victoroff 2006). They "made it" but want to make a statement for the family they left behind. So "both" often refers *vertically* to the same person at different stages in life.

Second, "both" refers *horizontally* to opposite group origins and status at the same time: both individuals who never left their lower-class poverty and others who are presently part of the middle class can become terrorists. Many terrorists are educated, earn a good living, and have families and, apparently, a good future ahead of them. Studies of South Asian (Afghan, Pakistani) terrorists also show that they are often undereducated or uneducated, live in poverty, and are recruited from religious schools (madrassas) (UNAMA 2007). Similarly, many North African (Moroccan, Algerian) terrorists come from the slums and are unemployed or menially employed. So a path map, to be accurate, must show both conditions.

A special category refers to eventual terrorists from abroad, notably Europe. They tend to cross the seas—usually Mediterranean, occasionally Atlantic—with a double background of failure (Sageman 2004). Persistently unemployed, they seek material satisfaction that they cannot obtain in their home economies. Semimodernized, they seek spiritual satisfaction that they cannot find in their own societies. So they flee to Europe in search of material achievement, which then frequently eludes them as much as it did at home. In the words of an Amsterdam mosque spokesman, "He is not accepted by society and he is not accepted at home" (Frankel 2004). Rejected by the host society, they come together as "a bunch of guys" and gravitate for a "home moment" to the local mosque, where the PEs are waiting for them with a message of welcome and indoctrination. Again, for foreigners adrift in an alien society, a readily available group is important as a refuge, a home away from home.

It is important to note that before moving ahead along the trajectory, most terrorists live amid foreign occupation (real or perceived) or armed rebellion (such as a nationalist movement). Real occupation includes Palestine but also Northern Ireland during the "Troubles," and shades into perceptions of Saudi Arabia when U.S. troops were there, Afghanistan and Iraq under Western military presence, and then, by extension, the entire Arab world, Tamil areas of Sri Lanka and Muslim areas of Mindanao "occupied" by government troops, and so on. In this context, potential terrorists' family members and peers indoctrinate them at a young age against such targets to vent their hostility, and create an in-group/out-group mentality. As an out-group, they become a target for ambient hostility, creating lowered self-esteem (Kakar 1996). In cases perceived as occupation (Israel-Palestine, Afghanistan, Pakistan, Iraq), the context operates directly. A Fatah member said, "I belong to the generation of occupation . . . the [1967] war and my refugee status were seminal events that formed my political consciousness and provided the incentive for doing all I could to help regain our legitimate rights in our occupied country" (Post 2005). In cases where occupation is not apparent, the reigning conspiracy theory atmosphere portrays the mood as one of helplessness. People see themselves as event "takers," not event makers, unable to control their own destiny collectively or personally, victims of a foreign domination that decides their fate for them.

The out-group in society enjoys reactive and compensatory cohesion and relies on enhanced social pressure and approval—the context for Lambert's analysis in chapter 3. Thus, examining a terrorist's childhood can reveal much about psychology and motives (Maleckova 2006). As children, many terrorists faced personal injury or trauma, sometimes referred to as a "lost childhood." This can take the form of derision or insult at a young age—from being rejected or ignored by one's family or group, for example—and is generally referred to as *narcissistic injury*, defined as massive, profound, and permanent damage or harm to an individual's self-image or self-esteem (Pearlstein 1991; Brooks 1999). "I was born in a painful environment. I have lived in painful circumstances and I will die in this way, too," said a Tajik Taliban member in Afghanistan. "When you do not have guns or bomber planes, then your body is the only weapon that you use to resist people killing your families" (UNAMA 2007; Barber and Olsen 2006). But stopping at this level of analysis is incomplete, for many who suffer narcissistic injuries do not resort to violence. Terrorism may offer psychological rewards that compensate for the damage inflicted on the individual's self-esteem, but evidence does not demonstrate that narcissistic injuries lead directly to terrorism. Rather, narcissistic injuries tend to lead to one's seeking a group for support.

Humiliation, coupled with the learned hatred for the out-group, leads potential terrorists to develop a sense of identity attached to their (perceived) territorial or religious symbols, and a need for an ideology to explain past ills and identify friends and enemies (Zartman 1966; Hudson 1999; Kruglanski and Victoroff 2009). They turn to activism for personal growth, but their shared trauma leads to group dependency and enhanced in-group feeling. Their perceived disenfranchisement and absence of control over their own destiny, associated with belonging to a marginalized ethnic (or political) group, contributes to a need for group adherence and acceptance. They look to the group to regain a heightened sense of self, acceptance, and personal growth.

Individual grievances motivate some people to become recruits, but this alone does not motivate them to perform terrorist acts. The turning point is joining a group and shifting individual grievances into ideologically driven reasons (Atran 2004; Alonso 2006; Akhmedova and Speckhard 2006). Because many feel they have no other path to pursue, they join a group to share collective perceptions of the world. Many, especially those under occupation (whether real or perceived), feel there is no compromise; what was taken by force must be gotten back by force. Individuals who are motivated to commit atrocities cannot survive without support from their groups, and terrorist groups cannot survive without some level of support from their community. Therefore, it is essential to examine the ideological appeal and indoctrination methods of groups that obtain terrorists' commitments.

Once Inside the Group

A terrorist organization reinforces self-esteem and gives members a privileged status akin to a hero's. Members feel they have demonstrated their worth to society by belonging to the group. Diverse accounts show that groups are effective at mobilizing resources to compel the individual to disengage from morality as defined by the government, occupier, and mainstream society and to engage with morality as defined by the group.

They also provide a unifying message that conveys a religious, political, or ideological goal to their various followers, not all of whom have precisely the same personal motivations. Most prominent among these motivations are personal and national revenge, a belief that one is advancing the liberation cause, a belief in posthumous rewards, and an expectation that one's family will receive material and immaterial benefits, social prestige, and religious impetus.

The destruction that terrorists pursue in groups is presented as valid and justifiable means of instigating change. Ultimately, many of these terrorists regain a sense of strength and power from their indoctrination. Joining a terrorist organization is a way of creating positive identities for themselves (Corera 2008). By submerging into a collective identity, they find meaning in their lives, and a sense of coherent structure. The group elevates their status in society and confirms their commitment to their cause or ideology. It also reinforces their perception they are acting altruistically for the welfare of future generations. "I wasn't allowed to go just like that," explained a terrorist aspirant. "I had to agree with the idea of jihad, with the ideology behind it, before I was ready to act. It wasn't enough just to say I want to go to be a martyr; I had to know why" (MacFarquhar 2004).

The recruitment process is a critical step in joining an organization. The accounts show that youth, already suffering humiliation or victimization, are easily influenced by their peers and by the use of religious or political symbolism (myths and legends). This occurs in schools, religious institutions, and social groups, where recruits are taught about honor and dignity and are reminded that war, conflict, and terrorism are part of the social landscape. They receive intense training in the terror message. Those fighting religiously based battles are trained in religious militancy, subjected to intense spiritual exercises, and taught about the spirit of the power, with intense devotion to God. Sheikh Ahmed Yassin, founder of Hamas, said, "The only aim is to win God's [Allah's] satisfaction. That can be done in the simplest and speediest manner by dying in the cause of God. And it is God who selects the martyr." A (failed) suicide bomber in Ghaza, when selected, echoed, "We were in a constant state of worship. We told each other that if the Israelis only knew how joyful we were they would whip us to death. Those were the happiest days of my life!" (Hassan 2001). All terrorists are taught that violence is an acceptable and justifiable form of revenge, defense, and liberation of self and society.

Community support is also an important part of the recruitment process. Rituals and ceremonies are used to venerate group members and especially suicide attackers. These celebrations have two purposes: to attract new recruits and to gain community support by displaying a member's newfound empowerment against the adversary. A Fatah member recounted, "After recruitment my social status was greatly enhanced. I got a lot of respect from my acquaintances and from the young people of the village" (Post 2005). Paintings and posters are used to glorify martyrs, and often religious imagery is tied in. This is especially useful for children who cannot read but can understand the imagery and subconsciously absorb it into their early lives. Also, groups distribute pamphlets and use public displays to honor members and martyrs.

Terrorist organizations create a family, a tightly knit brotherhood whose members depend on each other in a closed community kept together by ideological bonds. As François Soudan explains, "The three social rejects were looking for identity and signposts. The Organization answers their needs perfectly. . . . The Islamist family replaced their native one, the one that never helped them grow up" (Soudan 1996, 14–15). Under the watchful eye of the PE, individual identities are forged into the group identity that makes members inseparable. Data show that charismatic leaders of these organizations turn ordinary desires for kinship and religion into desires for the mission the organization is pitching (Sageman 2004). This is obviously to the benefit of the organization, though presented as a benefit for the individual (Atran 2004). Also, groups weed out unstable candidates that may not be firm in their commitment. In the process, planners in these organizations keep a close watch on recruits to note their self-discipline.

In many cases, two other reinforcing experiences are at work: exile and prison. The two do not operate at the same moment in the terrorist's path. Terrorists in training are sent abroad as part of the socializing process, whereas individuals are sent to prison as a result of some infraction, not necessarily terrorist related. The trip abroad—to Europe, Afghanistan, Iraq—gives experience. If in Europe, it is as part of the out-group; if in another Mideast location, as part of on-the-job training. Prison is a different matter. Prison is a badge of commitment, a living martyrdom, and Islamists are eager to proselytize in prison, where the confined conditions are a perfect setting for such education. "Poverty is the soil, prison the fertilizer," was an apt comment on Algerian conditions (Bennhold 2007). Up against the Western notion of prison as punishment or as reintegration is the practical experience of prison as the reinforcer and the converter.

It should be noted that this description is the ideal, often but not always realized. In some cases, the individual has a relatively short time in training and socialization in the group and is sent on his martyr's mission only to get cold feet or bumble his instructions at the crucial moment. Operatives in the second Casablanca bombing in 2005 were poor in training and short on faith, with uneven results.

The Suicide Attacker

As our model indicates, the suicide bomber has a slightly different path from other recruits (Seale 1992; Hoffman 2003). In Palestine, there is no shortage of willing recruits for martyrdom. As one Hamas leader said, "It is difficult to select only a few. Those whom we turn away return again and again, pestering us, pleading to be accepted" (Hassan 2001). Therefore, it is an honor to be selected for a suicide mission, and it endorses the potential attacker's moral character and commitment to the goals of the organization. In Palestine, a young man found in tears explained that it was not his friend's suicide that saddened him but the fact that his friend was chosen for martyrdom after only a few weeks in the organization, whereas he himself had been a member for years without being chosen.[4] Elsewhere, from Morocco and Algeria to Pakistan and Indonesia, individuals are attracted to the mission—in Spain, Kenya, Iraq, Afghanistan, and at home—and carefully selected by the group leaders.

Terrorist organizations carefully scrutinize the motives of a potential bomber, and the strength of his or her commitment. Candidates lead a life of secrecy and are constantly watched over. They are put into "martyrdom cells" with another member and are focused on being in the presence of God. At this stage on a terrorist's path, all feelings of fear and revenge are removed. Rather, the candidate is trained in self-discipline and piety and is taught that the attack is purely a military response. Suicide attacks allow potential attackers to punish the enemy and concurrently execute God's command to exact justice.

In Asia, the Middle East, and Africa, where suicide attacks are more frequent, potential attackers prepare a will on paper, audiocassette, or video. The videos are always shot against the background of the sponsoring organization's banner and slogans, with the potential Islamist attacker reciting the Quran while posing with guns. The violent attack is justified as jihad, and the potential attackers encourage their comrades to do the same (Hassan 2001). The videos are meant also to encourage the attacker to confront death and not fear it.

As mentioned previously, community support is vital to a terrorist organization's success. This is even truer after a successful suicide operation. An attacker's act becomes the subject of praise in talk and sermons and appears in the pamphlets that show new candidates the honors that they, too, will receive. Chants and songs are also used to honor martyrs. Also, in Palestine a bomber's family and sponsoring organization celebrate martyrdom much like a wedding. Many will talk about the honor that God has bestowed on their family. However, this response, too, seems to be socialized. When a mother was asked what she would have done if she had known her son was planning an attack, she said, "I would have taken a cleaver, cut open my heart, and stuffed him deep inside" (Hassan 2001).

Negotiations: Compete, Control, Cooperate

The above analysis has made some important points in the understanding of the terrorist's life cycle ("growing up terrorist") (Crenshaw 2000; Bjørgo and Horgan 2009). The first is to recognize that terrorists come from many sources. They are not just poor, alienated slum and camp dwellers but also educated, frustrated middle-class members, all joined in a feeling of being victimized. The second is to establish a varying number of steps ("lily pads") on which terrorists hop as they move on the path to violent action in accordance with their beliefs (Bjørgo and Horgan 2009, 3). The third finding is that wherever they come from and whatever steps they take, a centralizing moment in their evolution is the decision to join a militant group.

Militant membership does not determine terrorist action; that is, not all members of a militant group become terrorists. After this centralizing step, they then take off in different directions on the path toward or away from terrorist action. So membership becomes the necessary (though not sufficient by itself) element in the decision to use violence. Those who go on to act are carefully socialized, selected, trained, and nurtured. This analysis has not studied those who did not make it to action but has concentrated on identifying the steps of those who did. These steps can be reversed or negated to provide hypotheses for the further analysis separating the two categories, although data may be harder to gather (Cronin 2008).

This picture fits into the original model proposed for the study, to provide a further guide for the analysis of negotiation or other types of prevention possibilities *before* the terrorist act takes place—the ultimate purpose of this analysis. This section of the chapter does not have the same empirical base as the first part; rather, it examines logically or conceptually the potentialities that can be claimed to exist (Herz 1982). Finding empirical evidence is more difficult, although some does exist, notably in the chapters by Goerzig, Lambert, and Pettyjohn. The best the present analysis can do is to undertake similar logical evaluation, offer ideas and opportunities to practitioners, and incite a search for empirical data to test the ideas.

Combining the model and the analysis, there are four potential moments, or stages, for engagement that call for evaluation: the initial sociopolitical context, the personal steps to militant group membership, the group itself, and the subsequent steps to violent action. Potentialities vary in each case, and the moments can be evaluated one by one.

Sociopolitical Context

It is too easy to say that if only the basic grievances had been handled properly, the terrorism would not have occurred, or that we must look at ourselves as the basic cause rather than at the terrorist, who is simply the logical consequence of our mistakes. This is good material for the confessional, but it does not help us understand or handle the situation. That said, the possibilities for preventive engagement are not to be neglected, either (Zartman 2001, 2005, 2010; Denoeux 2008). While many elements of the current Middle East situation are beyond negotiation, others have been both handled creatively and neglected irresponsibly. A brief categorization may be helpful, although an extended analysis is beyond this chapter.

The broadest and least reachable level of basic grievances contains such components as globalization and the perceived marginalization of the local and surrounding populations, which see themselves as "event-takers" rather than "event-makers," in personal as well as global affairs. The spread of globalization represents a cultural as well as socioeconomic invasion of Arabo-Muslim society that—as the final insult to some—is craved by the affected populations themselves.[5] Some may call for a more equitable distribution of the benefits of globalization, but the globalization movement is simply too broad and too inevitable to be the subject of preventive negotiation. While the perception that the region is powerless to affect world events is historically erroneous (as the Crusaders' defeat, colonial withdrawal, oil pricing, and isolation of Israel show), that may be a debating point but hardly a negotiating subject.

On a more specific and manageable level, there is no doubt that the United States frittered away moments to weigh in creatively and committedly in the Israeli-Palestinian and -Syrian disputes from 1993 to 2008 (Hampson and Zartman 2011). Instead of recalling that the peace process was a U.S. invention that returned Arab territories to their rightful owners and never the reverse, and instead of staying that course despite the disruption of September 11, 2001, the United States let itself be sidetracked into a war on terrorism as an exclusive concern. Carrying negotiations on the Israeli problem to their conclusion would have been preferable in the 2000s, and committed persistent mediation would have been preferable in the 1990s. Lack of progress on the peace process was not one of the causes of al-Qaeda, but evidence of engagement and progress would have made easier the battle for the hearts and minds of the Arabo-Muslim Middle East.

Steps to Group Membership

It is hard to see specific moments or events, and easier to identify general conditions, that provide an opening for negotiations to prevent increasingly disaffected individuals from heading toward group membership. At this point, such efforts seek to accomplish three goals: to deal with manageable grievances and feelings of anomie, to remove action from doctrine (means from ends), and to separate political entrepreneurs from the community. Preventive engagement and negotiation must distinguish between two settings: in a foreign host country and at home. Marc Sageman has said that the relative absence of sleeper cells in the United States compared to Europe is explained by the welcoming and integrating atmosphere in the melting pot compared to the social and economic isolation suffered by Muslim immigrants in Europe. Exceptions have arisen, notably among Somalis, in recent years (Sageman 2004; Elliott 2009). That is a broad and doubtless ultimately unverifiable explanation, and one that helps little in explaining the paths of adolescents in refugee camps, but it does indicate the importance of opening communications or even negotiations on specifics with immigrant populations, as Lambert discusses in chapter 3. The need to show concern, provide better services, and talk with the young rioters in the north Paris and Hamburg suburbs, although they are not yet terrorists, provides a supportive example.

Efforts at integration, often involving negotiation, are needed at two levels. The more challenging is on the level of personal relations—challenging because it demands discernment and widespread person-to-person activities. Often intense personal measures are needed to remove a sense of alienation; the object is not to meet the need for personal fulfillment but to overcome that need. It is possible that the sense of class that has dominated European history, modernized in colonialist attitudes, reemerges when the formerly colonized peoples colonize the metropolis, and that sense underlies personal attitudes toward "invading" foreign populations.

The more efficient effort is on the social level, removing from societal attitudes the sense of out-group status. The more diverse a modern society, the more pluralistic group identities are present, none of which need be defined or self-defined as exclusive out-groups. Out-group definition begins within the surrounding community and becomes a cause for defensive identity efforts within the out-group—the basic element for an attitude that sees and seeks victimization, creating a one-sided security dilemma. An enormous amount of work is needed locally in European communities where Muslim populations have exploded in number, outpacing the local governments' capacities for satisfactory attention to living conditions and turning deprivation into discrimination (Arnson and Zartman 2005).

Muslim communities have a hard time integrating into European social fabric and, hence, become ghettoized, when they need proactive, affirmative actions to bring them into the mainstream of community life and—even in their communities—to find space to work, play, shop, and worship. Human rights become particularly important in this context, both as a rallying cause for averting group resentments and also as a symbol of guiding "Western" (actually universal) values. Much of this description also applied and still applies to Northern Ireland, where the whole society is separated and ghettoized, and to Uganda, where the Achole are alienated from the system as punishment for a previous regime, plundered by the national army, and terrorized by the Lord's Resistance Army (LRA).

There is much room for preventive negotiations on this level, before conditions make the communities hothouses for raising terrorists (Merriman and DuVall 2007). Local authorities can negotiate with immigrant community representatives about group needs and perceptions, and then with local councils and businesses to provide resources and redress. Consociation at the local level provides a formula for negotiation and a path to integration, while at the same time maintaining protective group identity and solidarity (Lijphart 1972). Universities, found in practically every large city, can provide study groups and service projects to accompany such negotiations. Lambert's experience in London, recounted in chapter 3, shows how potential terrorists can be weaned away from the attraction of al-Qaeda by responsive attention to their concerns.

In the second setting, the home country, efforts at dealing with grievances and loneliness, belief systems, and political entrepreneurs are even harder to undertake, since it is the home setting that provides a collective grievance, a cultural base, and a hive for organizers. External efforts are often delegitimized as foreign. Much depends on a responsive state, which may be part of the problem. The state needs to increase its own services, augmented by the efforts of moderate private organizations. Moderate political parties with a religious appeal undercut extremism; moderate religious leaders return to the sources and contest the scriptural justification of violence. Parties and religious leaders can be encouraged from abroad, but the effort to block the path to extremist groups must come from within the country where they reside.

Militant Group Membership

The militant group provides both a container for the prospective terrorists and a collective entity to engage in negotiations. Engagement at this stage avoids the problem of dealing with a range of individuals, as in the previous stage, but encounters the obstacle of engaging a group whose existence and appeal are based on contesting the authorities and providing an alternative basis of identity and action. The goal of negotiation is to provide and encourage alternative group adherence and acceptance that is divorced from violence. Violence is by no means a necessary ingredient in in-group solidarity but is fostered by the intensity of rage, hurt, anomie, and out-group feelings and by the in-group justification of violence as a means of expression. Thus, providing alternative nonviolent in-groups means lowering the level of anger and removing the tolerance for violence while at the same time providing havens for people who feel the need for support and solidarity.

There are strategies for overcoming the problem. One is to insert negotiations between the previous step and joining the group, by finding a counterleader (PE), creating one's own group, inviting discussions, and creating preemptive group cohesion through active dialogue and implementing response. Such efforts have borne fruit in Italy and the UK and doubtless elsewhere on the domestic level, and Pettyjohn's chapter shows the importance of such development on the international level. This type of measure is particularly relevant to neighborhood groups and block and professional associations, where improvement of local living conditions can become a subject for citizens' discussion with other community groups and for their petition to the local authorities. Such constructive groups can engage efforts and imaginations in dealing with real issues and solving real problems for the local population (Staub 2010). It is important to note that the two ingredients are necessary: dialogue is fine, but implementation of corrective measures is crucial. Otherwise, the absence of real (however limited) constructive responses merely intensifies feelings of discrimination, relative deprivation, and alienation.

A second strategy is to work the neighborhood once the militant group has been formed, paying particular attention to those still outside it—the potential water that is necessary to the swimming fish. Affirmative action showing the passive populations that they do have rights and opportunities is important, even as a belated response, as in the Community Relations Council in Northern Ireland. The militant group could claim that the action is a response to its own demands, but it is unlikely to do so, since religious revival, not affirmative action, is its primary focus. Usually the group is in its consolidation phase, past co-optation and petition in its relations with authorities (Zartman 1995). On the other hand, if even belated responsiveness can capture the attention of moderate group leaders, it can delay or disrupt the formation of a militant group. Separating the tinder from the pyromaniacs can be accomplished physically, when the imam invites arrest or deportation for his messages, but also substantively, by taking measures to overcome the feelings of hurt and helplessness in the community.

Another moment for negotiation is a later use of the same strategy, of dividing the group once it has been formed, identifying more moderate members from within the militant groups, and using alternative imams to create more amenable clubs and circles (Faure and Zartman 2010). This approach offers competition to the terrorist group and provides alternative but nonviolent organizations that bear the group's basic message, as discussed in Pettyjohn's chapter. The remaining extremist group becomes smaller and easier to monitor, while the breakaway group becomes a partner to work with, whether on the local level or in dealing with a nationalist cause. The Hamas-Fatah situation in Palestine provides an imperfect and reverse example of the strategy. There the original group gradually became the partner to work with, but its insufficiencies let a more radical group take its place as terrorists.

These are strategies of preventive engagement aiming at competition and control. A subtle but important shift in stance evolves from talking at, or even to, terrorists to talking *with* them, moving to persuasion and cooperation. The most direct strategy is to engage the group, listening to its grievances and responding to its concerns (Horgan and Taylor 2006). The group can be engaged either on the practical level, examining and handling concrete grievances, or on the spiritual level, using other believers to debate and negotiate aspects of doctrine, as illustrated in Goerzig's chapter (Ashour 2007). The point is not to sell the state's goals and policies but to listen and respond to the group's concerns and grievances. City authorities in France, the UK, and Germany have worked with Muslim associations to facilitate young people's transition from school to work (Masters and Deffenbaugh 2007, 127). Such an approach does justify and legitimize the militant group as a mouthpiece for its community, but it has the outweighing advantage of opening up talks and discussions, learning more about the group's images and missions, and pulling at least a wing of the group out of clandestinity and total opposition and into negotiation and conciliation.

In direct engagement, the principal aim is to wean the group away from its tactics of violence. To do so requires delegitimizing the violence directly, offering alternative paths toward its political goal, or changing that goal. Delegitimizing (deradicalizing) the use of violence with the help of alternative religious authorities has been practiced in Algeria, Saudi Arabia, Libya, Yemen, and, as Goerzig's chapter details, Egypt. This usually involves a liberal policy of amnesty wedded to a tough policy of military control (Ashour 2007, 2009, 2010). There are plenty of Muslim authorities who can cite scripture to show that violence, and especially violence against civilians, is not condoned, and they need to be employed to overcome the arguments of those who maintain that it is (CSID 2002). Changing the goal is more difficult and can be attained only by showing that the existing goal is simply unattainable—primarily by showing that efforts to attain it are blocked and unrewarding, at least for the moment. The Aceh Liberation Army in Indonesia was finally convinced in 2005 that attainable "self-government" was preferable to the unattainable goal of independence, and the Kurdish Workers' Party (PKK) is on the path to a similar realization. Firdous Syed, who founded the Janbaz Force in Kashmir, "realized the futility of violence . . . used to serve the interests of Pakistan" instead of the Ummah (Stern 2003, 135). The National Liberation Army in Macedonia agreed to join other, nonterrorist Albanian parties in reducing its demands to something less than independence, and Renamo in Mozambique came to an agreement on open participation and political competition rather than the overthrow of the Frelimo Party government. Alternative paths are primarily political rather than violent. Most former supporters of the Islamic Salvation Front in Algeria have rallied behind the moderate Islamic parties—Movement of the Society for Peace ([Algerian] Hamas) and the Islamic Renaissance Movement (Nahda)—as a means to their goal, and the Justice and Development Party in Morocco has turned to procedural and substantive reforms as its platform, although the extent to which it has also modified its goal of state takeover is unclear (Khalfi 2010). After various negotiations on details, such as prisoner exchanges and siege conditions, Fatah and the PLO were brought into negotiations with Israel at Oslo in 1993, providing a temporary meeting of the signatories (if not of the minds). The few Taliban who rallied to the government in the mid-2000s apparently felt that they had better prospects with those in power than with those trying to get in.

Frequently, weaning a group off violent tactics means weaning it off the spiritual leader. Abdullah Ocalan of the PKK and Afonso Dhlakama of Renamo may be the exception, but the experiences with Joseph Kony of the LRA in Uganda (and now Congo), Velupillai Prabhakaran of the Tamil Tigers (LTTE) in Sri Lanka, Jonas Savimbi of the National Union for the Total Independence of Angola (UNITA), Shamil Basayev of the Chechen separatist movement, Abimael Guzmán of Sendero Luminoso in Peru, Manuel Marulanda Vélez of the Revolutionary Armed Forces of Colombia (FARC), and even Yasser Arafat of the PLO, among others, support the findings. The spiritual leader has made his external reputation and personal mission his very identity. To turn his coat (or his hair shirt) is to deny his very self. (Note that this applies to heads of state as well, at least to some extent.) Better, then, for engagers to go back to the previously noted tactics: split the group, reach out to the lieutenants, reward rivalries, and woo and buy off followers.

Such actions need to keep in mind some basic axioms of negotiation:

- Begin with listening and respect, not with selling and compelling.
- Do not seek to negotiate a belief system; negotiate *within* a belief system.
- Give something to get something.
- Show that there is something to gain from negotiation.
- Help separate attainable from unattainable goals.
- Show alternative paths to similar goals that do not entail violence.

The two pairs of strategies of engagement—compete and control, convince and cooperate—go together, as in a bad cop, good cop routine. When negative engagement has shown that the terrorists' means and, possibly, ends are blocked, positive engagement can come into play. It is important to remember that the terrorists have no reason to respond to the second pair of strategies unless the first has been effective.

Steps from Group to Violence

The final step returns to the individual and is perhaps the least promising. It calls for efforts to identify vulnerable members of the group and to negotiate matters of motive on the way to the justification of violence (Barrett and Bokhari 2009). At this point, the individual is supported and protected by the group and, therefore, is hard to identify among others and difficult to isolate and contact. As we have seen, the individual is heavily indoctrinated and mesmerized by his opportunity to join the extremist group—he has already left the diving board and is hard to arrest in flight. A former fighter in Afghanistan, years later, answered unhesitatingly why he committed terrorist violence: "to go to heaven" (ICSR 2008). And a failed suicide bomber in Ghaza declared, "By pressing the detonator, you can immediately open the door to Paradise: It is the shortest path to heaven" (Hassan 2001). Even nonsuicidal and nonreligious zealots are similarly committed to carrying out their mission.

The job of negotiation is labor intensive, and the fork in the road that separates those who carry out the mission of violence from those who stay behind is still not well marked. However, a recent burst of attention to reasons why individuals leave terrorist movements has produced some important insights that can be put to work to facilitate more exits (Ross and Gurr 1989; Crenshaw 1991; Horgan 2003; Bjørgo and Horgan 2009; Cronin 2008). The exit paths result from extremist group members' being variously beaten, burned out, brought in, and backlashed. Strategic negotiations can be carried out to divide the group, as discussed in the preceding step. Talks, engagement, and negotiations to turn individual group members away from the ultimate act and develop policy debates within the group, or exit options from the group, can occasionally be promising if the engager can establish contact (Dominus 2005). Group excesses and leaders' ego trips can turn off members and make them vulnerable to efforts to win away followers or can turn off host populations and isolate terrorist groups as well (Abdul-Ahad 2004). The 2002 openings to negotiations within the LRA in Uganda and the LTTE in Sri Lanka were the product of internal splits from Kony's and Prabhakaran's lieutenants respectively, who were dissatisfied with their superiors' long-standing leadership styles (Lilja 2010, 101).

Amnesty programs can be powerful tools to attract individuals disillusioned with their group's ideology, who have lost faith in the cause or in their self-interested leaders due to what is often termed "burnout" or "backlash" (Ross and Gurr 1989). These programs, such as those set up in Italy in the 1970s or in the United States (witness protection programs), can serve both the state and the individual (della Porta 2009, Ashour 2009). They provide the individual with a route out of a clandestine and dark life, and the government with a source of information about the group in exchange for an incentive—such as a reduced sentence, protection, or reintegration into society (Post 2006). Amnesty programs worked well in dealing with the mafia in Italy, but the programs must be culturally acceptable within a society. They cannot be seen by others in the community as rewarding terrorists for their previous criminal activity.

Additionally, efforts need to be made to reintegrate these individuals into society, much as former paramilitaries are reintegrated in a post-conflict environment. Preventive DDRRR (disarmament, demilitarization, reintegration, reemployment, repatriation) should be considered. Such policies involve both civil society and the state and are not an easy or short-term task. They essentially go back to reducing support for terrorist groups within the community and the diaspora abroad. If terrorists understand that there are available options to defect from a group, they may consider them. Northern Ireland, for example, uses innovative strategies to integrate former paramilitaries into society by positioning them as community leaders. Ex-combatants feel empowered as community leaders and, thus, genuinely want to tackle problems faced by their community and engage them to find sustainable solutions. This, in turn, elevates their status in their community and offers them a heightened sense of self—a very important aspect. With this social program, the state is acting as a catalyst, not determining methods for reintegrating former terrorists but allowing the communities to deal with them at their own pace. Also, as was done in South Africa, they can ask for forgiveness for their crimes—but this, again, is very dependent on the culture of a society. In Afghanistan, former terrorists have been reintegrated into the Afghan Auxiliary Force, and Pakistan is trying to do the same within its security forces.

For amnesty, DDRRR, and social programs to work, states and the international community must be committed to see them through. This commitment includes financial resources as well as patience, because such programs do not provide a quick fix. As seen, luring away someone who is psychologically deeply embedded in a terrorist organization is the hardest of all the tasks.

Conclusion

This research has sought to provide a more accurate portrayal of the steps ("lily pads") that individuals of various origins in an offending sociopolitical situation take as they move into a welcoming group that then sends some of them out to do acts of terrorism. The analysis has then sought to identify moments in that path that provide opportunities for preventive engagement and negotiations. The most effective preventive measure is to deal with the causes of the grievance and anomie that characterize the sociopolitical situation, thereby undercutting the urge to move toward terrorism in protest. While a proactive policy can certainly reduce the causes for grievance, there are limits to the preventive actions that government can take in anticipating terrorist outbreaks.

The nexus of the paths from different origins to different outcomes is the welcoming group, which provides the best occasions for engagement and preventive negotiation. Engagement seeks to compete and control in an effort to weaken the terrorist groups; negotiation seeks to convince and cooperate with it. The twin strategies are the two sides of the same coin, aimed at turning the group's means from violence to politics and, eventually, its ends from zero-sum to positive-sum goals acceptable to both sides. The entire strategy holds together, but success requires combining some apparent opposites. The state must show that terrorism is a means that does not pay and does not achieve the terrorists' goals, but that alternative means are open and possible. In exchange for the disaffected group's rejection of terrorist means, the state must show that it is willing to pay with concessions on the group's goals. These are the terms of trade, but the devil, as always, is in the details. That exchange is the essence of engagement and negotiation.

Notes

1. See also Gupta 2008; McCauley and Moskalenko 2008.
2. Author interview with Palestinian analyst, January 2009.
3. For an excellent review of some of this literature, see Victoroff 2006.
4. Author interview with Palestinian analyst, January 2009.
5. The *thran*-related (insult-susceptible) position of the Northern Irish in relation to England is not too strained a parallel.

References and Data Sources

Abdul-Ahad, Ghaith. 2004. "Seeking Salvation in City of Insurgents." *Washington Post,* Nov. 11.

Akhmedova, Khapta, and Anne Speckhard. 2006. "A Multi-Causal Analysis of the Genesis of Suicide Terrorism: The Chechen Case." In Victoroff 2006.

Alonso, Rogelio. 2006. "Individual Motivations for Joining Terrorist Organizations: A Comparative Qualitative Study on Members of ETA and IRA." In Victoroff 2006.

Arena, M. P., and B. A. Arrigo. 2006. *The Terrorist Identity: Explaining the Terrorist Threat.* New York: New York University Press.

Arnson, Cynthia, and I. William Zartman, eds. 2005. *Rethinking the Economics of War: The Intersection of Need, Creed, and Greed.* Washington, DC: Woodrow Wilson Center Press and Johns Hopkins University Press.

Ashour, Omar. 2007. "Lions Tamed? An Inquiry into the Causes of De-Radicalization of Armed Islamist Movements: The Case of the Egyptian Islamic Group." *Middle East Journal* 61 (4): 596–624.

———. 2009. *The De-Radicalization of Jihadists: Transforming Armed Islamist Movements.* London: Routledge.

———. 2010. "De-Radicalizing Jihadists the Libyan Way." *Arab Reform Bulletin,* Apr. 7. www.carnegiendowment.org/arb/fa=show&article=40 (accessed Apr. 25, 2010).

Atran, Scott. 2003. "Who Wants to Be a Martyr?" *New York Times,* May 5.

———. 2004. "Trends in Suicide Terrorism: Sense and Nonsense." Paper presented to World Federation of Scientists Permanent Monitoring Panel on Terrorism, Erice, Sicily, Aug. http://sitemaker.umich.edu/satran/files/atran-trends.pdf (accessed Oct. 27, 2010).

Atran, Scott, Robert Axelrod, and Richard Davis. 2007. "Sacred Barriers to Conflict Resolution." *Science* 317 (5845): 1039.

Barber, B. K., and Joseph Olsen. 2006. "Adolescents' Willingness to Engage in Political Conflict: Lessons from the Gaza Strip." In Victoroff 2006.

Barrett, Richard, and Laila Bokhari. 2009. "Deradicalization and Rehabilitation Programs." In Bjørgo and Horgan 2009.

Bennhold, Katrin. 2007. "Privation and Despair Colored an Algerian Bomber's Life." *New York Times*, Dec. 14.

Bjørgo, Tore, and John Horgan, eds. 2009. *Leaving Terrorism Behind: Individual and Collective Disengagement*. London: Routledge.

Boustany, Nora. 2005. "A Look into the Minds of Suicide Bombers." *Washington Post*, Nov. 1.

Brockett, Charles. 1995. "A Protest-Cycle Resolution of the Repression/Popular-Protest Paradox." *Social Science History* 17 (3): 457–84.

Brooks, Geraldine. 1999. "Arms and the Boy." *Washington Post Magazine*, Feb. 14, 8–25.

Burgoon, Brian. 2006. "On Welfare and Terror." *Journal of Conflict Resolution* 50 (2): 176–203.

Butler, Christopher, and Scott Gates. 2010. "The Organization of Terror: Patterns of Recruitment, Allegiance and Support Networks." In *Coping with Terrorism: Origins, Escalation, Counter-Strategies, and Responses*, ed. Rafael Reuveny and William R. Thompson. New York: SUNY Press.

Center for the Study of Islam and Democracy (CSID). 2002. "American Muslims and Scholars Denounce Terrorism." *Muslim Democrat* 4 (3): 3.

Corera, Gordon 2008. "Al-Qaeda's 007." *Times* (London), Jan. 16.

Coser, Lewis. 2000. *Continuities in the Study of Social Conflict*. New York: Macmillan.

Crenshaw, Martha. 1991. "How Terrorism Declines." *Terrorism and Political Violence* 3 (1): 69–87.

———. 2000. "The Psychology of Terrorism: An Agenda for the 21st Century." *Political Psychology* 21: 2.

Cronin, Audrey Kurth. 2008. *How Terrorism Ends*. Princeton, NJ: Princeton University Press.

Davies, James. 1962. "Toward a Theory of Revolution." *American Sociological Review* 27 (1): 5–18.

della Porta, Donatella. 1992. "Introduction." In *Social Movements and Violence*, ed. Donatella della Porta. Greenwich, CT: JAI Press.

———. 1995. *Social Movements, Political Violence, and the State*. New York: Cambridge University Press.

———. 2009. "Leaving Left-Wing Terrorism in Italy." In Bjørgo and Horgan 2009.

della Porta, Donatella, and Dieter Rucht. 1995. "Left-Libertarian Movements in Context." In *The Politics of Social Protest*, ed. J. Craig Jenkins and Bert Klandermans. Minneapolis: University of Minnesota Press.

Denoeux, Guillain. 2008. "Guide to the Drivers of Violent Extremism and Terrorism." Unpublished paper prepared for USAID.

Dominus, Susan. 2005. "The Peacemaker of Flight 847." *New York Times Magazine*, Dec. 25.

Elliott, Andrea. 2009. "A Call to Jihad, Answered in American." *New York Times,* July 12.

Farnham, Barbara, ed. 1994. *Avoiding Losses, Taking Risks: Prospect Theory and International Conflict.* Ann Arbor: University of Michigan Press.

Faure, Guy Olivier, and I. William Zartman, eds. 2010. *Negotiating with Terrorists.* London: Routledge.

Frankel, Glenn. 2004. "From Civic Activist to Alleged Terrorist." *Washington Post,* Nov. 28, A18.

Gambetta, Diego, and Steffen Hertog. 2007. "Engineers of Jihad." Sociology Working Paper 2007-10, University of Oxford.

Gilbert, D. T., S. T. Fiske, and G. Lindzey. 1998. *The Handbook of Social Psychology.* 4th ed. Vol. 2. New York: McGraw-Hill.

Guimond, Serge, and Lise Dubé-Simard. 1983. "Relative Deprivation Theory and the Quebec Nationalist Movement: The Cognitive-Emotional and Personal-Group Deprivation Issue." *Journal of Personality and Social Psychology* 44 (3): 526–35.

Gunning, Jeroen. 2009. "Social Movement Theory and the Study of Terrorism." In *Critical Terrorism Studies,* ed. Richard Jackson, Marie Breen Smyth, and Jeroen Gunning. London: Routledge.

Gupta, Dipak. 2008. *Understanding Terrorism and Political Violence: The Life Cycle of Birth, Growth, Transformation, and Demise.* London: Routledge.

Gurr, Ted R. 1970. *Why Men Rebel.* Princeton, NJ: Princeton University Press.

Hampson, Fen Osler, and I. William Zartman. 2011. *The Global Power of Talk: Using Negotiation to Advance America's Interests and Global Security.* Boulder, CO: Paradigm.

Hassan, Nasra. 2001. "An Arsenal of Believers: Talking to the 'Human Bombs.'" *New Yorker,* Nov. 19.

Herz, Martin. 1982. "Diplomats and Terrorists: What Works, What Doesn't." Martin F. Herz Papers, Special Collections, Georgetown University Libraries.

Hewitt, Christopher. 2001. "Separatism, Irredentism and Terrorism: A Comparative Survey 1945–2000." In *Countering Terrorism through International Cooperation,* ed. A. P. Schmid. Milan: ISPAC.

Hirschman, Alfred. 1982. *Exit, Voice, and Loyalty.* Cambridge, MA: Harvard University Press.

Hoffman, Bruce. 2003. "The Logic of Suicide Terrorism." *Atlantic,* June. www.theatlantic.com/doc/200306/hoffman (accessed Nov. 3, 2010).

———. 2006. *Inside Terrorism.* New York: Columbia University Press.

Horgan, John. 2003. "Leaving Terrorism Behind: An Individual Perspective." In *Terrorists, Victims and Society: Psychological Perspectives on Terrorism and Its Consequences,* ed. Andrew Silke. Chichester, UK: John Wiley and Sons.

———. 2005. *The Psychology of Terrorism.* London: Routledge.

Horgan, John, and Maxwell Taylor. 2006. "Insurgency in Ireland: A Preliminary Analysis of the Provisional IRA Ceasefire 1994–1996 and Beyond." In *Understanding and Managing Insurgent Movements,* ed. Albrecht Schnabel and Rohan Gunaratna. London: Marvin Cavendish.

Hudson, Rex A. 1999. *The Sociology and Psychology of Terrorism: Who Becomes a Terrorist and Why?* Washington, DC: Library of Congress.

ICSR. 2008. "Pathways into Radicalisation: Why Do People Become Radicals?" Panel presentation, First International Conference on Radicalisation and Political Violence, London, Jan. 17–18.

Jamieson, Alison. 1989. *The Heart Attacked: Terrorism and Conflict in the Italian State.* London: Marion Boyars.

Jenkins, J. Craig, and Bert Klandermans, eds. 1995. *The Politics of Social Protest.* Minneapolis: University of Minnesota Press.

Kahneman, Daniel, and Amos Tversky. 1979. "Prospect Theory: An Analysis of Decision under Risk." *Econometrica* 47 (3): 263–91.

Kakar, Sudhir. 1996. *The Colors of Violence.* Chicago: University of Chicago Press.

Khalfi, Mustafa. 2010. "Understanding the PJD." Address to the Carnegie Endowment for International Peace Middle East program, Apr. 27, Washington, DC.

Krueger, Alan B. 2007. *What Makes a Terrorist? Economics and the Roots of Terrorism.* Princeton, NJ: Princeton University Press.

Krueger, Alan B., and Jitka Maleckova. 2003. "Education, Poverty and Terrorism: Is There a Causal Connection?" *Journal of Economic Perspectives* 17 (4): 119–44.

Kruglanski, Arie, and Jeffrey Victoroff, eds. 2009. *Psychology of Terrorism.* New York: Psychology Press.

Laraña, Enrique, Hank Johnston, and Joseph Gusfield, eds. 1994. *New Social Movements.* Philadelphia: Temple University Press.

Lijphart, Arend. 1972. *Democracy in Plural Societies: A Comparative Exploration.* New Haven, CT: Yale University Press.

Lilja, Jannie. 2010. "Disaggregating Dissent: The Challenges of Intra-Party Consolidation in Civil War and Peace Negotiations." PhD diss., Uppsala University.

MacFarquhar, Neil. 2004. "Lebanese Would-Be Suicide Bomber Tells How Volunteers Are Waging Jihad in Iraq." *New York Times,* Nov. 2.

Maleckova, Jitka. 2006. "Terrorists and the Societies from Which They Come." In Victoroff 2006.

Masters, Emane, and Alyssa Deffenbaugh. 2007. *The Lesser Jihad: Recruits and the al-Qaida Network.* Lanham, MD: Rowman and Littlefield.

McAdam, Doug. 1996. "Conceptual Origins, Current Problems, and Future Directions." In McAdam, McCarthy, and Zald 1996.

McAdam, Doug, John McCarthy, and Mayer Zald, eds. 1996. *Comparative Perspectives on Social Movements: Political Opportunities, Mobilizing Structures, and Cultural Framings.* New York: Cambridge University Press.

McCauley, Clark, and Sophia Moskalenko. 2008. "Mechanisms of Political Radicalization: Pathways toward Terrorism." *Terrorism and Political Violence* 20 (3): 415–33.

Merriman, Hardy, and Jack DuVall. 2007. "Dissolving Terrorism at Its Roots." In *Nonviolence: An Alternative for Countering Global Terror(ism)*, ed. Ralph Summy and Senthil Ram. Hauppauge, NY: Nova Science.

Miller, Greg. 2008. "Investigating the Psychopathic Mind." *Science* 321 (5894): 1284–86.

MIPT. 2007. "Terrorism Knowledge Base." Memorial Institute for the Prevention of Terrorism. www.tkb.org (accessed Dec. 11, 2007).

Moghaddam, Fathali M. 2005. "The Staircase to Terrorism: A Psychological Exploration." *American Psychologist* 60 (2).

Pape, Robert. 2003. "The Strategic Logic of Suicide Terrorism." *American Political Science Review* 97 (3): 343–61.

Pearlstein, Richard. 1991. *The Mind of the Political Terrorist*. Wilmington, DE: Scholarly Resources.

Piazza, James. 2006. "Rooted in Poverty? Terrorism, Poor Economic Development, and Social Cleavages." *Terrorism and Political Violence* 18 (1): 158–77.

Post, Jerrold. 2005. "Psychological Operations and Counterterrorism." *Joint Force Quarterly* 37: 105–10.

———. 2006. "Countering Islamist Militancy: An Epidemiologic Approach." In Victoroff 2006.

———. 2008. "Engaging Terrorists and Their Supporting Communities." Unpublished ms.

Post, Jerrold, Ehud Sprinzak, and Laurita Denny. 2003. "The Terrorists in Their Own Words: Interviews with 35 Incarcerated Middle Eastern Terrorists." *Terrorism and Political Violence* 15 (1).

Ross, Jeffrey Ian, and Ted Gurr. 1989. "Why Terrorism Subsides: A Comparative Study of Canada and the United States." *Comparative Politics* 21 (4): 405–26.

Sageman, Marc. 2004. *Understanding Terror Networks*. Philadelphia: University of Pennsylvania Press.

Seale, Patrick 1992. *Abu Nidal: A Gun For Hire*. New York: Random House.

Semelin, Jacques 2008. "Comprendre notre barbarie." *Justice & Démocratie* 23 (1er semester): 15.

Soudan, François. 1996. "Comment on fabrique un terroriste." *Jeune Afrique*, no. 1831.

Staub, Ervin. 1989. *The Roots of Evil*. New York: Cambridge University Press.

———. 2010. *Overcoming Evil: Genocide, Violent Conflict, and Terrorism*. Oxford: Oxford University Press.

Stern, Jessica. 2003. *Terror in the Name of God: Why Religious Militants Kill*. New York: HarperCollins.

Tamimi, A. S. 2001. *Rachid Ghannouchi: A Democrat within Islamism*. New York: Oxford University Press.

Tarrow, Sidney. 1996. "States and Opportunities." In McAdam, McCarthy, and Zald 1996.

Tilly, Charles. 2003. *The Politics of Collective Violence*. Cambridge: Cambridge University Press.

United Nations Assistance Mission to Afghanistan (UNAMA). 2007. *Suicide Attacks in Afghanistan 2001-2007,* Sept. www.unama-afg.org/docs (accessed Nov. 5, 2008).

Victoroff, Jeffrey. 2005. "The Mind of the Terrorist: A Review and Critique of Psychological Approaches." *Journal of Conflict Resolution* 49 (1): 3–42.

———, ed. 2006. *Tangled Roots: Social and Psychological Factors in the Genesis of Terrorism*. Amsterdam: IOS Press.

von Hippel, Karen. 2002. "The Roots of Terrorism." *Political Quarterly*. Suppl. no. 1 (August): 25–39.

Weber, Max. 1946. *From Max Weber: Essays in Sociology*. Trans. and ed. H. H. Gerth and C. Wright Mills. New York: Oxford University Press.

Wiktorowicz, Quintan, ed. 2004. *Islamic Activism: A Social Movement Theory Approach*. Bloomington: Indiana University Press.

Zartman, I. William. 1966. "Ideology and Interest." In *African Diplomacy: Studies in the Determinants of Foreign Policy*, ed. Vernon McKay. New York: Praeger.

———, ed. 1995. *Elusive Peace: Negotiating an End to Civil Wars*. Washington, DC: Brookings Institution Press.

———, ed. 2001. *Preventive Negotiation: Avoiding Conflict Escalation*. Lanham, MD: Rowman and Littlefield.

———. 2005. *Cowardly Lions: Missed Opportunities to Prevent Deadly Conflict and State Collapse*. Boulder, CO: Lynne Rienner.

———. 2010. *Preventing Identity Conflicts Leading to Genocide and Mass Killings*. New York: International Peace Institute.

2

Growing Out in Organization

William Donohue and Moty Cristal

A recent RAND Corporation study, seeking to inform policymakers, analyzed 648 terrorist groups that existed between 1968 and 2006, to determine how terrorist groups end (Jones and Libicki 2008). The study found that a transition to the political process is the most common end to groups that began with a violent mission (43 percent). These groups shift away from violence to achieve very narrow political goals. In 10 percent of cases, the groups ended their activities because they had achieved their very narrow terrorist objectives, whereas in 7 percent of cases, military force led to the end of the terrorist group. Other key findings of the study indicate that religion-based terrorist groups take longer to eliminate than other groups, that terrorist groups in general rarely achieve their objectives, and that big groups with more than 10,000 members are more likely to be victorious than groups with fewer than 1,000 members. Thus, keeping the size of the group from expanding is an important objective in fighting terrorism.

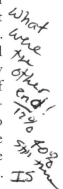

What were the other ends? 12% still too low. IS

Given that most terrorist groups end by making the transition to a political mission, it seems important to understand how they make this transition. What is the process by which groups evolve from forming on the basis of violence to adopting a primarily political mission? How do they begin, how do they take root and gain support, and how do they ultimately transform into some political entity or disperse altogether? If we assume that terrorist movements evolve as organizations or change as dynamic networks, a useful way to study them might be to draw on research in organizational life cycles. This chapter proposes a set of stages that might effectively describe how terrorist organizations progress to adopt a political, nonviolent mission. Certainly, not all such organizations evolve in the same way, as Boaz Ganor points out in his review of terrorist organization typologies (Ganor 2008). And yet, the proposed model helps academics and practitioners/politicians determine potential negotiation opportunities as they emerge as part of the larger strategy in dealing with terrorism.

The concepts presented in this chapter are meant to stimulate thinking about the value of identifying life cycles as a necessary part of creating more comprehensive intervention strategies (Bar-Tal 2000). Terrorist organizations are not, and should not be seen as, monolithic, static entities. Rather, they are dynamic, rapidly changing organizations whose structures, goals, and tactics are constantly shifting. This understanding should stimulate a dialogue about taking more of a process perspective in building effective counterterrorism strategies. A useful foundation for this perspective draws from work in organizational change. The idea is that organizations are not static institutions; they have a history and are always in the process of becoming something different. To understand this basic idea, we turn to the literature.

A Dune Approach to Understanding Terrorist Organizations

Previous thinking about terrorist organizations argues that terrorist groups typically exhibit a hierarchical organization with well-defined role structures and identities (Victoroff 2005; Ganor 2008). But it appears that emerging global terrorist organizations no longer operate in a hierarchical form typical of more localized or regionalized groups such as the Provisional Irish Republican Army (PIRA) or the Red Brigade. The hierarchical approach assumes that social identities, boundaries, and actors' choices are relatively fixed, stable, and consistent as individuals perform their routinized roles and assignments according to formal and unambiguous rules. A hierarchical frame tends to ignore the potential and real influence of constantly evolving and shifting formal and informal ties that cut across social categories and group boundaries. It also ignores other forms of informal everyday social relations that affect actors' identities, attitudes, and behaviors. Ganor argues that groups can take on many different kinds of organizational structures and shift between them quite readily.

Mishal and Rosenthal level this same criticism at research that seeks to classify Islamic terrorist organizations. Instead of seeing these organizations as networks or hierarchical structures, they use a dune organizational model to study al-Qaeda, Hezbollah, Hamas, and the Palestinian Islamic Jihad. A dunelike organization shifts with the wind and is continuously reshaped. The dune organization manifests key features such as (1) lack of affiliation with any explicit territorial rationale, making it difficult to monitor the organization's maneuvers; (2) no immanent institutional presence, resulting in an almost ghostlike organizational reality that is often built on its own disappearance; (3) dynamic activity that adheres to no sequential reasoning regarding interaction with other organizations; (4) command and communication chains that may be waived, intentionally fragmented, or severed at any time; (5) consequent maneuverability among various interests, and the attendant ability to align with different regional conflicts; and (6) adherence to a grand vision, such as global jihad, as a substitute for affiliation to a specific territory (Mishal and Rosenthal 2005).

In comparing the dune model with the hierarchical and network models, Mishal and Rosenthal conclude that the dune model has the advantage of a more open framework, which recognizes and accounts for the lack of institutional controls and boundaries that characterize the more contemporary terrorist organizations. The group can create institutional structures when necessary to carry out military missions, then revert to more blurred social, political, and operational boundaries that are often necessary to avoid detection. In this dune model, the mode of the intra- and interorganizational action is bargaining and negotiating rather than controlling. It is reinvention rather than coercion, steering rather than rowing. Players may not even know who is in command of the organization, or what the final action of the network might be. They take orders from one player and pass it on to another, without ever knowing the network's complete nature or characteristics. In a hub network, all orders come from the player located at the center, and all information must pass through that node. One player sees the whole picture, while all other players are subordinate to that central player, at least in the sense of receiving and transferring information.[1] In an all-channel network, on the other hand, information flows freely in a fully collaborative manner. Thus, no single player has real command and control over the others. But even in this form, the relevant players are defined and the organizational movement is not applied to outside players.

And yet, it is important not to assume that terrorist groups with a more dunelike profile are organizationally inept or chaotic (Mishal and Rosenthal 2005; Post, Ruby, and Shaw 2002). They still face structural demands, particularly as they grow and become institutionalized within some kind of organizational structure. If we identify the relevant organizational structures, then we can start thinking more dynamically about how terrorist

There's still structure, likes cells in the body

groups continuously reshape these structures. A terrorist group must face a variety of organizational constraints (e.g., flow of funds, distribution of resources, operational orders, reporting mechanisms, "credit" for committing terrorist acts, and decisions on claiming responsibility). For example, a March 2008 suicide attack in the Israeli town of Dimona was claimed by three terrorist organizations: the al-Aqsa Martyrs' Brigades (Fatah's military wing), the Abu Ali Mustafa Brigades (the Popular Front for the Liberation of Palestine's military wing), and the National Resistance Brigades. All these groups are out trying to build their brand as highly effective terror agents in order to keep funds flowing, attract members, and get "credit" for terrorist acts.

Terror operatives are subject to the same kind of leader-follower dynamics that any organization must deal with. That is, even though the group exhibits dunelike characteristics, it is still an organization that must adopt structures and processes that grow and change as its missions and tactics grow and change. This is a key assumption. Terrorist groups are not static but can alter their missions and approaches to take on different shapes as they move from one location to the next—much as a sand dune does. They must be described and understood according to how they evolve and change and what their internal and external organizational patterns are, rather than what they happen to be at any given moment. If we can begin to understand the patterns of these dunelike evolutions, we can start to identity the implications surrounding intervention. We can begin to see where negotiation and conflict management strategies can be effective in shifting the direction of terrorist groups away from violence and more toward political activity.

At this point, the question is, what kind of model can we use to describe the transformation of dunelike terrorist groups into political organizations with more traditional-looking structures? One model often used to describe changes in organizations is that of organizational life cycles. By applying that literature to terrorist organizational growth and development, we can better understand how terrorist groups shift from violence to politics.

Terrorist Organizational Life Cycles

The literature on organizational life cycles (most of it derived from studying for-profit businesses) indicates that typical organizations are born, grow, and eventually either decline or shift into some other form. This evolution can be modeled in four stages (Gray and Ariss 1985; Hwang and Park 2007). Collectively, this literature suggests that the typical developmental pattern includes (1) the *conception-and-development* stage, in which entrepreneurs develop their ideas and sell them to supporters and financial backers; (2) the *commercialization* stage, in which the entrepreneurs move into the marketplace to gain consumer acceptance and formalize organizational structures and processes; (3) the *growth* stage, in which the organization becomes larger and faces the challenges of managing volume and becoming more efficient to build market share; and (4) the *stability* stage, which evolves once growth slows and the organization's rigid structures and resistance to change make adapting difficult.

The Conception-and-Development Stage: Incubation

In applying this concept of life cycles to understand how dunelike terrorist organizations come into existence, grow their violent mission, and ultimately reshape themselves into more political entities, we must first examine how they approach the *conception-and-development stage*. In other words, how do terrorist entrepreneurs develop their ideas and sell them to potential supporters? Although chapter 1 in this book explores this issue specifically, the general idea is that any organization, including those with a terrorist mission, faces some key start-up challenges to move it along. It must sustain entrepreneurial leaders who can drive the organization's mission and secure funding, build the ideology about mission and vision, recruit qualified members to carry out the mission, and train them so they can implement the mission.

From this perspective, we might label this initial period the *incubation* stage, with leadership as its first start-up challenge. Who is the entrepreneur driving the ideology and crafting the group's structure? How is this leader consolidating power while also defining and communicating an ideological or revolutionary framework that will serve as the main form of indoctrination? From what sources do terrorists derive this ideological energy justifying the use of force to accomplish goals? The nature of this ideological framework is key in determining the rules and organizational structure for the terrorist's operation. Ganor provides a detailed description of how various Islamic-based terrorist leaders promote their ideology while working as entrepreneurs to creatively attract resources for their cause (Ganor 2008).

If fundamentalist religious beliefs serve as a main feeder of modern dunelike terrorist organizations, we can think of the leaders as ideological entrepreneurs using an established religious framework to promote extreme ideas to attract supporters toward their cause. These ideological entrepreneurs search for financial backers, seek acceptance from the more mainstream leaders' alienated constituents, and work to establish their violent brand and build market share, thereby strengthening themselves institutionally. Christine Fair describes how al-Qaeda uses a web of informal relationships and media tools to gain access to operational collaborators within Pakistan (Fair 2004). Timothy Thomas details how al-Qaeda uses the Internet not only to recruit and foment conflict across the globe but also to plan and execute its actions and manage its organizational structure (Thomas 2003).

Once the leaders have selected recruits, they begin indoctrination by creating or emphasizing the problem, picturing a common enemy, promoting a sense of humiliation and the desire for revenge, creating a virtual community, presenting an ultimate solution, and, in the case of Islamic-focused groups such as al-Qaeda, glorifying an extreme version of Islam, and its ideology. According to Fair, this process creates a peer group and a sense of belonging (Fair 2004). These indoctrination strategies become fairly routinized and sophisticated, and integrated with the group's religious practices. These peer groups are sustained not as a secular army but as a religious movement that is continuously building its commitment to make whatever sacrifice is necessary for "victory."

The ideological framework is also important in crafting the messages necessary to recruit, train, and indoctrinate members. The ideology must plug into a vital need within the recruits that justifies the commitment. As evidenced by the growth of terrorist activity in the Middle East, extremist groups make liberal use of various media platforms, both traditional (e.g., word of mouth) and new (e.g., Facebook, smart phones), to promote their message and pull individuals into the process. The entrepreneurs build influence during this incubation stage through strategic networking with like-minded terrorist organizations that share their ideological orientations. The al-Qaeda tactics in Pakistan, mentioned above, provide useful case examples of this activity (Fair 2004). The networking also helps develop intelligence and operational ideas.

Another key incubation process is training recruits, both ideologically and operationally. Though the training can range from military to various indoctrination strategies, its goal is to create a disciplined group of individuals who accept violence against innocents as a key strategy toward the ultimate objective, whatever it may be. And the training must continuously reinforce the social confirmation of the value inherent in suicide bombing or other extreme measures of violence. The acts must be publicized and celebrated within the community, both to legitimize the tactics and to recruit new members.

The incubation process must also continue to sell the organization's ideological foundation, to help legitimize it among constituents and make it grow. By 2008, Iraq had become a focal point for al-Qaeda's rhetoric, and statements continued to underscore al-Qaeda leaders' interest in Iraq and support for the ongoing insurgency. Statements released by Bin Laden

1. = developing / promoting ideology

and his deputy Ayman al-Zawahiri since late 2004 have rekindled public debate in Europe and the United States surrounding al-Qaeda's ideology, motives, and plans for future attacks. Statements released following the July 2005 al-Qaeda-linked suicide bombing attacks on the London transit system have characterized those attacks and al-Qaeda's ongoing terrorist campaign as a response to British and U.S. military operations in Iraq. Al-Qaeda in Iraq is an Iraqi insurgency group led by Abu Musab al-Zarqawi until his death in 2006; it is now believed to be led by Abu Hamza al-Muhajir. Zarqawi had his own insurgency, which was not affiliated with al-Qaeda but merged with it in 2004.

A key feature of terrorist rhetoric is its continual rededication to its ideologies and goals. Al-Qaeda follows a Sunni ideology and a Sunni militancy and has, since its inception, been violently anti-American. As evidenced by the rhetoric of certain members of the Salafi (or Wahhabi) ulama (body of mullahs) and militants such as al-Zarqawi, Sunni militancy is a two-pronged effort: to remove U.S. influence from the greater Middle East and to restore Sunni dominance there. The bombings in Karbala, Najaf, and other Shia holy sites make clear that Sunni militancy is designed both to combat the Shia revival and to provoke a sectarian civil war in Iraq in an effort to confound U.S. plans for the country.

Al-Qaeda suicide bombers and ambush units in Iraq routinely depend on the Web for training and tactical support, relying on its anonymity and flexibility to operate with near impunity in cyberspace. In Qatar, Egypt, and Europe, cells affiliated with al-Qaeda that have, since around 2005, carried out or seriously planned bombings rely heavily on the Internet. Al-Qaeda and its offshoots are building a massive and dynamic online library of training materials—some supported by experts who answer questions on message boards or in chat rooms—covering such varied subjects as how to mix poison, how to make a bomb from commercial chemicals, how to pose as a fisherman and sneak through Syria into Iraq, how to shoot at a U.S. soldier, and how to navigate by the stars while running through a night-shrouded desert. These materials are cascading across the Web in Arabic, Urdu, Pashto, and other first languages of jihadist volunteers. Potential al-Qaeda recruits can find links to the latest computer hacking techniques (in the discussion group called "electronic jihad"), the most recent beheading video from Iraq, paeans to the 9/11 hijackers, long Quranic justifications of suicide attacks, and al-Qaeda's online magazine *Sawt al-Jihad* (Voice of Jihad).

The Commercialization Stage: Strategic Violence

Once the terrorist organization has completed the incubation stage, it begins activities characteristic of the second stage in the organizational life cycle. In a legitimate business-focused organization, this is the *commercialization stage*, dedicated to gaining more customer acceptance and formalizing organizational structures and processes. That is, the company must put its products out there and make known the kind of business it wishes to pursue.

For the terrorist organization, commercialization means moving into the marketplace and growing the organization's ability to deliver on its mission to the target audience (funders, supporters, sympathetic governments). The organization now begins implementing violence to achieve its goals. Thus, we can more accurately term this life cycle stage *strategic violence*, since violence in the strategic service of ideology is the product the organization is delivering. To bring its violence product to market, the leadership must solidify its power over rival groups and develop the formal rules and procedures to secure its legitimacy in the marketplace.

The operational forces within the terrorist group function as a dunelike, self-organizing system. In the terrorist organization that must continuously evade or flee state-run authorities, cells shift continuously while still retaining the trappings of more formal organizations with leaders, defined roles, and command-and-control tactics. Strategically, the terrorist group uses its dunelike cell structure to select and target high-profile, symbolically significant individuals, buildings, and "venues," to gain legitimacy and draw attention to its differing values and interests from those of competing organizations. The goal is to appeal both to constituents, by demonstrating that the just war is indeed being waged, and to funders, who may be using the terrorists for their own purposes.

A good example of how an organization comes to establish and promote its legitimacy as an institution emerges from the Israeli-Palestinian conflict and Israel's continuing confrontation with Hezbollah in Lebanon. In April 1996, the Israeli armed forces launched Operation Grapes of Wrath, which was intended to wipe out Hezbollah's base in southern Lebanon. The killing on April 18, 1996, of over 100 Lebanese refugees in a UN base at Qana drew strong international condemnation. Shortly after the Qana incident, the United States mediated negotiations between Israeli and Syrian/Lebanese representatives who worked with Hezbollah. Following several days of negotiations, the two sides signed the Grapes of Wrath Understandings on April 26, 1996. Both sides agreed that civilians should not be targeted. In practice, this meant that Hezbollah agreed to refrain from firing Katyusha rockets into Israel, and the Israeli Defense Forces (IDF) would refrain from targeting civilians in southern Lebanon. Also, an international monitoring committee of American, French, Syrian, Lebanese, and Israeli representatives was set up to see that the understandings were observed. Many claimed that the understandings seemed to imply that Israel recognized Hezbollah's right to target IDF soldiers within the security zone.

Of interest in relation to terrorism, the life cycle model points out that during this second stage, individual managers or subunits tend to mobilize coalitions to advance their goals (Gray and Ariss 1985). Leadership structures and organizational practices become established and promoted. The Grapes of Wrath agreement turned Hezbollah into a semilegitimate institution as (1) Israel sat to negotiate with its "representatives" (i.e., Syria and Lebanon, which advocated its interests), and (2) Hezbollah gained implicit "legitimacy" to attack IDF soldiers. This is a textbook case of an organization establishing its legitimatization through the use of strategic violence.

An example of the strategic violence stage is Hamas's series of suicide bombings in 1996. Following the assassination of Israeli prime minister Yitzhak Rabin, the dovish leader Shimon Peres became Israel's prime minister. The prospect of progress in the political arena, together with the likely establishment of a Palestinian state in only parts of the West Bank and Gaza Strip, was unacceptable to the Hamas leadership. Hamas expressed fierce opposition to the newly created Palestinian Authority, led by Yasser Arafat, and hoped that jihad operations would sabotage the peace process.

The series of suicide attacks in February-March 1996, which caused more than 100 Israeli casualties, brought about a change in Israeli public opinion, resulting in the hawkish Benjamin Netanyahu's victory in the June 1996 elections. After the elections, it seemed that Hamas was satisfied with the result of its terrorist strategy: difficulties in the Israeli-Palestinian peace process, and the stalemate of the political process. This was in keeping with Hamas's conviction that any compromise with Israel is contrary to the interests of the Palestinian people, and with the long-term objectives of the Islamic movement: to liberate all Palestine and make it an Islamic state. These attacks, which actually undermined the peace process, gained popular support for Hamas within the West Bank and Gaza and forced the competing Palestinian Fatah movement to adopt the same strategy of suicide bombings in 2000, just to win back some public support, which favored Hamas since 1996.

To make sure that it is seen as delivering its violence products for the funders, the terrorist group becomes more reliant on external resources and logistics during this commercialization, or strategic violence, stage. This reliance requires some sort of command-and-control structure that enables the whole terror process to recruit members, secure resources, and attack targets. For example, Hezbollah's current structure, chain of command, and resources were all established after its strategic violence stage, which started to emerge during the 1980s with the taking of Western hostages and the bombings of U.S. Marine headquarters in Beirut and Tyre. As a result, Hezbollah became increasingly dependent on Iran and Syria to provide financial and logistical support for its activities.

To facilitate any military structure, a terrorist group must select a home base or set of bases in areas that will at least tacitly support the group's efforts. At a minimum, the locals must not interfere. But ideally, the locals must see the terrorist group's cause as legitimate and even assist in recruitment and logistical activities to sustain the violent mission. Initially, the group uses the local support simply to allow the violent mission's existence. But ultimately, the local supporters, who are typically resource starved, may come to embrace the terrorist mission, since they need jobs, infrastructure, clinics, and schools, and perhaps even reparations that could emerge in the conflict's aftermath. In Lebanon, the Shiite minority, residing mainly in the south and along the Israeli border, was the natural cradle for Hezbollah. And in the strategic violence stage, Hezbollah strengthened its stronghold in the south, though aiming to expand its support base throughout Lebanon.

A key need in sustaining the terror mission is funding. The leadership must continuously attract resources, either from a state that covertly supports terror or directly from supporters who engage in various legitimate or illegitimate commercial activities within recognized states. Funding strategies can often be very creative and indirect, but their purpose is always the same: to sustain the members and leaders and provide resources to the local communities that harbor the terrorist groups. The terror mechanism is expensive to create and support (Raphaeli 2003). Successfully sustaining it requires resources, and in recent years, terror financing networks, rather than state sponsors, are providing more of such patronage. While Iran and Syria continue to back international terrorist groups—mainly Hezbollah and Hamas—groups increasingly finance their own activities through a network of charitable and humanitarian organizations, criminal enterprises, front companies, illicit and unregulated banking systems, and the personal wealth of individual militants (Fitzgerald 2004).

In the course of carrying out its mission, the terrorist group will experience some kind of military, political, or economic retaliatory action from the hurt state or society. Since this retaliatory action typically occurs during the maturing strategic violence stage of the organization's life cycle, when leadership and command and control are well established, it can affect the organization in one of two ways. If the retaliation is minimal—say, largely

retaliation
- short = reinforce leaders
- long = diversification

economic or legal—it can serve to reinforce the leadership, since the leadership will still be seen as effective for avoiding retaliation or weathering it with minimal damage.

For example, Israel's policy of measures to disrupt freedom of movement, such as roadblocks and construction of the security barrier between the West Bank and Israel, may have resulted in significantly increasing Hamas's influence in Palestine, thereby actually advancing Hamas's goal of dominating the Palestinian political scene. Israel's conditioning political and, hence, economic progress on the immediate dismantling of Hamas's military infrastructure—in effect, demanding an improbable Palestinian civil war in exchange for more tolerable occupation conditions—has given Hamas a veto over the political progress. By thus weakening the Palestinian Authority (PA), Israeli policy has reduced the ability and, arguably, the incentive that either Hamas or the PA may have to contain the Islamists. Killing Hamas's leaders and militants, while perhaps temporarily dissuading the group from large-scale terror operations, has not reduced the numbers of Palestinians ready to undertake suicide attacks to advance their cause. This ability to perpetuate its mission is strong evidence that an organization has become institutionalized in the strategic violence phase.

On the other hand, if the retaliation is significant and prolonged, it can result in diversification, in which the terror group changes its operational mode, organizational structure, and leadership. The group must adapt to the threat and change, perhaps pulling itself back into an incubation phase to refocus its mission, select new leadership, and find new recruits. Israel made three such efforts during the 1990s, bringing mixed results. The most successful was the operation that resulted in the death of Palestinian Islamic Jihad leader Fathi Shikaki in Malta in October 1995. No competent successor emerged to replace Shikaki, thereby producing disarray in Islamic Jihad. The organization limped along for several years, unable to mount any serious attacks against Israel or Israelis. Less than a year later, Israel killed Yahya Ayyash, known as "the engineer." Ayyash had been one of Hamas's most skilled and prolific bomb makers, whose handiwork proved critical to many terrorist attacks against Israel. Although Israel had succeeded in removing a key figure from Hamas, Ayyash's death also unleashed four suicide bus bombings in the next two months, killing more than fifty Israelis. Finally, Israel failed to kill Khaled Meshal, the chief of Hamas's political bureau, in Amman in September 1997. Israeli agents succeeded in poisoning Meshal but were captured by Jordanian authorities before they could leave Jordan. To secure their return, Israeli prime minister Benjamin Netanyahu agreed to provide the antidote for the poison (thus bringing about Meshal's recovery) and released Hamas's founder,

Sheik Ahmed Yassin, from an Israeli prison. Yassin's return as a spiritual leader not only strengthened Hamas but also weakened Arafat because he was not involved in the dealings.

Typically, terrorist groups do not dissolve in the face of retaliation from military force, no matter how intense (Jones and Libicki 2008). One exception is Egypt's Gama'a Islamiya (Muslim Brotherhood), which did abandon its terror mission in the face of massive retaliation following the assassination of President Anwar Sadat (Munson 2001). The group now focuses on more prosocial activities. For an in-depth discussion of Gama'a Islamiya's change of heart, see Carolin Goerzig's chapter.

The Growth Stage: Political Violence

If the terrorist group can absorb the retaliation while promoting a political presence—even a legitimate one—it moves into a third, even more institutionalized phase of its life cycle. In the commercial model, this represents the *growth stage*, in which the organization becomes larger by building volume and becoming more efficient to build market share. In a terrorist organization, "*political violence*" is a more apt term, because the organization still retains its violent mission, yet the weight of its success forces it to become more institutionalized to be effective.

More institutionalization requires a larger political footprint, both within the supporting communities and within the organization itself. The organization must make more and more payoffs to the communities in terms of schools, clinics, and jobs, while also managing the internal politics of succession management and other growth challenges. At this point, then, the terror organization has moved beyond uniquely structured violent acts into almost an assembly line of violence. The funding streams, recruiting practices, and community institutions have become more efficient and routinized.

This success affords the terrorist group the ability to build buffers against threats from the injured state. The classic example of how terrorist organizations move into this political violence stage is the evolution of Fatah. Anat Kurz describes how Fatah moved through various institutional phases beginning in 1959, in the wake of the 1956 Sinai Campaign, in which Israel established its military dominance over its Arab neighbors (Kurz 2005). The first phase focused on regulative formation and a violence campaign, to be developed and carried out by a group of young Palestinians driven not by religious issues but by a need to reestablish a military counterweight to escalating Israeli dominance in the region. After this phase of sporadic violence and following the 1967 war, Fatah implemented a dual strategy that involved both violent mobilization and communal projects. The need for these projects became apparent as Israel's victory in the war made it clear that liberating Palestine was less and less likely, and Israeli occupation of Gaza and the West Bank presented Fatah with an opportunity to provide leadership in these captured territories. Following these efforts, Fatah entered a new phase of legitimacy after a series of confrontations with Israel that demonstrated Fatah's ability to provide a legitimate, even though ultimately ineffective, threat to Israel. By the end of 1973, that credibility began to translate into external political recognition, and by the end of the 1960s, several Arab states and Soviet bloc governments recognized the Fatah-led Palestinian Liberation Organization (PLO), with many of them providing logistical aid.

Through most of the middle and late 1970s and early 1980s, Fatah's two-pronged efforts gathered steam. While continuing its terrorist mission, it also initiated a diplomatic effort when it became clear in the aftermath of the October 1973 Yom Kippur War that the PLO had a role in the emerging regional political process. But Fatah did not abandon its terrorism mission, which remained a primary means for mobilizing support while also securing what diplomacy could not achieve (Kurz 2005).

In subsequent phases, while facing many challenges throughout the 1970s and 1980s, Fatah bounced back and forth between its terrorist and political missions and then finally solidified its political legitimacy in the run-up to the Oslo Accords in the early 1990s (Kurz 2005). From that time until the Camp David Peace Summit in 2000, Fatah tried to deal with the PA in managing the regional and international scrutiny that accompanied the high visibility of these various accords and peace initiatives. Then, following the collapse of Camp David, the intifada significantly eroded Fatah's legitimacy, which it subsequently tried to rebuild as it separates itself, at least politically, from Hamas and the Gaza Strip.

Fatah's evolution provides a useful example of how terrorist organizations evolve through the various stages, from incubation through strategic violence, and finally to political violence. This organization has evolved to sustain both violent and political/communal missions as it set up residence in the West Bank, having lost control of Gaza. In fact, Fatah initiated both roles typical of the political violence stage early on, with alternating emphases over time. The current situation finds it pursuing a more extensive political mission. This dual mission is difficult to sustain as Fatah seeks to emerge as a legitimate government. On one hand, maintaining the violent mission compromises its international standing, but on the other hand, abandoning that mission makes it appear weak internally, particularly on the commitment to expel Israel from its homeland. Straddling this fence is not easy, since communicating directly with its own terrorist wing is hardly

politically viable. Nevertheless, these kinds of political and operational efforts required to deal with the terrorist group change if or when it reaches
this political violence phase.

Israel, as well as other governments, faces this challenge daily. While
declaring that it is not negotiating with Hamas, Israel maintains at least
two channels of indirect communication: one concerning a prisoner exchange for the captured soldier held by Hamas in Gaza since June 2006,
and the second concerning humanitarian provision to the Hamas-ruled
Gaza Strip. To maintain political support within Israel while at the same
time making progress on both channels, Israel has to rely heavily on interested mediators or third parties (mainly Egypt)—a process that compli-
cates both the communication with Hamas and the terms of any potential
agreement. The government challenge is even more complicated when it
needs to deal with two "faces" of the same organization.

The British government, while conducting talks with IRA leadership
during the 1980s, faced the same challenge in communicating with both
Sinn Fein and the IRA. Modern terrorist organizations' institutional dynamics and fragmented, dunelike structures make negotiating with them
more and more challenging to governments, since the separation between
the terrorist arm and a legitimate political wing may hardly exist.

While dealing with its dual missions of political control and violent action, the terrorist group continuously weighs the effectiveness of each. In
this position, Zartman's issue of "ripeness" plays a significant role. A mutually hurting stalemate might cause the terrorist group to move away from
violence, whereas a mutually enhancing opportunity might create an incentive to become more political (Zartman 1989). Arafat's decision to negotiate at Oslo stemmed from the PLO's earlier failures to grasp power and
influence. Looking back at Arafat's 1988 agreement to accept UN Security
Resolution 242, it is important to understand the context. It was a difficult
period for Arafat, beginning as far back as Black September, in 1970, and
the king of Jordan's expulsion of the PLO from his territory. Then came
the Lebanon war (1982), the Palestinian losses of the first intifada (1987),
and the deteriorating status of the Soviet Union. All these challenges created ripeness for Arafat to move toward the political track. The Palestinian
loss of international support during the 1991 Iraq war, as well as the stalled
intifada, capped off the mutually hurting stalemate and enabled the Oslo
track (initiated in 1992) as a classic mutually enhancing opportunity.

The Stability Stage: Political Transformation

As institutionalization grows within the political violence stage, the terrorist organization may begin stretching its political initiatives and focus

more externally to influence the target audiences that originally incited its movement to violence. As in the example of Fatah, as the political process begins to dominate the violent mission, the group moves into its fourth phase, that of *political transformation*. Recall that this fourth stage corresponds to the *stability stage* in the evolution of commercial organizations. As a stage, stability reflects a stagnant or slow growth rate and the refocusing of its mission. When terrorist organizations begin to feel the weight of their political mission brought about by the quest for political legitimization, they begin to abandon a focus on the violent mission. A splinter group may emerge that wishes to retain the violent mission, but the main body of the group is committed to a transformation that really reflects a narrowing toward more stability.

As a result of the splintering in response to the terrorist group's decline or redevelopment, the politics intensify, as evidenced by increased power struggles and other political maneuvering aimed at preserving resource allocation. During this period, competition for leadership to define a new direction for the organization often threatens established power structures. A good example of this kind of decline is the Provisional Irish Republican Army, which became more politically institutionalized as it matured. As it gained more notoriety and political strength, leadership struggles emerged and ultimately resulted in an organizational split. (See McGarry and O'Leary 2004.)

We see another example of this split resulting from institutional pressures in the evolution of Hamas. Khaled Mashal, a physics teacher in his late forties, is currently the supreme leader of Hamas. He lives in exile in Damascus. He was thought of as the natural successor to Sheikh Ahmad Yassin and still leads the group's political bureau. But his authority was briefly challenged by Muhamad Rantisi, who sought to control the group's military wing, the Izz ad-Din al-Qassam Brigades. Mashal's "decision code" is a veto strategy that ultimately rejects virtually all internal military agreements to build political power. That is, he vetoes decisions regarding Hamas's future direction.

In contrast to Mashal, Ismail Haniya, the prime minister of the Hamas government in Gaza since 2007, presented the group's public face during the political campaign (2006), appearing in televised messages. Haniya was expelled from the Palestinian territories to Lebanon in 1992 and is a long-serving member of the group's political bureau. He is regarded as the leader of the more pragmatic wing of the group and has acted as a go-between with the Palestinian Authority. He has survived an assassination attempt. Haniya's decision code is influenced primarily by the political-organizational dimension (his relations with Mashal and with the Hamas military wing).

Haniya's decisions are constrained by the fact that he cannot afford to accept alternatives that will damage his position in the Hamas organization. The dilemma between the political-organizational dimension and the relationship with the military wing of Hamas leads him to reject compromise offers. Mashal is the only decision maker in Hamas who can decide on a deal with Israel or Fatah.

While the growth, or political violence, stage is characterized by moderate bargaining, the stability, or political transformation, stage exhibits much more intense bargaining, both internally among members of competing factions struggling for mission control and externally with various neighbor states and other states within the group's region. Again, the situation in the Mideast is a good example aimed at implementing or resisting new strategies.

The effect of international disengagement and sanctions was to polarize Palestinian politics. In late 2006 and early 2007, the violence between Fatah and Hamas began to escalate, in part because both sides were feeling stronger after months of reorganization and rearmament. The power struggle came to a head in the weeks before the Saudi mediation at Mecca in 2006. The unity government established at Mecca was precisely what Palestinians had been demanding for years. There is still the very real possibility of civil war between Fatah and Hamas, but the power-sharing arrangements agreed at Mecca have real legitimacy among Palestinians and, thus, offer a way out of the political crisis in Palestine. Mecca, therefore, is a prerequisite for a peace process, not an obstacle to it.

Without a Hamas-Fatah power-sharing agreement, and as long as the Islamists feel marginalized, unable to govern, and locked in an existential struggle for survival, there can be no sustainable diplomacy. With sizable public support, Hamas can deny Palestinian president Abbas the legitimacy required to make difficult concessions.

These power-sharing arrangements demonstrate the kind of intense internal bargaining typical of an organization entering the political transformation stage. The movement toward political transformation for Fatah and Hamas requires them to work through their differences while also constructively engaging neighboring states and other international states and organizations. The complexities of the power-sharing arrangements provide a glimpse into the kinds of bargaining challenges that politically transforming groups confront.

While the political transformation is slowly evolving for the Palestinians, it has developed even more thoroughly for the Provisional Irish Republican Army. The U.S. State Department no longer lists the PIRA as a terrorist organization. However, in the late 1990s, the Real IRA (RIRA) formed as a clandestine armed wing just before the PIRA signed the Good Friday Agreement in 1998 and decommissioned its weapons, essentially putting the PIRA out of the terrorist business and into the political scene in Northern Ireland (McEvoy, McEvoy, and McConnachie 2006). The RIRA has essentially splintered from the PIRA to continue the armed struggle to disrupt the Northern Ireland peace process and ultimately unite the Irelands. Its terrorist targets have included civilians, British army bases, and police stations in Northern Ireland. It has limited strength as an organization because the PIRA's political strength has intensified since 2005.

How, then, did the PIRA transform into a mainstream political group after thirty years of carrying out terrorist attacks? McEvoy, McEvoy, and McConnachie argue that this transformation was advanced by a community relations and education program called the Community Relations Commission, begun by the British government in the late 1960s. The commission's goal was to support cross-community contact initiatives alongside community development strategies, with the intent of raising the self-confidence of the two estranged Northern Irish communities, to help informal contact appear more normal. Throughout the 1970s, the commission conducted weekly rallies, sponsored small local groups holding social evenings, and promoted itself as an alternative to failed conventional political, constitutional, and military policies. After a brief restructuring, the commission became the Central Community Relations Unit within the Northern Ireland Civil Service and continued its grassroots efforts at peacebuilding. McEvoy et al. conclude that although subsequent political agreements, including the Good Friday Agreement and the decommissioning of the IRA, do not specifically reference community relations efforts, these efforts nonetheless played an important role in transforming the culture enough to make possible the acceptance of these initiatives (McEvoy, McEvoy, and McConnachie 2006).

According to Saul Smilansky, some specific circumstances made these initiatives possible (Smilansky 2004). Specifically, Northern Ireland is a comparatively prosperous democratic Irish country within the UK. Catholics who choose to stay in Northern Ireland, where they remain a minority group, are citizens of the UK and have attendant political rights. Their living conditions, while not as good as those of most Protestants, are not terribly harsh. Also, everyone in Northern Ireland has complete freedom of movement, and the communication infrastructures allow fluid exchange of information. Thus, citizens of Northern Ireland have the education, jobs, and political resources to transform their society toward more political expression and away from terrorism. They have a lot to lose by not making political progress.

For Fatah, this PIRA-like transformation has the benefit of increasing its separation from Hamas in Western eyes, since Hamas still embraces its violent mission while Fatah continues to search for a viable political voice. Unfortunately, the economic conditions in the West Bank are not nearly as healthy as they have become in Northern Ireland over the past two decades. Moreover, the complex political challenges that Fatah faces in its differences with Hamas and the complex relationships it faces with other Arab neighbors place much greater stresses on its political transformation. It will be interesting to see if those stresses yield a PIRA-like transformation.

Hezbollah's future is less clear than Fatah's. While it shows significant signs of local political activities in Lebanon, its military wing continues to dominate, thereby placing it more within a political violence phase. By contrast, the path away from a strategic violence phase for Al-Qaeda and the other dunelike terrorist groups that continuously shift their orientations may never occur. Are they likely to establish a more centralized political mission in the course of their prolific campaign of violence? There are no signs of this as al-Qaeda takes refuge in Northern Pakistan's tribal areas.

The Life Cycle Model

It is now possible to represent visually the life cycle model of terrorist organizations, particularly in relation to their violent mission, as a means of understanding both how they evolve as organizations and how to identity key intervention points for communication, negotiation, and conflict resolution. Figure 2.1 represents the life cycle stages of terrorist organizations as they evolve from incubation to political transformation.

Counterstrategies: Negotiation Policy Implications of the Life Cycle Model

The usefulness of the life cycle model lies in its ability to reveal opportunities for negotiation and other diplomatic interventions as the terrorist group moves through its various life cycle stages. The transition itself, the process of moving from one stage to the next, carries the potential for negotiation—whether a strategic engagement, tactical communication, or substantive negotiation. Any transformation results in changes in the personalities involved. Leaders change, some activists become more influential, and others lose control or disappear altogether. With changes in the personalities involved, engagement opportunities emerge. Moreover, the

Figure 2.1. The Life-Cycle Model of Terrorism

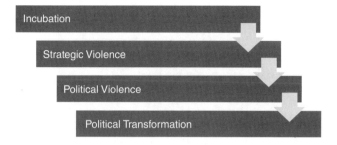

soil for planting negotiation seeds becomes richer as the terrorist organization moves away from its incubation activities, toward more politically involving stages. Strategically, the kinds of approaches best for negotiations involve some combination of front as well as back channels. Front channels can be very formal and public, or indirect and discrete. These are official channels, which governments use to engage with terrorist groups either directly or through third parties, publicly or far from the public eye. Back channels, on the other hand, are very informal and furtive and are carried out by nongovernmental organizations (NGOs). The links between these NGOs and the governments are unclear, thus allowing governments to be publicly protected by the "shield of deniability." Israel's negotiations with Hamas since Hamas won the Palestinian election in 2006 included back-channel meetings in Europe, formal indirect negotiations through Egypt that brought a cease-fire agreement in July 2008, and direct and discrete low-level humanitarian coordination.

Negotiations in the Incubation Stage

This stage presents the most significant set of challenges to negotiations (Hayes, Kaminski, and Beres 2003). At this stage, leaders are forming and starting to recruit members to their cause. Perhaps these groups are al-Qaeda cell start-ups or new wings of even more established groups. What might prevent these terrorist entrepreneurs from fomenting a culture of violence within their recruiting domains? Potentially the most useful option here is to pursue back-channel negotiations with the recruits and potential recruits. Shifting these young people away from a terrorist organization likely involves not mainline negotiation activity but, rather, a combination of a strategic counterterrorism policy and tactical communication with individuals. The "negotiations" may involve working with respected religious leaders, elders, academics/intellectuals, or other key community leaders in a grassroots effort to build nonviolent options for these potential recruits.

This is where we are losing

And, at the same time, it would also be useful to engage directly with those potential recruits by offering them religious, cultural, or status-related incentives to stay away from terrorism. Such incentives might include access to higher education, involvement in politically active community or religious organizations, or jobs helping rebuild the country. These efforts, directly and indirectly, seek to provide potential recruits with an alternative to terrorism.

Negotiations in the Strategic Violence Stage

Negotiations in this phase focus on counteracting the kinds of support activities that promote the violent mission. An organization such as al-Qaeda, which outwardly appears unlikely or incapable of evolving into a political entity, can still be subject to three different negotiation openings.

Tactical negotiations: If we consider negotiations a tactic in counterterrorism, a strategic extortion incident might be an opportunity for engaging the terrorists and ultimately lead to a change in their behavior. During the 1972 Munich Olympic Games, the German government missed several tactical opportunities to negotiate with the Palestinian terrorists, at a time when the PLO was still in its strategic violence stage. Could this tragic event have been averted if negotiations had taken place? In 2004, despite a firm policy of no negotiations with terrorists, Russian security forces negotiated tactically with the Chechen terrorists who kept 1,300 schoolchildren as hostages in the North Ossetia town of Beslan, but failed to conclude a deal. The event ended with the murder of more than 330 hostages who could possibly have been saved through a more disciplined negotiation process.

Commercial negotiations: Terrorist groups in their strategic violence stage conduct commercial negotiations, from buying and selling military equipment to acquiring logistical services, to enable their violent activities. These negotiations provide an intervention opportunity as long as they are one element in a comprehensive counterterrorism policy that includes creating a network of contact points within the terror organization, which can serve as messengers to and from the terrorist leadership.

Back-channel negotiations: In the late 1990s, Western forces made contacts with Afghan tribal leaders to agree on humanitarian assistance, knowing that the tribal leaders maintained close relations with al-Qaeda leaders. After all, before the 9/11 attacks, the United States had negotiated directly with the Taliban to give up the locations of al-Qaeda leaders (though the Taliban refused). The key purpose of these interventions is to create and simultaneously explore openings that might signal the ability or inclination of a terrorist organization to become more politically focused, and to create the necessary personal relationships to enter into a more substantive dialogue (Hoffman 2004; Cronin 2006).

Then why not the life cycle continue to this

Negotiations in the Political Violence and Political Transformation Stages

As terrorist groups adopt a more prominent political mission, they become increasingly open to negotiations. The political mission becomes very complex for groups such as Hezbollah as they work to provide essential social and military resources in Lebanon. They will certainly need help providing these services, but negotiating openly through front channels is not often politically viable. Here again, the use of intermediaries could be very useful. As Hezbollah continues its dialogue with Syria and even Iran, the organization's role as a primary negotiation player can be placed on the table and explored. Can these dialogues be expanded beyond negotiations with only supporters? It seems useful to determine how Hezbollah can be engaged by the international community. What is Hezbollah willing to concede in its violent mission in exchange for support for its social service and political missions? Krista Wiegand traces the diplomatic evolution of Hezbollah into a Lebanese political party. She argues that Hezbollah has made the choice to moderate its violent objectives in pursuit of domestic political goals (Wiegand 2009).

The point is that each stage of a terrorist group's life cycle presents different opportunities for negotiating toward reducing or completely removing the need for violence. Many Western governments embraced this approach in dealing with Yasser Arafat and the PLO by encouraging the PLO's political development and even providing resources for a police force. However, while maintaining open channels of communication, governments facing the dilemma of negotiating with a terrorist organization should take measures to reduce the chances of being manipulated by it. Hezbollah manipulated Israel's willingness to negotiate the release of its kidnapped soldiers, thereby strengthening the group's political power in Lebanon. In that case, a terrorist organization in its political violence stage managed to use the negotiations not to end the violence but to gain political support for its violent agenda.

The groups that are headed for political transformation present the most straightforward negotiation opportunities, since they indicate their willingness to exit from the pattern of violence. Fatah is perhaps the best example in the Middle East. It has become a legitimate, recognized organization, with many visits from prominent politicians and NGOs. Specifically, many Western governments are encouraging Fatah to expand its political missions and build a legitimate state. Of course, once this kind of engagement occurs, the governments bear the responsibility of following through with their negotiation intentions and initiating talks to further legitimize and grow the organization further away from terrorism. A terrorist organization that has chosen to distance itself from violence and turn into a political movement must provide its constituents with tangible achievements reached through negotiation rather than violence. A rich and productive "culture of talk" must occur across both front and back channels for there to be any real chance of countering a culture of violence.

Conclusions and Implications

A key implication of the life cycle model focuses on the need to gather additional data on the evolution of the new breed of terrorist group that seems to be evolving in dunelike structures. To the extent that these groups evolve in patterned ways, it becomes possible to make the dunelike structures more predictable, enabling governments to intervene earlier and more systematically. From this perspective, it would be wise to begin collecting data on each terrorist group, with the goal of charting its progression. Are there opportunities early in the group's development for even back-channel negotiations? Or, as the group becomes more politically active, how can the West reinforce the group's political legitimacy to aid in the transition to more peaceful means of change? Terrorist groups are organizations that grow and change, so those changes should be tracked to open up opportunities for problem-solving talks.

A second key implication of this chapter focuses on the need for policy coordination. Each nation appears to have different policies for engaging terrorist organizations. For example, in the Afghan war, coalition forces have gone back and forth about negotiating with Taliban leaders. As of 2010, negotiations have undergone fits and starts as Pakistan and U.S. and other Coalition forces have grappled with how to conduct these negotiations and what strategies to use in engaging the Taliban. Since the Taliban are probably in the strategic violence stage of development, should the goal be to facilitate their integration into the legitimate political process in both Afghanistan and Pakistan? This is the sort of question that countries facing the challenge of negotiating with terrorist groups must ask as they coordinate their policies around some framework that moves away from violence and toward more substantive problem solving.

Note

1. For a discussion of how self-organizing systems function, see Camazine 2006.

References

Bar-Tal, Daniel. 2000. "From Intractable Conflict through Conflict Resolution to Reconciliation: Psychological Analysis." *Political Psychology* 21 (2): 351–65.

Camazine, Scott. 2006. *Self-Organizing Systems*. New York: John Wiley and Sons.

Cronin, Audrey. 2006. "How al-Qaida Ends: The Decline and Demise of Terrorist Groups." *International Security* 31 (1): 7–48.

Fair, Christine. 2004. "Militant Recruitment in Pakistan: Implications for al Qaeda and Other Organizations." *Studies in Conflict and Terrorism* 27 (6): 489–504.

Fitzgerald, Valpy. 2004. "Global Financial Information, Compliance Incentives and Terrorist Funding." *European Journal of Political Economy* 20 (2): 387–401.

Ganor, Boaz. 2008. "Terrorist Organization Typologies and the Probability of a Boomerang Effect." *Studies in Conflict and Terrorism* 31 (4): 269–83.

Gray, Barbara, and Sonny Ariss. 1985. "Politics and Strategic Change across Organizational Life Cycles." *Academy of Management Review* 10 (4): 707–23.

Hayes, Richard E., Stacy R. Kaminski, and Steven M. Beres. 2003. "Negotiating the Non-negotiable: Dealing with Absolute Terrorists." *International Negotiation* 8 (3): 9–25.

Hoffman, Bruce. 2004. "The Changing Face of al-Qaeda and the Global War on Terrorism." *Studies in Conflict and Terrorism* 27 (6): 549–60.

Hwang, Yong-Sik, and Seung Ho Park. 2007. "The Organizational Life Cycle as a Determinant of Strategic Alliance Tactics: Research Propositions." *International Journal of Management* 24 (3): 427–37.

Jones, Seth G., and Martin C. Libicki. 2008. *How Terrorist Groups End: Lessons for Countering al Qa'ida*. Arlington, VA: RAND.

Kurz, Anat N. 2005. *Fatah and the Politics of Violence: The Institutionalization of a Popular Struggle*. Tel Aviv: Jaffe Center for Strategic Studies.

McEvoy, Lesley, Kieran McEvoy, and Kirsten McConnachie. 2006. "Reconciliation as a Dirty Word: Conflict, Community Relations and Education in Northern Ireland." *Journal of International Affairs* 60 (1): 81–106.

McGarry, John, and Brendan O'Leary. 2004. *The Northern Ireland Conflict: Consociational Engagements*. Oxford: Oxford University Press.

Mishal, Shaul, and Moaz Rosenthal. 2005. "Al-Qaeda as a Dune Organization: Toward a Typology of Islamic Terrorist Organizations." *Studies in Conflict and Terrorism* 28 (4): 275–90.

Munson, Ziad. 2001. "Islamic Mobilization: Social Movement Theory and the Egyptian Muslim Brotherhood." *Sociological Quarterly* 42 (4): 487–510.

Post, Jerrold M., Keven G. Ruby, and Eric D. Shaw. 2002. "The Radical Group in Context 2: Identification of Critical Elements in the Analysis of Risk for Terrorism by Radical Group Type." *Studies in Conflict and Terrorism* 25 (2): 101–26.

Raphaeli, Nimrod. 2003. "Financing of Terrorism: Sources, Methods, and Channels." *Terrorism and Political Violence* 15 (4): 59–82.

Smilansky, Saul. 2004. "Terrorism, Justification, and Illusion." *Ethics* 114 (4): 790–805.

Thomas, Timothy L. 2003. "Al Qaeda and the Internet: The Danger of 'Cyberplanning.'" *Parameters* 33 (11): 112–24.

Victoroff, Jeff. 2005. "The Mind of the Terrorist: A Review and Critique of Psychological Approaches." *Journal of Conflict Resolution* 49 (1): 3–42.

Wiegand, Krista E. 2009. "Reformation of a Terrorist Group: Hezbollah as a Lebanese Political Party." *Studies in Conflict and Terrorism* 32 (8): 669–80.

Zartman, I. W. 1989. *Ripe for Resolution: Conflict and Intervention in Africa.* New York: Oxford University Press.

3

Community Intervention as a Negotiation Strategy:

Al-Qaeda in London

Robert Lambert

This chapter stems from a case study reflecting on the experience of police and Muslim community representatives working in partnership to counter al-Qaeda influence in Brixton, London. The study demonstrates how both police and Muslim community partners need negotiation skills as they seek to build the trust and confidence needed for such demanding partnership work. Negotiation skills also come into play when Muslim community partners engage with local youth to challenge their understanding of al-Qaeda and al-Qaeda-related propaganda. The study therefore describes two kinds of interventions in a community-based approach to counterterrorism policing, in which high-level negotiation skills are key. It offers useful insights into how governments and police chiefs can build trust and safeguard credibility while better distinguishing between "moderates" and "extremists" in Muslim communities. The study also demonstrates the importance of understanding not just life cycles and processes of al-Qaeda influence but also fine-grained ideological complexities within broader currents of thought. Throughout, the study cautions against stereotyping either the terrorist threat or the potential partners in tackling it.

By 2010, the UK counterterrorism strategy known as CONTEST had become a sophisticated and well-resourced multiagency program with four major components: *protect, prepare, prevent, and pursue* (UK Home Office

2010). This chapter draws on the experience of a small police and Muslim community partnership project in London that largely predates the CONTEST strategy but anticipates the concept, if not the method, of the *prevent* strand (Lambert 2010). Politically, the catalyst and main driver for *prevent* was the "homegrown" suicide bomb attack on the London underground in July 2005, whereas the police and community partnership experience described in this chapter derives from the presence of al-Qaeda–inspired strategists and propagandists in London from 1993 onward. The author, for his PhD thesis, analyzed the legitimacy and effectiveness of that partnership experience and developed case studies in Finsbury Park and Brixton, in North and South London respectively (Lambert 2010). This chapter focuses primarily on the Brixton case study, drawing on the interviews and participant observations in that research to elucidate the notion of community intervention as a counterterrorism negotiation strategy. The discussion also benefits from the pioneering research conducted by Abdul Haqq Baker in the same arena (Baker 2010).

Several interviews with Muslim volunteer youth workers in London first germinated the idea of an intervention by a Muslim youth worker as a community counterterrorism negotiation strategy. One interview in particular illustrates this in dramatic fashion (Lambert 2010). The youth worker recalled sitting up all night counseling a troubled Muslim youth in the late 1990s. Long before the terms "homegrown terrorism" and "radicalization" had gained currency, the youth worker assessed that Raheem was under the influence of local violent extremists, and regretted that he did not have more time and resources to help him return to "the straight path" (Lambert 2010, 319).[1] That earlier regret was shockingly amplified on December 28, 2001, when the youth, Abdul Raheem, a.k.a. Richard Reid, tried to blow up a U.S.-bound airplane with a "shoe bomb" (Dodd 2006). Raheem was clear and credible when he later claimed that he was motivated by al-Qaeda (Dodd 2006). Indeed, in the opinion of London lawyer Peter Herbert, who met Raheem in his prison cell after his conviction and sentencing, Raheem's sane, reflective, and self-possessed articulation of an al-Qaeda rationale was striking: "'I am not crazy as they suggest, but I knew exactly what I was doing,' [Reid] said. 'Of course I would have been sad to have those people die, but I knew that my cause was just and righteous. It was the will of Allah that I did not succeed.' His motivation for turning to violence, he said, was the foreign policy of the US government, which, he said, had resulted in the murder of thousands of Muslims and oppressed people around the world from Vietnam to southern Africa to Afghanistan and Palestine" (Dodd 2006).

By 2010, the notion of intervention strategies to "deradicalize" youth inspired in similar ways as Raheem to become al-Qaeda terrorists had become a major area of interest for practitioners, policymakers, and researchers, with immediate implications for the *prevent* strand of CONTEST (Bjørgo and Horgan 2008). By examining Brixton police and community activity that in many ways anticipates *prevent* deradicalization initiatives, we can see the negotiation and partnership skills that may prove beneficial in this complex arena in both the short and the long term. The Muslim youth worker who counseled Raheem before he became a terrorist was confident that had he then enjoyed the trust and confidence he later established with police officers, he would have been able to alert police to the potential danger Reid posed. And more important, he might have developed his own community intervention strategy to the point that it could counter al-Qaeda's influence.

By addressing negotiation and partnership skills in a local context, this chapter points up a distinctive feature of this particular police and community project: the value of long-term trust building. This long-term view introduces a significant departure from conventional police negotiation scenarios, in which trust building is always instrumental and exploitative, used as it is to secure a short-term objective. Similarly, the chapter introduces the notion that a community partner of the police should enjoy a wholly different relationship from that of a police informant.

Three Al-Qaeda Propagandists in London

From the mid-1990s onward, three al-Qaeda propagandists played a major role in fostering terrorist support in small sections of Muslim communities in the UK. During the 1990s, only a small number of Muslim community groups were aware of the problem. One community group, which noticed the problem as early as 1993, is best described as the Brixton Salafi community in South London (Lambert 2010; Baker 2010). This community, a small part of London's diverse Muslim population, performed a key role in combating that al-Qaeda influence. Both the al-Qaeda propagandists and their Brixton Salafi opponents possessed the religious and street credibility necessary to make their voices count in a small but dangerous arena. Both sides also possessed negotiation skills that enabled them to influence the attitudes and behavior of their Muslim youth audiences. From 2002 on, the counterpropaganda work of the Brixton Salafis was supported by a small police unit, the Muslim Contact Unit (MCU), which itself employed negotiation skills to win the trust of the Brixton Salafis, who had become suspicious of police. By adopting both police and community negotiating skills, this London-based partnership initiative presented a viable and complementary approach to mainstream counterterrorism in reducing the negative effects of al-Qaeda propaganda and recruitment in susceptible segments of the community. The initiative attracted criticism, however, when the Salafi community partners themselves were described pejoratively by opposing community groups and influential media commentators as "extremists" or "fundamentalists" (Lambert 2010, 189). The police side of the partnership effectively countered this disparaging assessment and highlighted instead the expertise and credibility that the Brixton Salafi community group brought to bear in persuading Muslim youth that al-Qaeda propaganda was wrong. Throughout, the London police and community partnership initiative was grounded in an expert understanding of al-Qaeda strategy.

Abu Hamza (from Egypt), Abdullah el-Faisal (from Jamaica via Saudi Arabia), and Abu Qatada (from Jordan) are three of the most notorious, though by no means the only, al-Qaeda propagandists to have settled in London in the 1990s before being imprisoned in the UK in the following decade.[2] That each has been cited in recent UK terrorism trials as having influenced the phenomenon of "homegrown" British Muslim terrorism adds significance to their role as al-Qaeda propagandists in London. Describing them as al-Qaeda propagandists is not intended to establish conclusive organizational or network links between any of the three men and al-Qaeda's strategic hub, most publicly epitomized by Osama bin Laden and Ayman al-Zawahiri. But their own speeches and talks—freely available then and now and used as trial evidence against two of them—as well as the London Muslim interviewees who attended their talks and otherwise knew them, substantiate that relationship (Lambert 2010). What emerges with surprising clarity is that all three had established street-level reputations as effective communicators of a narrative that was al-Qaeda's in all but name long before 9/11. After that landmark event, their support for, and public allegiance to, al-Qaeda became more explicit. It is therefore sufficient for the purpose of this chapter to posit their roles as effective holders of a UK al-Qaeda franchise, adapting al-Qaeda's worldview to the express demands of UK audiences. This often allowed them to address specific local grievances while maintaining a wider focus on the need for a global jihad against the United States and its allies.

Indeed, once Prime Minister Tony Blair demonstrated his willingness to stand shoulder to shoulder with U.S. president George Bush in the "war on terror," it became increasingly apposite for al-Qaeda propagandists to describe the UK as an acolyte of the U.S. enemy (Lambert 2008a, 2008b).

In this, they were conforming to an adaptive model of al-Qaeda as a social movement with an ability to engage with the domestic profiles of different countries and regions, as David Leheny argues concerning al-Qaeda's influence in Southeast Asia (Leheny 2005). Al-Qaeda's iconic spokesman Osama bin Laden ensured that his UK supporters had templates to adopt and use as the terrorist movement stepped up its propaganda responses to the war on terror:

> What happened in September 11 and March 11 is your own merchandise coming back to you. We hereby advise you . . . that your definition of us and of our actions as terrorism is nothing but a definition of yourselves by yourselves, since our reaction is of the same kind as your act. . . . Our actions are a reaction to yours, which are destruction and killing of our people as is happening in Afghanistan, Iraq, and Palestine. By what measure of kindness are your killed considered innocents while ours are considered worthless? By what school [of thought] is your blood considered blood while our blood is water? Therefore, it is [only] just to respond in kind, and the one who started it is more to blame. . . . (Lawrence 2005, 234)

Bin Laden's powerful propaganda messages provided fuel for local events in London, such as Abu Hamza's meeting, provocatively billed as "a towering day in history," at the Finsbury Park Mosque on the first anniversary of 9/11 (Lambert 2010, 233). While that event alerted the wider community to the activities of Abu Hamza and like-minded extremists, the fact is that Hamza, el-Faisal, and Qatada had by then assiduously cultivated small but strong UK followings over a period of several years. One of their great attributes as community leaders was in helping young Muslims with a wide range of welfare issues. Very often new converts to Islam, no less than Muslims newly arrived in London, would need help with religious practice, diet, housing, benefits, relationships, employment, and many other matters. And their new leaders were adept at providing practical help, often at times and places where more conventional community leadership was lacking. Whereas many mainstream Muslim community leaders appeared remote and detached, the three London-based extremists were approachable, demonstrative, and in touch with street issues. For instance, many firsthand accounts pay tribute to Abu Hamza's and Abdullah el-Faisal's skills in helping young Muslims move away from drug and alcohol use (and related crime) and into strict religious observance. This is not to suggest that all mainstream Muslim community leaders lacked such skills, or to overlook an instrumental purpose on the part of Hamza and el-Faisal, but rather to acknowledge the caliber of their interpersonal and leadership skills when dealing with young people.

In addition, Abu Hamza skillfully used a close circle of loyal followers to act as intermediaries and conduits for communication with his wider following. A first-floor office at the Finsbury Park Mosque served as a headquarters for his "Supporters of Sharia" and as a place to hold interviews. Many Muslim newcomers to the UK (especially from Algeria) knew that the Finsbury Park Mosque would be a good place to seek help and shelter immediately upon arrival in London. Similarly, Abu Qatada established a regular presence at a youth club near Baker Street and the Regent Park Mosque (officially the London Central Mosque). His lack of fluent English was more than compensated by his reputation as a senior scholar and by the willingness of loyal supporters to translate his teachings for eager audiences. At various times, el-Faisal established strong community bases in Willesden, Edmonton, and Brixton. All three, however, were mobile and traveled regularly to Muslim communities around the UK.

It is also germane to recognize the influence that charismatic individuals can achieve through their personal commitment and availability to a small group of followers and supporters. Very often the scorn poured on the three men by outsiders (Muslim and non-Muslim) enhanced their credibility, in their followers' eyes, as leaders who were perceived to act on principle and could not be swayed by hostile criticism. Indeed, such positioning became a stock in trade for these three committed activists, who never missed an opportunity to contrast the bravery of characters such as Bin Laden with the timidity of Muslim leaders who became enamored of their home comforts and tacitly condoned injustices against Muslims. This theme was most notably reiterated by Mohammad Sidique Khan, the senior member of the 7/7 al-Qaeda martyrdom cell: "By turning our back on this work, we are guaranteeing ourselves humiliation and the anger of Allah. Jihad is an obligation on every single one of us, men and women.... Our so-called scholars of today are content with their Toyotas and semi-detached houses. They are useless. They should stay at home and leave the job to real men—the true inheritors of the prophet" (BBC News 2005).

Not least in the style and manner of his delivery, Khan reveals the influence that propagandists such as Abu Hamza and Abdullah el-Faisal had on him. The case of Abdullah el-Faisal is broadly representative for all three propagandists. By 9/11, he had become a familiar speaker on a national, though fringe, UK circuit of Muslim student and Muslim community events. While some of these events were public, with audiences of up to 500, in most cases they consisted of small study circles of around twenty, with attendance by invitation, in which young Muslims were encouraged to adopt an al-Qaeda worldview. At various times, Abdullah el-Faisal appeared with Hamza, unofficially his senior though they agreed on all key points and enjoyed cordial relations. Unlike the other two, el-Faisal, being

Jamaican, was especially influential with members of the black Muslim convert community, where he enjoyed high status. Significantly, the UK Home Office narrative of the July 7 bombings records that his calls to violence had found a receptive audience in Jermaine Lindsay, who killed himself and twenty-six others in the July 7, 2005, terrorist attack on a Piccadilly line underground train near Russell Square. Lindsay, also originally from Jamaica and also a convert to Islam, was found to have attended at least one lecture by el-Faisal and to have listened to tapes of other talks by him. Moreover, during el-Faisal's trial in London, the jury heard recordings of him telling his audiences to kill Hindus, Jews, and other non-Muslims, likening them to "cockroaches" (BBC News 2006).

El-Faisal was born William Forrest, the second of four children in a fervently Christian family, in St. James on Jamaica's western coast, near Montego Bay. On leaving Jamaica in 1983, he traveled first to Guyana, where he took a course in Arabic, before studying at the Imam Mohammed ibn Saud University in the Saudi capital, Riyadh. During searches of specialist Islamic bookshops and el-Faisal's rented house in Stratford, East London, police found recordings of him saying, "This is how wonderful it is to kill a *kuffar* [a nonbeliever] . . . You crawl on his back and while you are pushing him into the hellfire you are going into paradise" (BBC News 2006). During his four-week trial in 2003, followers came to the Old Bailey and watched as the court heard el-Faisal exhorting young Muslims to accept the deaths of women and children as "collateral damage" and to "learn to fly planes, drive tanks . . . load your guns and to use missiles" (BBC News 2006). All this came as no surprise to a small group of Muslim Londoners—Brixton Salafis—who had by then been combating this man's adverse influence in London and around the UK for much of the preceding decade. Significantly, when these Salafis sought police help to oppose el-Faisal's extremist demagoguery in 1996, they were rebuffed. Nor was their expertise sought when the authorities began legal proceedings against el-Faisal in 2002. They were not seen as an effective counterweight to el-Faisal's influence, because their own adherence to Salafism (or "Wahhabism," as their detractors preferred to call it) was generally described as being a central and defining component of al-Qaeda's ideology (Olivetti 2002; Murad 2001).

When the Metropolitan Police Service (MPS) Muslim Contact Unit (MCU)[3] first opened a dialogue with Muslim Londoners in January 2002, it became clear that el-Faisal, Abu Hamza, and Abu Qatada had become key figures in disseminating and promoting al-Qaeda propaganda over a significant period (Lambert 2010). Not many Muslim Londoners had intimate knowledge of their work; the overwhelming majority were merely aware of their reputations from a safe distance. Indeed, only a handful of groups within London's diverse Muslim population knew firsthand of any kind of al-Qaeda propaganda activity in the UK. One group came from what can best be described as a Salafi community. According to *The Oxford Dictionary of Islam*, "Salafi" is "a name derived from 'salaf,' 'pious ancestors,' given to a reform movement that emphasises the restoration of Islamic doctrines to pure form, adherence to the Qur'an and Sunnah, rejection of the authority of later interpretations, and maintenance of the unity of umma," that is, the Muslim community (Esposito 2003). On this basis, there is nothing to warrant such a community's stigmatization or pejorative religious profiling in ways that have become all too common-place. Much of the demonization of Salafi groups originates with compet-ing strands of Islamic practice, especially some Sufi groups, which regard Salafis as anathema (Olivetti 2002; Murad 2001). In the aftermath of 9/11 (and with more vigor after 7/7), leading media commentators and UK neoconservatives would join in the clamor against the "subversive threat" posed by Salafis. Thus, paradoxically, one of the most effective groups from the small list of Muslim Londoners identified by the MCU as having a track record of confronting al-Qaeda propagandists were themselves vili-fied as dangerous extremists.

The Brixton Salafi Community

Members of the Salafi community based in Brixton, South London, gave the MCU compelling accounts of their success in combating the propa-ganda of Abu Hamza, Abu Qatada, and Abdullah el-Faisal at close quar-ters over a sustained period from the mid-1990s on (Lambert 2010; Baker 2010). Initially, this community-based work consisted of resisting the ef-forts of Qatada, Hamza, el-Faisal, and their hard-core supporters to win influence in the community and take over control of the mosque (or *masjid*, as the Salafis prefer to call the building, a former residence converted to religious use). Indeed, the Brixton Salafi leadership was then made up of relatively new Muslim converts, who candidly admitted that for a brief time they were almost seduced by Qatada's claims of legitimate Islamic authority allowing him to assume control of the mosque and leadership of their local Salafi community. Qatada's outwardly impressive religious credentials were exposed as a sham only when the Brixton Salafi leader-ship consulted authoritative Salafi scholars in Saudi Arabia and Jordan. Later, the same line of inquiries enabled them to rebut Abdullah el-Faisal's challenges to their authority. But for the many young British-born, British naturalized, or British resident Muslims who gathered in circles in Brixton to listen to el-Faisal (in English) and Qatada (largely in Arabic at first but with some simultaneous English translations), the lack of religious authority was not apparent. Indeed, like their contemporary Hamza in Finsbury Park, Qatada and el-Faisal turned that lack of official license to good advantage. When the official Salafi scholars based in Saudi Arabia and Jordan denounced them as extremists, the al-Qaeda propagandists dismissed the scholars as "sellouts," "dollar scholars," and corrupt lackeys of the West, who were part of the very corruption that al-Qaeda sought to abolish.

By endorsing the so-called dollar scholars against the extremist influence of London-based al-Qaeda propagandists, the Brixton Salafis inevitably sustained the same kind of criticism themselves. While this criticism might undermine their credibility on occasion, they simply took it on as a challenge to overcome when addressing the same Muslim youth audiences that the al-Qaeda propagandists were seeking to influence. Whether at public meetings, in study circles, or in one-on-one counseling sessions, the Brixton Salafis were able to offset the charge of subservience to corrupt Arab regimes, through strict adherence to mainstream Salafi interpretations of Islam, which valued public security above political conflict or agitation. When dealing with the widely felt political grievances that al-Qaeda sought to exploit, the Brixton Salafis acknowledged the legitimacy of a sense of political injustice (e.g., over the treatment of the Palestinians by Israel and the West). But they adhered to a policy of nonintervention, on the basis of British Muslims' primary duty to attend to their religious, social, and family obligations at home in the UK. For example, during the conflict in Bosnia, the Brixton Salafis (following the advice of Salafi scholars in Saudi Arabia and Jordan) felt a duty to provide charitable aid to fellow European Muslims who were facing hardship, but no duty to wage jihad with their Bosnian brothers on the front line.

This restrained approach stood in sharp contrast to the pronouncements of Abu Hamza, who consolidated his power base at the Finsbury Park Mosque in North London during the mid- to late 1990s. In a transcript of a 1999 talk he gave to a circle of supporters in London, Hamza seeks to demonstrate the superiority of his call to violent action over the responsible approach of his South London neighbors:

> Don't you know Allah is happy when a kaffir is killed? Don't you know that? Don't you know Allah is happy when a Muslim is taken out of his prison by force and you are humiliating the kaffirs who put him in? Don't you know that? Don't you know that Allah is happy when you stop the evil from every society so the people can have good ears and they go have good listen to the reality of Islam. Don't you know that? Don't you know that the Prophet has praised people who will change people in life so they can change them into janaah also in the hereafter. . . . I am telling you what the ulama have failed to tell you. Because simply they cannot say this because they have

sold the religion of Allah. They are giving you now a very blunt statement everywhere, simply because the money is too sharp in their mind. (Lambert 2010, 211)

By this time, Hamza and his hard-core supporters had become well used to the Brixton Salafis' countermanding their violent messages. In 1999, Hamza delivered some 200 talks to Muslim audiences around the UK. On at least thirty occasions, Brixton Salafis made it their business to attend the same venues the following week (or soon thereafter), to challenge his accounts and reduce his adverse impact. Meanwhile Hamza lumped the Brixton Salafis with corrupt "dollar scholars" and Saudi sheikhs who could not be trusted to speak uncomfortable truths: "Look at the sheikhs they are giving you a very poor kind of fatwa. Every kind of fatwa to disable you to make sure you gonna be slaughtered.... If you can't protect yourself can you protect Islam? If you can't protect your brother do you expect anybody else to protect you when it comes you turn? If you don't help your brothers do you expect Allah to help you? And if you don't say the word of truth do you expect Allah will even raise your voice when you are humiliated and killed?" (Lambert 2010, 159).

At defining moments in the mid-1990s, the Brixton Salafis confronted Abu Qatada and Abdullah el-Faisal in circumstances where "street" credibility mattered more than religious credibility. Eyewitnesses report that on one occasion, Brixton Salafi management, in an impressive display of physical resistance, rebuffed attempts by el-Faisal and his supporters to wrest control of the mosque. The ability to stand up to this kind of bullying had often been absent elsewhere in Muslim London. But the staunch adherence to mainstream Salafism, combined with a willingness to face intimidation with steadfast physical resistance, earned the relatively young black convert management of the Brixton Mosque the respect of local Muslim youth and the grudging regard of their al-Qaeda opponents, who were used to getting their own way through intimidation elsewhere in London. As a result, word spread on the grapevine that even when threatened with violence, the Brixton Salafis had faced down el-Faisal's bullyboy tactics.

Brixton is also an important case study site because el-Faisal regarded himself as being well qualified to attract other black convert Muslims to the al-Qaeda flag. Although he encountered effective opposition from the Brixton Salafis, he found it easy enough to operate in the vicinity, away from the direct notice and influence of the Brixton Mosque. This is what he did during the second half of the 1990s and right up to his arrest in 2003, attracting black convert Muslims to his wider Muslim youth audiences, many of whom had family backgrounds in Islam. Typically, he would praise 9/11 and any other al-Qaeda attacks that his impressionable audiences might see on the television or read about on the Internet, and condone the lesser street crimes that many in his audiences engaged in. In the latter case, it would be commonplace to allow young street robber converts to Islam to continue their criminal activity as long as they robbed only non-Muslims, the *kaffir*. When the opportunity arose, the Brixton Salafis were extremely effective at countermanding this kind of advice to new converts with a background in street crime, because they could relate to them on their own terms and put el-Faisal's erroneous analysis in its proper context. Here again, in direct street-level negotiations between Brixton Salafi leaders (in their twenties or thirties during the 1990s) and local street criminals new to Islam (typically fifteen to twenty years old), the street credibility of the Brixton Salafi leaders was key to their legitimacy and effectiveness. Their physical presence underscored their religious authority.

The Brixton Salafis were not always bound to win this kind of argument. The well-documented cases of Abdul Raheem and Zacarias Moussaoui amply attest the ability of al-Qaeda propagandists to radicalize and recruit young members of the Brixton Muslim community during the late 1990s and early 2000s before 9/11. As noted in the introduction, one Brixton Salafi youth worker recalls how his informal counseling with Abdul Raheem failed to move Raheem away from the influence of Abdullah el-Faisal and company—the "Takfiris," as they became known on the streets. Significantly, that unsuccessful deradicalization interview took place before Raheem/Reid embarked on the international travels that culminated in his abortive attempt to explode a "shoe bomb" in the name of al-Qaeda on a transatlantic flight. Equally significant, it took place before the Brixton Salafis had established a partnership with the MCU. Before cementing that relationship with the MCU in January 2003, the Brixton Salafis had largely negative experiences with the Metropolitan Police. Indeed, in the aftermath of Reid's arrest in December 2001, they were approached by police (and media) with much suspicion. This was premised on the superficial notion that they themselves were part of a radicalizing process that had caused or allowed Raheem's progression to would-be suicide bomber.

The Muslim Contact Unit

Although the MCU was formed in January 2002, almost a year passed before police officers in the unit could embark in earnest on a trust-building project with the Brixton Salafi leadership. One of the questions that MCU officers posed at the time was, which sections, if any, of London's diverse and burgeoning Muslim communities had any expertise in undercutting al-Qaeda's influence among those susceptible to it? Clearly, the Brixton Salafis had a wealth of experience and expertise in this field. Their reluctance to engage with members of a police service that had displayed only suspicion toward them was gradually overcome by patient trust building and a willingness to engage the Salafis as partners, not recruit them as informants. The input of a Muslim police officer who shared much of the Salafi-oriented approach to Islam was enormously helpful in this effort. Indeed, his integrity and reputation were key to overcoming mutual distrust in the early stages. Thanks in part to this cooperative effort, Brixton became and remains the touchstone for relations between the Metropolitan Police and black Londoners.

The community relations background is significant. In response to Lord Macpherson's 1999 landmark verdict that the MPS was institutionally racist, a committed cadre of police officers was licensed to foster a new model of "diversity policing" (Lambert 2010, 15, 180). The defining feature of the new model was a commitment to support black and Asian ethnic minorities, Jewish communities, gay and lesbian communities, and women, both in the workplace and in all policing encounters. The diversity movement was further marked by an intense commitment to ensure that the catastrophic damage done to the MPS's reputation by Lord Macpherson's damning verdict never happened again. In practice, the MPS Diversity Directorate, serving as internal consultants, brought this new diversity alliance to roundtable policing discussions at every opportunity. Unlike trust building between the MCU and Salafi community groups, the new diversity alliance conducted business along familiar secular lines and would typically conclude meetings and enhance team bonding over a drink in a London pub. In contrast, MCU officers, rather than seeking to impose secular rules of engagement, respected their partners' religious practice, including strict Muslim gender segregation and abstinence from alcohol. Salafi communities (and other religiously observant Muslim Londoners) have been grateful that MCU officers respected their rules of engagement. A useful reference in understanding a British Salafi woman's perspective is Na'ima Robert's book *From My Sister's Lips,* which challenges most popular secular preconceptions and misconceptions about the "misogynist" and "paternalistic" nature of Islam and Muslims (Robert 2005). On the other hand, powerful secular lobbyists have pushed against forming close partnerships with "extremist," "oppressive," "homophobic," "anti-Semitic" Salafis, Islamists, and other Muslim "fundamentalists" (Gove 2006; Phillips 2006; Cox and Marks 2006).

Although the Brixton Salafis had worked hard and effectively against al-Qaeda propagandists for several years, they had become disillusioned by the lack of recognition and the constant criticism they received in the wake of the Abdul Raheem and Zacarius Moussaoui cases. Building a close partnership with the MCU enabled them to achieve small but important additions to their team, including bringing additional expertise from abroad in the form of a trained imam. Equally important, whereas the Brixton Salafis had become used to intrusive, confidence-sapping interviews with police and immigration officials at airports whenever they traveled abroad, that frustration diminished thanks to support from their new police partners. And MCU officers benefited from an insider's perspective on the way al-Qaeda propagandists went about their work in the capital. Such shared knowledge is the basic building block of good community policing, whether of gang crime, drug crime, or terrorism. Similar success occurred in North London, where an MCU partnership with a local Islamist community led to the 2005 overthrow of Abu Hamza supporters who had taken control of the Finsbury Park Mosque (Lambert 2010, 193–260). Unfortunately, however, widespread antagonism and suspicion toward Salafis and Islamists prevented the MCU model from being adopted more widely in London or nationally.

In 2007, with MCU support, key members of the Brixton Salafi community launched a new youth outreach scheme called "Street," which sought to extend their local work to a wider audience. Football and boxing were among the regular activities provided for the benefit of young Muslims. Typically, throughout the winter of 2007-08, crowds of around eighty youths attended Saturday evening football sessions in Kennington Park. Before kickoff, the players were given a Salafi pep talk encouraging them to give their best effort on the field and treat their opponents with respect, for Allah's sake. The Street leadership, aware that imprisonment had done nothing to diminish the adverse influence of Hamza, el-Faisal, and Qatada in Muslim communities, sought the facilities and resources to counsel young Muslims who had come under their extremist influence. Given the inevitable sensitivity surrounding this kind of work, the MCU played a key role in supporting the Street project with potential funders in central and local government. Considering all the counterextremist work the Brixton Salafi community had done, entirely voluntarily, for several years, the collaborators thought it appropriate for central and local government to help fund this more cohesive project. Crucially, MCU support was extended in 2007 to include the Brixton police, who had rebuffed the Brixton Salafis' appeal for support in 1996.

Terrorist trials in UK courts have highlighted the value that al-Qaeda strategists attach to training Muslim youth in outdoor pursuits. Paintball, camping, white-water rafting, mountaineering, martial arts, and survival skills have all featured as "innocent" activities that serve to build and bond teams in ways familiar to police and army recruits the world over. The Brixton Salafis' ability to offer the same sorts of environments and activities to

Muslim youth audiences, while presenting a wholly different account of UK citizenship and responsibility, has been key. Needless to say, however, a farmer in the Brecon Beacons may not immediately distinguish between Brixton Salafis and al-Qaeda supporters, and it is therefore important that a unit such as the MCU be able to vouch for its London community partners when they venture to remoter parts of the country. This kind of support work by the MCU also helps distinguish its and its partners' roles from those of traditional "police handlers" and their informants. Policy designed to enable the efficient police management of informants ("covert human intelligence sources") does not encourage the trust-building and partnership-building approach but, to the contrary, seeks to avoid the kind of close relationship that has worked for the MCU and its Brixton Salafi partners.

Police and Community Negotiating Skills

The role of an MCU officer is usefully contrasted with that of a police hostage negotiator. An experienced police hostage negotiator who succeeds in establishing an active dialogue with the leader of a terrorist group holding hostages will be acutely aware that attempts to negotiate a nonviolent outcome to a volatile crisis are contingent on superior orders that may invoke an armed response at any time. On occasion, therefore, a negotiator's own assessment of what negotiations can achieve may be countermanded by the person in overall charge. When this happens, the conditional nature of a hostage negotiator's relationship with a hostage taker is exposed and terminated in an instant. This is to acknowledge that a hostage negotiator is trained to work in a stressful environment where the relationship-building skills employed are inherently fragile and subordinate to a wider strategic purpose. Essentially, the police commander of a hostage crisis invokes a classic "good cop, bad cop" strategy that is manifested on city streets the world over every day: the "good cop" offers the cornered criminal a peaceful, negotiated route to settlement and justice, while the "bad cop" stands in the shadows, ready to intervene forcefully at a moment's notice. Whatever the context, an experienced police commander will judge when the decisiveness of the "bad cop" outweighs the usefulness of the "good cop's" negotiating skills, and at the moment of decision to switch from one resource to the other, the symbiotic relationship of the two policing styles becomes evident. Needless to say, experienced criminals and well-trained terrorists (no less than viewers of television crime dramas) are fully aware of such timeless policing strategies. Not surprisingly, however, in the heat of a crisis and in the hands of skilled police negotiators, "good cop" tactics may still retain an element of valuable distraction while executive "bad cop" resources are prepared and deployed.

In partnership with the Brixton Salafis, MCU officers were concerned with soft policing tactics of a fundamentally different sort. Trust building was premised on transparency and a mutual respect for each side's role and legitimacy. Community partnership work of this kind is proactive, preventive police work—unlike negotiation involving hostages or potentially violent incidents, which are reactive in nature. The MCU's aim was to empower and support Muslim community representatives with the skills and commitment to help prevent susceptible Muslim youth from being recruited into al-Qaeda (or al-Qaeda-inspired) terrorist activity. In this context, *empowerment* and *support* are soft skills more commonly associated with community policing and social work than with counterterrorism policing. Indeed, while partnership skills might well be compatible with hostage negotiation skills, they differ in important respects.

And yet, there is nothing in the innovative methodology of the police unit's empowerment approach that restricts hard counterterrorism from pursuing terrorist suspects in more familiar ways. In interviews, Muslim youth workers express an awareness that any of their youth "clients" may, at any time and unbeknownst to them, be the subject of a covert terrorist investigation. Indeed, the same Muslim youth workers express an understanding that if their efforts to guide a young person away from terrorist influence are unsuccessful, they will be obliged to report the individual to the police (Lambert 2010).

On occasion, MCU officers have been required to defend their Brixton Salafi partners from allegations that the partners themselves were intrinsically linked to terrorism. In interviews, MCU officers judged stereotyping, profiling, and conflating of Salafis with al-Qaeda terrorism to be misleading and counterproductive (Lambert 2010). The mere fact that al-Qaeda terrorists adapt and distort Salafi approaches to Islam does not mean that Salafis are implicitly linked to terrorism or extremism, much less that individual Salafis are likely to be terrorists or extremists, any more than Catholicism is a key pointer to Provisional IRA terrorism.

UK recruits to al-Qaeda have a diverse range of Muslim family backgrounds. However, it is axiomatic that by the time they become al-Qaeda suicide bombers (or other active terrorists), they have bought into an ideology using distorted strands of Salafi thinking. This is why Salafis often have the best antidotes to al-Qaeda propaganda once it has taken hold. Thus, according to MCU interviewees, conflating Salafis with the problem just inhibits their willingness and ability to immunize their communities against it.

Significantly, a local partnership policing project that points up the con-
tinuity and longevity of London's al-Qaeda terrorist threat from 1993 to
2007 sits at odds with an authoritative strand of terrorism studies literature
that seeks to use 9/11 as the marker of a "new" exceptional terrorist threat
and the beginning of a "global war on terror" to defeat or disrupt it (Berman 2003; Ben-Dor and Pedahzur 2004, 71–90). As Marie Breen Smyth
notes, this view has three problems: (1) it "tends towards a-historicity . . .
ignoring the historical experiences of numerous countries"; (2) it "excep-
tionalizes the experience of the U.S. and al-Qaeda"; and (3) it "tends towards 'state-centrism,' with the 'terrorist' defined as the (security) problem and inquiry restricted to the assembling of information and data that
would solve or eradicate the 'problem' as the state defines it" (Smyth 2007).
Especially relevant to the London partnership between the MCU and the
Brixton Salafis is Smyth's observation that this account "ignores the roots
of terrorism and the contribution of the state itself to the creation of the
conditions in which terrorist action by non-state actors occurs" (Smyth
2007, 2). The partnership approach also sits at odds with mainstream accounts (both academic and popular) of countering al-Qaeda by offering a
bottom-up perspective against the full weight of post-9/11 discourses that
approach the issue from a decidedly top-down vantage point (Carter 2001;
Coker 2002, 40; Walt 2002).

Partnership Skills

Both sides of the partnership—MCU police officers and Brixton Salafis—
make credible claims to possessing privileged insight into the terrorist's
perspective. Brixton Salafi community partners present compelling accounts of the extent to which long-term exposure and proximity to individual London-based terrorist strategists has given them unique insider
understanding of the psychology and methodology of organizing and recruiting strategically minded terrorists. Just as crucially, they share experience of a Muslim London street culture in which terrorists and those they
have recruited move and operate. Added to this, they bring what might
best be interpreted as cultural proximity to the strands of religious and political thinking that al-Qaeda strategists and propagandists use to convince
young London Muslims to become terrorists or terrorist supporters. This
kind of knowledge, a rare find in counterterrorism, was insufficiently understood and valued by policymakers and senior police management during
the research period that concluded at the end of 2007. The Brixton Salafi
partners' knowledge is best described as providing five interdependent and
vital attributes when engaged in proactive preventive counterterrorism

community work: (1) an understanding of al-Qaeda ideology, (2) an understanding of al-Qaeda indoctrination methodology, (3) the specialized knowledge to challenge it, (4) religious credibility, and (5) street credibility. Research shows, however, that none of this counts for much if it is not allied with outstanding commitment and bravery of the kind displayed consistently by the Brixton Salafis.

As an example of the qualities listed above, when a Brixton Salafi community partner vividly recalls listening to private and powerful accounts of al-Qaeda ideology in a recruitment setting, his insider experience is invaluable in helping the partnership assess the strengths and weaknesses of the al-Qaeda narrative, and the points at which to make effective interventions. Broadly speaking, this analysis requires an insider's religious, community, and political knowledge. The Brixton Salafi analysis will often accord with academic accounts of al-Qaeda ideology, but what sets this perspective apart is its high level of community context and empathy. Similarly, experienced community members who understand all of the recruitment methodology's religious, political, and community impact are best equipped to intervene against it. Thus, one seasoned community insider has commented on the significance of the recruiter's recurring theme of "manhood," wherein young, inexperienced, and sometimes convert Muslims are encouraged to see their strict daily religious practice as but one important half in their new religious lives. The other half is fighting the "enemy" and acquiring the prerequisite skills, both mental and physical, to do justice to the task, themselves, and their families. Needless to say, a community intervention at any stage of a terrorist radicalization or recruitment process will be successful only if it has the specialized knowledge and credibility to challenge it on three fronts: religious, political, and community.

Religious and street credibility are best illustrated by an interviewee who had joined the Brixton Salafis after being involved in violent extremism: "I was in Feltham for street robbery.[4] Same as Richard Reid. Later [than Reid]. Same call from el-Faisal. Sounded good to me. Rob the kafir. Could have got me killed. Or back in prison. Stupid. Three years with that erroneous belief till I came to Mr. Baker's khutbah."[5]

"Erroneous belief" and "erroneous call" are two of a handful of stock terms in the Brixton Salafi counterextremism tool kit that have been used to good effect over the past fifteen years. The interviewee here had switched his allegiance from Abdullah el-Faisal and Osama bin Laden to Abdul Haqq Baker and the Brixton Salafis and adopted a new vocabulary as well as a new sense of citizenship. These terms, used repeatedly throughout interviews and discussions with Brixton Salafis—who themselves often have been involved in extremism or street crime—serve to underscore their dual motivations: correcting a false call to Islam and helping local youths become responsible citizens.

Muslim MCU officers played a valuable role in trust building, and this, in turn, enhanced the shared expertise of the partnership. According to an MCU officer who had worked doing surveillance on domestic and international terrorist targets in London, understanding al-Qaeda became a process of shared learning:

> I would ask [a Muslim MCU officer] about the way [an al-Qaeda propagandist and strategist] spoke to a young audience in London. We would listen to the tape together. He would explain the religious and community context and what he called the pressure points in the talk to me. How effective [the al-Qaeda propagandist] was at conveying a sense of authority and instilling in the audience a feeling that they should follow his leadership. Then he would ask me about the way terrorist groups behaved when they were planning an attack and were concerned that they might be under surveillance. What kind of counter-surveillance tactics they employed. What kind of street skills were needed in a terrorist group. I would explain what I had learned over the years doing this kind of work. Later on, I would have the same kind of discussions with [a Muslim youth worker] who [a Muslim MCU officer] introduced me to about al-Qaeda terrorists [four names mentioned] he knew well. This was the way we got a feel for the calibre of the people we were dealing with and built up a picture of al-Qaeda influence in London. (Lambert 2010, 103)

Michael Kenney is one of a small number of academics who have explored the informal learning processes that take place in counterterrorism policing and who have compared them with similar processes within terrorist and organized crime groups (Kenney 2007). His fieldwork with the MCU in 2007 tends to confirm the importance of what he calls *metis* learning, where skills are honed on the streets, over *techne,* or classroom, learning, which does not always adequately test the individual's ability to operate in real counterterrorism scenarios (Kenny 2008). In his detailed comparative study of Colombian drug traffickers and al-Qaeda terrorists, Kenney elucidates key similarities in the learning experiences of two very differently motivated groups and usefully separates their taught skills (techne) from their learned-on-the-job skills (metis). For both groups—one economically driven and the other motivated by political and religious zeal—the pressure of intrusive and coercive policing serves to ensure that the subjects' techne and metis skill sets are honed and sharpened in covert, high-risk environments. "Techne" and "metis" are ancient Greek terms that Kenney uses to describe abstract technical knowledge such as drug- and bomb-making procedures (techne) and experiential, intuitive knowledge such as "ingenuity, elusiveness . . . cunning and deceit" (metis) (Kenney 2007). Invariably, metis skills are employed by drug traffickers and terrorists to safeguard the products of their techne skills—such as drug shipments and primed and timed bombs—and to counter security and policing tactics that seek to disrupt their activities.

An MCU officer says that the same street skills separate effective counterterrorism operatives from those who do not make the grade—just as terrorist recruits who lack metis skills may be given a safe job in propaganda dissemination, poor counterterrorism operational trainees will return to the safety of desk jobs (Lambert 2010, 104). The combination of street skills that converged in the MCU gave it a unique insight into the way al-Qaeda-directed or -inspired terrorists operated in London, and the mutual learning between police and the Muslim community grew as the new unit matured. This shared learning experience helps explain how responses to al-Qaeda came about on the MCU.

Street expertise provides a nexus between police and community skills that bears directly on the Brixton partnership. Axiomatic for both partners is the need to cultivate skills that will enable negotiations to take place with targets of recruitment for dangerous and illegal activity.

Mohammad Sidique Khan, the leader of the 7/7 al-Qaeda London tube bombers, demonstrated his expert techne and metis skill sets when he was unexpectedly and casually approached by an old school friend on a busy Leeds shopping street just days before he led the first-ever suicide terrorist attack in the UK. While taught techne skills might have reminded him of the importance of maintaining cover at all times, only developed metis skills allowed him to engage happily in small talk for a long period with a non-Muslim he had not seen for several years. Khan presented an alter ego that concealed his all-consuming covert terrorist purpose so successfully that his old school friend could not recognize the man he met in the street as the mass murderer of innocent civilians days later. Against such skilled performers, admonitions from government ministers and police chiefs to communities to report suspicious behavior are likely to prove fruitless. This is not to overlook the fact that Khan had appeared on the UK counterterrorist radar in 2004, but rather to illustrate how effectively terrorists may become experts at concealment and deception, both through taught procedures (techne) and improvised aptitude (metis).

The available evidence surrounding the preparations of the 9/11 bombers shows a similar use of well-honed metis skills (National Commission 2004). Mohamed Atta, like Khan a key player in a carefully managed conspiracy, displays similar expertise that techne teaching alone cannot produce. In both cases, it may be reasonable to speculate that al-Qaeda strategists had previously identified exactly this potential in both men: metis, or, more simply, street, skills. Their ability to succeed in such critical tasks was not a matter of chance but an indication of expert preparation and recruitment—the strategic acumen that is essential to the effectiveness and longevity of any significant terrorist movement. Indeed, in important respects, al-Qaeda recruiters are no different from experienced military, security, and police trainers who select specialist officers to perform dangerous undercover operations against organized-crime and terrorist targets. In consequence, covert terrorist metis (just as much as its counterpart techne) is passed on from teacher to apprentice in the same way that it is done by the very individuals being trained to disrupt them.

Conclusion

The MCU's role in the Brixton partnership was aimed at empowering Muslim communities with the needed street skills to counter al-Qaeda propagandists' efforts at subverting and recruiting young Muslims to their cause. In important respects, the project adopted the same "soft" community policing approaches used to combat drug problems, in which susceptible youths are engaged as potential victims and differentiated from unscrupulous traffickers and pushers, who are targeted for long-term imprisonment. In UK counterterrorism (as elsewhere in the West), there is no precedent for treating young potential terrorist recruits as victims who should be rehabilitated into the community, rather than as criminals to be targeted and prosecuted for serious terrorist offenses. To allow credible grassroots Muslim community groups to perform much of this work with minimum supervision is to push well beyond the boundaries of conventional counterterrorism. Indeed, even in drug and gun crime policing, there is skepticism about the ability of soft community initiatives to rehabilitate offenders or divert susceptible youths away from criminal behavior. How much more resistance, then, will rally against soft approaches when the subject is the most politically charged of the day: terrorism?

By supporting and empowering Brixton's Salafi community leadership to counsel and negotiate with Muslim youths, MCU officers were extending and applying the notion that "communities defeat terrorism." For many years before 9/11, Londoners lived and worked against the backdrop of a tangible terrorist threat, often dramatically demonstrated during Provisional Irish Republican Army, Irish National Liberation Army, and Real Irish Republican Army (RIRA) bombing campaigns in the 1970s, 1980s, and 1990s (and concluding with a RIRA campaign in 2000–2001). Notable cases of public vigilance leading to the detection or disruption of such terrorist activity attested to the health of active and vigilant citizenship in the capital. But the detection, disruption, and prevention of terrorism are greatly enhanced if all sections of society—especially those sections where terrorist propaganda is prevalent—are active in their support of counterterrorism policing. It has long been recognized that terrorists should, wherever possible, be denied community support and sympathy (Arblaster 1977). Would-be terrorists in London maximize their opportunities to successfully surmount counterterrorist security measures and carry out violent attacks if they have tacit support—or at least a willingness to turn a blind eye—of sections of the community that they either belong to or frequent.

The Brixton partnership project was novel in introducing to counterterrorism a bottom-up, community-based approach that is better understood in community policing strategies targeting drug, gun, and other street crimes. A decade later, it is even clearer that organized crime and terrorism operate beneath the radar of conventional politics, where only civil society networks will have an impact on potential recruitment. The London partnership project was, in fact, located in the field of multiagency partnerships aimed at taking a holistic view of crime problems where community buy-in is essential. Its absence, up to now, from counterterrorism arenas may indicate how minor a role community policing has played in the global "war on terror" since 9/11.

On several occasions, Brixton Salafi youth workers have, through negotiation, successfully steered susceptible Muslim youths away from supporting and potentially engaging in al-Qaeda terrorism. In doing so, they have not tried to challenge or water down the fundamental religious beliefs of the young persons they were negotiating with. On the contrary, successful Brixton Salafi interventions are best characterized by their clarification of a correct Salafi interpretation that exposes the paucity of religious understanding in al-Qaeda's propaganda. More conventional "hearts and minds" approaches designed to validate U.S. and UK policy in wider Muslim communities would only have undermined any chance of success—especially if the negotiations had been done by "outsider" Muslim community groups who lacked credibility.

As police officers know only too well, successful crime prevention of any kind is less measurable and, therefore, less attractive than the apprehension of offenders. A young drug user who is successfully persuaded by a reformed drug addict to avoid further drug use will not feature in the kind of performance statistics that police or social services compile for the Home Office. The same holds true in counterterrorism, where nine cases of successful community intervention against al-Qaeda propaganda and recruitment will count for nothing if one other intervention fails and a young man goes on to become a suicide bomber. The political risk is magnified when the intervention work involves Salafi communities that are often deemed a threat to social cohesion. No modest success by the Salafis and their police partners on the streets of London will outweigh the risk of political disapprobation at the bar of tabloid judgment. On the other hand, the ongoing threat posed to Londoners by al-Qaeda terrorism suggests that the proven negotiation skills of the Brixton Salafis in reducing that threat should be highly valued and not discarded lightly.

Notes

1. "The straight path"—a fundamental tenet of Islam.
2. At the time of this writing (January 2010), Abu Hamza was serving a prison term in the UK for incitement to murder while simultaneously awaiting extradition to the United States to face terrorism charges there; el-Faisal, having completed a prison term in the UK for incitement to murder, was deported to Jamaica in 2007; and Abu Qatada remained in preventive custody in the UK without having faced trial.
3. In 2002 the MCU consisted of two officers; in 2007 it had a staff of eight.
4. Feltham Young Offenders Institute, in the London borough of Hounslow.
5. Abdul Haqq Baker's talk at jummah prayer at Brixton Mosque most Fridays during 1994–2001, and occasional Fridays during 2002–07.

References

Arblaster, Anthony. 1977. "Terrorism: Myths, Meanings and Morals." *Political Studies* 25 (3): 413–24.

Baker, Abdul Haqq. 2010. "Countering Terrorism in the UK: A Convert Community Perspective." PhD diss., University of Exeter.

BBC News. 2005. "London Bomber Video Aired on TV." Sept. 2. http://news.bbc.co.uk/1/hi/uk/4206708.stm (accessed Oct. 4, 2010).

———. 2006. "Bomber 'Influenced' by Preacher." May 11. http://news.bbc.co.uk/1/hi/uk/4762123.stm (accessed Oct. 4, 2010).

Ben-Dor, Gabriel, and Ami Pedahzur. 2004. "The Uniqueness of Islamic Fundamentalism and the Fourth Wave of International Terrorism." In *Religious Fundamentalism and Political Extremism*, ed. Leonard Weinberg and Ami Pedahzur. London: Frank Cass.

Berman, Paul. 2003. *Terror and Liberalism*. London: Norton.

Bjørgo, Tore, and John Horgan, eds. 2008. *Leaving Terrorism Behind*. London: Routledge.

Carter, Ashton B. 2001. "The Architecture of Government in the Face of Terrorism." *International Terrorism* 26 (3): 5–23.

Coker, Christopher. 2002. *Globalisation and Insecurity in the Twenty-first Century: NATO and the Management of Risk*. London: International Institute for Strategic Studies.

Cox, Caroline, and John Marks. 2006. *The West, Islam and Islamism: Is Ideological Islam Compatible with Liberal Democracy?* London: Civitas.

Dodd, Vikram. 2006. "I Knew Exactly What I Was Doing." Interview with Peter Herbert. *Guardian*, Aug. 26. www.guardian.co.uk/world/2006/aug/24/alqaida. terrorism (accessed Oct. 3, 2010).

Esposito, John, ed. 2003. *The Oxford Dictionary of Islam*. Oxford: Oxford University Press.

Gove, Michael. 2006. *Celsius 7/7*. London: Weidenfeld and Nicholson.

Kenny, Michael. 2007. *From Pablo to Osama: Trafficking and Terrorist Networks, Government Bureaucracies, and Competitive Adaptation*. University Park, PA: Penn State University Press.

———. 2008. "Organizational Learning and Islamic Militancy." Report, National Criminal Justice Service. www.ncjrs.gov/pdffiles1/nij/grants/226808.pdf (accessed Oct. 6, 2010).

Lambert, Robert. 2008a. "Empowering Salafis and Islamists against Al-Qaeda: A London Counterterrorism Case Study." *PS: Political Science and Politics* 41 (1).

———. 2008b. "Salafi and Islamist Londoners: Stigmatised Minority Faith Communities Countering al-Qaida." *Crime, Law and Social Change* 50 (1–2): 73–89.

———. 2010. "The London Partnerships: An Insider's Analysis of Legitimacy and Effectiveness." PhD diss., University of Exeter.

Lawrence, Bruce, ed. 2005. *Messages to the World: The Statements of Osama bin Laden*. London: Verso.

Leheny, David. 2005. "Terrorism, Social Movements, and International Security: How Al Qaeda Affects Southeast Asia." *Japanese Journal of Political Science* 6 (1): 87–109.

Murad, Abdal-Hakim. 2001. "Recapturing Islam from the Terrorists." www. masud.co.uk/ISLAM/ahm/recapturing.htm (accessed Oct. 4, 2010).

National Commission on Terrorist Attacks upon the United States. 2004. *The 9/11 Commission Report: Authorized Edition*. London: Norton.

Olivetti, Vincenzo. 2002. *Terror's Source: The Ideology of Wahhabi-Salafism and Its Consequences*. Birmingham, UK: Amadeus.

Phillips, Melanie. 2006. *Londonistan: How Britain Is Creating a Terror State Within*. London: Gibson Square.

Robert, Na'ima R. 2005. *From My Sister's Lips*. London: Bantam.

Smyth, Marie Breen. 2007. "A Critical Research Agenda for the Study of Terrorism." Paper presented at the European Consortium for Political Research Symposium, Pisa, Italy.

UK Home Office. 2010. "The UK Counter-terrorism Strategy (CONTEST)." www.homeoffice.gov.uk/counter-terrorism/uk-counter-terrorism-strat/ (accessed Oct. 3, 2010).

Walt, Stephen M. 2002. "Beyond bin Laden: Reshaping U.S. Foreign Policy." *International Security* 26 (3): 56–78.

4

Terror, Muscle, and Negotiation:

Failure of Multiparty Mediation in Sri Lanka

Maria Groeneveld-Savisaar* and Siniša Vuković

The unyielding and uncompromising positions of conflicting sides have often represented a crucial challenge for international mediators. Even though such rigid stands are a common feature in conflicts involving a terrorist organization, mediation activities are not predestined to fail. But the mediators need to develop a well-tailored set of strategies to steer inflexible parties to a negotiated solution. This chapter discusses the need for strategic strength in the mediation process in case the warring parties lack the motivation to settle. Several authors in the field of external mediation of intrastate conflicts have argued that where the warring parties lack the motivation to settle, there is a need for a mediator "with muscle"; that is, to bring the parties in conflict back to the negotiation table requires stronger, more manipulative mediation strategies (Sisk 2009; Bercovitch 2009; Pruitt 2002). The key factor that drives a mediating state to employ the most coercive measures to resolve the conflict, thus investing considerable resources, is its strategic interests. That is, if the parties lack sufficient motivation to settle, strategic strength is needed, but the wielder of that strength must have a strategic interest in order to use that power. Sri Lanka's fifth peace process, which started off promisingly in 2002, became stalled in 2003, and was defunct by 2006, shows the crucial importance of this link.

105

One of the longest modern-day civil wars in Asia, waged for twenty-six years by the Liberation Tigers of Tamil Eelam (LTTE), also known as the Tamil Tigers, against the government of Sri Lanka, ended in a clear victory by the government in May 2009. Ending an intrastate war with a military solution and not through some sort of peace settlement is rather rare these days. The last peace process in Sri Lanka was enriched by a group of international actors: Norway, the United States, Japan, and the EU. This "dream team" was assembled by Norway and the Sri Lankan government in the hope that including members of the international community would motivate the warring parties to keep the talks going. The LTTE was labeled a terrorist organization by the United States but not by the EU, Norway, or Japan. In principle, this should have provided a scenario in which the outside actors could divide the work of mediation and, using specific leverages at their disposal, provide necessary incentives for the conflicting sides to move toward a settlement. Therefore, while the United States was unwilling to engage directly with the LTTE, Norway, the EU, and Japan could engage with both parties. But as the peace talks stalled in 2003 and 2006, hostilities resumed.

Contemporary practice has shown that civil wars are effectively managed from the outside only when there is an unequivocal commitment by the international community to use a well-tailored combination of carrots and sticks and, when necessary, apply aggressive measures such as deployment of military forces to the troubled area (Sisk 2009). This chapter will show that in addition to the internal factors behind the suspension of the peace talks, reasons for the failure can also be found in the intrinsic dynamics of the process and in the characteristics of the third parties that acted as mediators. The "dream team" of international actors lacked sufficient motivation to intervene in a way that would employ all the leverages each actor had at its disposal in the process. This lack of sufficient motivation, especially by the most powerful mediators, can be traced back to the fact that Sri Lanka was not strategically important. For this reason, powerful actors were reluctant to invest considerable resources in managing the conflict and bringing the negotiations between a political terrorist organization and the state to a successful conclusion.

In recent years, the most frequent type of third-party involvement has undeniably been mediation (Frazier and Dixon 2006). *Mediation* is generally described as "a process of conflict management, related to but distinct from the parties' own negotiations, where those in conflict seek or accept the assistance of an outsider (whether an individual, an organization, a group, or a state) to change their perceptions or behavior, and to do so without resorting to physical force or invoking the authority of law" (Bercovitch 2009, 343). Such an idealistic view of the mediation process and the mediator's presumed neutral stance might be misleading unless we emphasize the importance of the third party's self-interest to get it involved and get it marshaling its resources to move the conflicting sides toward a mutually acceptable solution. In fact, for a lot of actors, international mediation is a useful (foreign) policy instrument through which they can pursue some of their interests without creating too much opposition (Touval 1992). As Touval and Zartman point out, "Mediators are no less motivated by self-interest than by humanitarian impulses . . . the mediator is a player in the plot of relations surrounding a conflict, and has some interest in the outcome (else it would not mediate)" (Touval and Zartman 1985, 8).

Experience shows that mediation is rarely undertaken by a single trustworthy mediator; rather, most cases involve numerous mediators, which are often intertwined in mediating coalitions. Today a multiplicity of mediators is less a matter of choice than a fact of life (Sisk 2009). The increase in numbers, both of peacemaking efforts and of actors involved in those efforts, has undeniably stretched the traditional meaning of mediation. Theoretically, "multiparty mediation refers to different things in different contexts: it can refer to simultaneous, sequential, and composite mediated interventions" (Crocker, Hampson, and Aall 1999, 666).

Despite some unfavorable features, multiparty mediation has become a necessity for terrorist conflicts that require elevated levels of commitment to manage them. Since a single entity (whether a state or an international/regional organization) is seldom both able and willing to invest as much as is really required, more than one third party represents a good alternative. Not every mediator enters the process with the same level or type of leverage and commitment. But a combination of mediators with different leverages can contribute to the efficiency of collective activity, since the process may rely on "borrowing leverages" from various parties. At the same time, the costs of mediation get divided among the mediators. The costs of mediating alone usually reach a point where the outside player sees its resources overstretched. By reducing the costs of intervention, mediators can deploy more focused strategies, which may help move one or both conflicting parties toward a peaceful settlement of their dispute.

Ultimately, the participation of influential regional and global actors in the mediating coalition can contribute to "restructuring" both domestic and regional relationships that hamper the achievement of a negotiated solution, through the creation of necessary incentives to manage the conflict. Following this line of thought, Sisk stresses the importance of a "powerful state to play the 'heavy.'" One state, usually an interested regional state or a global power with considerable influence in the region, is supposed to provide necessary "communications, diplomatic consistency, intelligence, and finance to make the mediation effort effective" (Sisk 2009, 53). This actor, which Sisk refers to as the "lead state," should be ready to use a well-thought-out blend of carrots and sticks to guide the parties toward a mutually acceptable solution.

Coordination of leverages, which is essential for a successful multiparty mediation, is generally done through coordinating specific strategies that mediators use throughout the process, since each strategy is exemplified by a particular set of leverages. This research uses the typology put forward by Touval and Zartman, who classify the mediators' behavior and corresponding strategies on an intervention scale ranging from low to high, from facilitation (both communication and formulation) to directive-manipulation strategies (Touval and Zartman 1985, 1989, 2006; Zartman and Touval 1996).

Strategic versus Tactical Strength

In mediation, *leverage*—"the ability to move a party in an intended direction"—derives from the very fact that disputing sides need mediators' assistance in finding solutions to their problems (Touval and Zartman 1985, 2006, 436; Touval 1992). Since leverage has to be channeled through collective action, mediators face a crucial challenge in achieving internal agreement on the necessary combination of inducements they can produce given their individual social power.

Carnevale identifies two main forms of power in mediation, based on actors' "will and skill." On one hand, there is the resource-based aspect of mediating power, which he calls "strategic strength." On the other hand, there is a behavioral aspect of mediating power, exemplified in the mediator's premeditated choice of specific techniques and in its ability to follow a particular procedure. Carnevale calls this "tactical strength." According to that classification, "strategic strength in mediation refers to what the mediator has, to what the mediator brings to the negotiation table; the tactical strength refers to what the mediator does at the negotiation table" (Carnevale 2002, 28).

Contemporary practice shows that in some cases the mediating coalition must be prepared to employ considerable resources, ranging from targeted financial incentives to military deployment. Sisk identifies three very important rewarding, or noncoercive, measures that mediators can use as leverage: First, they can transfer financial means to the parties in conflict to encourage them to alter their positions. Second, they can promise to deploy neutral peacekeeping forces to "induce weaker parties to accept vulnerabilities in the post-accord environment ... guaranteeing non-defection by other parties" (Sisk 2009, 54). Third, they can confer legitimacy on a faction's cause, which would otherwise be marginalized. This way a terrorist group can obtain an affirmation that it is a "representative of those it purports to represent" (Sisk 2009, 55).

In recent mediations between states and political terrorist organizations, coercive power (a specific form of strategic strength) has proved highly instrumental. Coercive measures are generally exercised through various forms of threat or punishment. Diplomatic pressure is the softest coercive mechanism at the mediators' disposal, and usually it includes different types of "persuasion, mass media appeals, withdrawing recognition, or public shaming" (Sisk 2009, 55). This tool has been used quite often, especially by lead states, as the U.S. roles in the Dayton peace talks and the Sudan north/south dispute show. A more rigorous coercive measure is the imposition of sanctions, which transmits the mediators' discontent with a party's behavior and attitude in the process. Over time, different forms of sanctions have been exercised all over the world, varying from "smart sanctions" to specific lists of terrorist organizations, as discussed in Kristine Höglund's chapter in this volume. Finally, the most intrusive and violent form of coercive power is the use of military force. Several scholars have shown that an intense conflict with a high number of casualties necessitates a more powerful coercive intervention than does a low-intensity conflict, mainly because the cost of not reaching a solution is exceptionally high (Rubin 1980; Hiltrop 1989). Whereas weak mediators excel when the parties are motivated to settle but lack the necessary optimism or communication facilities to move forward, strong mediators such as the United States are especially needed when the parties lack sufficient motivation to settle (Bercovitch 2009, 348; Pruitt 2002, 51).

Isak Svensson shows that "most effective are those mediation attempts when both power and pure mediators are active as third parties" (Svensson 2007, 229). In state conflicts with political terrorist organizations, a combined intervention of both types of mediators allows them to produce agreements that regulate both the military dimension (through the involvement of a powerful mediator) and the power-sharing dimension (through the involvement of a "pure" mediator that relies on tactical strength), as required.

Self-interest in Mediation

Even though mediators' involvement is primarily justified through the aim of resolving a conflict, additional motives complement the aspiration to produce a peaceful solution. Mediators play their role in negotiations and expend resources not only because they aim to resolve a dispute but because they also seek to gain something (Greig 2005). Thus, although a wide variety of motives might drive mediators to intervene, in nearly all cases these motives are "tainted" with the mediators' self-interest. For states, self-interest is reflected in attempts to produce settlements that will "increase the prospects of stability, deny their rivals opportunities for intervention, earn them the gratitude of one or both parties, or enable them to continue to have a role in future relations" (Zartman and Touval 1996, 446).

In principle, the activities of states as mediators reflect a blend of both defensive and offensive motives. *Defensive* reasons are seen when the conflict's prolongation directly threatens the outside state's interests or could induce other states to join; thus, a fear of such escalation encourages states to become involved. *Offensive* motives of state intervention are, in short, "the desire to extend and increase influence" (Zartman and Touval 1996, 447). Through its power, the mediator can enhance its own influence and create an environment in which the mediation's success depends on the mediator's involvement. This occurs in situations where the conflicting sides depend on the mediator to garner concessions from the other party and where the mediator assumes the role of guarantor of the agreement. Nevertheless, since mediation bears inevitable costs for mediators, third parties will seek to share these costs with fellow countries or pursue these activities through collective entities such as international organizations.

This is especially true for small and medium-size powers. Even though these actors usually have domestic issues (e.g., fear of the conflict's spillover onto the mediator's soil) as their key motives for intervening, it is not unusual for them to use mediation as a tool for strengthening their influence and prestige abroad. Since small and medium-size states have limited maneuvering space on the international level, "mediation increases their usefulness and independence in relation to their stronger allies" (Touval and Zartman 2006, 430).

When and Why to Flex a Muscle

Manipulation strategies that imply powerful interventions by mediators are most needed when the conflict has escalated to the point that the costs of continuing become too high. In contemporary mediation literature, these costs are generally attributed to the conflicting sides. The ripe moment to negotiate is when conflicting sides have reached a "mutually hurting stalemate," and any further continuation would only be costlier than resorting to peace talks (Touval and Zartman 1985).

But current scholarship fails to address another important issue: what about the costs that mediators face, especially when they resort to the most coercive measures at their disposal? The mere fact that a state is prepared to take very costly measures to change the dynamics in a conflict in which it is not directly involved implies that the state has something more at stake.

The size of the country in conflict is rarely a factor. Even the smallest countries, whether islands or landlocked, may represent something of strategic importance for more powerful states. A good example in this regard is the case of Taiwan and its strategic relevance for the United States (Ross 2006; Wu 2006). A terrorist conflict, regardless of the size of the country involved, attracts attention from outside and induces third parties to intervene as mediators. Quite often, civil wars can involve participation of a group whose methods project the image of a terrorist organization. But the fact that some outside actors label one side in the conflict terrorists does not diminish the likelihood of a third-party intervention to manage the conflict. "Party arithmetic" actions, done by outside actors to affect which entities are involved in a given negotiation—that is, adding and subtracting parties—often indicates that it may be possible to deal with the terrorists (Lax and Sebenius 1991, 162). Third parties can be necessary to help the conflicting sides bridge the deep gap produced by rigid stands on both sides: an almost absolutist position and demands by the "terrorists," and a refusal by the central authorities to negotiate with terrorists.

According to Pruitt, there are at least three types of terrorist groups, classified by representational level and ideology. According to this classification, the most problematic to negotiate with are groups with high levels of representation and strong ideological foundation, such as al-Qaeda or the Ku Klux Klan (Pruitt 2006). Organizations with strong ideological convictions but a very weak representation base (such as the Red Brigades or the Baader-Meinhof Gang), though generally less successful in achieving their goals in the long run, are still very difficult to negotiate with. The third type comprises the less ideological ethnonationalist groups, whose aim is "to gain power, autonomy, or independence for their ethnic group" (Pruitt 2006, 372–73). Even though they are hard to beat, they are often reasonable enough to allow a negotiated solution (Pruitt 2006, 372–73). Among the most well-known terrorist groups of this third kind are the Irish Republican Army (IRA), the Palestinian Liberation Organization, and Sri Lanka's LTTE.

Interestingly, each conflict involving any of these three terrorist groups was managed through a multiparty mediation effort, with varying levels of success (Crocker, Hampson, and Aall 1999). Whereas the Good Friday Agreement ended the civil strife in Northern Ireland, and several rounds of negotiations in Oslo and Madrid moved the Israelis and Palestinians closer to a negotiated solution, the multiparty mediation efforts in Sri Lanka failed completely. In all cases, the United States played the role of powerful mediator. However, the United States' level of involvement and its readiness to use the leverage it possessed differed greatly from case to case, directly affecting the conflict management process. The question arises, what explains such different treatment of each conflict by a powerful actor such as the United States?

Powerful states that might assume the role of lead state are driven by geopolitical considerations much wider than the resolution of any specific conflict—considerations that embrace both defensive and offensive motives. The capability to "mediate with muscle" is what distinguishes strong mediators. The mediator's power to punish the disputants—coercive power—encourages respect for the mediator, and greater cooperation in making concessions (Carnevale et al. 1989). In cases when the conflict has escalated to the point that disputants cannot engage in joint problem solving, forceful mediator intervention becomes most effective (Carnevale 2002).

Strategic power is never applied aimlessly. Rather, it is a direct consequence of the powerful mediator's premeditated decision on whether applying that power is in its best interest. These strategic interests are rarely found in an official document that sets the guidelines for future involvement. However, by looking at the different elements that influence state behavior, we may well discern what is strategically important for a powerful state. Reflecting on the U.S. role in Northern Ireland and the Middle East, we can see that specific features of the United States' relations with actors in those areas determine the likelihood of a U.S. intervention in specific conflicts. Here are the most recognizable elements:

- Proximity to vital economic resources (e.g., water, oil, gas) and corresponding infrastructure
- Economic relations
- Proximity to the source of security instability
- Political relations and ideological compatibility
- Proximity to a rival-power state, and relations with it
- Proximity to a partner state, and relations with it
- Historical record

Current multiparty mediation scholarship falls short in explaining under which circumstances we can expect a powerful state to intervene in its full capacity. Instead, it focuses either on the possibility of "borrowing leverage" from a powerful state or on the importance of having a powerful state in the mediating coalition. While less coercive measures have become the norm in mediation activities, especially because of the lower costs they produce for mediators, coercive power has not been applied as often. Although one might expect a powerful state to use its leverage whenever necessary, this is seldom the case in reality. The key factor that drives lead states to employ the most coercive measures, thus investing considerable resources, to resolve the conflict is its strategic interests. In other words, when the parties lack sufficient motivation to settle and strategic strength is needed, the strategic power must have a strategic incentive to use that power. The case of Sri Lanka illustrates this relationship between strategic interest and coercion.

Background to Sri Lanka's Conflict

The civil war in Sri Lanka, an ethnic conflict between the government and the LTTE, has been one of the longest, most intractable intrastate conflicts in Asia. According to the International Crisis Group (ICG), more than 70,000 people were killed in the north and east from the 1980s to 2006 (ICG 2006). Hundreds of thousands have been displaced, many of them more than once. Several unmediated and mediated peace talks have taken place, but none has ever produced a peace agreement. The last peace attempt, which formally lasted from 2002 to 2006, producing the cease-fire agreement (CFA), six rounds of peace talks in 2003, and two rounds in 2006, became defunct in 2006, when the warring parties once again started exploring a military solution to the conflict. This chapter discusses Sri Lanka's fifth peace process during 2002–06, for this was the duration of the peace talks before hostilities resumed.

The fifth Sri Lanka peace process was highly internationalized, involving several important world players that had both tactical and strategic means at their disposal. Also, as Goodhand argues, the case is interesting because of "the emergence, more by default than by design, of a strategic complementarity between different international actors. . . . Each had different approaches, different sets of alliances within Sri Lankan society and consequently different points of leverage" (Goodhand 2006a, 39–40).

The events that developed into the Sri Lankan ethnic conflict started after the end of the British colonization, with the new constitution of 1948. According to Rotberg, the 1948 constitution "lacked a bill of rights like India's," or anything that could provide "effective formal protection for minorities" (Rotberg 1999, 5). The state's discriminatory policies led to anti-Tamil riots in 1956, followed by the deadlier riots of 1958, 1977, 1981, and 1983. The infamous 1983 riot caused thousands of Tamil refugees to flee to

India and Western countries—the beginning of the large Sri Lankan Tamil diaspora. This diaspora later played a major role in financing the war waged against the government (DeVotta 2007). All these developments led to the further development of Tamil militant groups, most notably the LTTE, founded in 1976 and led by Velupillai Prabhakaran. The central goal for the LTTE was an independent country, the Tamil homeland called Eelam. The full-scale war between the Sri Lankan defense forces and the LTTE started in 1983 and ended on May 19, 2009, with the government declaring victory over the rebels.

Sri Lanka's civil war has produced five distinguishable rounds of peace talks.[1] Significantly, some of these talks avoided the core political issues, instead concentrating on humanitarian, logistical, or military issues (Rupesinghe 2006c). Also, the negotiations were occasions for the warring parties to rearm themselves and, as Uyangoda puts it, "discover new differences" and "reconstitute the conflict" (Uyangoda 2007, viii). Biswas observes, "While the party in power tends to adopt a more conciliatory position, the one in opposition follows a more belligerent and critical path. This, in turn, impacts the progress of talks between the government and the Tamil separatists. Ultimately, this has created a situation where facilitative intervention does create room for talks but no agreement is reached" (Biswas 2006, 59).

The Peace Process of 2002–06

Prelude to the Fifth Peace Process

The significant developments preceding the peace process were the economic recession in Sri Lanka, the escalation of the war in 1999–2001, which made for a war-weary population, and the post-9/11 atmosphere worldwide. Until then, the LTTE, through its strong lobby abroad—particularly in countries with a large Tamil diaspora—had been able to sell itself as an organization of freedom fighters, protecting a Tamil minority that had been harassed by the majority rule for decades. As Paikiasothy Saravanamuttu, head of the local nongovernmental organization (NGO) Centre for Policy Alternatives, points out, "11 September impacted on the LTTE's political psyche and its room for manoeuvre internationally in respect of funds, legitimacy and acquisition of weapons" (Saravanamuttu 2003, 132). In the changed environment, it became more difficult for the LTTE to keep up its freedom-fighter image and thereby ensure the same level of fund-raising from its diaspora and NGOs in Western countries. Moreover, several powerful countries had already listed the LTTE as a terrorist organization, further limiting its ability to operate in these countries:

in India since 1992, the United States since 1997, and the UK since 2001. All these developments made the LTTE revise its tactics and increased its motivation to look for a settlement. At the end of 2001, the economic crisis and the escalation of the war led to the government's fall, and a coalition of parties called the United National Front (UNF), led by the United National Party (UNP), won the elections in December 2001. This coalition was led by Ranil Wickremesinghe, Sri Lankan prime minister during 2001–04 and the so-called architect of the peace process. Chandrika Bandaranaike Kumaratunga, of the Sri Lanka Freedom Party (SLFP), remained president, which led to an uneasy cohabitation.

The UNF government, and Wickremesinghe in particular, made very clear from the start that its priorities were the peace process, with the inclusion of the international community, and the revival of the economy (Bastian 2006). After Wickremesinghe took office, things started to move rapidly. The cease-fire agreement, signed in February 2002, provided for the end of hostilities and the establishment of the Sri Lankan Monitoring Mission (SLMM) to monitor implementation of the cease-fire between the parties. From September 2002 to March 2003, six rounds of direct negotiations were held between the LTTE and the government of Sri Lanka.[2] Another significant achievement was the statement, made by the parties at an Oslo press conference in 2002, on their intention to explore the federal option.[3] This was the first time the parties considered a federal solution and the LTTE backed down from its secessionist goal (Höglund and Svensson 2006).

But in 2003, the United States barred the LTTE from attending a seminar held in Washington to discuss the peace process, on the grounds that the United States listed the LTTE as a terrorist organization. In response, the LTTE suspended the talks and refused to attend the Tokyo conference of June 2003, where donors had pledged $4.5 billion to the peace process. The LTTE stated that the international community and the Sri Lankan government had failed to recognize it as an equal party to the process. The peace process stalled. This was complicated by the cohabitation crisis between President Kumaratunga, of SLFP, and Prime Minister Wickremesinghe, of UNP. The crisis had been simmering since the beginning of the peace process, because the president, who was the commander in chief, head of state, and head of the cabinet—with the power to call for elections at any time she liked after the government had been in office for a year—was largely excluded from the peace process. The crisis culminated in the president's taking over three key ministries in November 2003, followed by the dissolution of the parliament and, finally, the downfall of the UNF government (Fernando 2006). But Oslo's facilitation continued after the government changed and also after the newly elected president, with a nationalist and pro-military-solution platform, Mahinda Rajapaksa of the SLFP, came to power in 2005.

In 2006, the no-war, no-peace period that had lasted since the peace process stalled in 2003 descended into a low-intensity conflict, then into open war, particularly in the east. Nonetheless, two rounds of peace talks (Geneva I and II) did take place in 2006 in Geneva. The first round was held on February 19–20, and the second on October 28–29. But the 2006 efforts to get the peace process moving essentially failed. The failure to implement the agreements of Geneva I severely undermined the prospects for further talks.

Failure of the Peace Process

The peace talks, which had started off so promisingly, led by a deeply committed prime minister and experienced Norwegian mediators, stalled in 2003 and failed in 2006, for a variety of reasons. For one, Sri Lanka's ethnic conflict has repeatedly demonstrated a capacity for intense reescalation (Uyangoda 2007). As Höglund and Svensson point out, one of the motivations for the cease-fire, for both sides, may have been the opportunity to rearm and reorganize for the future (Höglund and Svensson 2009). Therefore, it appears that one of the reasons the peace process failed was because the parties never really lost the appetite for a military solution (Smith 2007). Second, the parties failed to sign even an interim settlement agreement. With no political agreement, the relationship between the government and the LTTE was based entirely on the CFA. Uyangoda points out that the basis for the negotiations and the CFA "was the preservation of the parties' strategic interests through a condition of no-war.... Consequently, the problem-solving and conflict transformation approach became entirely absent" (Uyangoda 2006, 4). Third, the peace process was focused exclusively on two parties: the government, led by Wickremesinghe, and the LTTE. President Kumaratunga and other southern political elites were largely excluded from the process, and non-LTTE Tamil parties and Muslim parties had no role at all. As pointed out by the ICG, "Much of the dynamic of this conflict is within ethnic communities, and the failure of the peace process to address this, made a lasting peace less likely" (ICG 2006, i).

In 2004, two significant developments changed the balance of power between the parties. The defection of the LTTE's eastern commander, Vinayagamoorthy Muralitharan, known as Colonel Karuna, and the losses suffered by the LTTE's naval wing in the tsunami of December 2004 led some sections of the government and armed forces to believe that the LTTE's offensive capacity was weakened and that a highly concentrated war against the LTTE, with the help of the breakaway faction, would be winnable (Uyangoda 2006).

In conclusion, all the above-mentioned developments induced the parties to start exploring their military options again and contributed to the subsequent failure of the talks. But without discounting the internal developments that contributed to the failure of the peace talks, it is important to understand the part that the international mediators and their self-interest played in the peace process.

The International Community's Role and Interests in the Peace Process

A conscious effort to create an "international safety net" was one of the most important strategies of the UNF. Prime Minister Wickremesinghe's first policy statement, before the CFA was signed, made it clear that he considered international opinion a key factor in guaranteeing peace in Sri Lanka. As Sunil Bastian points out, this strategy brought in the United States, Japan, and the EU as cochairs of the peace process, in addition to Norway. "In doing so, the UNF managed to secure the involvement of a 'superpower,' its major trading partners and Sri Lanka's largest donor, in the peace process" (Bastian 2006, 247). The common motivator for the external actors was the perception of the Sri Lanka case as an "easy win" (Goodhand 2006b). Goodhand argues that in 2002, international actors were willing to "prioritize peacebuilding because it appeared to be a low risk-high opportunity situation" (Goodhand 2006a, 15). And Uyangoda criticized the international community for focusing mainly on short-term success and approaching the peace talks "as an exercise that should produce an early peace deal" (Uyangoda 2006, 4).

The mediating actors were divided into those that engaged the LTTE (Norway, the EU, and Japan) and the United States, which did not. However, the United States did signal to the rebels "that a change in LTTE behavior could lead to a change in the U.S. approach" (Lunstead 2007, 16). Donors encouraged the establishment of joint government-LTTE mechanisms, such as the Post-Tsunami Operational Management Structure, but these initiatives did not succeed.

Norway

Norway, a small country with no specific geopolitical interests or colonial past, has had a good record of conflict mediation since the early 1990s.[4] There are perhaps three main reasons for Norway's becoming involved as a mediator in several peace processes. First, its political and social culture is considered suitable for mediation activities, since it has a tradition of development assistance. Second, an image as a peacemaker and a "great moral power" is important for Norway's self-perception (Höglund and Svensson 2009, 179). Third, engaging in the peace talks of intrastate wars has enabled Norway, a small and distant Nordic country, to be an arbiter between the global powers and the developing countries, thereby taking a much more significant role in the international arena than it would have otherwise (Moolakkattu 2005; Höglund and Svensson 2009). Kelleher and Taulbee point out that Norway has a consistent approach to peacemaking, the key components being time, patience, secrecy, funding, and activist facilitation. By taking a leading role in Sri Lanka, Norway seemed to deviate from its preference to hold more of a supportive and low-profile role and to "conduct relevant activities under the 'radar screen' of public scrutiny" (Kelleher and Taulbee 2005, 80).

Norway first became involved in Sri Lanka's peace process in 1999–2000. Erik Solheim was appointed as a special adviser to the Norwegian Department of Foreign Affairs in March 2000 and took a full role as facilitator after the UNF government took office in December 2001 (Bullion 2001). One of the main reasons the actors chose Norway as the mediator was that it had no strategic interests in Sri Lanka. As Foreign Minister Lakshman Kadirgamar stated, Norway was considered suitable since it is a small, faraway country with no colonial background and, therefore, was seen as not having an agenda of its own. Moreover, it also had experience in peacemaking (Ram 2001). Also in Norway's favor, India accepted it as an external mediator, because India did not see this small, remote country as a threat to its own strategic interests in the region (Moolakkattu 2005). Norwegians themselves have pointed out that they got involved for a mix of reasons, beginning with its long-term development aid projects in Sri Lanka and also including personal contacts through Norwegian NGOs and individuals (Rupesinghe 2006b). And Norway's interest in Sri Lanka may not have been related to the conflict itself but rather to the possibility of getting access to the highest offices of the global powers (Höglund and Svensson 2009). Although Norway's wider reputational concerns may explain why it stayed involved in Sri Lanka's conflict long after the peace process became defunct, they were not likely a main reason for Norway's original involvement in the process in 1999–2000. For one thing, at that time Norway could not have foreseen a regime change and subsequent successful start of the process, which would attract other players.

According to the statements made by Norwegian mediators, Norway's primary role was as a facilitator. Its involvement ranged from facilitating communication between the parties to more concrete formulator roles in drafting the CFA and the Oslo Declaration. Norway made it clear from the beginning that it saw itself as merely a "postman" between the two sides (Economist 2001). It defined its job as finding the common ground that integrated the most important concerns of both parties that both might later accept. The Norwegian facilitators stated clearly that ownership of the conflict was with the warring parties and not with themselves. Erik Solheim stressed that "it has to be remembered that at the end of the day President Mahinda Rajapaksa and the LTTE leader Prabhakaran will decide. If they want peace, we are here to assist. If they want war, there is nothing we can do" (Rupesinghe 2006b, 344–45). The Norwegians' job of postman was also endorsed by the Sri Lankan government. In April 2001, Foreign Minister Lakshman Kadirgamar said in an interview, "But when it comes to substantive negotiation, the Norwegians will have no particular role at all. . . . They will have no mandate to propose solutions. They will certainly have no mandate to make any judgmental decisions. In that sense, they're not arbitrators, they're not judges, they're not mediators" (Ram 2001). This strategy of staying out of ownership of the conflict and focusing on the "two-party model" has been later criticized as having reduced Norway's legitimacy, and when the peace process became stalled, Norway did have rather limited leverage to stop the escalation of the conflict (Höglund and Svensson 2009). It was also suggested that this neutral role of low-key facilitator was alien to the collectivist culture of Asia, thereby creating confusion (Moolakkattu 2005).

Norway's second tactic was, in cooperation with Prime Minister Wickremesinghe, to widen and strengthen the international safety net. As a result of this strategy, the Unites States as the global player, the EU as the biggest trading partner, and Japan as the biggest donor became the cochairs to the process. Although India was not officially involved in the process as a cochair, Norway held regular consultations with India throughout the process and considered its consent on the different steps of the peace process crucial to progress.

Third, Norway tried very hard to appear impartial to both parties and to the public of Sri Lanka. As the Norwegian facilitators themselves put it, "Our only principle is that of not excluding talking to anyone" (Martin 2006, 125). Engaging directly with the LTTE, thereby giving legitimacy to a group that several powerful countries had already listed as a terrorist organization, was not making them many friends among Sinhala nationalists. Also, as Harriet Martin states, "In becoming facilitators for the peace process in Sri Lanka, the Norwegians were taking on a pariah insurgency group with whom none of their natural political allies could even, officially at least, have tea with" (Martin 2006, 126).

But this tactic of impartiality failed, partly because the image of impartiality is difficult to uphold in asymmetrical conflicts, and thus, right at the beginning of the process, Norway (through Erik Solheim) came under criticism for being biased in favor of the LTTE (Höglund and Svensson 2009). Additionally, wearing a hat of a monitor of the cease-fire violations by being involved in the SLMM did not help maintain Norway's reputation as a neutral mediator. In their attempt to treat both parties as equal, the Norwegians were not helped by the LTTE's enthusiastic comments calling them "the white tigers" (Martin 2006, 113).

Fourth, as in previous peace processes, one of Norway's tactics was to be patient and keep focused on long-term goals. During the peace talks, Norway demonstrated laudable patience with the warring parties. The realities of working under this level of criticism created a survivalist attitude in the facilitating team. As one of the facilitators put it, "If you want to get involved in this process, you should not expect not to get your fingers burned, you should expect to get them electrocuted" (Martin 2006, 116). Norway did put up with the fierce attacks from Sinhala nationalists, and personal abuse in the local media. During the peace process, the Norwegian embassy was picketed by protestors carrying coffins with dead bodies inside and burning the Norwegian flag (ICG 2006). Considering all this pressure, Norway's commitment to the peace process was consistent and intrepid. Its mediation activities relied primarily on low-key tactical strength. But Norway did seem to realize that more strategic strength was needed to keep the parties at the negotiating table. To that end, it brought in big powers that had the necessary sticks and carrots, as custodians of the process, in the hope that they might compensate for Norway's lack of strategic strength. This seemed reasonable because, as discussed earlier, mediations that combine strategic and tactical strength tend to be more successful than those with only one or the other. The remaining part of the chapter will discuss why this strategy did not prove successful.

The United States

The United States has repeatedly demonstrated, in peace processes all over the world, that it can and will use its manipulative strength. Strong involvement in very visible conflicts has contributed to the perception that if the United States is involved, it likely has a strong, even hidden, agenda in that particular country and is ready to deploy its strategic strength. But the United States had neither a historical record nor strong trade and economic relations with Sri Lanka, and U.S. development assistance had already decreased significantly since the end of the Cold War and was slated to be cut even further, from around $5 million annually in 2001–04 to

$2 million in 2005 (USAID 2000). Although some Sri Lankan Tamils live in the United States, the diaspora there, at 35,000 people, is too small to significantly influence U.S. politics or policymaking (Bandarage 2009, 21). It has been argued that the United States has military interests regarding Trincomalee Harbor and runway facilities in Sri Lanka (Noyahr 2006). But Jeffrey Lunstead, U.S. ambassador to Sri Lanka in 2003–06, has stated that the United States does not have "significant strategic interests in Sri Lanka" (Lunstead 2007, 11). Lunstead contrasts Trincomalee with Singapore, where the U.S. Navy has a major facility: "Singapore is ideal because of its internal stability, its superb facilities and infrastructure, and its position. Trincomalee currently lacks all of these, and is unlikely to gain any of them in the foreseeable future" (Lunstead 2007, 11). Moreover, even within South Asia, U.S. strategic interests are focused on India as a nuclear power and a growing economic partner but also, to some extent, a political partner in the region. The United States also has strategic interests in Pakistan as a nuclear power and in the tensions between India and Pakistan and Afghanistan regarding the battle against al-Qaeda (Kronstadt 2004; Lunstead 2007). Also, since India has made clear that it demands primacy in its immediate neighborhood and since both political and military relations between the United States and India have been improving significantly over the past few years, the United States was not interested in stepping on India's toes over Sri Lanka.[5] As Lunstead argues, the United States shared information and, to lesser extent, coordinated its policies with India during its involvement in Sri Lanka's peace process (Lunstead 2007).

The only area where the United States had certain strategic interests in Sri Lanka was in "political relations and ideological compatibility," namely, the war on terror. But it is important to keep in mind that the LTTE was a very localized terrorist organization that carried out its activities, especially in recent times, mainly in Sri Lanka. Its ties with worldwide terrorist organizations such as al-Qaeda are either insignificant or nonexistent; therefore, its power to threaten U.S. interests is minimal compared to that of terrorist groups with worldwide activities (Lunstead 2007).

So why did the United States get involved in Sri Lanka's peace process in the first place? Lunstead points out that it was not due to any dramatic change in U.S. strategic interests, but because regime change in Sri Lanka brought to power a pro-West, pro-free-market prime minister and because of Deputy Secretary of State Richard Armitage's personal interest (Lunstead 2007, 13). In a speech delivered in Washington in 2003, Armitage asked, "Why should the United States invest significant attention and resources to Sri Lanka, especially at a time when we have such overwhelming competing interests?" (Armitage 2003, 89). He admitted that self-interest did not truly justify U.S. involvement, yet his reply when questioned was nevertheless straightforward: ". . . because it can be done. And because it is the right thing to do. Because the parties to the conflict appear to be ready to reach a resolution, more so than at any other time in the past twenty years." The most significant part of his answer, "because it can be done," was also supported by Teresita Schaffer, another former U.S. ambassador to Sri Lanka, who also gave as one of the reasons for U.S. involvement in the Sri Lankan conflict that "there was the real possibility of success" (Noyahr 2006, 373). This perception of an "easy win" was, as Goodhand points out, common for all the main international actors in this peace process (Goodhand 2006a, 2006b). It was the main reason for the United States and others getting engaged in the process and then sneaking away when success proved more elusive.

The U.S. position consisted of three components: "pressuring the LTTE, engaging with the government and supporting activities aimed at peaceful transformation" (Frerks and Klem 2006, 43). Since the United States had banned the LTTE in 1997, it could not provide material assistance, and LTTE officials could not obtain visas to the United States. The condition for U.S. engagement with the LTTE was that the LTTE give up the violent struggle. It would have been politically untenable in the post-9/11 world to meet with terrorist representatives, and therefore, the United States had no direct talks with the LTTE. The United States was the only cochair to give military aid to the Sri Lankan government. Although military assistance funding never reached high levels, it could have contributed to a feeling within the LTTE that the international community was reducing its options (Lunstead 2007). At first, the U.S. policy not to engage with the LTTE seemed to work out well enough within the framework of the cochairs, in which the United States took the role of "bad cop" while the EU played the "good cop," engaging directly with the LTTE. But the LTTE suspended the talks after the U.S. decision not to let it attend the Washington Development Conference in April 2003. Although some have argued that this occasion was rather a ready excuse for the LTTE to get out of the peace process, the U.S. decision provided that excuse nonetheless. In response, the United States maintained its pressure, stating that the movement's reasons to withdraw were "not convincing" (Asian Tribune 2003).

The limited U.S. strategic interest in Sri Lanka showed also in the waning U.S. interest in the peace process. According to Lunstead, it was first the deterioration of the peace process and then the beginning of a second George W. Bush administration, in January 2005, that resulted in Deputy Secretary Armitage's departure (Lunstead 2007, 33). But it is also important to note that in March 2003, the United States started its military operation in Iraq—an operation that became highly criticized and was clearly one of the Bush administration's main strategic foreign policy interests. The stalled peace process in a small, faraway country "with minimal strategic interests for the US, with a deteriorating security situation based in part on the inability of Sri Lankan political elements to cooperate," was not a priority for the United States (Lunstead 2007, 33). The United States remained engaged in the peace process through the cochairs framework, but its visible involvement did not go beyond condemning statements regarding the escalation of the hostilities, and human rights and humanitarian concerns.

The European Union

The EU has also been called a "reluctant cochair" due to its modest involvement in Sri Lanka before and at the beginning of the peace process (Noyahr 2006, 387). Similar to the U.S. involvement, the EU's involvement in Sri Lanka was minimal before the 2002 peace process. In 2001, the European Commission downgraded the delegation in Colombo, leaving a nonresident head of delegation based in Delhi, and only one diplomat based in Colombo. Heavy lobbying from Sri Lankan officials brought the EU reluctantly to involve itself in the peace process, which led to its role as a cochair (Noyahr 2006). The EU's main strategy seemed to be to "stick with the Norwegians," and it kept a low profile throughout the peace process because of "the absence of major direct interests" (Frerks and Klem 2006, 46). Most EU member states do not have strong interests in Sri Lanka, and only seven of the twenty-seven members have diplomatic missions there.[6] The country with the closest ties to Sri Lanka is its former colonizer, the UK, which had 300,000 Sri Lankans living in its territory. Other EU member states do have Tamil diasporas, but these are small.[7] With the EU cast as the "good cop," in November 2003 EC Commissioner on External Relations Chris Patten met with the LTTE's leader, Prabhakaran, in Kilinochchi (European Commission 2003). Some saw this as swimming against the current, since some other top officials, such as UN Secretary-General Kofi Annan, had decided not to visit the LTTE (Frerks and Klem 2006). Sri Lankan media heavily criticized the EU for the visit, with local newspapers screaming, "Keep Patten out of the country," and accusing him of "bloody European gumption and insolence of the highest order" (Martin 2006, 116). The EU was keeping to its "stick with the Norwegians" tactics by visiting Kilinochchi after the Norwegians' statement to the diplomatic community in Colombo that the LTTE needed to see people in order to grow into the political mainstream.[8] But after the visit, the EU issued a strong statement on the LTTE's human rights violations and warned the group that it must comply with international human rights standards if it wished to obtain "recognition as a political player in Sri Lanka" (Martin 2006, 128).

The LTTE lost its "good cop" in May 2006, when the EU used one of its sticks and listed the LTTE as a terrorist organization in response to the August 2005 assassination of Sri Lankan foreign minister Kadirgamar, and other human rights violations.[9] The Council of the EU's declaration stated that the decision should not come as a surprise to anybody. "Several warnings have already been provided to the LTTE, which the LTTE has systematically ignored" (Council of the European Union 2006). Although the EU did not focus that much on denouncing terrorism, it did concentrate on human rights violations such as child recruitment and political killings (Frerks and Klem 2006). Therefore, although it was ready to engage with the LTTE despite the LTTE's reputation and the overall "war on terror" environment, it was the use of specific methods typical of terrorist organizations, such as assassinations of top officials and other grave human rights violations, that made Brussels take a strong stance.

The success of this stick (or carrot, from the perspective of Sri Lanka's government) regarding the progress of the peace talks was not really clear and seemed rather limited. The EU remained committed to the process in Sri Lanka, issuing condemning statements, alone and in cooperation with other cochairs, regarding humanitarian and human rights concerns. However, after the peace process stalled, the EU did not do much beyond this.[10] Also, it has been argued that the conflict got little attention in Brussels— for example, the ICG observed, "While fighting raged in August 2006, the situation did not even reach the agenda of EU foreign ministers meeting in Brussels." The ICG also suggested the "limited geopolitical impact" of Sri Lanka's conflict as the reason for this low interest (ICG 2006, 19).

Japan

Until recent years, Japan, despite being an economic superpower, was not active in global politics but remained satisfied in the role of a passive donor. Recent years have seen a gradual shift in its international positioning, with it emphasizing noneconomic sources of power, such as military and diplomatic power. Laurence argues that one of the most important reasons for this change is concern over China's increasing influence (Laurence 2007). Japan assumed a prominent role one month after the peace talks started, when Yasushi Akashi, a former UN undersecretary for humanitarian affairs, was appointed special envoy for the Sri Lankan peace process. The Japanese government hosted the donors' conference in June 2003, to discuss the peace negotiations and international assistance for development and reconstruction in Sri Lanka (Noyahr 2006). Japanese policy in

Sri Lanka's peace process was to position aid as a major engine of peace. But Japan did not want to resort to conditionalities or political pressure. Moreover, Japanese ties with Sri Lanka have traditionally been very government focused, and this policy continued in the peace process. Although Japan had not banned the LTTE, it refrained from making funds available to it. It was not that Japan wanted to punish the LTTE as a terrorist organization, but rather that Japanese aid in general flowed through governments and, in exceptional cases, through UN agencies. According to Frerks and Klem, "It was clear that Japan wants to enter the international arena of peacebuilding and also wants to keep the money flowing. They were sucked into the Tokyo process but were not very happy about it" (Frerks and Klem 2006, 45).

India

India is the only country with strong strategic interests in Sri Lanka. For decades, India has perceived itself as the regional manager of South Asia and has not allowed other external forces' involvement in the region[11] (Rao 1988). "India has always had substantial intelligence resources in Sri Lanka, including being involved in counterinsurgency initiatives against the LTTE, whose autonomous power India seeks to crush" (Philipson and Thangarajah 2005, 47). The Sri Lankan conflict has influenced India's political situation, since already in the 1980s the conflict spilled over into the south Indian state of Tamil Nadu, where Tamil guerrilla groups set up and where thousands of Sri Lankan Tamils fled following the anti-Tamil riots in 1983 (Samaranayake 2006). Several Tamil Nadu political parties used the resulting large-scale sympathy in Tamil Nadu. The Indo-Sri Lanka Peace Accord, signed by the governments of India and Sri Lanka in 1987, and the subsequent mission by the Indian Peace Keeping Force (IPKF) in Sri Lanka were failures: the Indian armed forces failed to disarm the LTTE while losing some 1,300 troops (Bullion 2001). This was a shock for India, and it showed the limits of India's capacity to deploy strategic strength and act as a security manager in South Asia. The peacekeeping saga ended for India with the LTTE's assassination of former prime minister Rajiv Gandhi in 1991. India banned the LTTE as a terrorist organization the following year and issued an arrest warrant for Prabhakaran. Thereafter, India has kept a firm stand in not getting formally involved in Sri Lanka's peace process. After the fifth process started off, Indian foreign secretary Kanwal Sibal visited Sri Lanka and admitted that though "logically we should be involved," the "legal complexities" were such that "our options are certainly limited" (Sambandan 2002). These legal complexities are based on the LTTE's banning for crimes in India, including the assassination of Rajiv Gandhi. But because all parties recognized India's strategic interests in Sri Lanka, both the government and the LTTE, as well as the mediators, regularly consulted India. The Norwegians stressed that all the key points were discussed with India since the peace could not be achieved without India's support and since "India's interest in Sri Lanka is legitimate" (Rupesinghe 2006b, 339). Nonetheless, India accepted the Norwegian involvement only with great reluctance and generally resented the increased internationalization in its own "backyard" (Philipson and Thangarajah 2005).

Although India had clearly stated that it would not become a formal party to the fifth peace process, there were still voices calling for its stronger intervention after the fighting resumed. As the CPA report points out, in the case of more limited international interest in Sri Lanka, India would have been the only candidate for high-profile intervention as the regional power, but in this case it was "conditioned by the 'once bitten twice shy' effect of the IPKF experience in the late 80s." The CPA further states that Indian interest in Sri Lanka has also changed as economic interests are increasingly taking the central place. "Consequently, high profile political or in the extreme case, military intervention, carries with it the risks of upsetting and even undermining the growing economic stake" (CPA 2007, 5).

The Cochairs

The cochairs of the peace process—Norway, Japan, the United States, and the EU—became institutionalized as a group at the Tokyo Conference on Reconstruction and Development of Sri Lanka, which took place in June 2003 without the LTTE's participation. At this conference, the donors collectively pledged foreign aid of approximately US$4.5 billion over the four-year period 2003–06 and closely linked this to the progress of the peace talks (Shanmugaratnam and Stokke 2004). This conditionality policy, perceived as a big carrot, was about to become a big failure by the international community. Positive incentives did not succeed in getting the parties back to the negotiating table. Neither Sri Lanka nor the LTTE was aid dependent, and the conference added to the LTTE's increasing unhappiness, since it felt that it was not being treated as an equal party. Also, the LTTE saw no point in international fund-raising when "it did not have a legally constituted instrument under its control to receive the funds for reconstruction" (Shanmugaratnam and Stokke 2004, 16). Since several important donors still banned the LTTE, it was not clear how the organization could enjoy the benefits of the policy of incentives. In the end, the tsunami that struck Sri Lanka in December 2004 flushed away the remnants of the conditionality policy because "the threat of withholding aid in an 'over-aided' environment will have very little effect" (Good-hand and Klem 2005, 14). The "donors dangled the carrot assuming the process was moving in the right direction, but when this proved to be a false assumption they did not replace the carrot with a stick" (Frerks and Klem 2006, 54).

Relations between cochairs were considered good: they were mainly speaking with one voice by issuing common statements, with no signifi-cant spoilers among them. The cochair mechanism provided a broad base as well as a division of labor (ICG 2006).

But this division of labor was accidental and "based purely upon the policies of the home foreign ministry and aid ministry policies, not on the needs of the peace process in Sri Lanka" (Philipson and Thangarajah 2005, 48). Moreover, the way the mediators split the tasks did not seem to put to good use the different types and degrees of leverage that each could apply to the warring parties. Although it could be argued that the U.S. strategy of being a biased mediator who would deliver the government could have produced important results, this potential was never used to the fullest (Touval and Zartman 1985). On one hand, the United States lacked the strategic interest to motivate its use of more decisive carrots and sticks in its relations with the government in Colombo. On the other, by widely ignoring the LTTE, the United States weakened the chances of making the LTTE more flexible in peace talks. The United States has engaged with terrorist organizations before, when engagement furthered its own strategic interests. Not talking to the LTTE was a policy choice, not a le-gal requirement (Lunstead 2007). Therefore, this suggests that the limited role of the United States resulted from its limited strategic interests in the conflict.

The cochairs' use of sticks was limited to condemning statements. Sev-eral scholars and organizations, including Uyangoda, Bouffard and Car-ment, Smith, and the CPA, have criticized this level of involvement that does not go beyond scolding. As the parties to the conflict became aware of the mediators' limited interests and restrained use of sticks, the mediating parties' leverage was also limited. The CPA stated that the government of Sri Lanka was aware of the limits to international interests in Sri Lanka, which paved the way to the "let's see what we can get away with" attitude toward international opinion." Moreover, the government also realized that it could engage with other, non-Western international actors, such as Paki-stan, Iran, China, and Russia, which were willing to offer their assistance without any conditions (CPA 2007). That prediction proved true. The new kid on the block, offering unconditional financial, military, and diplomatic support, has been, since early 2007, a player with straightforward—and certainly strategic—interests: China. After the March 2007 agreement that allowed China to build a $1 billion port in southern Sri Lanka, allegedly to use as a refueling and docking station for its navy, Beijing appears to have significantly increased arms sales to Sri Lanka. China has also provided crucial diplomatic support in the UN Security Council, blocking efforts to put Sri Lanka on the agenda, and also boosted financial aid to Sri Lanka, even as Western countries have reduced their contributions (Page 2009). A spoiler had indeed emerged.

Conclusion

This chapter argues that in civil wars involving terrorists, when the warring parties are not motivated to settle, a mediator with strategic strength is needed. Since strategic strength requires high diplomatic pressure and resources, the mediating parties are more likely to deploy it when they have strategic interests in the country. This assumption was applied to explore the link between the mediating parties' lack of strategic interests and the failure of the fifth peace process in Sri Lanka.

Principal among the obstacles in the Sri Lanka peace process was the international actors' inability to make a credible commitment. Sisk has pointed out that "neither India as a regional hegemon, nor external actors such as the UN have demonstrated the willingness and capacity to deploy sufficient peacekeeping forces as this would require tens of thousands of troops" (Sisk 2009, 164). Second, external mediators seemed unable or unwilling to leverage the parties into peace. Further complicating the process was the manner in which the mediators treated the conflicting sides. Especially problematic was the U.S.-LTTE relationship. One of the main reasons the LTTE suspended the talks was the United States' refusal to talk to it and invite its representatives to Washington to discuss the peace process, because it was labeled a terrorist group.

Thus, U.S. leverage on the LTTE was limited. It was not clear how the LTTE could benefit from the financial support promised by the international community, since several countries that acted as mediators were prohibited from financing a terrorist organization. In such circumstances the LTTE did not perceive the offers made by the outside actors as significant carrots. And sticks were absent, too. The presence of a strong mediator could have brought to bear more coercive methods for getting the parties back to the peace talks, but these cards were never played. Several authors have proposed a variety of tools that could have had more influence on the parties. In the LTTE's case, Sisk argues that a strong mediator could have raised the possibility of an International Criminal Court indictment for the LTTE leadership, since "the very threat of the indictment before the world court could be the kind of leverage to stimulate progress in war-torn Sri Lanka" (Sisk 2009, 164). Bouffard and Carment argued for direct UN involvement in the form of a peacekeeping mission to monitor the cease-fire (Bouffard and Carment 2006). A less costly option could have been to further strengthen the SLMM's mandate as truce monitors. At the same time, various forms of targeted sanctions, ranging from specific travel bans for government officials or rebel leaders to full-scale economic sanctions, were never fully considered. Ultimately, along with the employment of clear-cut sticks and carrots, mediators should have been very careful not to irritate the disputants, especially when they were signaling a willingness to negotiate. For instance, the U.S. decision to exclude the LTTE from the conference in Washington certainly did not contribute to engaging the group in achieving a peaceful solution to the conflict. It is true that after the peace process became stalled and parties gradually returned to war, the international community became more anxious over the situation, but it never went beyond verbal censure. Obviously, the third parties' interests in Sri Lanka were limited, which prevented them from exerting any hard pressure.

The Sri Lankan case is an important illustration of the intrinsic dynamics of the multiparty mediation process. It suggests that in cases where the parties are unwilling to settle, the mediator with muscle is needed. Powerful mediators contribute to an effective peacemaking process by providing the necessary leverage that allows for "tough measures first" and "soften[ing] if cooperation is forthcoming" (Sisk 2009, 197). At the same time, the case unequivocally demonstrates the importance of specific interests that would drive powerful actors to intervene with full leverage. Terming these interests *strategic interests,* this case study has sought to demonstrate how only once the conflict is jeopardizing strategic interests of a powerful state will the coercive power be applied. But the case study also suggests that if a powerful mediator has very low strategic interests in the conflict, its involvement can turn into a liability that actually jeopardizes the peace process. More precisely, the unwillingness to use all the available resources (as was the case with the United States in Sri Lanka's peace process) will only create a false impression of strength that in reality is never deployed. Lacking such strategic interests in the case of Sri Lanka, the mediating parties contributed to the peace talks' failure, since they did not employ any strategic strength to bring the parties back to the negotiating table. The mediators' leverage weakened further still after the parties to the conflict became aware of the lack of strategic interests and consequently started to dismiss the mediators' criticism as empty talk that would not be followed with concrete actions. This left room for spoilers to come in and fill the third-party void.

In cases where one of the warring parties is a terrorist organization, chances are that some mediators will find it difficult to engage fully in talks with its representatives. But despite apparent difficulties, such conditions do not predetermine the outcome of the peace process. Part of the intrinsic value of a properly coordinated multiparty approach is a division of the mediation workload, so that different mediators may engage more closely with the appropriate conflicting sides. If a terrorist organization is involved in a conflict, and mediators lack the necessary strategic interests to use strategic power in moving the parties toward an agreement, the mediators still need to find suitable, less coercive and more rewarding measures to keep the parties motivated to negotiate a settlement. But if the mediating parties do not have strategic interests to deploy the necessary combination of carrots and sticks, it becomes unclear whether the mediators can create any positive value. This puts into question the prospects for a successful mediation, since without such strategic interests, efforts may be destined to fail. Rather, to develop the combination of sanctions and incentives necessary for successful mediation, powerful mediators need to have clear strategic interests in the conflict.

Notes

*Maria Groeneveld-Savisaar's research for this chapter was funded by the European Social Fund's Doctoral Studies and Internationalisation Programme DoRa.

1. The Thimpu talks in 1985, the Indo-Lanka Accord in 1987, the Premadasa/LTTE talks in 1989–90, the Kumaratunga/LTTE talks in 1994–95, and the Wickremesinghe/LTTE-Rajapaksa/LTTE talks in 2002–06.

2. The SLMM was a monitoring team comprising Norway, Sweden, Finland, Denmark, and Iceland, whose role was to be an impartial instrument to monitor the CFA and facilitate the resolution of disputes over implementation. With the resumption of hostilities, the SLMM became more war monitor than peace monitor. Its operations were further complicated in the summer of 2006 when, following the EU ban on the LTTE, the LTTE demanded the departure of all EU countries from the mission. The SLMM remained in Sri Lanka until the abrogation of the CFA by the Sri Lankan government in January 2008 (SLMM 2008).

3. The parties stated that they had agreed "to explore a solution founded on the principle of internal self-determination in areas of historical habitation of the Tamil-speaking people based on a federal structure within a united Sri Lanka" (Daily Mirror 2002).

4. Norway has played a role in the following peace processes: the Oslo Accords (until 1993); Guatemala (1996); Haiti, Sudan, Cyprus, and Kosovo (1999); and Colombia (2000) (Bullion 2001).

5. On India's foreign policy interests, see Mohan 2006; on India-U.S. relations, see Kronstadt 2004.

6. The UK, Sweden, the Netherlands, France, Italy, Germany, and Romania.

7. Some 100,000 Sri Lankan Tamils live in France, 60,000 in Germany, 24,000 in Italy, 7,000 in the Netherlands, 6,000 in Sweden, and 600 in Finland (Bandarage 2009, 21).

8. This was after President Kumaratunga had instructed the diplomatic community in spring 2004 not to visit the LTTE areas anymore. The international community accepted the statement. But in July 2004, the Norwegians had gotten the president to soften her firm stand, and the diplomats were allowed to go if they had a reason (Martin 2006, 127).

9. Canada also banned the LTTE in 2006.

10. The EU's involvement became more visible in 2007 regarding the "battle" (as perceived by the Sri Lankan government and media) over the "GSP+"—the extension of the Generalized System of Preferences (GSP). The GSP+ is a trade concession granted by the EU to developing countries that have ratified and implemented certain UN conventions on sustainable development, labor, human rights, and good governance. The GSP+ allows the beneficiary countries to export their products to EU member states with reduced or no tariffs. As Sri Lanka came up for review on GSP+ eligibility for 2009–11, the question arose whether it had complied with the GSP+ regulation on effective implementation of the UN human rights conventions. Human rights activists took this issue up as a possible way to pressure Sri Lanka to comply with international human rights law. But Sri Lanka perceived this as unfair pressure and lobbied for GSP+ status. The EU proceeded to investigate Sri Lanka's compliance with regulations, and in February 2010, it withdrew GSP+ trade benefits (European Commission 2010).

11. This policy was set by the so-called Indira doctrine (named for Indira Gandhi), which stated, "India will neither intervene in the domestic affairs of any state in the region unless requested to do so, nor tolerate such intervention by an outside power. If external assistance is needed to meet an internal crisis, states should first look within the region to help" (Rao 1988, 422).

References

Armitage, Richard L. 2003. "Sri Lanka Prospects for Peace." *Defense Institute of Security Assistance Management Journal* 25 (3): 89–92.

Asian Tribune. 2003. "Way Out of Ethnic Conflict Is through negotiations—US Envoy." *Asian Tribune,* Apr. 26. www.asiantribune.com/news/2003/04/26/way-out-ethnic-conflict-through-negotiations-us-envoy (accessed Nov. 4, 2010).

Bandarage, Asoka. 2009. *The Separatist Conflict in Sri Lanka: Terrorism, Ethnicity, Political Economy.* New York: Routledge.

Bastian, Sunil. 2006. "How Development Undermined Peace." In Rupesinghe 2006a.

Bercovitch, Jacob. 2009. "Mediation and Conflict Resolution." In *The Sage Handbook of Conflict Resolution,* ed. Jacob Bercovitch, Viktor Kremenyuk, and I. W. Zartman, 340–57. London: Sage.

Biswas, Bidisha. 2006. "The Challenges of Conflict Management: A Case Study of Sri Lanka." *Civil Wars* 8 (1): 46–65.

Bouffard, Sonia, and David Carment. 2006. "The Sri Lanka Peace Process: A Critical Review." *Journal of South Asian Development* 1 (2): 151–77.

Bullion, Alan. 2001. "Norway and the Peace Process in Sri Lanka." *Civil Wars* 4 (3): 70–92.

Carnevale, Peter J. 2002. "Mediating from Strength." In *Studies in International Mediation*, ed. Jacob Bercovitch, 25–40. New York: Palgrave Macmillan.

Carnevale, P. J., D. E. Conlon, K. A. Hanisch, and K. L. Harris. 1989. "Experimental Research on the Strategic-Choice Model of Mediation." In *Mediation Research: The Process and Effectiveness of Third-Party Intervention*, ed. Kenneth Kressel and Dean G. Pruitt. San Francisco: Jossey-Bass.

CPA. 2007. "War, Peace and Governance in Sri Lanka." Centre for Policy Alternatives, Dec. 31. www.reliefweb.int/rw/RWB.NSF/db900SID/AMMF-6ZPDGQ?OpenDocument&rc=3&cc=lka (accessed Nov. 5, 2010).

Crocker, Chester A., Fen Osler Hampson, and Pamela R. Aall. 1999. *Herding Cats: Multiparty Mediation in a Complex World*. Washington, DC: United States Institute of Peace Press.

Council of the European Union. 2006. "Declaration by the Presidency on Behalf of the European Union Concerning the Listing of the LTTE as a Terrorist Organisation." Council of the European Union, May 31. www.consilium. europa.eu/uedocs/cms_Data/docs/pressdata/en/cfsp/89790.pdf (accessed Nov. 5, 2010).

Daily Mirror. 2002. "LTTE Comes Two Steps Down." *Daily Mirror,* Dec. 6.

DeVotta, Neil. 2007. "Sinhalese Buddhist Nationalist Ideology: Implications for Politics and Conflict Resolution in Sri Lanka." Policy Studies 40, East-West Center. www.eastwestcenter.org/fileadmin/stored/pdfs/ps040.pdf (accessed Nov. 4, 2010).

Economist. 2001. "Hitting the Tigers in Their Pockets." *Economist,* March 8.

European Commission. 2003. "Commissioner Patten Visits Sri Lanka on 25–26 November 2003." Nov. 21. www.dellka.ec.europa.eu/en/whatsnew/2003/pdf/pr-031121.pdf (accessed Nov. 5, 2010).

———. 2010. "EU Temporarily Withdraws GSP+ Trade Benefits from Sri Lanka." Feb. 15. http://trade.ec.europa.eu/doclib/press/index.cfm?id=515 (accessed Nov. 5, 2010).

Fernando, Austin. 2006. "The Peace Process and Security Issues." In Rupesinghe 2006a.

Frazier, D. V., and W. J. Dixon. 2006. "Third-Party Intermediaries and Negotiated Settlements, 1946–2000." *International Interactions* 32 (4): 385–408.

Frerks, Georg, and Bart Klem. 2006. "Conditioning Peace among Protagonists: A Study into the Use of Peace Conditionalities in the Sri Lankan Peace Process." Netherlands Institute of International Relations "Clingendael," June. www.clingendael.nl/publications/2006/20060600_cru_frerks_klem.pdf (accessed Nov. 5, 2010).

Goodhand, Jonathan. 2006a. "Conditioning Peace? The Scope and Limitations of Peace Conditionalities in Afghanistan and Sri Lanka." Netherlands Institute of International Relations "Clingendael," June. www.clingendael.nl/publications/2006/20060800_cru_goodhand.pdf (accessed Nov. 4, 2010).

———. 2006b. "Internationalization of the Peace Process." Lecture presented at the international seminar "Envisioning New Trajectories for Peace in Sri Lanka," Zurich, Apr. 7–9.

Goodhand, Jonathan, and Bart Klem. 2005. "Aid, Conflict and Peacebuilding in Sri Lanka 2000–2005." *Sri Lanka Strategic Conflict Assessment 2005.* Vol. 1. Asia Foundation. http://asiafoundation.org/publications/pdf/208 (accessed Nov. 5, 2010).

Greig, J. Michael. 2005. "Stepping into the Fray: When Do Mediators Mediate?" *American Journal of Political Science* 49 (2): 249–66.

Hiltrop, Jean M. 1989. "Factors Affected with Successful Labor Mediation." In *Mediation Research: The Process and Effectiveness of Third-Party Intervention,* ed. Kenneth Kressel and Dean G. Pruitt. San Francisco: Jossey-Bass.

Höglund, Kristine, and Isak Svensson. 2006. " 'Sticking One's Neck Out': Reducing Mistrust in Sri Lanka's Peace Negotiations." *Negotiation Journal* 22 (4): 336–87.

———. 2009. "Mediating between Tigers and Lions: Norwegian Peace Diplomacy in Sri Lanka's Civil War." *Contemporary South Asia* 17 (2): 175–91.

ICG. 2006. "Sri Lanka: The Failure of the Peace Process." International Crisis Group, Nov. 28. www.crisisgroup.org/en/regions/asia/south-asia/sri-lanka/124-sri-lanka-the-failure-of-the-peace-process.aspx (accessed Nov. 4, 2010).

Kelleher, Ann, and James Larry Taulbee. 2005. "Building Peace Norwegian Style: Studies in Track 1½ Diplomacy." In *Subcontracting Peace: The Challenges of NGO Peacebuilding,* ed. Oliver P. Richmond and Henry F. Carey. Aldershot, UK: Ashgate.

Kronstadt, Alan K. 2004. "India-U.S. Relations." In *CRS Issue Brief for Congress,* Nov. 4. Congressional Research Service, Library of Congress. http://fpc.state.gov/documents/organization/37996.pdf (accessed Nov. 4, 2010).

Laurence, Henry. 2007. "Japan's Proactive Foreign Policy and the Rise of the BRICS." *Asian Perspective* 31 (4): 177–203.

Lax, David A., and James K. Sebenius (1991). "Thinking Coalitionally: Party Arithmetic, Process Opportunism, and Strategic Sequencing." In *Negotiation Analysis,* ed. H. Peyton Young, 153–93. Ann Arbor: University of Michigan Press.

Lunstead, Jeffrey. 2007. "The United States' Role in Sri Lanka's Peace Process 2002–2006." Asia Foundation. http://asiafoundation.org/publications/pdf/209 (accessed Nov. 4, 2010).

Martin, Harriet. 2006. *Kings of Peace, Pawns of War: The Untold Story of Peacemaking.* London: Continuum.

Mohan, C. Raja. 2006. "India and the Balance of Power." *Foreign Affairs* 85 (4): 17–32.

Moolakkattu, John Stephen. 2005. "Peace Facilitation by Small States: Norway in Sri Lanka." *Cooperation and Conflict* 40 (4): 385–402.

Noyahr, Keith. 2006. "The Role of the International Community." In Rupesinghe 2006a.

Page, Jeremy. 2009. "Chinese Billions in Sri Lanka Fund Battle against Tamil Tigers." *Times* (London), May 2.

Philipson, Liz, and Yuvi Thangarajah. 2005. "The Politics of the North-East." *Sri Lanka Strategic Conflict Assessment 2005.* Vol. 4. Asia Foundation. http://asia foundation.org/publications/pdf/212 (accessed Nov. 5, 2010).

Pruitt, Dean G. 2002. "Mediator Behavior and Success in Mediation." In *Studies in International Mediation,* ed. Jacob Bercovitch, 41–54. New York: Palgrave Macmillan.

———. 2006. "Negotiation with Terrorists." *International Negotiation* 11 (2): 317–84.

Ram, N. 2001. "I Can Confirm That the Peace Process Is Moving." Interview with Lakshman Kadirgamar, *Frontline* 18 (8): 124–27. www.hinduonnet.com/fline/fl1808/18081230.htm (accessed Nov. 4, 2101).

Rao, P. Venkateshwar. 1988. "Ethnic Conflict in Sri Lanka: India's Role and Perception." *Asian Survey* 28 (4): 419–36.

Ross, R. S. 2006. "Comparative Deterrence: The Taiwan Strait and the Korean Peninsula." In *New Directions in the Study of China's Foreign Policy,* ed. A. I. Johnston and R. S. Ross, 13–49. Stanford, CA: Stanford University Press.

Rotberg, Robert I. 1999. "Sri Lanka's Civil War: From Mayhem toward Diplomatic Resolution." In *Creating Peace in Sri Lanka: Civil War and Reconciliation,* ed. Robert I. Rotberg. Washington, DC: Brookings Institution Press.

Rubin, Jeffrey Z. 1980. "Experimental Research on Third-Party Intervention in Conflict." *Psychological Bulletin* 87 (2): 379–91.

Rupesinghe, Kumar, ed. 2006a. *Negotiating Peace in Sri Lanka: Efforts, Failures and Lessons.* 2nd ed. Vol 1. Colombo, Sri Lanka: Foundation for Co-Existence.

———. 2006b. "Interview with Erik Solheim, Minister of International Development." In Rupesinghe 2006a.

———. 2006c. "Introduction." In Rupesinghe 2006a.

Samaranayake, Gamini. 2006. "Of Phases and Paces." In *Sri Lanka: Peace without Process,* ed. B. Raman, N. Sathiya Moorthy, and Kalpana Chittaranjan. Colombo, Sri Lanka: Vijitha Yapa.

Sambandan, V. S. 2002. "Our Options Limited in Sri Lanka: Sibal." *Hindu,* Dec. 9.

Saravanamuttu, Paikiasothy. 2003. "Sri Lanka: The Best and Last Chance for Peace?" *Conflict, Security and Development* 3 (1): 129–38.

Shanmugaratnam, N., and Stokke, Kristian. 2004. "Development as a Precursor to Conflict Resolution: A Critical Review of the Fifth Peace Process in Sri Lanka." Department of International Environment and Development Studies, Noragric, Norwegian University of Life Sciences. www.docstoc.com/docs/3574465/Department-of-Internationl-Environment-Development-Studies-Noragric-Norwegian-University-of (accessed Oct. 18, 2010).

Sisk, Timothy D. 2009. *International Mediation in Civil Wars: Bargaining with Bullets.* New York: Routledge.

Smith, Chris. 2007. "The Eelam Endgame?" *International Affairs* 83 (1): 69–86.

SLMM. 2008. Sri Lankan Monitoring Mission. www.slmm.info (accessed Nov. 4, 2010).

Svensson, Isak. 2007. "Mediation with Muscles or Minds? Exploring Power Mediators and Pure Mediators in Civil Wars." *International Negotiation* 12 (2): 229–48.

Touval, Saadia. 1992. "The Superpowers as Mediators." In *Mediation in International Relations,* ed. Jacob Bercovitch and J. Z. Rubin. New York: St. Martin's Press.

Touval, Saadia, and I. William Zartman. 1985. *International Mediation in Theory and Practice.* Boulder, CO: Westview.

———. 1989. "Mediation in International Conflicts." In *Mediation Research: The Process and Effectiveness of Third-Party Intervention,* ed. Kenneth Kressel and Dean G. Pruitt, 115–37. San Francisco: Jossey-Bass.

———. 2006. "International Mediation in the Post-Cold War Era." In *Turbulent Peace: The Challenges of Managing International Conflict,* ed. Chester A. Crocker, Fen Osler Hampson, and Pamela Aall, 427–43. Washington, DC: United States Institute of Peace Press.

USAID. 2000. "USAID/Sri Lanka Country Strategy Paper 2001–2005." http://pdf.usaid.gov/pdf_docs/PDABT334.pdf (accessed Oct. 17, 2010).

Uyangoda, Jayadeva. 2006. "Sri Lanka's Crisis: The Peace Process Wears Thin." *Polity* 3 (1).

———. 2007. "Ethnic Conflict in Sri Lanka: Changing Dynamics." Policy Studies 32, East-West Center. www.eastwestcenter.org/fileadmin/stored/pdfs/PS032. pdf (accessed Nov. 4, 2010).

Wu, X. 2006. *Taipingyang shang bu Taiping (Turbulent Water: U.S. Asia-Pacific Security Strategy in the Post–Cold War).* Shanghai: Fudan University Press.

Zartman, I. William, and Saadia Touval. 1996. "International Mediation in the Post-Cold War Era." In *Managing Global Chaos: Sources of and Responses to International Conflict,* ed. Chester A. Crocker, Fen Osler Hampson, and Pamela R. Aall, 445–61. Washington, DC: United States Institute of Peace Press.

5

U.S. Policy toward Nationalist Terrorist Organizations:

Isolate or Engage?

Stacie L. Pettyjohn

In January 2006, Hamas stunned the world by winning the Palestinian Legislative Council elections. Although the United States had pressured Israel to let Hamas participate in the elections, it had not expected the Islamist group to win enough votes to gain control of the Palestinian Authority (PA). Hamas's victory presented the George W. Bush administration with a dilemma: deal with a government led by a terrorist organization, in the hope of convincing it to moderate, or continue to declare the organization not moderate enough and refuse to deal with the terrorists, thereby isolating the Hamas-led PA? The Bush administration obviously chose the latter policy; once Hamas took office, the United States pursued a strategy of isolation and quickly cooperated with Israel to isolate the branches of the PA controlled by Hamas. The United States hoped this policy of economic coercion would diminish Hamas's public support, lead to the government's collapse, and bring Fatah, the other main Palestinian political party, back to power (Sayigh 2007; ICG 2006, 2). Given the Bush administration's hard-line posture toward terrorism generally, its response to Hamas's victory is hardly surprising. Nevertheless, it does raise an important question: when will the United States break its stated policy of nonnegotiation and engage a nationalist terrorist organization (NTO)?[1]

An enduring principle of the United States' counterterrorism strategy has been to "make no concessions to terrorists and strike no deals" (U.S. State Department 2002). In other words, the United States' default policy toward terrorist organizations is isolation and nonnegotiation. Although the United States has seldom chosen to engage an NTO, it has done so. To take one recent example, the United States engaged Sunni insurgents in Iraq in an effort to divide the insurgency, incorporate disaffected Sunnis into the government, and, in the words of Ambassador Zalmay Khalilzad, "deal with their legitimate concerns" (Ware 2005). Similarly, in Afghanistan the United States has supported an initiative to disengage low-level Taliban fighters by offering them incentives to lay down their arms (Nordland 2010). There are even signs that the Obama administration may be willing to negotiate with some high-level members of the Taliban, though not with Mullah Omar, who is believed to be unwilling to compromise (Lander and Cooper 2010). Typically, however, the negotiation question does not involve a terrorist organization in direct conflict with the United States but one that is merely an interested third party. As an external party, the United States has intervened on several occasions in various conflicts by engaging an NTO. For instance, the Reagan administration began a dialogue with the African National Congress (ANC) in 1986, even though the ANC was at that time escalating its use of violence against the South African government.[2] In 1988, Secretary of State George Shultz reversed the long-standing U.S. policy prohibiting negotiations with the Palestine Liberation Organization (PLO), despite the objections of the Israeli government. Similarly, in 1994, President Bill Clinton infuriated the British government by giving a visa to Sinn Fein leader and alleged former Irish Republic Army (IRA) commander Gerry Adams.

Because psychological, international, and domestic political constraints often make it extremely difficult for a government combating a terrorist organization to shift unilaterally to a policy of engagement, a third party may be needed to persuade the principals that negotiations are necessary (Spector 1998, 45; Pruitt 2006, 380; Zartman and Alfredson 2010). It is important, therefore, to examine the policies of one of the most influential third parties: the United States. If the United States wishes to foster a durable peace agreement, it must deal with all the major parties in the conflict. The question then becomes, under what conditions will the United States decide publicly to engage an NTO?

The argument in this chapter is restricted to terrorist organizations that (1) pursue nationalist goals, (2) target states allied or aligned with the United States, and (3) possess a dual structure—a political as well as a military division. Nationalist terrorist organizations—the *nationalist-separatist* types discussed in the volume's introductory chapter—are distinct because their goals are tied to a particular homeland, making their aims potentially attainable, which, in turn, means that a compromise settlement may end the conflict (Laqueur 1987, 203–08; Byman 1998; Miller 2007, 335; Sánchez-Cuenca 2007).[3] They differ from terrorist organizations that have more expansive goals—perhaps to change an entire region or even the world. In contrast to groups with nihilistic aims, an NTO's geographically bounded goals can potentially be addressed through negotiations.[4] Second, the decision to engage a terrorist organization is truly puzzling only when the group targets an ally of the United States. The logic of realism or realpolitik would lead one to expect that states may be willing to support or condone the actions of groups in conflict with their enemies.[5]

Third, the dual structure of an NTO opens up the possibility that the group may lay down its arms and pursue its goals through legal means. The political wing participates in party politics, or aims to do so, while the military arm remains committed to a strategy of violence (Weinberg and Pedahzur 2003). If an NTO has only a military wing, there is very little chance that an agreement will peacefully end its armed struggle. In these cases, the NTO has not shown enough interest in diplomatic strategies even to take the very preliminary step of creating a political branch. From the perspective of the United States, the dual structure of an NTO is important for two reasons: first, the presence of the political wing suggests that the NTO's leaders may be interested in peacefully resolving the conflict; and second, the political wing provides an interlocutor that is more acceptable than the armed branch.

This is not to say that the presence of a political wing necessarily means an NTO is ready to end its use of violence. Rather, it merely opens the possibility that this could occur. For instance, Hezbollah created a political party in 1992, but it also has maintained its military wing, the Islamic Resistance (Hamzeh 2004). Since the Taif Agreement ended the Lebanese civil war, Hezbollah has participated in all of Lebanon's elections and has led a parliamentary coalition, appropriately named "Loyalty to the Resistance." As the name of Hezbollah's coalition suggests, its main objective is to protect the organization from attempts to disarm it (Ranstorp 1998). In other words, Hezbollah entered into politics not because it was considering giving up its arms, but so that it might work from within the Lebanese government to stymie efforts to take the Islamic Resistance's weapons, and to protect the organization's other core interests.[6] In addition, creating a political party endowed Hezbollah with a veneer of legitimacy, which helped limit the amount of international pressure on the organization.

While this dual nature creates the possibility for a political solution to the conflict, it also raises questions about the terrorists' aims. It is unclear whether the NTO is truly moderating or whether its efforts to cooperate are just a ruse to gain popular support and buy time. This situation creates a dilemma for the United States and the targeted nation: should they engage the terrorists in an effort to end the violence peacefully, or is engagement a reward for bad behavior and a signal of weakness?

This chapter addresses the dilemma posed by NTOs and offers an argument for when the United States is likely to choose a policy of public engagement. Existing studies of engagement have three major shortcomings: First, they do not specify the conditions under which a state will implement a public policy of engagement. Second, they fail to apply the logic of engagement between states to the relations between states and substate actors. Finally, they overlook the fact that third parties can also adopt a policy of engagement. The third-party dimension is particularly crucial for studies of U.S. foreign policy because, with the exception of its involvement in Iraq and Afghanistan, the United States is not in direct conflict with any NTOs. Nevertheless, as the sole superpower, the United States is involved or expected to intervene in a number of ongoing conflicts in which NTOs are participants.

This chapter argues that the United States will engage an NTO only in the absence of preferred interlocutors and when it believes that the NTO is moderating. In addition to these two necessary conditions, a catalyst seems to be needed to alter the expected utility of engagement, pushing a reluctant U.S. administration to adopt this politically and strategically risky policy. The remainder of this chapter proceeds in three parts. The first section discusses the general logic of engagement and the costs and benefits of engaging an NTO. The second section presents the argument in greater detail. The conclusion summarizes the chapter's arguments and considers the question of whether the United States will publicly engage Hamas.

Engagement: What and When?

Three general policies—reassurance, appeasement, and engagement—are considered *soft-line strategies,* as opposed to hard-line strategies such as deterrence, containment, and coercion. While soft-line strategies use conciliatory actions to prevent conflict, hard-line strategies use force or the threat of force to check aggression. More specifically, a state uses a policy of reassurance when it wants to demonstrate its own lack of aggression, thereby decreasing the possibility of an unwanted conflict with an adversary (Stein 1991). Similarly, appeasement occurs when a state unilaterally offers concessions to its adversary, often as a short-term strategy to avoid conflict by satisfying the adversary's demands (Treisman 2004; Rock 2000).

Engagement differs from both these strategies and can be defined as a noncoercive, long-term policy based on interaction, dialogue, and positive incentives that aims to induce an instrumental change in the behavior of the target (Haass and O'Sullivan 2000; Suettinger 2000; Cha 1999, 2001; Schweller 1999). A more ambitious policy of engagement also strives to effect a more enduring change by socializing the target into a particular set of norms, thereby modifying its preferences.[7] Engagement can be used to achieve a number of goals and has been implemented to deal with dissatisfied rising powers, rogue nations defying international law, and states that violate their citizens' human rights. Today engagement is most often employed in an effort to socialize the target into liberal or democratic norms (Adesnik and McFaul 2006).

The ultimate goal of engaging an NTO is a peaceful and durable solution to an ongoing conflict. In other words, successful engagement results in an NTO's choosing to disarm permanently and pursue its goals through peaceful means. Only a lasting peace can justify incurring the potential costs of what is by definition a long-term strategy. However, this definition of success does not specify whether there has to be a change in the terrorists' ultimate *ends* or solely in their *means:* forgoing violence. Resolving a conflict may sometimes require an NTO to change its underlying goals, especially if these involve destroying an enemy; but at other times, it may only be necessary for the NTO to pledge to pursue its goal peacefully. Therefore, the United States endeavors to convince the terrorists, at a minimum, to abandon violence, even though this usually begins as a calculated move to secure gains from engagement and avoid punishment. Even if an NTO's compliance is initially instrumental, tactical actions can be internalized over time, resulting in more enduring outcomes (Risse 1999, 531; Schimmelfennig 2005, 831; Checkel 2005, 804). Under certain conditions, a U.S. policy of engagement can facilitate an NTO's moderation by bringing both parties to the table and convincing them that they are trapped in a mutually hurting stalemate, with negotiations the only way out of the situation.[8] Also, engagement gives the United States significant leverage over both disputants, enabling it to push them to make the necessary concessions to reach a settlement.[9]

Nevertheless, a decision to engage an NTO has numerous *costs and benefits* at both the international and domestic levels (Byman 2006, 403–08). Once a group has been classified as a terrorist organization, a state is expected to respond with a policy of isolation. Moreover, having branded a group with the terrorist label, a state is hard put to convince international and domestic audiences that the organization is now reformed and worthy of engagement.

At the international level, the primary security concern is that engagement will be taken as sign of weakness and will encourage other terrorists to escalate their violent campaigns. Engagement may also backfire and give the NTO legitimacy even while it continues to use violence. Similarly, a terrorist organization may cooperate to gain and increase its strength before relaunching its armed struggle from a better position. In addition to the concern that engagement will ultimately strengthen the NTO, there is the parallel fear that a conciliatory policy demonstrates that violence will be rewarded, which may in turn encourage further violence. If so, this would also weaken those within the NTO's society who are committed to nonviolent tactics (Bueno de Mesquita 2005). Also, beginning a dialogue with an NTO may estrange the United States from its ally and incur considerable international criticism. Finally, the search for a permanent solution is tempered by the low probability that a terrorist organization will give up violence, and by the fact that even when this does come about, it usually occurs slowly, over a long period.

At the domestic level, engagement is potentially costly because it is likely to invite criticism and provide fuel for the U.S. president's rivals to diminish her popularity and influence. This is especially true if the NTO takes advantage of the United States and does not end its armed struggle. In addition to hurting the president's chances for reelection (if she is not in her second term), unsuccessful engagement will weaken the president, diminishing her ability to achieve other policy goals.

Although a policy of engagement may have numerous downsides, it may also offer many benefits. From the perspective of the United States, the best possible outcome is a permanent solution to the conflict. If this occurs, the United States is strengthened because a source of international instability is removed and its ally no longer has to devote its resources to combating the NTO. Moreover, if engagement succeeds at integrating the NTO into a political system, the president will be seen as a peacemaker and receive a considerable boost in popularity and power (Touval 1982, 322).

There are two *types of engagement:* clandestine and public. Clandestine engagement takes place without the public's knowledge and is therefore less costly for a government or third party, as well as less beneficial for the NTO. Secret meetings between a state's officials and members of an NTO may be used solely as a channel of communication, or they may also serve as a forum for political discussions. In the first instance, a law may forbid meeting with terrorists, but circumstances may necessitate some form of interaction or coordination; thus, a secret channel is used to avoid the legal and political consequences of overtly talking with terrorists. For example, during the civil war in Lebanon, the PLO was in control of large parts of the country, including the neighborhood where the U.S. embassy was located. Despite the ban on negotiations with the PLO, CIA officer Bob Ames met secretly with high-ranking PLO members. In these meetings, the PLO agreed to provide security for the evacuation of U.S. diplomats in 1976 and, afterward, continue to ensure the safety of the Americans remaining in Lebanon (Wallach and Wallach 1990, 349). When it was absolutely necessary to communicate with the PLO, the U.S. government opted to use an intelligence officer because the meetings were more likely to remain confidential and because, even if knowledge of the meetings became public, the meetings were deniable since the United States government does not discuss intelligence operations.

If covert meetings with members of an NTO are discovered, an administration can typically dissociate itself by using intermediaries outside the government, who can easily be renounced as acting without official approval. The Clinton administration, for example, established a back channel to discuss political issues with Sinn Fein. Messages were relayed from the White House to Senator Edward Kennedy's office, which in turn contacted a prominent Irish American journalist who dealt directly with Sinn Fein leader Gerry Adams (O'Clery 1997, 66–68). Layered and indirect means of communicating, like those used by the Clinton administration, insulate both parties from criticism if the interaction becomes public.

Given that secret meetings involve significantly less risk, it is not surprising that both parties are often willing to set up such exchanges. Secrecy protects both the terrorist leaders and U.S. officials from the inevitable attacks that would come if the meetings were in the open. Sometimes more accommodating members of an NTO may agree to covert meetings with U.S. officials in the hope that these discussions will evolve into a public policy of engagement. This seems to have been the case when the PLO arranged with Secretary of State Henry Kissinger to meet with an American official in the wake of the October 1973 Arab-Israeli War. In these meetings, PLO members met with deputy CIA director general Vernon Walters in Rabat. PLO chairman Yasser Arafat hoped that the secret dialogue would develop into an open policy of engagement, which would in turn legitimize the PLO and enable it to participate in the peace process (Walker and Gowers 2003, 112–15). In the end, Arafat's hopes were unfounded, since Kissinger had no intention of deepening the United States' relationship with the PLO. Rather, the secretary of state tactically misled the PLO to guarantee its quiescence during the sensitive stage before Egyptian-Israeli negotiations began (Kissinger 1982, 627).

Although clandestine engagement with an NTO is less risky than public engagement, the engager also typically gains less leverage over the terrorists. And yet, secret meetings and dialogue can be beneficial; a face-to-face dialogue conducted by a few individuals outside the public eye is a conducive setting for persuasion and building trust (Lynch 2002, 204). As

Kristine Höglund develops in her chapter of this volume, prenegotiations are usually needed if a government wants to negotiate openly with an actor it has previously vilified (Spector 1998, 45; Pruitt 2006, 381–83). But as the Kissinger example above demonstrates, clandestine negotiations do not always lead to a policy of engagement. Nevertheless, the legitimacy and material benefits that NTO leaders often desire, and which give a mediator the influence necessary to bring both sides to the negotiating table and push them toward a settlement, come only from public engagement.

When Is the United States Likely to Choose a Policy of Public Engagement?

One of the major limitations of the literature on engagement is that it does not specify the conditions under which states will adopt this policy toward other states, let alone toward groups such as NTOs. While international relations theories do not usually apply to substate actors, the three dominant approaches—realism, liberalism, and constructivism—do suggest plausible hypotheses for when the United States would choose to engage NTOs; however, none can accurately explain the variation in U.S. policy choices or in the timing of those choices.

Two variables influence whether the United States is likely to engage an NTO publicly: (1) the presence of preferred alternative groups representing the same population as the NTO and (2) perceptions of the NTO's degree of moderation. First, the United States will prefer to engage alternative and more acceptable groups that represent the same population as the NTO, because doing so is far less costly than dealing directly with the terrorists. Another group may be preferred to an NTO for a number of reasons, but the most important is that the group is willing to compromise in order to end the conflict. Second, the United States will choose engagement only when decision makers believe that the NTO is willing to negotiate an end to the conflict and to work through institutionalized procedures to achieve its goals. In other words, the United States must believe that the terrorist leaders are moderating. Without these two conditions, the costs of engaging an NTO are very high and the odds of producing an agreement very low; therefore, engagement is avoided. Both these conditions are necessary, but not sufficient, for the shift to a public policy of engagement. Additionally, in all the cases in which the United States has ultimately engaged an NTO, a catalyst has pushed a reluctant U.S. administration to adopt this strategically and politically risky policy.

The first variable is the *alternative representative* factor. Often in nationalist conflicts, several parties—such as terrorist organizations, legitimate political parties, grassroots associations protesting the current political arrangement, and even other states—claim to represent the aggrieved population. This presents the government and interested third parties with the option of negotiating either with the terrorists or with one of these other representatives. For many reasons, the latter are often the preferred interlocutors, particularly if they are willing to compromise and also shun violent tactics. In short, the United States usually chooses the most viable alternative that is also moderate—or, in Devashree Gupta's words, the principle of minimal harm (Gupta 2007, 332). Negotiating with representatives that work peacefully to realize their goals minimizes or even eliminates the potential political and strategic costs of engaging an NTO. Thus, engaging a moderate alternative presents little risk to the United States and may appear to offer a better prospect of successfully resolving the conflict.

Sometimes, however, it is difficult to find a viable alternative to an NTO that is willing to negotiate an end to the conflict and also abstains from using violence. For example, take the situation in the Palestinian territories today. While most observers agree that Palestinian President Mahmoud Abbas is committed to nonviolence, the same cannot be said for Fatah, his political party, or Hamas, his rival movement. In 2002, the United States designated the al-Aqsa Martyrs Brigade (AMB), which is affiliated with Fatah, a foreign terrorist organization. Despite this, the Bush administration maintained close contact with the mainstream Fatah organization; its willingness to deal with Fatah seems to stem from three factors: (1) Abbas is willing to negotiate with Israel; (2) he does not have control over radical factions of Fatah, such as AMB; and (3) the main alternative to Fatah is Hamas, also identified as a foreign terrorist organization. The Bush and Obama administrations have continued to interact with Fatah because, for the most part, its leadership is more moderate than Hamas's and has been working to curb the activities of radical factions such as AMB. In other words, many of Fatah's most prominent leaders remain willing to negotiate a permanent-status agreement with Israel and are opposed to using violence. By contrast, Hamas's leadership has refused to recognize or negotiate with Israel and defends the Palestinian population's right to attack Israel.[10]

Although the alternative representative's moderation is the key characteristic that makes it more attractive than the NTO, other attributes—such as its legal status, ideology, and malleability—may also explain why it is preferred over competitors. A representative may be chosen because it is a sovereign state rather than a substate actor lacking status under international law. For treaties or international agreements to be legally binding, the signatories must be recognized states or, in some cases, international organizations. This makes nonstate actors such as NTOs undesirable partners, because it is questionable whether they are legally obligated to adhere to any accord that may be reached. For example, over the course of two decades, the United States considered King Hussein of Jordan the legitimate representative of the Palestinian people and sought to have him come to terms with Israel over the status of the West Bank. At least part of the reason that the Reagan administration chose to push for negotiations between Jordan and Israel was that the PLO, as a nonstate actor, had an undefined status under international law.[11]

In some instances, the potential representative's ideology influences the choice of interlocutor. A representative's beliefs are important because they may have a natural affinity or enmity with liberal democratic norms. If decision makers believe that a particular representative would implement policies harmful to U.S. interests, they will be less likely to support that alternative. For example, during the Cold War, the United States was hesitant to deal with nationalist organizations such as the ANC, because of the ANC's ties to the South African Communist Party and its close relationship with the Soviet Union.

Finally, all things being equal, decision makers would rather deal with a representative that is susceptible to American influence than with a more independent and unreliable alternative. One could argue, for instance, that in 2003 the Bush administration pushed Arafat to create the position of prime minister and appoint Abbas to the office because Abbas did not have a comparable base of popular support and was therefore more pliable than Arafat.

Although the United States would rather deal with its chosen alternative to the NTO, there are three reasons why it may be forced to abandon negotiations with its handpicked interlocutors. First, the selected representatives may relinquish their claim to lead the population in question. Public renunciations of leadership occur infrequently and are most likely to take place when an existing state has attempted to speak for a population with nationalist aspirations. This occurred in July 1988 when King Hussein, struggling to deal with the Palestinian intifada, renounced his claim to the West Bank and stated that the PLO would be accountable for the Palestinian territories. Hussein's announcement brought about the collapse of Secretary of State George Shultz's peace plan—which envisioned a joint Jordanian-Palestinian (though not PLO) delegation negotiating first a transitional agreement and then a final-status agreement with Israel—and opened the door for the Reagan administration to initiate a dialogue with the PLO (Quandt 2005, 275).

Second, while the preferred alternative maintains that it is the legitimate leader of a population, events on the ground can belie this claim. In other words, the United States may be compelled to recognize that the representative, given its lack of public support, is not a viable alternative to the NTO. For example, the township uprisings in South Africa revealed that the United States' preferred interlocutor, Inkatha leader Mangosuthu Buthelezi, did not have sufficient backing within the black population to continue to serve as an alternative to the ANC (Jung, Lust-Okar, and Shapiro 2005). Similarly, in October 1974, Secretary of State Kissinger feared that the Arab League's Rabat Declaration—stating that the PLO was the "sole legitimate representative of the Palestinians"—denied King Hussein the ability to continue to speak for the Palestinians. At the end of the day, the Rabat Declaration was not nearly as absolute as it seemed at the time, and before long, King Hussein reasserted his claim to speak for the West Bank (Quandt 2005, 159).

Third, the chosen representative may push to incorporate the terrorist organization into negotiations. For example, after an extended secret dialogue with Sinn Fein leader Gerry Adams, John Hume concluded that Adams was prepared to negotiate an end to Northern Ireland's troubles. Recognizing that peace depended in large part on the IRA's acceptance of such an agreement, Hume lobbied U.S. leaders, asking that they support Adams's 1994 application for a visa. Because Hume had always been committed to nonviolence, he had enormous credibility with many prominent Irish Americans who had historically opposed the IRA (O'Clery 1997, 83–86, 98–99). The Clinton administration heeded Hume's advice and issued the visa to Adams, initiating the long process of drawing Sinn Fein into negotiations. In each of these examples, a policy of excluding the NTO in favor of preferred representatives became ineffective and unsustainable, leading the United States to consider the previously unacceptable policy of beginning a dialogue with an NTO.

The second variable—the NTO's *perceived level of moderation*—highlights the fact that a decision to engage an NTO is strategic, meaning that the preferred course of action depends on the expected reactions of the terrorist organization (Lake and Powell 1999, 3). Since the United States makes significant gains only if the parties peacefully resolve the conflict, the likelihood that the NTO is willing to do so influences whether a policy of engagement is chosen (Zartman and Alfredson 2010). A negotiated settlement, in turn, depends largely on whether the NTO's leaders favor peacefully resolving the conflict and are willing to make concessions in an effort to reach a mutually agreeable accord. In short, the United States must believe that the NTO's leaders are moderating before it will begin the process of engagement.

What do the terrorists have to do to be seen as a viable candidate for a policy of engagement? By definition, all NTOs use terrorism, but each group has its own distinct goals. The extent to which an NTO must go to convince the United States that it is moderating depends on how sympathetic the United States is to the NTO's ultimate aims. That is, the concept of moderation can be disaggregated into two separate but related concepts: ends, or motives, and means, or strategies. Motives refer to an actor's fundamental aims and are distinct from intentions or strategies, which are the actions taken to realize those ultimate goals (Montgomery 2006, 156). Regardless of a group's aims, the United States condemns the use of terrorism. Nevertheless, the United States may either agree with or be fundamentally opposed to the terrorists' objectives.[12] The degree of sympathy with which an NTO's ends are viewed depends largely on what U.S. policymakers consider an acceptable settlement, and how well this idea tracks with the terrorists' aspirations. In cases where the United States sympathizes with the NTO's goals but opposes its tactics, the NTO need only show a willingness to forgo violence to demonstrate that it is moderating. On the other hand, if the United States objects to the goals as well as the means, the NTO has the more difficult task of credibly signaling that it has limited its aims as well.

For example, because the United States was not fundamentally opposed to the ANC's or Sinn Fein's aims, it engaged both groups without their modifying their goals. To this day, Sinn Fein remains committed to securing independence for Northern Ireland and unifying the southern and northern parts of the island. Similarly, the ANC never wavered in its goal of ending apartheid and instituting a truly democratic government in South Africa. In both these cases, the terrorists' goals did not change, but their leaders persuaded the United States that they wanted to come to terms with their adversaries and would be willing to give up their arms.

In contrast, the United States stipulated that the PLO and Hamas must limit their aims before it would even consider beginning a dialogue with either group. This requirement was implemented because the United States objected to these NTOs' central purpose, which was (and, in the case of Hamas, still is) to regain all of mandatory Palestine and destroy, or at least subsume, Israel into a larger polity that would dilute its unique Jewish character. Before the United States was willing to open a dialogue with the PLO, Arafat had to publicly accept Israel's right to exist, announce his willingness to negotiate a solution to the conflict by accepting UN Security Council Resolutions 242 and 338, and renounce terrorism.[13] The United States demands a similar tempering of Hamas's aims and tactics as a condition to engagement.

It is more difficult for an NTO to demonstrate a change in ends than a change in means. Strategies are largely epiphenomenal to the constraints facing an organization. Terrorists use violence because the political system does not provide them with an avenue to redress their grievances. Therefore, it is reasonable to assume that if an NTO indicates that it is willing to give up violence when provided with the right incentives, it will actually do this, at least momentarily, to let negotiations take place. On the other hand, altering one's motives requires a more fundamental change. The situation is further complicated because motives are declared but unobservable, which forces one to use the imperfect measurement of gauging preferences by behavior (Frieden 1999, 40). The difficulty with judging motives by actions is that the two do not correlate perfectly. Actions or strategies are a function of an actor's motives as well as of the opportunity structure, meaning that the actor may cooperate because the other available courses of action are too costly, not because of a transformation in the actor's fundamental preferences. For example, Hamas has proposed a *hudna,* or long-term truce, in exchange for Israel's withdrawing from the territories it occupied in the June 1967 war (Mishal and Sela 2006, 108). Both the Israeli and U.S. governments have rejected this cooperative offer, claiming that it is a tactic intended to buy enough time to shift the balance of power in favor of Hamas. In other words, they suspect that Hamas remains committed to regaining all of mandatory Palestine (i.e., that its motives are unchanged) and that the offer of a *hudna* is simply due to the recognition that Hamas cannot currently achieve its objective.

Since it is difficult to distinguish between genuine signals of moderation and feints intended merely to give the terrorists enough time to regroup, decision makers are typically very skeptical of cooperative gestures from terrorists. Consequently, the United States usually requires that an NTO's leaders repeatedly prove their moderation with their words and deeds. Given that each U.S. president has his own predispositions and beliefs about a situation, the terrorists will have to go to varying lengths to convince different administrations that they have genuinely changed (Kydd 2000, 341).[14] For example, President Carter was inclined to include the Palestinians in negotiations in an effort to realize a comprehensive Arab-Israeli peace agreement, but he was legally forbidden to do so until the PLO accepted UN Security Council Resolutions 242 and 338.[15] Understanding the PLO's misgivings about these resolutions, Carter was willing to let the PLO accept them with reservations (Quandt 1986, 60). This stands in contrast to the Reagan administration, which was averse to soft-line policies and required PLO Chairman Yasser Arafat to assent to the UN resolutions without any qualifications (Quandt 2005, 283–85).

In 1977, Arafat was unwilling to endorse even a modified version of the UN resolutions, but by 1988, he publicly accepted the resolutions and renounced terrorism a number of times in order to meet Secretary of State Shultz's specifications.

What would impel a nationalist terrorist organization such as the PLO to make such extensive unilateral concessions? In general, the leadership of an NTO moderates in response to a decline in the organization's influence. This weakness may be the result of many factors, including loss of support of an external benefactor, or the emergence of rival organizations, which siphon public support away from the NTO. When a terrorist organization faces possible elimination or irrelevance, it is forced to reconsider its tactics and sometimes even its goals and often becomes more pragmatic. In other words, an NTO's leaders usually decide to pursue a political solution because the costs of continuing the armed struggle rise and the probability that their tactics will succeed declines.

For instance, between 1977 and 1988, the PLO experienced what appeared to be a very deep, perhaps even inevitable decline in its power. First, when the PLO was expelled from Lebanon in 1982, it lost the sanctuary that had enabled it to launch raids inside the Israeli border. As it became increasingly apparent that the Palestinian commandos were not going to defeat Israel, the PLO's exiled leadership increasingly feared being marginalized in Tunis. The outbreak of the first intifada, and the concomitant emergence of rivals to the PLO in the occupied territories, proved that these concerns were not unfounded, impelling Arafat to try to raise the status of the PLO by reaching out to the United States. In short, the PLO's seemingly irreversible decline led the mainstream exiled leadership to temper its goals and its tactics in an effort to join the diplomatic process.

Even though engagement is a product of the terrorists' moderating, these nascent signs of pragmatism do not guarantee that the conflict will be resolved, nor do they suggest that U.S. mediation is unnecessary to realizing a peace agreement. Shifting from terrorist organization to political party is usually a very slow and uneven process, in which the organization's leaders must persuade their constituents that they can make gains through diplomacy. Signals of moderation do not mean that the NTO's leaders have fully renounced violence—only that they are increasingly willing to forgo violence as long as they believe that the NTO can advance its goals through peaceful means. For example, Gerry Adams had not yet given up violence or convinced the IRA to institute a standing cease-fire when President Clinton granted him a visa. Even more remarkably, the Reagan administration began a high-level dialogue with the ANC even as the ANC launched an unprecedented number of attacks against Pretoria. Even when an NTO's leader has repudiated terrorism, as Arafat did in 1988, such a proclamation does not ensure that the leadership will actually stop using violence or try to restrain others within the organization from doing so.

Also, to peacefully resolve a conflict involving an NTO, the state as well as the terrorists must be willing to negotiate. As noted earlier, third-party engagement not only helps bring the terrorists to the negotiating table, it is often necessary in persuading the opposing state to engage in negotiations with the NTO. The third party does this by legitimizing the NTO, which in turn inhibits the opposing state's ability to use hard-line strategies against it.

Although perceived moderation influences U.S. decision making, it alone does not determine whether the terrorists will end their armed struggle. Even when an NTO and its adversary truly want to negotiate an end to the conflict, they still have to agree on a specific settlement.[16] Moreover, for a conflict to be fully resolved, the NTO's renunciation of violence needs to be permanent, meaning that its members internalize the norms of compromise and nonviolence. Otherwise, there is no guarantee that if the circumstances change, the terrorists will not again resort to terrorism. This occurred at the outset of the second intifada, when many members of the PLO, who had abstained from violence since 1993, resumed their attacks against Israel. To resolve a conflict permanently, an NTO and the state must first agree to negotiate, they must reach an agreement, and the NTO must believe that violence is not an acceptable means of pursuing its goals.

There are five general ways that an NTO can *signal its moderation:* (1) soften its rhetoric, (2) display a willingness to engage in negotiations with its adversary, (3) participate in elections or join a government, (4) limit its attacks to its adversary only, and (5) implement a cease-fire. A rhetorical softening occurs when the terrorists accept the notion of compromise and recognize that their enemies have legitimate rights. For example, in the midst of the township uprising in South Africa, ANC leader Oliver Tambo announced that the ANC was not seeking a military victory but that it was using violence to pressure Pretoria to negotiate (McKinley 1997, 78). Although moderate rhetoric may not always be backed up by the group's actions, it is a significant change because it generates domestic and international audience costs (Fearon 1994, 580–81, 1997, 69). That is, a rhetorical change can create pressure on the NTO's leaders to act in accordance with their public statements. This occurs because moderate speeches have two interrelated effects: First, they alienate hard-line domestic and international supporters. Second, they lead the NTO's followers to expect a negotiated settlement. Moreover, as the leaders lose the support of extremists, they increasingly rely on their moderate constituents to stay in power. If they renege on their promises to seek peace, they risk losing the support of their domestic followers as well as their recently gained international backers. In short, a return to extremist tactics can threaten the position of the leaders in the NTO and the strength of the organization itself.

Second, terrorists' motives are also judged by the organization's willingness to engage in negotiations with its enemy in an effort to end the conflict peacefully. Even secret negotiations, such as those that occurred between imprisoned ANC leader Nelson Mandela and the South African government, signal the willingness of the terrorist organization's leadership to make concessions. Public negotiations are a stronger signal because they generate audience costs, but secret negotiations may enable the terrorist leadership to convince its adversary of its sincerity and may also build trust between the negotiators. Third, an NTO's decision to participate in elections and within a government indicates a willingness to consider strategies other than violence in pursuit of its goals. By participating in elections, the NTO implicitly recognizes the legitimacy of the government that is the target of its armed struggle. If an NTO goes further and actually joins a government, it is demonstrating an even greater readiness to compromise. However, an NTO's decision to work through a state's institutions does not necessarily indicate a willingness to end its military strategy, for it may simply be adding another track to its unchanged ends—testing the water of politics while retaining the use of violence. For example, until the 1980s, Sinn Fein adhered to an abstentionist policy, refusing to recognize or participate in any government associated with British rule (Lynn 2002, 74). Waning public support forced leaders such as Gerry Adams to deviate from abstentionism by running for, and then eventually participating in, local and, eventually, national elections, as a part of a mixed strategy that used both "the Armalite and the ballot box."[17] Hamas and Hezbollah both participate in elections but maintain their armed wings and continue to launch violent attacks against both Israel and the government they are part of. Nevertheless, for terrorists initially relying on violence to achieve their goals, broadening their strategy to include nonviolent tactics is a nascent but necessary step toward compromise and forgoing violence altogether.

An NTO's level of moderation can also be gauged by whether the group uses violence indiscriminately or limits its attacks to its principal adversary. When an NTO increases the scope of its targets to include other nations, it signals that the group remains extremely radical and that engagement is not likely to have any positive effect. Conversely, if an NTO limits its attacks to its primary adversary, it demonstrates that the organization is pursuing particular goals instead of nihilistically causing death and destruction and that engagement could succeed. For example, by the late

1970s, Fatah, the largest constituent group of the PLO, had stopped perpetrating high-profile international terrorist attacks and directed its strikes only against Israeli targets (Sayigh 1997, 311).

Finally, if an NTO implements a cease-fire, it suggests that the group is willing and able to halt its attacks and that it may also be willing to compromise with its opponents. On March 28, 1978, Arafat committed the PLO to a cease-fire along the Lebanese-Israeli border. This was a significant act for the PLO, which had never before accepted even a temporary truce with Israel. This act, coupled with the continuing stream of statements from Arafat to Western journalists indicating that the PLO was ready to coexist peacefully with Israel, could have been interpreted as important signs that the PLO was moderating (Cobban 1984, 96).[18] Nevertheless, the Carter administration was justifiably more focused on the PLO's fervent opposition to Israeli-Egyptian negotiations, and its recent attempt to use violence to spoil the peace talks. Similarly, for six months in 2008, Hamas agreed to, and largely upheld, a cease-fire, or *tahadiya* (calming), with Israel. Nevertheless, when the *tahadiya* expired in December, Hamas decided not to renew the truce and resumed launching rockets from the Gaza Strip in what appears to have been an effort to secure better terms from Israel (Scham and Abu-Irshaid 2009, 3). Hamas's 2008 truce demonstrated that the organization was disciplined, but given how the cease-fire ended, it failed to convince most observers that Hamas was ready to live in peace with Israel.

A solitary cooperative statement by the NTO's leaders without an accompanying significant shift in their rhetoric and actions is not sufficient to convince a U.S. administration that the organization is truly moderating. The leaders have to undertake a prolonged and multifaceted campaign to persuade others that they sincerely wish to resolve the conflict peacefully. Any one of the five indicators alone is unlikely to be adequate; rather, the terrorists need to make many cooperative public statements that are supported by actions such as negotiations, implementing a cease-fire, or taking part in elections. There is no objective threshold that an NTO must meet in order to prove its moderation to the United States, because each administration is different and its personal views color its perceptions.

In addition, *an exogenous catalyst* appears necessary to alter the expected utility of engaging an NTO, by making this the preferred course of action. In the cases of the ANC and the PLO, the rising levels of violence increased the costs of a policy of isolation and triggered a shift to engaging the terrorist organizations. The United States initiated contacts with the ANC to appease domestic public opinion, and it began a dialogue with the PLO in an effort to stabilize the region. In both cases, increasing levels of violence induced the United States to begin dialogue, but for different reasons. In the first case, the increasing violence mobilized transnational organizations and domestic groups that lobbied the Reagan administration to end its support for the white South African government. Domestic pressures thus made the policy of isolating the ANC unsustainable, impelling the Reagan administration to end its constructive engagement of the apartheid government in Pretoria and initiate talks with the ANC—the group considered to be a terrorist organization. In the second case, the rising level of violence created a strategic imperative to act, by threatening to destabilize Israel and even the entire Middle East. Both cases illustrate how rising violence raised the costs of inaction either domestically or internationally. Alternatively, in the case of Sinn Fein, a perceived opportunity for peace, which raised the expected benefits of engagement, was the proximate reason for the change to a soft-line policy. The British and Irish governments' announcement of the Downing Street Declaration greatly increased the probability that an agreement to end the conflict could be reached between all parties in Northern Ireland, raising the probability of realizing the benefits from a policy of engagement.

Conclusion

This chapter argues that intervention is often necessary to peacefully resolve conflicts involving nationalist terrorist organizations, and that the United States, as the sole superpower, has the military, financial, and diplomatic resources needed to facilitate the realization of such a peace agreement. A decision by the United States to engage a terrorist organization can force the disputants to begin talking to each other, and its continued involvement can help locate a mutually agreeable settlement and sustain cooperation.

But American presidents are understandably reluctant to engage an NTO. Even in the best-case scenario, where the terrorists cooperate and eventually disarm, beginning a dialogue with a designated terrorist organization exposes the president to potentially high costs internationally and harsh criticism domestically. As a result of these constraints, the United States is likely to initiate talks with an NTO only if two conditions are present. First, the United States must be compelled to interact with the terrorists by a lack of alternative representatives. If viable, preferred interlocutors exist, the United States will try to work with them instead of the terrorists. Second, the key U.S. policymakers must believe that the terrorists' leaders are prepared to compromise and forgo violence. If the NTO's leaders are believed to remain committed to achieving an absolute victory, negotiations will be considered a futile policy and, moreover, one that will lead only to further violence. In addition to these two necessary conditions, an external catalyst appears necessary to raise the expected utility of a policy of engagement, impelling the United States to abandon a policy of isolation in order to begin talking with the terrorists.

What does this framework suggest about the prospects of a shift in American policy toward Hamas? As discussed at the beginning of this chapter, since the organization's unexpected electoral victory, the United States has unequivocally refused to deal with Hamas. In addition to isolating the Hamas-led government and, now, the Hamas-controlled Gaza Strip, the Bush administration implemented a multilateral policy of economic coercion aimed at reducing Hamas's popularity and undermining its rule. The administration's focus on combating terrorism, combined with its unprecedented support for Israel, made engagement highly unlikely. Moreover, these predispositions led the Bush administration to establish demanding and unyielding criteria that Hamas would have to meet in order to prove that it had moderated.

In the end, however, two factors convinced the Bush administration to support a policy of isolating Hamas: the presence of a rival Palestinian party, Fatah, and Hamas's continued commitment to reclaiming all of mandatory Palestine. Despite the electoral loss, Fatah and its leader, Palestinian president Mahmoud Abbas, still retained considerable influence and offered a moderate alternative to Hamas. Moreover, although some Hamas leaders have made conciliatory statements toward Israel, their messages have been undercut by radical speeches, the continued launching of Qassam rockets into Israel, the conquest of the Gaza Strip in the summer of 2007, and Hamas's steadfast refusal to meet the three conditions of the Quartet (the United States, Russia, the EU, and the United Nations): recognize Israel's right to exist, renounce terrorism, and accept previous agreements signed by the PLO.

Is the Obama administration likely to change course and engage Hamas? Although President Obama appears to have a worldview significantly different from President Bush's, it is doubtful that he will begin a dialogue with Hamas unless the United States' preferred interlocutors, namely Abbas and Fatah, are unavailable and Hamas's leaders credibly signal that they are moderating. Despite having run on a platform that the United States should talk with its enemies, Obama has distinguished between holding discussions with the governments of legitimately recognized nation-states and talking to substate actors such as Hamas (National Public Radio 2009). Moreover, while the Obama administration has taken a tougher line on the construction of Israeli settlements in the West Bank, it remains

committed to its ally and is therefore hesitant to adopt too many policies that Israel will certainly oppose. Perhaps more important, the Obama
White House has repeatedly affirmed its desire to support President Abbas, who remains opposed to entering into a power-sharing agreement unless Hamas's leaders first accept the Quartet's conditions. Therefore, even
as the United States pressured Israel to ease its blockade of Gaza after the
fatal Israeli commando raid on the Gaza-bound flotilla in May 2010, it has
remained unwilling to reach out to Hamas (Kershner 2010). Instead, in an
effort to bolster President Abbas, the White House has sponsored the resumption of direct negotiations between Israel and the Abbas government
in the West Bank (Bronner 2010). Hamas's recent actions seem to have
confirmed the Obama administration's assessment that the group remains
militant and should be isolated. After Hamas launched two shooting attacks in the West Bank at the end of August and beginning of September
2010 Obama denounced "the tragedy . . . where people were gunned down
on the street by terrorists who are purposely trying to undermine these
talks" (Haaretz Service, Mozgovaya, and News Agencies 2010). Although
President Obama is more open to engaging Hamas than was his predeces-
sor, the conditions necessary for engagement are absent.

Nevertheless, there are two plausible though unlikely scenarios that
could prompt a change in U.S. policy toward Hamas. First, it is possible
to imagine a situation in which President Abbas concludes that he needs
Hamas's support, or at least its acquiescence, to reach a settlement with
Israel on the permanent-status issues. Accordingly, Abbas could convince
Hamas to accept the Quartet's conditions or otherwise signal its willingness to live in peace with Israel, and then convince the United States that it
is necessary to deal with Hamas. Second, President Abbas and Fatah could
be discredited because of their failure to reach a permanent-status agreement with Israel. At the same time, Hamas's leaders could also decide to
accept the Quartet's conditions in order to break out of the isolation that
is slowly suffocating the Gaza Strip.

In either instance, Hamas's leaders would have to convince the United
States that they have limited aims, and the United States' preferred interlocutor, Fatah, must no longer be available. The scenarios differ because, in
the first, Fatah insists on bringing Hamas into negotiations, whereas in the
second, Fatah loses the support of its constituents, leaving Hamas as the
only Palestinian party with significant popular support. Yet the chance that
either scenario will come about in the short term seems unlikely. Abbas
seems determined to pursue negotiations without reconciling with Hamas.
Moreover, since the conquest of Gaza, radicals seem to have gained the
upper hand within Hamas, making it extremely unlikely that Hamas will

accept the Quartet's conditions in the near term. Thus, the United States is not likely to engage Hamas as long as the safer alternative of President Abbas still exists, and until Hamas credibly demonstrates that it is willing to live in peace with Israel.

Notes

1. Defining "terrorism" and identifying groups as terrorists is a contentious and highly subjective task. This chapter refers to radical nationalist organizations as terrorists because that is how the U.S. government officially categorizes these groups. For more on the difficulties of defining "terrorism," see Gibbs 1989, 329–40; Hoffman 1998, 13–44.

2. The term "engagement" was first popularized as a result of the Reagan administration's soft-line policy toward South Africa's apartheid government (Crocker 1980, 81).

3. NTOs have goals, such as independence or equality, specific to a particular homeland or nation. This definition extends beyond separatist groups seeking autonomy or independence to include any group whose goals are geographically bounded, usually to a particular nation (Sánchez-Cuenca 2007). Those more narrowly described groups include what others have called ethnonationalist terrorist organizations, ethnic terrorists, and nationalist-separatist organizations.

4. This distinction between NTOs and nihilistic terrorist organizations is similar to Hoffman's distinction between traditional and new terrorists (Hoffman 1998). However, NTOs include only those traditional terrorists with nationalist aims. This is also similar to the typology used by Zartman, who distinguishes between total absolute terrorists, which have unlimited goals, conditional absolutes, and contingent terrorists (Zartman 2003, 444–46).

5. For example, the United States considers the Kurdistan Workers' Party, which is combating Turkey—a U.S. ally—a foreign terrorist organization. But it has not similarly labeled—and has, in fact, had discussions with—the Party for Free Life in Kurdistan, another Kurdish terrorist organization but one that targets Iran (Oppel 2007).

6. In addition to preserving its weapons, Hezbollah would like the government to officially accept the Islamic Resistance's presence. Hezbollah also seeks to gain political power and eliminate Lebanon's confessional political system, which underrepresents Shiites (Hamzeh 1993, 334, 2004, 112).

7. "Socialization" is defined as the "process of inducting actors into the norms and rules of a given community" (Checkel 2005, 804). This differs from inducing compliance based solely on a cost-benefit calculation because, once the actor is socialized, compliance is the result of internalized beliefs that dictate the appropriate course of action (March and Olsen 1998, 951–52; Fearon and Wendt 2002, 60).

8. For more on mutually hurting stalemates and the impact of mediators, see Touval and Zartman 1985, Zartman 1985, Zartman and Touval 2007, Rubin 1981, and Princen 1992.

9. For more on the effects of engagement on NTOs, see Pettyjohn 2009, 41–69.

10. This is not to say that Fatah as a whole is against using violence. Fatah leader Marwan Barghouti organized attacks against Israel during the al-Aqsa intifada, which is why he is currently serving five life sentences in an Israeli prison. Barghouti argued that the Palestinians should negotiate with Israel, but in tandem with "action on the ground." Barghouti personally has significant popular support, but more moderate leaders such as Mahmoud Abbas, Muhammad Dahlan, Ahmed Qurei, Nabil Shaath, and Saeb Erekat continue to

dominate the party apparatus and the PA. For more on Barghouti and the Fatah Tanzim, see Usher 2000. For more on U.S. plans to have Abbas incorporate AMB into the PA's security forces, see Sayigh 2007, 20–21.

11. Author's interview with Charles Hill, Feb. 6, 2007, New Haven, CT.

12. If the United States agrees with an NTO's objectives, it is less likely to label the group a terrorist organization.

13. UN Security Council Resolution 242, passed after the June 1967 Arab-Israeli War, vaguely calls for a peaceful settlement in which occupied land is exchanged for peace. It also only mentions the Palestinians as nameless refugees, which was the PLO's main objection to the resolution (UN Security Council 1967). During the October 1973 war, the Security Council passed Resolution 338, which called for an immediate cease-fire, the implementation of Resolution 242, and negotiations under appropriate auspices (UN Security Council 1973).

14. Kydd points out that individuals with lower levels of trust required more signals of reassurance from the Soviet Union to be convinced of its benign intentions (Kydd 2000, 341).

15. As part of the Sinai II agreement, Secretary of State Henry Kissinger pledged in a secret memorandum of understanding with Israel not to recognize or negotiate with the PLO unless it first recognized Israel's right to exist and accepted UN Security Council Resolutions 242 and 338 (Kissinger 1999, 456). Later Congress added that the PLO also had to renounce terrorism (Quandt 2005, 482, fn 24).

16. In this situation, the parties are said to have stag hunt preferences (their most preferred outcome is cooperation), but they still must resolve what is known as the distributional conflict. (See Powell 1994, 338–43.)

17. "The Armalite and the ballot box [or "bomb"]" refers to a famous speech by Sinn Fein leader Danny Morrison to the party's annual conference (ard fheis) in 1981. In this speech, Morrison asked why the Republicans could not seize power "with a ballot paper in one hand and the Armalite in the other" (Hannigan 1985, 34).

18. Arafat's soft-line statements were correctly viewed as not representative of the organization as a whole. Since Sadat's visit to Jerusalem, sentiment within the PLO had become more bellicose, and there was considerable dissatisfaction within the rank and file at Arafat's continued talk of coexistence (Walker and Gowers 2003, 170). There was also opposition to the PLO's implementation of the cease-fire with Israel. Those opposed sought to undermine the truce by continuing to use violence, but Arafat and Khalil al-Wazir thwarted their plans (Cobban 1984, 96).

References

Adesnik, David, and Michael McFaul. 2006. "Engaging Autocratic Allies to Promote Democracy." *Washington Quarterly* 29 (2).

Bronner, Ethan. 2010. "Mideast Leaders Hopeful after Opening of Talks." *New York Times,* Sept. 5.

Bueno de Mesquita, Ethan. 2005. "Conciliation, Counterterrorism, and Patterns of Terrorist Violence." *International Organization* 59 (1).

Byman, Daniel. 1998. "The Logic of Ethnic Terrorism." *Studies in Conflict and Terrorism* 21 (2).

———. 2006. "The Decision to Begin Talks with Terrorists: Lessons for Policymakers." *Studies in Conflict and Terrorism* 29 (5).

Cha, Victor. 1999. "Engaging China: The View from Korea." In *Engaging China: The Management of an Emerging Power*, ed. Alastair Ian Johnston and Robert S. Ross. New York: Routledge.

———. 2001. "Japan's Engagement Dilemmas with North Korea." *Asian Survey* 41 (4).

Checkel, Jeffrey. 2005. "International Institutions and Socialization in Europe: Introduction and Framework." *International Organization* 59 (4).

Cobban, Helena. 1984. *The Palestinian Liberation Organisation: People, Power, and Politics*. New York: Cambridge University Press.

Crocker, Chester A. 1980. "South Africa: A Strategy for Change." *Foreign Affairs* 59 (Winter).

Fearon, James D. 1994. "Domestic Political Audiences and the Escalation of International Disputes." *American Political Science Review* 88 (3).

———. 1997. "Signaling Foreign Policy Interests: Tying Hands versus Sinking Costs." *Journal of Conflict Resolution* 41 (1).

Fearon, James, and Alexander Wendt. 2002. "Rationalism v. Constructivism: A Skeptical View." In *Handbook of International Relations*, ed. Walter Carlsnaes, Thomas Risse, and Beth A. Simmons. London: Sage.

Frieden, Jeffrey A. 1999. "Actors and Preferences in International Relations." In *Strategic Choice and International Relations*, ed. David A. Lake and Robert Powell. Princeton, NJ: Princeton University Press.

Gibbs, Jack. 1989. "Conceptualization of Terrorism." *American Sociological Review* 43 (3).

Gupta, Devashree. 2007. "Selective Engagement and Its Consequences for Social Movement Organizations: Lessons from British Policy in Northern Ireland." *Comparative Politics* 39 (3).

Haaretz Service, Natasha Mozgovaya, and News Agencies. 2010. "Two Israelis Wounded in Second West Bank Shooting Attack in Two Days." *Haaretz*, Sept. 1.

Haass, Richard N., and Meghan L. O'Sullivan, eds. 2000. *Honey and Vinegar: Incentives, Sanctions, and Foreign Policy*. Washington, DC: Brookings Institution Press.

Hamzeh, Ahmad Nizar. 1993. "Lebanon's Hizbullah: From Islamic Revolution to Parliamentary Accommodation." *Third World Quarterly* 14 (2).

———. 2004. *In the Path of Hizbullah*. Syracuse, NY: Syracuse University Press.

Hannigan, John A. 1985. "The Armalite and the Ballot Box: Dilemmas of Strategy and Ideology in the Provisional IRA." *Social Problems* 33 (1).

Hoffman, Bruce. 1998. *Inside Terrorism*. New York: Columbia University Press.

International Crisis Group (ICG). 2006. *Palestinians, Israel, and the Quartet: Pulling Back from the Brink*. Middle East Report no. 54, June 13.

Jung, Courtney, Ellen Lust-Okar, and Ian Shapiro. 2005. "Problems and Prospects for Democratic Settlements: South Africa as a Model for the Middle East and Northern Ireland?" *Politics and Society* 33 (2).

Kershner, Isabel. 2010. "Israeli Easing of Blockade of Gaza Draws Praise of U.S." *New York Times*, June 20.

Kissinger, Henry. 1982. *Years of Upheaval*. Boston: Little, Brown.

————. 1999. *Years of Renewal*. Boston: Little, Brown.

Kydd, Andrew. 2000. "Trust, Reassurance, and Cooperation." *International Organization* 54 (2).

Lake, David A., and Robert Powell. 1999. "International Relations a Strategic-Choice Approach." In *Strategic Choice and International Relations*, ed. David A. Lake and Robert Powell. Princeton, NJ: Princeton University Press.

Lander, Mark, and Helene Cooper. 2010. "U.S. Wrestling with Olive Branch for Taliban." *New York Times*, Jan. 27.

Laqueur, Walter. 1987. *The Age of Terrorism*. Boston: Little, Brown.

Lynch, Marc. 2002. "Why Engage? China and the Logic of Communicative Engagement." *European Journal of International Relations* 8 (2).

Lynn, Brendan. 2002. "Tactic or Principle? The Evolution of Republican Thinking on Abstentionism in Ireland, 1970–1998." *Irish Political Studies* 17 (2).

March, James G., and Johan P. Olsen. 1998. "The Institutional Dynamics of International Political Orders." *International Organization* 52 (4).

McKinley, Dale T. 1997. *The ANC and the Liberation Struggle*. Chicago: Pluto Press.

Miller, Gregory D. 2007. "Confronting Terrorisms: Group Motivation and Successful State Policies." *Terrorism and Political Violence* 19 (3).

Mishal, Shaul, and Avraham Sela. 2006. *The Palestinian Hamas: Vision, Violence, and Coexistence*. New York: Columbia University Press.

Montgomery, Evan Braden. 2006. "Breaking Out of the Security Dilemma: Realism, Reassurance, and the Problem of Uncertainty." *International Security* 31 (2).

National Public Radio. 2009. "Transcript: Obama's Full Interview with NPR." June 1. www.npr.org/templates/story/story.php?storyId=104806528 (accessed Oct. 14, 2010).

Nordland, Rod. 2010. "Lacking Money and Leadership, Push for Taliban Defectors Stalls." *New York Times*, Sept. 6.

O'Clery, Conor. 1997. *Daring Diplomacy: Clinton's Secret Search for Peace in Ireland*. Boulder, CO: Roberts Rinehart.

Oppel, Richard A. Jr. 2007. "In Iraq, Conflict Simmers on 2nd Kurdish Front." *New York Times*, Oct. 23.

Pettyjohn, Stacie L. 2009. "Engagement: A Path to Disarmament or Disaster?" *International Negotiation* 14 (1).

Powell, Robert. 1994. "Review: Anarchy in International Relations: The Neorealist-Neoliberal Debate." *International Organization* 48 (2).

Princen, Thomas. 1992. *Intermediaries in International Conflict*. Princeton, NJ: Princeton University Press.

Pruitt, Dean G. 2006. "Negotiation with Terrorists." *International Negotiation* 11 (2).

Quandt, William B. 1986. *Camp David: Peacemaking and Politics*. Washington, DC: Brookings Institution Press.

———. 2005. *Peace Process: American Diplomacy and the Arab-Israeli Conflict since 1967*. 3rd ed. Washington, DC: Brookings Institution Press.

Ranstorp, Magnus. 1998. "The Strategy and Tactics of Hizballah's Current 'Lebanonization Process.'" *Mediterranean Politics* 3 (1): 125.

Risse, Thomas. 1999. "International Norms and Domestic Change: Arguing and Communicative Behavior in the Human Rights Area." *Politics and Society* 27 (4).

Rock, Stephen R. 2000. *Appeasement in International Politics*. Lexington: University of Kentucky Press.

Rubin, Jeffrey Z., ed. 1981. *Dynamics of Third Party Intervention: Kissinger in the Middle East*. New York: Praeger.

Sánchez-Cuenca, Ignacio. 2007. "The Dynamics of Nationalist Terrorism: ETA and the IRA." *Terrorism and Political Violence* 149 (3).

Sayigh, Yezid. 1997. *Armed Struggle and the Search for State: The Palestinian National Movement, 1949–1993*. New York: Oxford University Press.

———. 2007. "Inducing a Failed State in Palestine." *Survival* 49 (3).

Scham, Paul, and Osama Abu-Irshaid. 2009. "Hamas: Ideological Rigidity and Political Flexibility." United States Institute of Peace Special Report 224 (June).

Schimmelfennig, Frank. 2005. "Strategic Calculation and International Socialization: Membership Incentives, Party Constellations, and Sustained Compliance in Central and Eastern Europe." *International Organization* 59 (4).

Schweller, Randall. 1999. "Managing the Rise of Great Powers: History and Theory." In *Engaging China: The Management of an Emerging Power*, ed. Alastair Ian Johnston and Robert S. Ross. New York: Routledge.

Spector, Bertram I. 1998. "Deciding to Negotiate with Villains." *Negotiation Journal* 14 (1).

Stein, Janice Gross. 1991. "Reassurance in International Conflict Management." *Political Science Quarterly* 106 (3).

Suettinger, Robert Lee. 2000. "The United States and China: Tough Engagement." In *Honey and Vinegar: Incentives, Sanctions, and Foreign Policy*, ed. Richard N. Haass and Meghan L. O'Sullivan. Washington, DC: Brookings Institution Press.

Touval, Saadia. 1982. *The Peace Brokers: Mediators in the Arab-Israeli Conflict, 1948–1979*. Princeton, NJ: Princeton University Press.

Touval, Saadia, and I. William Zartman. 1985. *International Mediation in Theory and Practice*. Vol. 6. Boulder, CO: Westview Press.

Treisman, Daniel. 2004. "Rational Appeasement." *International Organization* 58 (2).

UN Security Council. 1967. *Resolution 242,* Nov. 22, 1967. http://daccess-dds-ny.un.org/doc/RESOLUTION/GEN/NR0/240/94/IMG/NR024094.pdf?OpenElement (accessed Oct. 25, 2010).

———. 1973. *Resolution 338,* Oct. 22, 1973. http://daccess-dds-ny.un.org/doc/RESOLUTION/GEN/NR0/288/65/IMG/NR028865.pdf?OpenElement (accessed Oct. 25, 2010).

U.S. State Department. 2002. *Patterns of Global Terrorism 2001.* May. www.state.gov/s/ct/rls/crt/2001/pdf/index.htm (accessed Oct. 25, 2010).

Usher, Graham. 2000. "Fatah's Tanzim: Origins and Politics." *Middle East Report* 217. www.merip.org/mer/mer217/217_usher.html (accessed Oct. 13, 2010).

Walker, Tony, and Andrew Gowers. 2003. *Arafat: The Biography.* Rev. and updated ed. London: Virgin.

Wallach, Janet, and John Wallach. 1990. *Arafat: In the Eyes of the Beholder.* New York: Carol.

Ware, Michael. 2005. "The New Rules of Engagement." *TIME,* Dec. 12.

Weinberg, Leonard, and Ami Pedahzur. 2003. *Political Parties and Terrorist Groups.* New York: Routledge.

Zartman, I. William. 1985. *Ripe for Resolution: Conflict and Intervention in Africa.* New York: Oxford University Press.

———. 2003. "Negotiating with Terrorists." *International Negotiation* 8 (3).

Zartman, I. William, and Tanya Alfredson. 2010. "Negotiating with Terrorists and the Tactical Question." In *Coping with Terrorism: Origins, Escalation, Counterstrategies, and Responses,* ed. Rafael Reuveny and William R. Thompson. Albany, NY: SUNY Press.

Zartman, I. William, and Saadia Touval. 2007. "International Mediation." In *Leashing the Dogs of War: Conflict Management in a Divided World,* ed. Chester A. Crocker, Fen Osler Hampson, and Pamela Aall. Washington, DC: United States Institute of Peace Press.

PART II

HOW TO ENGAGE

Devising Strategy and Tactics

Guy Olivier Faure and I. William Zartman

Extremist political organizations use terrorism to further broad goals of political and societal change. These goals can range from a change in political status of a defined territory or population to the total reform of society, to the millennial and even eschatological aims of the absolute terrorists. The goals of engagement and negotiation are also wide-ranging, for both sides. They involve not only ending an incident but also taking broader steps into the political realm. Engagement is not just a matter of extracting hostages. It requires digging into the underlying causes and issues, which involves wider policy considerations and higher decision-making levels. No longer simply a job for policemen and specialists, it becomes the work of diplomats and policymakers.

Beyond the temporal determinants of the negotiation process lie the issues themselves, and the need to take a hard look at the relationship between ends and means, as discussed in Pecastaing's chapter. While the state needs to eliminate the extremists' violent means of protest if it is to make itself whole, it can do so only by addressing their goals, understanding them, clarifying them, and sorting out the adoptable from the unadoptable—all actions that require engagement and, eventually, negotiation. Like the state, terrorists in political organizations find it difficult to conceive of engagement with their adversary, whose nature and policies they see as inextricably mixed. It is this commingled identity of the two elements that both sides need to break, as the starting point for examining the ways of engagement and as a step back from mutual Manichaean demonization and toward a search for exchangeables and partial outcomes of common interest.

States and extremist political organizations must be able to communicate with each other, overcoming both physical and psychological barriers. Since confrontation has demonized the opponent and prohibited contact, any attempt at contact is regarded with distrust and suspicion. The parties must think of possible deals that will meet their minimum demands, combining the elements of recognition, violence, and grievances. Since the conflict has centered on the impossibility—indeed, the immorality—of even considering the other party's demands and positions and, hence, the legitimacy of the opponent's violence, it is hard to conceive of an acceptable deal with the evil opponent. Since the enemy has little to offer the state other than the end of its violent tactics, additional elements may be needed to make the agreement worth its cost.

Such efforts by terrorists and states to enter into each other's webs of thought are best done preventively, to limit future damage. But prevention can also occur even after violent action has already taken place. In Egypt, for example, the imprisoned leaders of the Islamic Group (Gama'a Islamiya) restudied their doctrines and came to the conclusion that their millennial ends did not justify diabolical means. The story of their efforts at negotiating among themselves to prevent further outbreaks of terrorism is told in the chapter written by Carolin Goerzig after in-depth interviews with members of the group.

Tactics of engagement are often ambiguous—a further complication examined by Kristine Höglund. Cease-fires and other conflict management techniques, even temporary ones, tend to favor negotiations, although much has been written about the inadvisability of counting too much on cease-fires as a prelude to, rather than a consequence of, settlement. Similarly, antiterrorist measures such as labeling and banning do not appear to help negotiations, although generally the carrot and the stick, used together, give impetus to negotiation rather than undercutting it. The general finding is that negotiation and other tactics affect each other and must be used strategically.

In the chapter by Aldo Civico, these ideas are tested in application involving the role of mediators in a notable case in Colombia. The important role of mediators has already been introduced in part I—unless constrained by powerful mediators, the parties can be tempted to look at negotiations simply as an occasion for rearming for another round of conflict. Civico's chapter examines engagement attempts between Colombia and the National Liberation Army (ELN) to show how continued confrontation over time produced moderation in the terrorists but then left the government unwilling to go beyond merely an end of violence as its demand and concession. The mediator, President Hugo Chávez of Venezuela, became too involved in his efforts and turned into a manipulator without bringing benefits to both parties, ending the attempt at engagement.

These chapters do not cover all the possible tactics for engaging and negotiating between terrorists and states, but they do give insights into the types of efforts necessary to bring those contacts and efforts to fruition. There is much to investigate between issues of ends and of means—topics of exchange that can be used to dissuade the extremists (and the state) from using violence and that can soften the absolute doctrines that justify it.

6

Facing Terrorism:

Engagement and De-escalation

Camille Pecastaing

There was a time when terrorists were, at least to some, sympathetic, heroic figures. They were the modern bandits, rebels against the absolutism and injustice of states and empires. It helped if they had a discernible moral vision. In the 1949 play *Les Justes,* Camus presented Ivan Kaliayev, a real-life social revolutionary who, in 1905, aborted throwing a bomb at an archduke, to spare the wife and children accompanying him. Camus had made a name for himself during World War II as the editor of a publication of the French Resistance—a just cause if ever there was one. And yet, the partisans' first celebrated act was the assassination of a random German naval officer in a Paris subway. Was this terrorism or heroism?

Jump ahead to the twenty-first century, to the daily suicide bombings indifferent to the presence of civilian women and children. That these attacks take place mostly in Afghanistan, Pakistan, and Iraq is only a matter of opportunity. Others have occurred at a school in Beslan, discos in Bali, restaurants in Tel Aviv, and trains in Paris, London, Madrid, and Mumbai. If twenty-first-century terrorism has a moral vision, it is vastly different from Kaliayev's.

This essay explores what happened to terrorism—how it got from there to here. Many variables can plausibly account for terrorism's drift toward unchecked lethality and gore. One is that high-value targets (today's archdukes) are so well protected, they have been replaced by masses of low-value targets (Crenshaw 1995, 31). There is also the general fascination with weapons. And with weapons now having entered the age of mass casualties, suicide bombings use simple explosives in densely populated areas to mimic on a small scale the devastation of weapons of mass destruction. Also, with czarism a thing of the past, democracy makes people—that is, everyone—responsible for the acts of the reviled state, and, thus, a legitimate target for retaliation (Chaliand and Blin 2007, 8). And then there is the question of religiosity: the possibility that the moral compass of Islamist terrorists is skewed by religious fervor (Juergensmeyer 2000; Stern 2003, xxvi–xxviii).

Terrorism is communication. It is a discourse about sovereignty, punctuated by acts of force, because of the intimacy between force and sovereignty at the heart of the Weberian definition of statehood. This essay postulates a correlation between the escalation in forms of violence, and the state's growing efforts to silence terrorists and refusal to engage with them on any field other than that of violence. Shut down the discourse, and all that is left is the punctuation—and the punctuation has become louder.

States and terrorists come in all shapes and calibers, but this chapter more specifically considers situations where, despite the asymmetry in coercive power, both parties share substantial popular legitimacy. States are not political aberrations, predatory apparatuses occupying a foreign land and exploiting the local population, but a form of social organization recognized by many as legitimate. Likewise, terrorists are not self-appointed, inspired, politicized criminals but, rather, the violent outgrowth of broader social movements clamoring for reasonable rights. Terrorists do have a *potential support base:* a population under direct or indirect control of the state and whose rights they can claim to represent, as discussed further in the first chapter; a population that can identify with them, although not necessarily unconditionally. Support for the ends pursued by terrorists is not the same thing as support for the means they use.

Another way to look at the difference between means and ends is to distinguish between the diminution and renunciation of violence (conflict management) and the closure of a social situation that fueled the conflict in the first place (conflict resolution). Formal negotiations are often expected to resolve the conflict, but the asymmetry between the parties is necessarily brought into the framework of negotiations. States can be expected to make concessions proportional to the irritation caused by terrorists, but no more. In return for those concessions, terrorists are expected to reconcile themselves with the reality of the state's needs and its ultimate authority. The kind of negotiating is a reflection of the military/security situation: it is the transformation of physical power into contractual power in order to halt the disruptive cycle of violence.

Closing a genuine social conflict is not like closing a business deal. It is not about who gives what to whom; it is not about getting as much, and giving as little, as one can in a process of formal negotiations. Conflict was constructed in the minds of belligerents. Resolution will have to be, too. Real closure requires from all sides a sweeping social evolution and a redefinition of concepts such as "national interest" and national identity. Formal negotiations may be a final step on that road, to work out the details, but they are not the journey.   *engagement ≥ terrorism*

Communication, or engagement, is a more diffuse form of negotiation, aimed not at producing a final settlement but, at a minimum, at framing the terms of the conflict to de-escalate from lethality and gore. In the long run, communication is also the way to familiarize all parties with the terms of the cognitive revolution that can one day enable genuine closure through mutual recognition—that is, through reconstructing perceptions of the other and of the other's place in the world. This chapter explores the possibility that it is when communication is impeded—usually as a result of deliberate state policies—that terrorism drifts into lethality and gore. The chapter also reviews some of the many ways that communication can take place, even outside formal negotiations, in order to frame the terms of conflict and prevent a drift toward greater violence.

Closing the Space of Communication

Tactically, "no negotiation" policies aim at neutralizing hostage taking, putting an end to the rounds of prisoner exchange whereby captured terrorists are traded for civilian (or military) captives. Strategically, these "no negotiation" paradigms are of a different nature. They tend to accompany heavy sentencing for participation in terrorist activity, and public stances prohibiting arrangements of any kind with terrorists. Such measures are not just deterrents; they are denials. They intend to seal terrorists off at all possible levels: not just from the use of force but also from the right to make legitimate demands. In the long run, this intransigence not only limits the government's options but has the potential of radicalizing terrorists.

Terrorists are complex characters, one half angel, martyred to redeem humanity, the other half demon, devouring the flesh of innocents. They are also extrovert: they have a point to make, and throughout most of the modern history of terrorism, they have sought and found people to listen to them. Anarchists, social revolutionaries, and nationalists of all kinds have had their detractors and their advocates. In the past, they generated far more noise than actual human death. Sympathy for terrorism was particularly common between World War II and the mid-1970s. Partisans were the heroes of the Resistance against Nazi Germany, and their aura passed on to the freedom fighters of the decolonization struggle. A simple snapshot of Ernesto Guevara became a universal sign, carrying a meaning of youth and freedom.

Terrorists also had long understood that stylistic choices they made helped or hurt their public relations. From their beginnings in the nineteenth century, they had worked to depict themselves as victims. Exposing the repressive nature of the state was at the core of the strategy to conquer power (Zamoyski 2001). This was particularly true of "pure" terrorists, who, like anarchists and social revolutionaries, operated primarily at a symbolic level. As a vanguard, they left the actual business of revolution to the masses they hoped to enlighten with their "propaganda of the deed." Fastidious about targets and methodologies, most restrained themselves to bombing empty government buildings or carrying out political assassinations. In that era, the target was emblematic of abusive authority, and the attack was a political message inviting popular defection: it meant not to terrorize but to inspire. There were occasional drifts into lethality, but those were more the function of individual dispositions than of serious strategic thinking. By bombing a crowded café in 1894, French anarchist Emile Henry tested the limits of the methodology (Merriman 2009).

Compared with most attempts to trigger a social revolution in the name of class struggle, campaigns for self-determination were broader affairs, in which acts of terrorism per se were inscribed in an attrition strategy backed by extensive social action. The objective was not to overthrow the state by demonstration but to *substitute for* the state—something the Irish Republican Brotherhood took decades to accomplish. Targets could be symbolic (communication) or tactical (attrition or polarization). Moral finesse mattered less, because identity lines were discernible and could fracture under the pressure of violence. Vietnamese Communists would throw bombs in cafés to bleed foreign occupiers, awaken Vietnamese nationalism, and punish collaborators (Karnow 1991; Summers 1999, 33, 342; Currey 1997). The mobilization of the potential support base was actively pursued and not left to a demonstrative effect. Through grassroots efforts like the work of political commissars, rebels reached out to a civilian population that suffered indiscriminate state reprisals—reprisals provoked in the first place by acts of sabotage or terrorism. The Algerian Front de Libération Nationale (FLN), which had no qualms about terrorizing a potential support base, grew in popularity among Muslims when vigilante outfits from among the European colonists started attacking Muslim neighborhoods (Horne 1978, 529; Stora 2004, 82–100; Slama 1996).

In those serious conflicts, terrorism was not an isolated behavioral anomaly, a crime wrapped in political garb, but a disagreeable facet of greater historical events, judgment about which could legitimately go either way. This complexity kept public perceptions focused on warfare and not just on terrorist acts, affording terrorists considerable leeway in their modes of action. Yet nationalists kept an eye on the lines in the sand. The Irgun had bombed bus stops in Arab villages during the 1930s Arab Revolt, but it was embarrassed by the ninety-odd deaths at the King David Hotel in 1946 and blamed the British for not heeding the warnings it sent (Parker and Farrell 2006).

In Algeria in 1957, the FLN timed a general strike to coincide with debates of the United Nations General Assembly in order to provoke a favorable resolution (Watson 2003, 121; Crenshaw 1978). In the early decades of the Cold War, most actions still had a strong component of communication: terrorists and revolutionaries knew that the people would tune in through their newspapers and radios and, increasingly, their television sets. It was their strategy to expose the public to messages that might progressively change their worldview and accustom them to a new order of things. The strategy worked with maximal effect during the Vietnam War, with Hanoi monitoring the progress of the antiwar movement in the United States. In the end, that conflict was reduced to the seminal 1972 image of Kim Phúc, a young girl burned by napalm, running naked down a country road: a snapshot of victimization, waging the most effective form of psychological warfare. Leaders of the civil rights movement had accomplished the same feat by crossing that bridge in 1965 in Selma, Alabama, and being trampled by the police in front of cameras.

To get those violent images that would change history, revolutionaries needed to provoke the authorities, and that was the function of run-of-the-mill terrorism. But the tide turned in the early 1970s, when a variety of factors contributed to global "terrorism fatigue." The revolutionary ideal, forged in 1776 in Britain's American colonies, was in terminal agony. The Soviet Union was irretrievably tainted by Stalinism, and Mao's apocalyptic Cultural Revolution was progressively exposed for the imposture that it was. The postmodern revolution that seemed to gain traction in the spring of 1968—a global rising of all things oppressed, a flowering of Maoist and neo-Trostkyist sentiments—failed to resist the embourgeoisement of baby boomers. All the media stars of that era—Weather Underground, Black Liberation Army, Red Army Faction, Brigate Rosse—faded away, leaving but an anecdotal legacy.

The ideal of self-determination was also on the decline. As imperialism wound down and more states gained independence, many revolutionary leaders turned into reactionary rulers and joined the camp of the status quo. The Biafran war that began in 1967 was a sign of times to come. The compact of the United Nations—nonaggression and mutually recognized sovereignty—became entrenched with time, and freedom fighters found themselves on the wrong side of history. The main enemy of the Polisario Front in the Western Sahara has been global indifference—all the more striking considering that fifty-three countries recognize the Sahrawi Arab Democratic Republic the Polisario represents. The Kurds, the world's largest nonsovereign ethnic group, never got to be a cause célèbre, because their nationalist champions were too parochial and too late in the game. European integration would have a similar effect, making claims of once popular sovereigntist groups such as Basque Homeland and Freedom (ETA) and the Provisional Irish Republican Army (PIRA) increasingly anachronistic in a postnationalist Europe.

It was not just that the ends had become elusive—public opinion had grown weary of the means as well. Throughout the 1970s, the live TV revolution made bombings and hostage crises a routine household spectacle, while the rise of transnational terrorist operations became an irritant for the populations of liberal countries where the killing took place. Western Europe was particularly exposed, with probably the most notable operation there being the hostage crisis at the 1972 Munich Olympics. Palestinians would remain a darling cause of a certain European left, but too much was too much: Abu Nidal, Carlos "the Jackal," and the Armenian Secret Army for the Liberation of Armenia (ASALA) were never popular heroes.

The Palestinian nationalist movement illustrates this epochal shift from inspirational to destructive, which coincides with increases in the intensity and efficiency of counterterrorism. There were the hijackings as public relations operations, such as that of TWA flight 840, seized in August 1969, and there was Yasser Arafat's groundbreaking trip to the United Nations in November 1974. But there also were the volleys fired and grenades thrown at airport crowds—Lod in 1972, and Vienna and Rome in 1985. Somewhere along the way, communication had broken down, and the fedayeen had drifted off message, indulging in bloodletting just as they lost the ability to influence political events on the ground. The implacable success of the Shin Bet had shut them off from Palestine; exiled in Amman, then from Amman to Beirut, then from Beirut to Tunis, Palestinian factions sank into lethality as the Palestine Liberation Organization (PLO) sank into irrelevance (Black and Morris 1991).

Governments, given freer rein because of diminishing popular sympathy for revolutionaries, more secure in their sovereignty thanks to new technologies of power (e.g., wiretapping, satellite imagery), and more aware of the common interests they shared, hardened their stance on terrorism. Israel, which made few efforts to glorify its own terrorist past, had pioneered the counterterrorist methods for the new era. There was a special unit (Sayeret Matkal) to free hostages; there would be no negotiations; there were retaliations (Operation Gift) and death squads (Operation Wrath of God) (Ensalaco 2008, 47–48).

France, Germany, and even the United States were inspired to form commandos trained to break hostage situations. Those units shone in Djibouti (1976), Entebbe (1976), and Mogadishu (1977) and advised in Mecca (1979), giving no quarter (Trofimov 2008). Meanwhile, the historical leadership of the German Red Army Faction was wiped out in prison under odd circumstances (1977), and Bobby Sands and his Irish Republican Army (IRA) fellows were left to take their hunger strike to the grave (1981). Everywhere the doors of dialogue were preemptively closed and punishment stepped up. Intergovernmental cooperation was on the rise. In the 1970s, the autocratic regimes of South American countries had joined forces in Operation Condor to eliminate opponents throughout the continent. Paris and Madrid collaborated with great effectiveness against ETA after Spain joined the European Union in 1986.

Ironically, the myth of the popular revolution was finally laid to rest by the 1979 overthrow of Iran's Pahlavi regime. Ayatollah Khomeini, the black-clad Robespierre of the Iranian revolution, was no romantic figure. And he was not alone in failing to live up to the inspiring, mythical character that Ernesto Guevara had embodied only a generation before. By 1979, once-glorious revolutionaries such as Fidel Castro and Yasser Arafat were obsolete when not farcical; Pol Pot had joined the ranks of the mass murderers of the twentieth century; and revolutionary-in-chief Muammar Gadhafi was lost in the absurd.

Too many revolutionaries and ever more dubious causes meant that people were tuning out just as pressure was put on the media to control the message. States sponsoring terrorism were put on short notice: Libya was bombed in 1986, in retaliation for a disco bombing in Germany, and embargoed for good measure. Listening to and accommodating terrorists was over.

There were a few exceptions. Iran was amply rewarded for the mayhem it inspired in Lebanon—from the spectacular bombings of 1983, which forced the multinational force to depart, to the wave of long-term abductions of foreign nationals. The PIRA's political branch worked doggedly throughout the 1980s to keep lines of communication open, while the operational side tested the limits of the acceptable. The African National Congress (ANC) managed to improve its standing in the global media because of Mandela's plight, because its terrorism was neither very effective nor very violent, and because the public diplomacy of the apartheid Republic of South Africa was so terribly poor.

The Cold War allowed for one last great heroic insurgency: the Afghan jihad, feted by the West as a victory for freedom. But that romance soured as soon as the Soviet threat dissipated. The West failed to imagine a place for political Islam in the new order of things, and the mujahideen veered onto a collision course with their former sponsors. Within a couple of years of the victory in Afghanistan, jihad flared up in new fronts across the Muslim world—Algeria, Bosnia, Egypt, Kashmir, Chechnya—and jihadist support networks followed Muslim immigrants deep into the West's heartland (Vidino 2005, 137; Coolsaet 2008, 113).

Jihad flared from the embers of revolutionary socialism and nationalism. It was the new class struggle, mixed with nativist revival. The jihadists pledged to end the corrupting effect of Western hegemony and secularism, but the unipolar world of the 1990s had no forbearance for their anti-imperialist claims. For one thing, American imperium was not as imposing as earlier forms of Western dominion—the Muslim world had already gone through its round of independence. For another, the 1990s were not a political decade: attention was on economic globalization and the benefits of market-based democracies.

It was easy to dislike Islamism: its aesthetics were reactionary, and its campaign for legitimacy was punctuated by episodes of extraordinary brutality quite beyond the standards of terrorists past. Jihadism did not seem to understand that psychological warfare was a popularity contest, or did not seem to care—perhaps because, with God on one's side, what humanity thought was of little importance. But the lethality of jihadism was not about God; it was more about the effects of a feedback loop. Just as a large part of global public opinion shut off the message that jihadists were trying to peddle, jihadists drifted into a self-indulgent quest for lethality and gore. What in the nineteenth century were isolated, pathological cases of targeting civilians had become the norm.

Islamists attracted little sympathy from the international community when they were brutally crushed in Egypt and Algeria in the mid-1990s. If the West stood by during the siege of Sarajevo, it was in part because of suspicions that Bosniaks were covert Islamists (Sells 1998; Maček 2009, 130, 133), and it took the massacre in Srebrenice to persuade the West to act against Serb militias. Europe easily accepted that the slogan "one man, one vote, one time" represented the attitude of Algeria's Islamist party, the Islamic Salvation Front, toward democracy. No one caught the irony that doubts about the democratic credentials of a party running in democratic elections should justify a military interruption of the electoral process (Sammakia 1997, 9). The atrocities Russia committed in 1994–96 during the first Chechen war were barely more noticed than the Indian military's brutal occupation of Kashmir under the Armed Forces Special Powers Act of 1958, which allows detention without charges and provides for lax rules of engagement (Reveron and Stevenson 2006, 316). And in 1993, while the world applauded as the first intifada gave birth to the Oslo peace process, it missed that an irrelevant Fatah in exile had essentially been resurrected at the expense of such up-and-coming groups as Hamas, in essence starting a Palestinian civil war (Shikaki 2002).

On the flip side, the Armed Islamic Group, manipulated or not by the Algerian government, was slaughtering whole villages in 1995–96 (Souaïdia 2001; Samraoui 2003). Gama'a Islamiya was gunning down tourists in Luxor (1997), and Chechens were making snuff videos of Russian prisoners being beheaded (1993–94). The Taliban were defacing World Heritage monumental sculptures and applying the *hudud* (punishments fixed in traditional Islamic law) literally, in a monstrous caricature of Islamic justice. Gama'a Islamiya was blowing up churches on Christmas Day (1999), and the holiday season was to be a period of choice for jihadist operations. And al-Qaeda, of course, was getting into the business of provoking the United States with extraordinary, senselessly lethal PR stunts. The performative, declaratory, theatrical terrorism of the 1960s had given way to a gory spectacle of suicide bombings and mass killings. For many around the world, jihad read like an apocalyptic fantasy of destruction.

Alienation, Repression, and Lethality

A well-evidenced psychological phenomenon is the "fundamental attribution error" (Ross 1977). Individuals will tend to attribute their own actions to circumstances, and the actions of others to their nature. Islamist circles attribute the violence of American counterterrorism since 9/11—torture of prisoners, killing of civilians—to the deep imperialistic and racist essence of the West. Conversely, successive U.S. administrations have justified U.S. counterterrorism policy as dictated by the circumstances of a grave threat from a fanatical lot. There is no space for dialogue, no forum for the exchange of ideas—just a mirroring effect: evil looking at evil.

In the eyes of many Westerners, jihadists' brutality, this quantum leap in the scale of revolutionary violence, has something to do with their being Muslim—whether because they are believers or because of something specific to Islam (Wike and Grim 2007). It seems chronologically plausible that the 1979 Iranian Revolution inserted an odious religious fanaticism into a romantic tradition of revolutionary terrorism. But that cut-off point misses the drift into lethality and gore already apparent in the 1970s in some ultrasecular Palestinian factions—a drift that was to be fully consummated in the global jihad, though not initiated by it. Abu Nidal precedes Bin Laden.

The perpetration of atrocities is facilitated by the degree of identity alienation between parties—what is commonly known as "pseudospeciation" and "dehumanization." Multiple factors can contribute to this alienation: an agrarian background (which implies limited exposure to "others" and familiarity with killing animals); low levels of education (associated with rural origins); feelings of anomie resulting from migration and recent urbanization; anxiety related to inadequate socialization and low self-esteem; personal receptiveness to chauvinist messages; collective hysteria induced by a xenophobic hegemonic discourse; and the buildup of trauma in a protracted conflict. Religion is a marker of identity and, as such, an instrument of alienation. But religion—the act of dogmatic faith that is religion—is not by itself a behavioral primer for committing atrocities. In that respect, Islam is no different from other creeds, monotheistic or not.

We can reexamine in that light the radicalization of terrorism over the past forty years. No-negotiation and no-recognition paradigms and heavy punishments have come in parallel with dehumanization processes. Contrary to the opinion of experts, the public has been led to believe that violent extremists are ontologically different from other humans, that terrorism is the individual expression of a perverted free will that exists in finite supply within a population (Post 2006, 17). Order will return when the right (or enough) individual troublemakers are eliminated; violence will eradicate violence. Like ritualized human sacrifice, counterterrorism operates from the assumption that the annihilation of some (by death squads or life sentences) can make a difference and change the course of history.

This is how the "global war on terror" was framed in the mass media in its early years, allowing for all sorts of tolerable exceptions to the rule of law as it applies to terrorists. By contrasting the humanity of Muslims with the inhumanity of terrorists, the global war on terror started as an exorcism: the corpus of peace-loving Muslims has to be purified of the jihadist cancer that infected it. Those who were not marked to be killed by drone attacks were corralled in otherworldly areas such as Guantánamo and Supermax detention centers, where the limits of suffering were explored in search for humane forms of torture (Metzner and Fellner 2010). The correspondence between crime and punishment was severed. In the United States, conspiring to commit a terrorist act warrants the same punishment as committing the act (U.S. Code 2009a, 525). Thus, the most clumsy, inchoate plots, or even mere inflammatory statements, can be met with decade-long sentencing. Providing material support to terrorists is punished by fifteen years' imprisonment, but counts can be cumulative and thresholds are low (U.S. Code 2009b, 533). Even legal or negotiating advice to an organization on a terrorist watch list is now deemed a crime equivalent to terrorism (U.S. Supreme Court 2010).

Not everyone can and will become a full-fledged terrorist—in any society, only a small fraction ever embraces armed struggle (della Porta 1995b, 205). But it is misguided to look for the etiology of terrorism in a flawed personal disposition. The belligerence of activists is the consequence of complex psychological dynamics, the product of a social experience as well as a social construct (Stout 2002; Moghaddam 2006, 26, 123; Sageman 2008). Their action can be sustained only if nourished by a "cause," by perceptions of iniquity shared among a population that hosts the many "sympathizers," without whom the few "terrorists" could not operate. This insight has inspired the shift in U.S. policy after 2006 from counterterrorism to counterinsurgency—from the ontological to the sociological (Kilcullen 2009, 250–51; Nagl 2005, 141). This shift from counterterrorism back to counterinsurgency (COIN), implemented first in Iraq, required a revolution in thinking from where public perceptions were in 2005.

Along those lines, Muslim states such as Saudi Arabia, Indonesia, Egypt, and Libya have set up deradicalization programs for jihadists. Rather than being dehumanized, inmates are held in relative comfort and engaged in a dialogue about Islam and the context of armed struggle in Muslim life, as analyzed in the chapters by Goerzig and Lambert in this volume. While the experiment is too recent to produce definitive results, early signs are encouraging. It seems that a majority of militants can be rehabilitated, that dialogue offers opportunities missed by a repression-only approach (Boucek 2008). It is interesting to note that the premise for rehabilitation is that participants in the program have been deceived by a separate class of hard-liner militants. Conceptually, it is difficult to do without the existence of an ontological evil.

The insight that COIN brings to the table is that when a "cause" has enough depth to reverberate across society, repression will not reach a breaking point, at least not within acceptable levels of so-called kinetic action. Unless the entire society is "broken" by state terror, terrorism will replenish its ranks at an equal or faster rate than counterterrorism depletes them; and the greater the repression, the greater the differential rate between recruitment and attrition.

In fact, the effectiveness of repression follows a J curve. Counterterrorism works best when it operates within the parameters of law enforcement:

when repression is targeted and is limited to violent activists and when punishment is perceived by the social corpus as fair and reasonable (Commonwealth Human Rights Initiative 2007, 10). Routine law enforcement paired with open dialogue and some political concessions is the strategy most likely to prevent defiant responses from the opposition's potential support base. The preemptive method was pioneered by Prussian chancellor Otto von Bismarck in the 1870s, when social laws defanged the German revolutionary movement and eventually gave birth to reformist social democracy.

On the other hand, broader, indiscriminate repression often has the counterproductive effect of radicalizing a population not necessarily committed to political violence. Martial laws, curfews, random searches, mass arrests, torture, and killings are the main causes of radicalization. The case of Northern Ireland in the 1970s offers a good example: whereas British troops intervened at first to protect Catholics, harsh counterinsurgency policies adapted from the decolonization struggle managed to turn large segments of the Catholic population against the UK (LaFree and Hendrickson 2007).

Repression becomes effective again when it reaches a certain threshold. A regime of terror, denying the population any capacity to organize or communicate beyond small circles of trust, has a shot at finding the societal breaking point. In the 1970s, the military regimes of Latin America effectively decimated the ranks of the opposition. Since 2000, Russia has tolerated egregious violations of human rights in reinstating its authority over Chechnya.

Only authoritarian societies can step up their counterterrorism operations to that last level, unavailable to regimes constrained by some form of rule of law. Repression in democracies, therefore, has decreasing marginal utility and negative rates of return. Excesses will fuel resistance without rising to the level of intensity that would effectively suppress it. A rule-of-law-oriented society embroiled with a somewhat legitimate cause contemplates the necessity of cohabiting ad infinitum with a violent opposition. ETA, IRA, and the various incarnations of the Palestinian resistance have been cases in point for decades. The endurance of the Pashtun Taliban is a more recent example, and the issue in that situation is not to *end* but to *frame* violence.

Terrorists do not plot from a blank slate. Their actions are shaped by projections of reality and by images of themselves, of the society they oppose, and of their place in that society. Giuseppe Mazzini, Sergei Nechaev, Michael Collins, George Grivas, and Ernesto Guevara defined for their times what it is to be a terrorist. But aesthetics change; fads spread from locale to locale, from conflict to conflict, before being eventually eclipsed.

Suicide bombing is to the early twenty-first century what hijacking and hostage taking were to the 1970s: the embodiment of a terrorist operation. There is something cyclical here. Terrorist attacks in the nineteenth century often involved martyrdom. The political assassinations common in that era required physical proximity to the target, with few other options but capture or suicide. Ignacy Hryniewiecki died when throwing the bomb that killed Alexander II in 1881, and the Pervomartovtsi, his fellow conspirators from Narodnaya Volya, had not made particular plans to avoid arrest. The Black Hand assassins who killed Archduke Ferdinand in 1914 kept cyanide capsules (Remak 1959).

By the twentieth century, however, the largest terrorist organizations were protecting their members, either through the practice of revenge killing (e.g., Michael Collins's IRA targeting of the infamous G-men) or prison escape (e.g., IRA commandos' breaking Irish congressman Eamon de Valera out of prison in 1919). The most ambitious prison escape attempted by a terrorist organization was probably the Acre Prison break by Irgun and Lehi members in 1947.

The Russian Revolution and the IRA's success in 1921 raised expectations that martyrdom was not inevitable, that terrorists and revolutionaries could live to see their cause vindicated. In the 1960s and 1970s, many operations aimed either to exact revenge for executed comrades (thereby preventing further executions) or to liberate interned ones. Death and life imprisonment were risked but not inevitable, and the successive hostage crises were a form of dialogue on that point. That dialogue set thresholds that terrorists and states should not cross if they wished to keep violence within bounds.

But by the 1980s, improvements in counterterrorism, stepped-up punishments, no-negotiation paradigms, and purposefully built high-security prisons had considerably reduced the odds of escape or liberation. The 1980s also saw martyrdom reappear, in the form of the suicide bomber. At first, the reasons were tactical: martyrdom operations were easier to put together because they did not require an escape plan, and the death of the attacker provided additional shock value, sending a message about the opposition's determination. This seems to have been the moral calculus of Sri Lanka's Liberation Tigers of Tamil Eelam when dozens of young women, veiled by the grace of innocence normally attributed to their gender and age, went to their deaths against high-value targets and whoever stood near (Gonzalez-Perez 2008, 63). The effect was spectacular, and the victimizer could still claim victimhood. Suicide operations also gratified the Shia ethos of martyrdom then cultivated in revolutionary Iran, from where it was exported to Lebanon. But martyrdom remained the exception, and the candidates a handful, often wired to a remote detonator as insurance against a change of heart.

Suicide operations became more frequent in the 1990s and commonplace in the following decade. The growing frequency of martyrdom changed the norms, and martyrdom *became* the norm. By accepting death, the assailants robbed the state of its power of deterrence: they no longer had to contemplate the repression that would be unleashed against them. By the same token, death freed them of moral limits. Since they were preemptively paying the highest price for their act, they didn't need to be too fussy about how they used force. Somewhere along that road, the most common target of suicide operations became crowds of civilians.

Suicide operations against civilians were not an ideal base for engaging in dialogue with state and society. Over the decades, terrorists of all stripes had shown a great attachment to rationality. The societies they proposed to build out of the revolution may have resembled nationalist or socialist utopias, yet they went to great lengths to explain and justify their projects, to appear reasonable. In the wake of operations, communiqués were routinely issued to provide the public with cognitive elements so that it could appreciate the latest developments in the broader context of the struggle.

Not all societies offered equivalent opportunities for communication. Rule-of-law societies have free media, which do not exist in authoritarian environments, where effective censorship dampens the effectiveness of psychological warfare. In the West, the relationship between terrorists and free media has long been symbiotic, and the "theater" of terrorism was orchestrated by clever strategists feeding content to journalists eager to break the news (Nacos 2007).

This situation changed in the mid-1980s, in the wake of protracted hostage crises in Tehran and Beirut. Governments chided media for offering terrorists a complicit platform and used incentives to crowd their adversaries out of the airwaves. The famously independent BBC has been under continuous attack for its principled neutrality in reporting on incidents involving acts of terrorism. Most networks chose self-censorship. Either way, states got better at controlling the message. Trials were staged so that they would no longer offer a platform to send a political message: media coverage was reduced to a trickle of parsed statements from defendants. In Italy, special courts were set up to display *pentiti*, former revolutionaries who publically denounced violence. That method was replicated more recently throughout the Middle East.

By the time global jihad erupted, mainstream media were already filtering terrorist communiqués. Jihadists have communicated ceaselessly but have done so through alternative channels, from sympathetic imams and veterans of the Afghan jihad scattered across the globe to new media such as Al-Jazeera in its early days, and the ubiquitous websites that modern technology allows (Lynch 2006). Very little of that noise crosses over outside a sympathetic ghetto, and jihadists have never gained direct access to global audiences. For the average Western observer, information available about the motivations of jihadists has been filtered several times over by pundits and talking heads and is biased toward the egregious, such as the calls to establish a global Islamic caliphate.

The nauseating brutality of jihadist violence, from the suicide bombings in crowded areas to the snuff videos of beheadings, seems to justify the lack of interest in the jihadists' signals. After all, why listen to bloodthirsty criminals? But indifference to their motivations obviates the need to understand what made them so violent in the first place. Jihad came into its own in Egypt in the 1970s, in Afghanistan in the 1980s, and around the same time in Israeli-occupied Lebanon and Palestine. During these formative years, much of the dialogue with Islamist activists and terrorists took place in interrogation chambers. Israeli counterterrorism got into trouble with its Supreme Court over the use of torture and sometimes outsourced interrogations to Lebanese employees in Khiyam prison in Southern Lebanon. Another infamous prison, Pul-i-Charkhi, in Kabul, was the scene of countless atrocities during the Soviet adventure in Afghanistan. The famous video of a young Ayman al-Zawahiri denouncing his torturers at his 1981 Cairo trial is a highlight of jihadist lore. The American rendition program for cases involving terrorism, to send captives for interrogation in countries with loose restrictions, was started under the Clinton administration (Mayer 2005). Indian security forces in Kashmir could use any method of interrogation with impunity, as did their Algerian and Egyptian counterparts. The geography of global jihad reads like an Amnesty International report about prisons that produced not great inspirational heroes such as Gandhi or Mandela but broken, vengeful men.

History had made countless other broken men. Public figures like Gandhi and Mandela could escape brutal treatment, making their lifelong ordeal a rallying cry until history made good on the legitimate rights of their people. But repression had been far worse on anonymous militants. To control insurgencies, colonial administrations pioneered mass internment and commonly tortured and executed rebels. Communists were hunted down, tortured, and massacred on countless occasions. Soviets tortured their prisoners, as did the Nazis, who also exterminated entire villages in retaliation for terrorist attacks, as in Lidice and Oradour-sur-Glane.

Conversely, irregular combatants, exposed to formidable risks, were capable of terrible violence. Partisans, from Spanish Republicans to Algerian nationalists, massacred civilian populations on a scale that exceeds the violence of today's jihadists. The Khmer Rouge purged its own population of whoever was tainted by collaboration with the foreign power. Extreme lethality is not an innovation of the past twenty years, but what shocks us about jihadist violence is that it has forced itself onto the imagination of Western societies that have become both exceptionally tame and wholly oblivious of their own violent history.

It is within that framework that we can most usefully study the activity of contemporary terrorists. It is in those cases where identity alienation is not complete, where terrorists somehow remain tethered to the society in which they operate, that they do show restraint. Restraint is a matter not just of morality but of strategy. In a somewhat open society, communiqués and public trials and the social and political work of sister organizations that operate aboveground compel terrorists to calibrate their action or lose all connection to the society they aim to influence. Terrorism is communication, each attack a statement. Harsh repression limits the dialogue of terrorism and counterterrorism to one register only: that of violence.

Jihadists may love death, as they often proclaim, but they may not be keen on pain. The younger generation of jihadists has not suffered pain. The angst of being an immigrant in London or Paris, ostracized because of skin and creed, does not quite amount to pain. Young recruits from Yemen and Saudi Arabia may be economically and culturally disoriented, but they have not endured pain. For that generation, lured by a subculture of relevance through martyrdom, it is better to go out in a flash, with as many others as possible, than to risk torture in a local prison, and a life sentence in the crushing isolation of an American penitentiary. Marwan Barghouti may one day leave Israeli jails to lead his people, but it is known to all that top al-Qaeda operatives such as Ramzi Yousef and Khalid Sheikh Mohammed have been swallowed whole by the American penal administration, never to resurface. Not even their trials could be used as meaningful political statements.

Terrorism is a dead end. There is no political calculation, no quid pro quo—only self-expression through the mechanics of the explosive device. Harsh punishments have eliminated incentives for restraint by terrorists who do not think politically, because there is no political process. Instead, they come to terms with an unenviable and mostly unavoidable fate by drifting toward ever more brutal and suicidal methods.

The empirical correlation between the inevitability of a terminal form of punishment (torture, death, lifelong imprisonment) and the intensity of terrorist violence does not demonstrate causality. One can plausibly argue that harsher repression came as a necessary consequence of the greater radicalism of modern terrorists. And there are cases that seem to point to sui generis brutality: the Taliban in its prime and al-Shabaab in Somalia had little repression to fear in the failed states where they came into being. But those outfits were not terrorists by any margin; they were parastates bent on establishing control over a population. Their violence came from a different place, akin to state terror.

The opposite causality, on the other hand, suggests a way out of the cycle of escalation. Today's suicide bombers may appear impervious to restraint when, in fact, their kind may have been driven to lethal suicide attacks by the very absence of alternative channels for interacting with their adversary. Communication, engagement, negotiations, whatever format they may follow and regardless of their ultimate objective, present an opportunity to steer the dialogue of deeds away from lethality and gore. This is the essence of counterinsurgency and deradicalization programs. The alternative is for governments, trapped by their own commitment never to negotiate with or engage their adversaries, to be at a loss to find an effective response to the ever more brutal violence. The caveat is that the situation may not be easily reversed: norms have changed over the past four decades as the result of an incremental and mostly unconscious process. They will not be rewritten overnight.

The Route to Communication

Terrorism is often considered the poor man's version of state terror, strategically aiming to terrorize a population into compliance. But the kind of mass terror that would seize a populace and corral it, herdlike, toward surrender is the preserve of states. Empirically, terrorism never forced populations to do anything out of fear unless a complete breakdown of order compelled people to emigrate en masse—for instance, in the last year of the Algerian war of independence, or in Iraq a couple of years into the U.S. occupation. As long as states hold, terrorism is hardly more than a nuisance, with low statistical lethality, encountered primarily through media reports (Jenkins 2006). Nationalist movements gained independence because their colonial masters feared for their treasury (and reelection), not for their lives.

The psychological impact of terrorism resides not in the terror it imposes but in other distinctive effects. An obvious one is that a successful attack alerts a larger segment of the population to the existence of a particular issue, usually evoked in a communiqué when someone claims responsibility for the operation. Another effect is that certain kinds of operations have the potential of mobilizing along identity lines. The element of deliberate human agency—the intentionality—evokes predation and elicits mobbing responses deep-seated in the human psyche, mobilizing the target community against the community the terrorists claim to represent. This phenomenon puts immediate pressure on the state because it reframes the incident from a mere lapse in law enforcement to a more warlike context.

The sovereignty of the state and the legitimacy that comes from providing security are best measured by the job performance of those in charge of public order, from heads of state down the law enforcement chain of command. Each successful terrorist operation affects the legitimacy of the state because it signals the professional failure of its civil servants. Revulsion over an attack translates into anger against the state. Just as 9/11 rallied the American people around a leader reborn as a war president, a parliamentary commission sought to establish responsibility for what had happened. In essence, the United States government owned up to the failure that allowed 9/11 to happen, in order to redraft a social contract around the global war on terror. Terrorists were denied initiative; the opportunity to strike had been given them by a dysfunctional bureaucracy (National Commission on Terrorist Attacks 2004).

The reaction to terrorism tends to be driven by those who have the most at stake personally, and those are not the potential victims within the civilian population but those in charge of public security. To maintain legitimacy in the position they occupy, they have to prevent future terrorist operations and, in accordance with the law, repair past attacks by capturing and punishing perpetrators. The more difficult that task, the more intense their frustration/anger/aggression response will be, taking counterterrorism up the path of escalation.

States confronted with a limited challenge to their authority—for instance, the occupation of public offices or a university—will often temporize, look for accommodation. But there is a threshold of provocation beyond which sedition becomes terrorism, forcing the state to step up the repressive machine. What differentiates activists from terrorists is that the latter aim to cross that threshold, using violence as bait to initiate a cycle of repression and popular reaction, until violence is profoundly entrenched and the conflict has become self-feeding.

In most cases, the state retains the initiative. Some governments may seek to balance repression with a political process. Others will proclaim their determination to extirpate the scourge of terrorism, with public assurances that they will never surrender, will never negotiate—and setting the stage for an all-out, zero-sum confrontation. The paradox remains that in all but a few cases, at some point down the road, both parties will enter into some form of negotiation. So there are powerful reasons to engage terrorists as soon as possible, avoiding the phase of escalation.

There are also powerful reasons *not* to engage. Negotiations can be a concession of legitimacy and, in some cases, a first step toward a transfer of sovereignty. Sovereignty is not limited to independence in a secessionist conflict; it is also about political rights. The civil rights movement in the United States used civil disobedience and, occasionally, violence to achieve a more equal distribution of sovereignty between black and white citizens. Contentious politics always involve discussions about sovereignty, and with such high stakes, states are legitimately reluctant to open channels of communication too soon and unduly reward intimidation. But there is a fundamental difference between a permanent, unalterable no-negotiation paradigm and a no-negotiation phase that allows time to test the staying power of contestation and to fathom the depth of the sociopolitical demands being pushed forward by activists and terrorists.

Cognitively, closing the dialogue with terrorists—including restricting their access to the space of public discourse, such as mass media—helps prolong all forms of denial about the claims they make. But only for a while. If the terrorists have staying power—and they would be hard put to sustain their operations without being the torchbearers of an issue that resonates with a popular base—their claims will eventually force their way into the broader consciousness. This is how a majority in Israel came to be the champion of Palestinian statehood (in principle) and how the United States was sensitized to problems of governance and development in Muslim countries and to the more direct issue of the footprint of pax Americana in the Middle East.

Once the state and its constituents have acknowledged, in some form, the validity of those claims from the opposition, there are no more reasons to postpone negotiating. In fact, opening negotiations is the recognition de jure of a political reality established de facto by the opposition's ability to sustain a political challenge over time, through terrorism or other means.

The transition from a no-negotiation stance to a phase of dialogue is fraught with peril for governments (Harmon, Pratt, and Gorka 2010, 176; Art and Waltz 2009, 515). Policy reversals cost political credibility, although good spin and a change in government can facilitate the shift. More problematically, the government could lose the support of the counterterrorist personnel, who may feel betrayed by the reversal. The risk is particularly acute when the military has been at the forefront of the counterterrorist effort. This was the case in France in 1961, when elements of the military attempted a coup against President de Gaulle, who was then negotiating with the Algerian FLN. Civilian (and particularly Islamist) Turkish governments have had to tread carefully over the Kurdish issue—a very sensitive one for the military, which has been on the front line against the Kurdistan Workers' Party since the 1980s.

Also, segments of the population can turn against the regime. This was the case with the Organization of the Secret Army, a group of hard-liner European colonists who turned to terrorism to oppose Algerian independence; and also with religious Zionist organizations opposed to the Oslo Accords between Israel and the PLO. De Gaulle escaped assassination attempts in 1961 and 1962 (Crenshaw 1995, 505). Israeli prime minister and Nobel Prize winner Yitzhak Rabin, assassinated in 1995, was less fortunate. For most states but especially for democracies, the decision to open negotiations, and the substance of those negotiations, ought to be broadly accepted by the populace. Sometimes that acceptance will need to be confirmed in a referendum on a peace accord. But over time, no-negotiation stances build up resistance within the state's constituents, which limits the state's freedom. Leaders then have to consume political capital to legitimize a policy shift of considerable magnitude, or show extraordinary skills at obfuscation. The shift that occurred in Iraq after 2005, with the formation of Sunni awakening movements, was facilitated by the 2008 economic collapse. A distracted U.S. public never quite understood how yesterday's insurgents wound up on the U.S. payroll.

States can mitigate the risk of popular backlash by engaging in implicit rather than explicit negotiations. The value of back-channel negotiations, sometimes carried out through third parties such as the Red Cross, Sant'Egidio, and diplomats of neutral countries, is that they remain deniable. The theme of the classic spy novel *Agents of Innocence* is a widely reported nonaggression arrangement in the 1970s, between the CIA Beirut station and the PLO's Ali Hassan Salameh, at a time when the United States officially refused to recognize that organization (Ignatius 2001).

States can also use gradual repression to establish implicit rules of engagement with terrorist organizations. Restrained attacks are met with restrained repression, which is stepped up only if terrorists cross thresholds that may not even be explicit but can be learned through experimentation. Such a dynamic seems to have prevailed between Hezbollah and Israel in the 1990s. In 1993 and 1996, the Israeli Defense Forces conducted two intensive aerial campaigns against Shia populations, to deter Hezbollah's rocket and mortar attacks against civilian populations in Israel. By July 1996, an Israeli-Lebanese Monitoring Group was created to monitor a cease-fire agreement that aimed to prevent attacks against civilians. Hezbollah would never cease to harass Israeli and South Lebanese Army—a Lebanese unit employed by Israel—forces in south Lebanon, but it would mostly desist from attacking civilians in Israel proper. Conversely, the Israeli response remained mostly limited to noncivilian objectives. When Israel evacuated south Lebanon in 2000, Hezbollah was left short of targets and had to reinvent a new mission for itself: the liberation of a few farms stranded on the wrong side of the border. But the broad principles of the arrangement remained in place until the events of summer 2006, when the Israeli army reentered south Lebanon and bombed Beirut following the abduction of two soldiers.

Those tit-for-tat, live-and-let-live arrangements are not limited to conflicts across international borders. Many conflicts between states and domestic terrorists have been through periods of truce, explicit or implicit. While those phases often end up in acrimony, with one party blaming the other for using the cessation of violence to rearm, they show that mutual understandings are possible. The existence of aboveground operations related to the combat organization (e.g., a political party, a trade union, social services) can facilitate this process, because the state can influence the modus operandi of terrorists by using gradual repression against those structures when attacks deviate from a tolerable norm. While such an accommodation is never foolproof, empirical evidence confirms that terrorists respond to incentives. In Northern Ireland, the relationship between loyalists and nationalists was fraught with tension as bridges were cut between the two communities. By contrast, a system of signals with the UK government allowed the PIRA to pursue its communication and manipulation campaign while avoiding the negative side effects caused by civilian casualties. In response, the UK government never sought to eradicate Sinn Fein. Moderation on the front of violence allowed the nationalists and the British to pursue on-again, off-again talks without too much outcry from their respective popular bases. Similarly, Israel waited until the intensity of Palestinian suicide bombings reached intolerable levels in 2003–04 to send a strong signal by assassinating Hamas's leadership. Leaving aside the question of proportionality and civilian victims, Operation Cast Lead of January 2009 in Gaza aimed not to destroy Hamas but to modify its behavior by damaging its noncombatant infrastructure.

Shutting down all structures associated with a terrorist movement exposes the state to losing all leverage over the militants. Spain's premier Aznar banned the Basque nationalist party Batasuna in 2002–03, along with other organizations associated with ETA. While effective police work in France weakened ETA during that period, the political situation festered in Spain. When Aznar's socialist successor looked for ways to restart a process of negotiation, he faced a more elusive and temperamental ETA. The history of the young Spanish democracy illustrates the political cost of ill-conceived counterterrorist policies. The first socialist era, in the 1980s,

was tainted by the scandal of anti-ETA death squads, and the Nationalist government that followed was discredited for rushing to attribute—
wrongly—the 2004 multiple attacks on the Madrid mass transit system
to ETA.

The next step after back-channel and implicit negotiations is to enter
into limited negotiations that do not seek to resolve the conflict but aim
to deal with practical issues, particularly the conditions of internment of
captive members of terrorist organizations. For example, the Oslo Accords
and subsequent agreements were limited to matters ranging from political
prisoners to local administration, while deliberately avoiding "final status"
questions.

In this kind of conflict, prisoners have always posed a challenge for
states. At worst, they motivate serial abductions or barricaded-hostage
crises, perpetrated in order to trade hostages for prisoners. Also, famous
prisoners can become martyrs—living symbols of hegemonic oppression.
And conditions of detention can be politically exploited. While a "political" designation elevates prisoners to the rank of combatants and is a
confession of gaps in the state's legitimacy, a "criminal" status may fuel
the hostility of the terrorists' potential support base. Hardship imposed
on relatives of prisoners as a result of detention policies—especially when
those relatives are respected or vulnerable members of their community—is
widely resented. The Spanish government policy to detain ETA members
far away from Basque provinces, often in overseas dominions, has been
a propaganda tool for the organization. The 1981 group hunger strike to
obtain from the Thatcher government political status for IRA prisoners
got Bobby Sands elected to Westminster and brought great publicity to
the republican cause. The "unlawful combatant" designation created by the
Bush administration to remove prisoners from national and international
law turned out politically onerous.

Concessions on the extent of repression and on the status of prisoners
are small steps for which the state can negotiate restraints to violence. No
breakthrough is likely to emerge from those accommodations, and resolution of the conflict is no closer. But arrangements of that sort help prevent
the erosion of moral norms that accompany an intense, no-limit conflict,
and ultimately keep the body count down. Decades-long terrorist insurgencies in states that are somewhat bound by the rule of law and open to some
form of compromise exact casualty tolls in the hundreds to low thousands
(e.g., in Northern Ireland, Spain, Israel). Moreover, populations on all sides
of the conflict tend to tire of violence, even though violence was never carried out on a large scale. Unbound repression may bring a quick (though
perhaps temporary) end to a conflict, but the human toll is generally in the

hundreds of thousands (Algeria, Chechnya, Egypt, Kashmir, Afghanistan, Iraq), and the societal tolerance for violence, while difficult to measure directly, seems considerably amplified rather than reduced. It is also apparent from this list that the states that are able to limit the intensity of violence are the strongest ones, with a developed rule of law. Only a strong state is in a position to determine the condition of internment in its prisons, or the conditions under which trade unions and political parties sympathetic to the violent opposition can operate in its sovereign territory.

Resolution: Transforming the Adversaries

Terrorists do not simply demand a space to exist, and magnanimous treatment when captured. Generally, they demand elements of sovereignty for their support base: economic rights, voting rights, all the way to the right of self-determination. The accession to those rights necessitates a more or less profound reformulation of national identity within the state the terrorists oppose. Hegemonic groups that most closely identify with the status quo have displayed formidable psychological resistance to change in the face of social protest, whether the cause is decolonization, desegregation, counternationalism, or wealth redistribution. The violence of counterterrorism is in part the outward, kinetic manifestation of an internal struggle to maintain a satisfying social identity in changing times—just as the violence of terrorism is an attempt to challenge the status quo and enfranchise a dominated identity. Closure will be achieved only when both parties have redefined their self-concept in ways that are both internally acceptable and externally compatible. What will it mean to be British if the empire is lost? What kind of superpower is the United States if it cannot bring insurgents to heel? What does it mean to be "white" in a desegregated society? What does it mean to be Christian—or Muslim—in a secular society? How can the Zionist narrative of victimization and redemption survive the recognition that Palestinians, too, have been despoiled? How can Palestinian identity define itself other than as a combatant identity engaged in an existential struggle with Zionism?

Psychological evolution faces built-in resistance as humans seek to adapt reality to their mind-sets before adapting themselves to reality. Empirically, it takes several years—sometimes decades—of sustained violence before parties can finally form new, mutually compatible, peaceful roles. In this transition, communication in a unified, public field is essential, because it is from that communication that a narrative emerges around which adversaries can reformulate their identity. The British Commonwealth was the new narrative that replaced the British Empire. The "two states" solution for

Israelis and Palestinians is, for now, just that: a narrative. It is an arbitrary model and certainly not the best by many measures, but at least it provides a vision, a core around which new, pacified identities could crystallize. At first, communication does not need to be direct for the narrative to emerge. Terrorists issue communiqués, states respond with counterstatements, and neutral third parties (the international community) echo and amplify this dialogue, giving it depth and substance. Over time, as the psychological process of adjustment and redefinition takes place, some form of convergence in the disparate threads of narrative should become perceptible. Al-Qaeda and the United States, despite their professed and deep-seated enmity, have both sent messages to the effect that Islam and the West should be able to live in peace and that the West should not have a permanent military presence in Muslim countries.

Actual negotiations between adversaries can improve the coherence of a unified narrative, but they should never preempt by much the speed of the psychological adjustment taking place within the consciousness of the populations. For the state, committing to a negotiation process with terrorists is not committing to an outcome. On the contrary, negotiations should not try to rush to closure—or even try to achieve a significant breakthrough. At best, leadership and dialogue guide and slightly accelerate the pace of history that has to run its course.

Sometimes the object of negotiation becomes no more ambitious than to keep dialogue alive, with the content narrowing to minor matters that seem easiest to resolve—or even to the format of negotiations. In the case of the Israeli-Palestinian peace process, the frustratingly slow pace and limited progress of this approach seemed to vindicate the advocates of radical solutions. Postmortems of that epoch have blamed the shortcomings and duplicity of the parties, but the second intifada could just as well have been the inevitable outcome of the flawed concept of too-incremental negotiations (Ross 2004; Finkelstein 2007). Violence erupted immediately after the breakdown of the most serious attempt to reach a settlement, at Camp David in the summer of 2000. What this reveals is that the various phases of negotiations in the preceding years, as futile and obsessed with minor details as they were, were too oblique to help both populations form a mutually compatible image of what a settlement would look like. Camp David 2000 was a case of going too fast.

Impatience carries the risk that dialogue will be discarded altogether. Negotiations—or, rather, the dialogue around them—are crucial for the parties to keep a footing in reality. Breakdown of the dialogue essentially frees populations to formulate their identity in opposition to each other and embrace exterminationist fantasies. In defense of the peace process, it achieved little but was better than what came after, with Palestinians attempting to break Israeli will via waves of suicide bombings, and Israelis walling off whole Palestinian communities. The death toll subsided, but the impasse remained. Unless one party has both the military and the political wherewithal to actually implement the extermination—through intimidation, assimilation, or even literally through physical extermination—those fanciful detours build rancor and may take adversaries further away from closure.

The Northern Irish conflict exemplifies the grounding effect of dialogue. Progress has been painfully slow—it stretched over two decades—and was marred by outbreaks of violence (Coogan 2001). But from the early 1980s onward, violence was only an accessory to the political solution in gestation (Hennessey 2001). Dialogue had escaped the confines of the nationalist and unionist adversaries: the UK and then Ireland and the United States got involved, contributing to shape a realistic way out of the Troubles. Those states had material leverage over the belligerents, but, just as important, they had moral leverage, expressed through the formulation of a shared vision. The realist streak imposed itself through a unified field of dialogue. *Linguistic intractability*

Maintaining a unified field of dialogue at all times is crucial for the perceptions of everyone to converge on a single model for a future social contract, for future arrangements. As progress is being made on that front, the state may start to negotiate an end to violence with the terrorist structure. The state has different options. First, it may wish to negotiate explicitly or implicitly, as discussed above. Also, states can negotiate from the top down or from the bottom up. Top-down negotiations can be preferred for traditional hierarchical organizations, where the command-and-control structure remains effective and the base is likely to follow the leadership.

A condition to top-down negotiations is quality intelligence about the structure and leadership of the organization—the internal rivalries, the relative legitimacy of various leaders, their respective goals, the solidity of command-and-control lines, and the popular legitimacy of the organization. Top-down negotiations will very likely create lost commands: operational groups, resenting political compromise, will splinter from the mainstream organization and initiate attacks to spoil the negotiations. The Real IRA's 1998 bombing in Omagh, for instance, was a reaction against the decommissioning program agreed upon in the Good Friday Agreement, as Donohue and Cristal have discussed in chapter 2. States have a proclivity for failing to distinguish between spoilers and partners in peace committed to a political solution; and all the while, the partners in peace run the risk of being delegitimized to the popular base. Arafat's predicament during the second intifada is a case in point. On one hand, Israel accused him of being duplicitous with the violence, and on the other, Hamas and junior Fatah members denounced him for selling out the cause of Palestinian nationalism. Israel had overestimated Arafat's legitimacy with the Palestinians: his personal credentials were not enough to counterbalance the magnitude of the sacrifice they felt they had to make for peace.

The absence of an effective command structure makes top-down negotiations difficult—a situation the United States encountered in failed states from Somalia to Afghanistan and, at one time, Iraq. But counterterrorism plays a part in creating circumstances adverse to top-down negotiations. A side effect of intense repression has been the transformation of organizations from hierarchical to networked, because established lines of command are too vulnerable to counterterrorism. Much has been made of the networked structure of al-Qaeda and affiliated jihadist groups (Sageman 2004). It is because those groups never developed adequate protection that they were forced to operate as loose networks. Israel's attempt, with the peace process, to reinforce the command structure of the PLO at the expense of Hamas only fragmented further the systems of authority within the Palestinian population—a fragmentation that would manifest in 2007, with Hamas taking over Gaza. The irony is that the PLO was weak because it had been thoroughly defeated by Israel between 1970 and 1985.

Other terrorist campaigns had been undertaken by movements that resembled the networked more than the hierarchical structure. The anarchists who carried out a wave of political assassinations at the turn of the twentieth century were isolated individuals inspired by a common ideology. The left-wing groups, such as the Weather Underground, that blossomed in Western democracies in the 1970s had a similar structure. While those groups had well-known historical founders and leaders, the lack of a sanctuary, combined with permanent police pressure, meant they could exist only as a network of underground, autonomous cells or communes of local sympathizers. Their structure existed only on paper, making them more susceptible to a bottom-up approach.

The point is illustrated by the case of the Italian Brigate Rosse. Allegedly the most developed leftist terrorist group operating in the West in the 1970s, it was easily defeated by a combination of effective, targeted counterterrorism—broadly respectful of democratic principles as they applied in Italy at the time—and bottom-up negotiations (della Porta 1995a). The Italian government initiated a partial amnesty program, offering lenient sentencing to recanters (*pentiti,* in popular parlance, most of whom were sympathizers who had not committed serious crimes) in return for cooperation and the public renunciation of armed struggle, in widely broadcast trials.

Bottom-up

The main advantage of the bottom-up approach is that defectors have access that states will never have, and are the best vehicle to reach out to active members in the terrorist organization (Jenkins 2006). Defectors are legitimized by their credentials as former members, and historical or high-profile defectors can be most influential. They provide a counternarrative that grows louder with each new defection and can eventually overwhelm the belligerent line, cutting radicals from their popular base. Whereas an elimination campaign does little to affect the dominant narrative and targets only dispensable personnel—even historical, charismatic leaders can be replaced—a delegitimization campaign changes the nature of the narrative and undermines the very act of armed struggle. It is the difference between making radicals into martyrs and making them obsolete.

To be effective, a bottom-up approach requires several conditions. First, people come to armed struggle with different motivations, and a key to successful rehabilitation is to provide individualized options for a way out of the pattern of violent behavior (Bjørgo and Horgan 2009). Second, those who renounce armed struggle should be protected from accusations of treason or selling out; thus, such loaded terms as "defector" should be avoided. Former members should not be required to betray their onetime comrades in arms or publicly embrace the policies of the state. Their discourse should simply be that armed struggle is not the optimal way to achieve the goals they remain committed to. María Dolores Catarain, "Yoyes," a former member of the ETA-militar executive committee, became disillusioned with armed struggle and returned to Spain under a reinsertion (amnesty) program. She came to symbolize a new era in which a political solution was possible. A threat for hard-liners in ETA-militar, she was falsely accused of turning informant, and killed in 1986 (Ibarra Güell 1987). The truth is that states' best assets have always been insiders. From infiltrated double agents to paid defectors to mere collaborators in a negotiated solution, insiders are the key to successful CT programs.

To move from CT to final resolution, the state has to open up non-violent (i.e., democratic) channels for the opposition to pursue its objectives. In Italy, the 1983 formation of the first socialist government broke the Christian Democrats' monopoly on power since World War II, taking wind out of the sails of the revolutionary left. Genuine reforms to redress issues that had fueled the movement of contestation in the first place will mollify the opposition and increase the credibility and legitimacy of those who renounce armed struggle.

In Jordan, militantism was vastly reduced by political openings, and amnesty programs have been mostly successful (Tal 2005, 220–21). Those who persisted with violence did so by personal inclination: Jordanian Abu

[handwritten margin notes: "→ NOT his brutality", "Have to give defectors a way out"]

Musab al-Zarqawi found fertile terrain for armed insurgency in Iraq, but the multiple hotel bombing he orchestrated in Amman in November 2005 was found abhorrent by the vast majority of the population, and his own tribe repudiated him. Jordan had no room for men like him. Amnesty programs in Algeria and Egypt have gotten many militants to renounce armed struggle, but underlying issues of political participation and economic justice have not been resolved (Volpi 2003, 74–82). Violence returned to Algeria in 2006 after a decade of relative peace, and incidents have occurred in Egypt since 2004.

Amnesty without political opening brings a temporary reprieve to an exhausted generation of fighters without fundamentally resolving the root cause of protest. If the populace sees no alternative to political violence in pursuing its cause or rights, defectors will be written off as losers or traitors until a new generation picks up the struggle. The historical leadership of Fatah faces that predicament, since its main legitimacy now seems to derive from international aid that pays for patronage—and even that is not much.

The question of political opening is particularly challenging for the United States in relation to its nonstate foreign opponents. The United States is a global hegemon, whose foreign policy affects populations across the globe. And while the United States is internally a democracy, it also holds itself to be absolutely sovereign in its foreign policy, unaccountable to global public opinion. This skirts the question whether a hegemonic democracy should somehow be responsive to the preferences of foreign populations affected by its policies—populations whose own repressive polity often prevents them from expressing themselves. The point is easy to illustrate. If an oil-exporting country is a democracy, its population may, through legitimate representatives, decide it will not sell oil to the United States, because it disapproves of a particular U.S. policy. If that same country is an autocracy whose security is guaranteed by the United States (either directly or through arms sales), it may appear to the people that their country's policies—such as the price at which it sells oil, or the weapon systems it buys from the United States—are imposed from abroad. This argument has been made extensively by Bin Laden, not without success among the Muslim radical fringe.

This dilemma has been obliquely acknowledged by recent American "public diplomacy" efforts, aimed to better "sell" American policies to the world, combined with efforts to spread democracy abroad in response to the jihadist challenge and to growing anti-Americanism. The ultimate question is the extent to which the United States will have to adjust its foreign policy in order to delegitimize terrorism directed against it (Scheuer 2004).

Promoting democracy presents its own risks. Washington's embarrassment following the 2006 electoral victory of Hamas exposed the intensity of the dilemma.

Another limitation of the bottom-up approach is that it is rarely compatible with top-down negotiations. Bottom-up negotiations have an effect similar to harsh counterterrorism: they erode the cohesion of the organization and undermine its structure of authority. While this can effectively reduce the number of active militants and, therefore, the scale of violence, it may leave behind pockets of hard-liners. The puzzling durability of a hardcore ETA-militar can be explained in part by the lack of central control within the Basque revolutionary movement at the time when the newly democratic Spanish government conceded autonomy to Basque provinces and allowed the reinsertion of former ETA members into civil society.

In extreme cases, successful policies against militant groups may leave the state facing a populace no longer controlled by the opposition structure—the terrorist organization or the political parties or religious organizations attached to it—resulting in chaos and civil war. Israel, for instance, was never quite able to calibrate how much to build up or undermine the autonomous authority of the PLO/Palestinian Authority. By shifting back and forth between top-down and bottom-up approaches, between repression and negotiation, Israeli policies amplified the intractability of the conflict. And by 2010, it appears that Hamas plays a positive structuring role in Gaza, inhibiting the rise of more radical, transnational forms of militant Islamism (Filiu 2009). Similarly, the Taliban became an amorphous, far more intractable adversary after it split into numerous local commands following the 2001 U.S.-led invasion of Afghanistan.

Whether bottom-up or top-down, negotiation programs should consider that the popular base will not automatically fall into place and that it is essential to design functional, democratic political institutions (e.g., parties, unions) to organize the population. For example, in 2003, the French government endeavored to reduce the appeal of radical Islamist currents by setting up a French Council of the Muslim Faith, an interlocutor with the state, to which French Muslims can elect delegates. In this respect, conflicts about limited sovereignty—about political rights—are more likely than conflicts about full sovereignty to deliver improvements in political participation. Those terrorist organizations that become sovereign are not automatically the matrix for democratic life and vibrant civil society. Topdown negotiations toward secession have often brought autocracy along with independence. The Vietminh in Vietnam, the FLN in Algeria, the ANC in South Africa, and the PLO in the West Bank have tended to monopolize power in the new polity. Sometimes terrorism in opposition morphs into state terror once the militants are in power: it is a matter of being accustomed to using violence for political ends. Peace brings its own challenges.

Conclusion: The Wastefulness of the Conflict Cycle

Political radicalism often crystallizes at a particular historical juncture—a popular demonstration turned bloody, a political assassination, or a foreign invasion—attracting droves of (mostly young) militants to armed struggle. Conflict will run its course from there, tracing its own idiosyncratic path that will profoundly influence the life cycle of political radicalism. Restrained, well-targeted police work combined with fair and lenient penalties, followed up with political openings and rehabilitation programs, is most likely to cut the wind of revolutionary passions. Rather than embark on a futile attempt to exterminate terrorists and terrorism, states would be better advised to negotiate the prompt reentry of sympathizers and militants into the social contract. They have many routes to do this: official or not, unilateral if necessary, top-down or bottom-up.

The reduction of radicalism is possible only with a reformed social contract, one that co-opts some of the social issues that inspired the protest, and that delegitimizes violence. Contrary to the knee-jerk reaction of most governments, the answer to terrorism is not emergency law but the strengthening of the rule of law, not less democratic consultation but more democracy. The state, and the elite groups that are its satellites, will have to make concessions in the way of rights claimed by the terrorists and their support base. Sometimes it is a material affair: moneys or lands or jobs have to be made available. But often the sacrifice is psychological. It is about reformulating one's sense of identity in the abstract; it is about shifting boundaries that were never more than mental representations but are nonetheless dear to those who hold them. The irony is that by the time the state has completed this mental work, it will often have forgotten that the reforms it now pursues in the name of fighting terrorism are generally those reforms put on the agenda by the terrorists. Once, a fledgling al-Qaeda demanded that U.S. personnel leave the sacred land of Saudi Arabia. Eventually, it managed to provoke the United States into a war that raged long after most U.S. personnel had redeployed outside the Saudi kingdom.

Is there value in considering the demands of terrorists? Should states rush to the negotiating table at or even before the first explosion? History has directionality. It is this directionality that generally—not always but almost—determines the outcome of conflict between states and terrorists, and it is this directionality that should inform realistic objectives for a negotiation process. If the sense of history is statehood for a given people, it is a waste of time not to have an open discussion about that, even if the national liberation movement of the people is a terrorist organization. How can one make that determination in foresight? Reading the course of history, rather than wasting resources trying to change it, is the essence of good leadership.

That said, some states and their leaders, sometimes, have a shot at changing the natural course of history. Sinicization may terminate the centuries-old, distinctive political and cultural experiences of Tibet and Xinjiang. Morocco may similarly assimilate the Sahrawi people. Kurds and Pashtuns may never be able to realize their national aspirations. But no one should be surprised that making that kind of history will come at the cost of contentious politics, violence, and terrorism for several generations.

References

Art, Robert, and Kenneth Waltz, eds. 2009. *The Use of Force: Military Power and International Politics*. Lanham, MD: Rowan and Littlefield.

Bjørgo, Tore, and John Horgan, eds. 2009. *Leaving Terrorism Behind: Disengagement from Political Violence*. New York: Routledge.

Black, Ian, and Benny Morris. 1991. *Israel's Secret Wars: The Untold History of Israeli Intelligence*. New York: Grove Weidenfeld.

Boucek, Christopher. 2008. "Saudi Arabia's 'Soft' Counterterrorism Strategy: Prevention, Rehabilitation, and Aftercare." Carnegie Papers. Carnegie Endowment for International Peace. www.carnegieendowment.org/publications/?fa=view&id=22155 (accessed Oct. 1, 2010).

Chaliand, Gérard, and Arnaud Blin. 2007. *The History of Terrorism: From Antiquity to al Qaeda*. Berkeley and Los Angeles: University of California Press.

Commonwealth Human Rights Initiative. 2007. "Stamping Out Rights: The Impact of Anti-Terrorism Laws on Policing." CHRI Report. www.human rightsinitiative.org/publications/chogm/chogm_2007/chogm_report_2007.pdf (accessed Oct. 22, 2010).

Coogan, Tim Pat. 2001. *The Troubles: Ireland's Ordeal and the Search for Peace*. New York: Palgrave.

Coolsaet, Rik. 2008. *Jihadi Terrorism and the Radicalisation Challenge in Europe*. Burlington, VT: Ashgate.

Crenshaw, Martha. 1978. *Revolutionary Terrorism: The FLN in Algeria, 1954–1962*. Stanford, CA: Hoover Institution Press.

———. 1995. "The Effectiveness of Terrorism in the Algerian War." In *Terrorism in Context*, ed. Martha Crenshaw. University Park: Pennsylvania State University Press.

Currey, Cecil B. 1997. *Victory at Any Cost: The Genius of Viet Nam's Gen. Vo Nguyen Giap.* Washington, DC: Brassey's.

della Porta, Donatella. 1995a. "Left-Wing Terrorism in Italy." In *Terrorism in Context,* ed. Martha Crenshaw. University Park: Pennsylvania State University Press.

———. 1995b. *Social Movements, Political Violence, and the State: A Comparative Analysis of Italy and Germany.* Cambridge: Cambridge University Press.

Ensalaco, Mark. 2008. *Middle Eastern Terrorism: From Black September to September 11.* Philadelphia: University of Pennsylvania Press.

Filiu, Jean-Pierre. 2009. "The Brotherhood vs. Al-Qaeda: A Moment Of Truth?" *Current Trends in Islamist Ideology* 9 (Nov. 12). www.currenttrends.org/research/detail/the-brotherhood-vs-al-qaeda-a-moment-of-truth (accessed Oct. 23, 2010).

Finkelstein, Norman G. 2007. "The Camp David II Negotiations: How Dennis Ross Proved the Palestinians Aborted the Peace Process." *Journal of Palestine Studies* 36 (2).

Gonzalez-Perez, Margaret. 2008. *Women and Terrorism: Female Activity in Domestic and International Terror Groups.* New York: Routledge.

Harmon, Christopher, Andrew Pratt, and Sebastian Gorka. 2010. *Toward a Grand Strategy against Terrorism.* New York: McGraw-Hill.

Hennessey, Thomas. 2001. *The Northern Ireland Peace Process: Ending the Troubles.* New York: Palgrave.

Horne, Alistair. 1978. *A Savage War of Peace: Algeria 1954–1962.* New York: Viking.

Ibarra Güell, Pedro. 1987. "Yoyes: ética y política." *Mientras Tanto* 29 (March): 69–76.

Ignatius, David. 2001. "Penetrating Terrorist Networks." *Washington Post,* Sept. 16.

Jenkins, Brian. 2006. *Unconquerable Nation: Knowing Our Enemy, Strengthening Ourselves.* Santa Monica, CA: RAND.

Juergensmeyer, Mark. 2000. *Terror in the Mind of God: The Global Rise of Religious Violence.* Berkeley and Los Angeles: University of California Press.

Karnow, Stanley. 1991. *Vietnam: A History.* New York: Viking.

Kilcullen, David. 2009. *The Accidental Guerrilla.* New York: Oxford University Press.

LaFree, Gary, and James Hendrickson. 2007. "Build a Criminal Justice Policy for Terrorism." *Criminology and Public Policy* 6 (4): 781-90.

Lynch, Marc. 2006. "Al-Qaeda's Media Strategies." *National Interest,* March 1. http://nationalinterest.org/article/al-qaedas-media-strategies-883 (accessed Oct. 23, 2010).

Maček, Ivana. 2009. *Sarajevo under Siege: Anthropology in Wartime.* Philadelphia: University of Pennsylvania Press.

Mayer, Jane. 2005. "Outsourcing Torture: The Secret History of America's 'Extraordinary Rendition' Program." *New Yorker,* Feb. 14.

Merriman, John. 2009. *The Dynamite Club*. New York: Houghton Mifflin Harcourt.

Metzner, Jeffrey L., and Jamie Fellner. 2010. "Solitary Confinement and Mental Illness in U.S. Prisons: A Challenge for Medical Ethics." *Journal of the American Academy of Psychiatry and the Law* 38 (1).

Moghaddam, Fathali M. 2006. *From the Terrorists' Point of View: What They Experience and Why They Come to Destroy*. Westport, CT: Praeger.

Nacos, Brigitte. 2007. *Mass-Mediated Terrorism: The Central Role of the Media in Terrorism and Counterterrorism*. Lanham, MD: Rowman and Littlefield.

Nagl, John. 2005. *Learning to Eat Soup with a Knife: Counterinsurgency Lessons from Malaya and Vietnam*. Chicago: University of Chicago Press.

National Commission on Terrorist Attacks. 2004. "Final Report of the National Commission on Terrorist Attacks upon the United States" (*The 9/11 Commission Report*). www.gpoaccess.gov/911/index.html (accessed Oct. 23, 2010).

Parker, Ned, and Stephen Farrell. 2006. "British Anger at Terror Celebration." *Times*, July 20. www.timesonline.co.uk/tol/news/world/middle_east/article 690085.ece (accessed Sept. 28, 2010).

Post, Jerrold. 2006. "The Psychological Dynamics of Terrorism." In *The Roots of Terrorism*, ed. Louise Richardson. New York: Routledge.

Remak, Joachim. 1959. *Sarajevo: The Story of a Political Murder*. New York: Criterion.

Reveron, Derek S., and Jeffrey Stevenson. 2006. *Flashpoints in the War on Terrorism*. New York: Routledge.

Ross, Dennis. 2004. *The Missing Peace: The Inside Story of the Fight for Middle East Peace*. New York: Farrar, Strauss and Giroux.

Ross, Lee. 1977. "The Intuitive Psychologist and His Shortcomings: Distortions in the Attribution Process." In *Advances in Experimental Social Psychology*. Vol. 10, ed. Leonard Berkowitz, 173–220. New York: Academic Press.

Sageman, Marc. 2004. *Understanding Terror Networks*. Philadelphia: University of Pennsylvania Press.

———. 2008. *Leaderless Jihad: Terror Networks in the Twenty-first Century*. Philadelphia: University of Pennsylvania Press.

Sammakia, Nejla. 1997. "Algeria: Elections in the Shadow of Violence and Repression." *Human Rights Watch/Middle East* 9 (4).

Samraoui, Mohamed. 2003. *Chronique des années de sang*. Paris: Denoel.

Scheuer, Michael. 2004. *Imperial Hubris: Why the West Is Losing the War on Terror*. Washington, DC: Brassey's.

Sells, Michael A. 1998. *The Bridge Betrayed: Religion and Genocide in Bosnia*. Berkeley and Los Angeles: University of California Press.

Shikaki, Khalil. 2002. "Palestinian Divided." *Foreign Affairs* 81 (1).

Slama, Alain-Gérard. 1996. *La Guerre d'Algérie: Histoire d'une déchirure*. Paris: Gallimard.

Souaïdia, Habib. 2001. *La sale guerre*. Paris: La Decouverte.

Stern, Jessica. 2003. *Terror in the Name of God: Why Religious Militants Kill.* New York: HarperCollins.

Stora, Benjamin. 2004. *Algeria, 1830-2000: A Short History.* Ithaca, NY: Cornell University Press.

Stout, Christopher, ed. 2002. *The Psychology of Terrorism.* Vol. 3, *Theoretical Understandings and Perspectives.* Westport, CT: Praeger.

Summers, Harry G. 1999. *The Vietnam War Almanac.* Novato, CA: Presidio Press.

Tal, Nachman. 2005. *Radical Islam in Egypt and Jordan.* Brighton, UK: Sussex Academic Press.

Trofimov, Yaroslav. 2008. *The Siege of Mecca.* New York: Anchor.

U.S. Code. 2009a. Title 18, § 2332b. *Acts of Terrorism Transcending National Boundaries.*

U.S. Code. 2009b. Title 18, § 2339a. *Providing Material Support to Terrorists.*

U.S. Supreme Court. 2010. *Holder v. Humanitarian Law Project.* 130 U.S. 2705 (June 21, 2010).

Vidino, Lorenzo. 2005. *Al Qaeda in Europe: The New Battleground of International Jihad.* Amherst, NY: Prometheus.

Volpi, Frédéric. 2003. *Islam and Democracy: The Failure of Dialogue in Algeria.* London: Pluto Press.

Watson, William. 2003. *Tricolor and Crescent: France and the Islamic World.* Westport, CT: Greenwood.

Wike, Richard, and Brian J. Grim. 2007. "Levels of Negativity: How Muslim and Western Publics See One Another." *Public Opinion Pros,* Oct. www.public opinionpros.norc.org/features/2007/oct/wike.asp (accessed Oct. 1, 2010).

Zamoyski, Adam. 2001. *Holy Madness: Romantics, Patriots, and Revolutionaries, 1776–1871.* New York: Penguin.

7

Egypt's Gama'a Islamiya:

Change through Debate?

Carolin Goerzig

ARCA index

A fter the Egyptian government sought an alternative approach to Gama'a Islamiya, that nation's biggest threat during the 1980s and 1990s, the terrorist group eventually announced that it was unconditionally renouncing and immediately halting all acts of violence against the state. It would cease all attempts to overthrow the government and would dedicate itself to peaceful coexistence with its former enemies. This surprising development brought suspicion and criticism from all sides, and the widespread belief that the Gama'a leadership had merely bowed to severe pressure by the government. Some moderates and secularists argue that in reality, Gama'a Islamiya has not changed at all. Skeptics remain suspicious and claim that the apparent transformation from militant jihadi group to nonviolent sociopolitical organization is just a trick to get out of prison and continue working through the system toward an Islamic Egyptian state.

Islamic hard-liners and other violent jihadi groups argue that Gama'a Islamiya simply surrendered to the government and betrayed the cause. According to Hossam el-Hamalawy, an Egyptian journalist who covers militant Islamic groups, "The Gama'a's leadership is trying to steer the wheel towards moderation, while the global Islamist scene is going through radicalization" (el-Hamalawy 2003). An infuriated Ayman al-Zawahiri, al-Qaeda's second in command, published the book *Knights under the Prophet's Banner,* in which he strongly criticizes Gama'a's peace initiative, calling its leaders traitors and infidels.[1] Al-Zawahiri's effort to discredit Gama'a's religious revisions with his personal rebuttals demonstrates the importance of the revisions. Although jihadi groups follow an unwritten code of not criticizing other Islamist groups regardless of what takes place, al-Zawahiri ignores this rule (al-Zayyat 2004, 73). He strongly criticizes Gama'a's spokesperson Montasser al-Zayyat for benefiting from security privileges, such as facilitated access to high-ranking prisoners, that are not accorded even to government ministers. According to al-Zawahiri, this proves where Al-Zayyat's true loyalty rests, since he promotes the cease-fire only to serve the profiteers of the initiative.

Contrarily, Gama'a Islamiya members insist that "there was no deal with the state" (Gama'a Islamiya 2004, 15). Instead, they delegated Montasser al-Zayyat "to promote the initiative and verify to their brothers inside and outside Egypt that it was truly issued by them" (al-Zayyat 2004, 75). They also reject the accusations that they are traitors and government agents, saying that "they lost the fight against the government. They lost, they are finished."[2] But why would a group that "lost" transform radically "from a jihadi group to a sociopolitical Islamic group . . . change their ideas radically vis-à-vis multipartism and other aspects, stop violence, and even scrutinize their ideas of the past"?[3] The fact that those who initiated the revisions will not be pardoned and will either spend the rest of their lives in prison or be executed speaks strongly in favor of Gama'a Islamiya's arguments. Indeed, the cease-fire was not declared spontaneously but came about as a result of multiple factors, one of them being the approach that Egyptian security and justice officials developed as part of the counterterrorism strategy now also being applied in Saudi Arabia and Yemen: debate. Islamic scholars who offered their services to the government entered into religious and political discussions with the imprisoned Gama'a Islamiya members to persuade them to abandon violence. Where torture and harsh prison sentences often failed, dialogue and debate succeeded.

Was the group's cease-fire initiative ultimately a result of severe government pressure on one end, or of intense debates on the other? The answer matters, for at least two important reasons. First, the perspective taken is consequential for counterterrorism policies. Whether we perceive repression, or debate, as the main driver of a terrorist group's transformation has implications for the kind of counterterrorism policy we advocate. Second, the answer is consequential for the intra-Islamic debate—the discussion sparked by Gama'a Islamiya's change of heart centers on the vital question of what is the right and true Islamic way. Perhaps al-Qaeda can steer this debate in its favor and convince others that to give in to government pressure is to betray the cause for worldly considerations. On the other hand, Gama'a Islamiya may establish its transformation as theologically sound. The outcome is consequential for either group's mobilization potential.

This chapter argues that debate played the key role in Gama'a Islamiya's change of mind. The reasoning hinges on the distinction between individual and collective rationality and—closely related—between ends and means. For a group to transform as Gama'a Islamiya did, individual and collective rationality must harmonize; that, is individual ends cannot oppose collective ends.

Martha Crenshaw has stated that what might seem irrational at the individual level can be thoroughly rational on a collective level. She exemplifies this statement with suicide terrorism. While suicide terrorism might not be rational from an individual point of view, it can bring a strategic advantage from a collective point of view (Crenshaw 1998, 9). In this context, the failure of repression as a deterrent becomes obvious, since deterring a committed suicide bomber with violence is basically impossible.

The question becomes more problematic, however, if preferences within a terrorist group are such that individual rationality butts up against collective *irrationality*. This problem becomes especially apparent in considering conflicts driven by greed. As Zartman points out, "Greed hijacks the conflict from social (group) to personal (individual) benefits" (Zartman 2005, 270). Yet the clash between individual and collective rationality is characteristic not only of greed-driven groups. In fact, taking into account that terrorism is, on the whole, unsuccessful, it is almost never a rational collective choice (Abrahams 2006). From this angle, even the suicide bomber aiming to die for the collective cause is not really doing something for the terrorists' collective good. The motivation to die for a higher cause can ultimately be traced back to a very personal end, such as revenge, prestige, or an elevated position in the afterlife.

In terrorist groups, the individual ends run counter to the collective ends. This was also the case with Gama'a Islamiya in the run-up to its transformation. Whereas the group's members had individual motives for resorting to violence, such as revenge, prestige, or simply hatred, violence did not bring the group closer to its unachievable end: an Islamic Egyptian state. In fact, violent means corrupted the group's ends, turning into the end itself. Now Gama'a Islamiya advocates ceasing violence to pursue its ends. Terrorism, according to the group, has brought only misery on the Muslim world. Thus, Gama'a members strongly criticize al-Qaeda in their book *Mistakes and Dangerous Consequences of al-Qaeda and Its Strategy*, saying, "The enemies of Islam became united and Muslims suffer more than ever" (Gama'a Islamiya 2004, 7). While al-Qaeda may have thought that it scared the West, it simply provided the United States with an opportunity to attack the Middle East and Islam. According to al-Zayyat, "Islamists across the globe were adversely affected by the September 11 attacks on

Individual Goal [handwritten annotation in margin]

the United States. Even Islamist movements that did not target the United States are paying the price of this folly. . . . Bin Laden's desire to take revenge . . . has given the Americans and other governments the power to destroy the Islamists before our eyes" (al-Zayyat 2004, 96).

Not only does al-Qaeda's struggle strengthen the enemies of Islam, it also divides the Muslim world, leading Gama'a to ask, "Is it after we have been through rivers of blood and Muslims fighting Muslims? . . . Has that reached our target?" (Gama'a Islamiya 2002a). According to Gama'a, it has resulted in the opposite: the Muslim world gets ever more divided and, hence, weakened.

Taking this perspective, al-Qaeda's argument about Gama'a Islamiya's betrayal of the Muslim cause can be neutralized and even turned on its head: al-Qaeda's members are not helping the Muslim cause and may ultimately be motivated by individual aspirations.

Seeking a collective end does not necessarily mean shunning individual preferences. But when individual ends are aligned with collectively rational ends, terrorism ceases. This is so because terrorists either achieve their collective ends and are no longer terrorists, or adapt by aiming at a more realistic achievement through peaceful ways, as evidenced by the case of Gama'a Islamiya.

But how does such a process of harmonizing individual and collective rationality come about? Can the alignment of personal and collective ends be better fostered through repression or through debate? To begin a process of realizing the collective irrationality of violence, debate is crucial. Repression, on the other hand, serves to keep the individual reasoning for violence alive—clearly to the detriment of a rational collective purpose. This is so because the group dynamics necessary to gain insights into the actual irrationality of terrorism are impeded by repression yet fostered by debate. This study begins by establishing Gama'a Islamiya's background as a terrorist group lacking a collective rationality. Then it observes the effects of repression before contrasting them with the implications of debate.

Background: Gama'a Islamiya as a Terrorist Group Lacking Collective Rationality

In the beginning, the Egyptian government strongly rejected any form of talks with the Gama'a Islamiya (Islamic Group). All the available evidence classified the group as a terrorist organization without a rational mind-set and, hence, with no possibility of ever changing its ideology and goals. The group lacked collective rationality because its ends were unattainable and, thus, were ultimately replaced by violent means. Although the group's primary strategy followed a nonviolent, bottom-up approach, a combination of factors eventually pushed it to pursue toppling the infidel government and replacing it with an Islamic state.

In the 1970s, young Egyptian students joined a group that called itself Gama'a Islamiya. Several factors lay at the heart of the group's radicalization, one being the inability of the more moderate Muslim Brotherhood to achieve substantial political gains during its parliamentary experience. This inability implied a loss of support, not merely for the Brotherhood but also for its moderate approach. Gama'a members became increasingly suspicious of the Muslim Brothers' true intentions. Accordingly, Gama'a leader Tal'at Fu'ad Qasim replied in an interview with Hisham Mubarak, "After we started al-Gama'a al-Islamiya, al-Sadat released a number of Muslim Brothers from jail to clamp down on us in Cairo. When they tried to take on our people, we developed our critical orientation toward the Muslim Brothers" (Mubarak 1997, 316).

Feeling that the Brotherhood had achieved little in all its years, Gama'a Islamiya eventually rejected the Brothers' accommodating path and decided that the way to achieve an Islamic state was through a revolutionary Islamic mass movement (Hafez 2003, 55). And so, to gain legitimacy, Gama'a Islamiya not only provided social services to the needy but also engaged in direct militant action, disrupting musical festivals and wedding ceremonies and attacking video clubs and beer bars (Hafez 2003, 52).

The emerging atmosphere of violence was nurtured by an intellectual justification for extremism, for example, by the ideas of Sayyid Qutb.[4] Qutb, known mainly as an Islamist theoretician, spent two years in the United States and returned a determined fundamentalist. He is widely regarded as "the father of modern fundamentalism . . . and was the most influential advocate in modern times of jihad . . . and doctrines that legitimize violent Muslim resistance" (Swenson 2005). To Sayyid Qutb, Muslims live not in an Islamic world but in *jahiliyya* (pre-Islamic ignorance): "The Muslim community has long ago vanished from existence. . . . The Muslim community vanished at the moment the laws of God became suspended on earth" (Qutb 1964). Therefore, according to Qutb, the government that does not apply Islamic law but suspends the law of God on earth has to be fought. This is so because a compromise with *jahili* society is simply unthinkable (Qutb 1964). When Nasser's government executed Qutb in 1966 for his radical views, he became a martyr for many young Egyptians. His book *Milestones* had a significant impact later on members of Gama'a Islamiya.

The members of the group were impatient to see their goals realized. The Muslim Brothers' lack of success confirmed the radicals in their conviction that the Islamic cause could not be advanced by institutional means (Hafez

2003, 54). Gama'a members waited impatiently for the Muslim Brotherhood to become effective, and when not much happened, they sought to
accelerate the path toward an Islamic state by violent means.

Even for the group's more radical elements, attacking civilians was highly
controversial, although Gama'a's ideology ultimately legitimized such attacks. Perceiving Islam and *jahiliyya* to be irreconcilable, it saw secularists, liberals, communists, and other "non-Qutbists" as infidels with whom
no compromise was possible. Because Gama'a believed it an obligation to
wage jihad against infidel regimes, it viewed jihad as an important part of
Islamic activism, which, in the beginning, calls for *da'wa* (the practice of
calling others to the right path, namely, to a life guided by Islam), progressing to the prohibition of vices and culminating in holy war.

These views are a recipe for escalating violence. The conclusive end
to the purpose of re-Islamizing society and fighting the infidel regime
is to topple the government: "If you like to clear the stairway, you begin
from the top not from down . . . so you have to remove this government,
hence the violence. The only way to change the regime is to engage in violence, because you can only dream of changing through democratic vote."[5]
Gama'a Islamiya therefore focused on fighting the "near enemy," with the
goal of assuming power in Egypt and re-Islamizing the Egyptian society.
In this, it stood in clear contrast to al-Qaeda: "At least we can take it as
given that Al-Qaeda belongs to that stream of international militant Islamist movements that espouse jihad against what they perceive as the
external enemies to Islam and the Muslim people. In this it differs from
such domestically grown jihadist movements, as the Gama'a Islamiya and
Jihad Organisation in Egypt, which targeted the regime within their own
country" (Rashwan 2005).

Gama'a Islamiya was clearly against multipartism and eventually published a book against it in 1985. Diaa Rashwan explains the differentia-
tion between "sociopolitical groups" and jihadi Islamists: "Sociopolitical
groups have a program in spite of Islamic sharia. They want to reorganize
society and adapt Islamic sharia to such reorganization—for example, to
multipartism."[6] But Gama'a Islamiya wanted the law of the book, not the
parliament, which did not represent God or sharia.[7] But what, exactly, this
law of the book means, the group never specified. It remained unclear what
should actually replace multipartism, and it never elaborated on its goal,
which was confined to toppling the government. In fact, Jihad had become
the goal: "Thus, people act out of anger, self-respect, et cetera. It does not
mean that they have a clear vision. They are just saying 'no way.' They never
had a project. The Gama'a Islamiya never had a project."[8]

Egyptian Islamist violence aimed increasingly at the state and its institutions, Coptic Christians, tourists, and secular intellectuals as well as ordinary civilians suspected of collaborating with the state. The 1997 massacre of sixty civilians in Luxor further distanced Gama'a Islamiya from the population, which felt that the violence was not accomplishing anything.[9] On the contrary, with tourism the main source of income for many, the increasing attacks on visiting foreigners turned the population against the group.[10] Gama'a Islamiya soon found itself isolated and without the support it had enjoyed in the beginning. Tal'at Fu'ad Qasim's statement that "it does not cost us much to strike at this sector" did not prove true. Indeed, the group "became more isolated in the society. They did not find shelter in the society, the normal people, anymore."[11]

When Omar Abdel Rahman tried to justify the violence, asking, "How can we cry for a tourist and not cry for the hundreds of thousands of the oppressed?" it became clear that the group had turned to indiscriminate violence (Hafez 2003, 183).[12] As members of Gama'a Islamiya now say of themselves, "We were very young and immature."[13]

Whereas the Gama'a members were strongly impressed by fundamentalist leaders and their literature, they had no "Islamic experience, they did not know the average school of Islam. They had no time to criticize."[14] Thus, they were very selective in interpreting religion and took these selections out of context to suit their uncritical, unexamined views. Also, because their goals were so far from attainment, they never thought about what, exactly, they were striving for or how to implement it. With jihad turning into an end in itself, a collective rationale based on applying Gama'a's views to reality became infeasible.

Repression and the Violent Gama'a Islamiya

Deterrence through repression serves only to foster the individual purpose of violence while feeding into the collective irrationality of violence. Moreover, deterrence strategies face a dilemma when confronting terrorists who lack collective rationality; that is, effective deterrence depends on the rationality of the potentially deterred. Lacking tangible goals, irrational terrorists cannot be deterred, simply because there is nothing tangible that one can threaten to take away from them.

A case in point: Egypt's military counterterrorist strategy from the 1970s through the 1990s bore no fruit. More than two decades of persecution resulted in the detention of most members of Gama'a Islamiya, the biggest terrorist threat in Egypt during this period. But despite thousands

Renarse?

So, more success by limited, precise terror.

of arrests, dozens of executions, and long-term prison sentences, the campaign of violence did not cease; in fact, it intensified. Gama'a members continued attacking Egypt's security and government officials as well as the tourism industry. They were involved in assassinating Egyptian president Anwar Sadat in 1981 and the speaker of the Egyptian parliament in 1990. In 1992, a Gama'a splinter group killed a leading Egyptian secularist figure and author for his views, which opposed its ideology of an Islamic Egyptian state. The group's violent campaign peaked in 1997, with the massacre of more than sixty foreign tourists and local tour guides in Luxor. Although this attack was the work of a few rogue members and not authorized by the Gama'a leadership, the international community now felt directly threatened by the organization, which was already labeled as terrorist in Europe and the United States.[15] The Egyptian government pushed international agreements to capture and extradite Gama'a members and other suspected Islamist extremists to Egypt. Through these agreements, militants from Afghanistan, Albania, Bulgaria, Bosnia, Sudan, Yemen, and other countries could be captured and extradited (Hafez 2003, 86).

Ninety-five percent of violence in Egypt in the 1980s and 1990s was blamed on Gama'a Islamiya (Rashwan 2008). The Egyptian government resorted to military means and arrested thousands of the group's members. Torture, while nothing new in Egypt, was now applied indiscriminately (Hafez 2003, 86). Those Gama'a members who were not executed, arrested, or killed in shootouts with security forces left for Afghanistan to fight the Soviets or sought refuge all over the world, including in the United States and Western Europe. Especially after the assassination of Sadat in 1981, the Egyptian government initiated a major offensive against Gama'a Islamiya. A Middle East analyst describes the offensive: "It was really very nasty what happened here. Nothing like Algeria, I mean Islamic Algeria. A nightmare, this was done very nasty. How many people were killed here!"[16]

Emergency laws, imposed after the assassination of President Sadat, allowed the security forces to detain thousands of Islamists without court order or judicial supervision. The police and military had a free hand in devising security strategies in the manner they deemed most suitable to the circumstances. And when the government adopted a shoot-to-kill policy in the 1990s, the number of injured Islamists declined, while the number killed rose dramatically (Hafez 2003, 86).

Despite the government's efforts, however, the jailed Gama'a Islamiya leadership still found ways to communicate with its members outside prisons. The attempted assassination of President Mubarak in Addis Ababa in June 1995 was coordinated by the group, even though most of its members were already jailed.[17] While the Egyptian government refused to speak or negotiate with terrorists, the campaign of violence and terrorist attacks continued unabated. The government, strongly supported by security forces, used all possible means at its disposal to fight the Islamists. Extrajudicial arrests, military tribunals, arrests without warrants, imprisonment without trials, torture, and executions all failed to deter the Islamists from their use of violence.

Deterrence through repression makes violence individually rational because deterrence nurtures the very thing it seeks to prevent: radicalization. According to Montasser al-Zayyat, Gama'a was initially very close to the Brotherhood, and this closeness changed only when the government pushed the group toward violence: "First the Gama'a Islamiya used peaceful means . . . but it was the result of the government's treatment and behavior towards the Gama'a Islamiya, so the group responded with violence."[18]

This view is confirmed by Mohammed M. Hafez, who feels that indiscriminate repression by the Egyptian government contributed to the group's radicalization. When the government killed Gama'a Islamiya's official spokesman in 1990, the group formed an armed wing and retaliated by assassinating the former speaker of Parliament. The state's massive reaction targeted not only militants but also their families and friends—"virtually anyone who had a beard with a trimmed moustache" (Hafez 2003, 85).[19]

As the state began taking Islamists' relatives hostage to pressure militants into turning themselves in, stepped up its mistreatment and torture of those captured, and imposed further restrictions such as curfews, Gama'a members saw violence as a justified response. As evidenced in the group's statements, the Gama'a Islamiya began its fight against the state to stop mass arrests and the takeover of private mosques (Hafez 2003, 86).

When one of Gama'a's historic leaders was asked to explain how and why the group resorted to violent jihad rather than follow the path of the moderate Muslim Brotherhood, the answer was straightforward:

> We tried the *da'wa* approach but were severely punished by the oppressive government. Although Sadat encouraged us in the beginning, and the *da'wa* was bringing positive results of bringing people back to Islam, we have become a perceived threat to his rule. Security forces closed our mosques, prevented us from entering universities, arrested us, and tortured us. We had a popular support. People saw what the repressive government was doing to us, so they were convinced that if the government is afraid of us coming to power, then we must be doing something right. And we took up weapons. . . .[20]

The government's brutal response served to augment the extremists' oversimplified theological reasoning. According to the theological reasoning for violent jihad, a strong desire to seek "justice, revenge, and defend honor" plays a crucial part (al-Hashimi and Goerzig 2010). In their published revisions, former fundamentalists point to torture and long, unjustified prison sentences as contributing to the rise of Islamic extremism (Gama'a Islamiya 2002a). While in prisons throughout the 1960s, many Islamic activists began to question the reasons for such harsh treatment: if they were true Muslims who had to be punished so severely, then could the police be Muslim as well? True Muslims did not cause harm to others; thus, the regime, the police, and all individuals who followed orders from the authorities must be infidels, or *jahiliyin* (Gama'a Islamiya 2002b).

By this reasoning, the notion of the enemies of Islam took hold and evolved into an ideology whose consequences we still see today. Mawil Izzi Dien also argues that Egypt's crackdown on Islamists in the 1960s created a backlash against Arab and Muslim regimes supported by foreign powers: "The crushing of the Muslim Brotherhood by Egyptian authorities created a ripple effect of 'Islamic resurgence,' 'government opposition,' and 'Islamic hero movement' which was duplicated in most of the Muslim world that was formerly part of the Ottoman empire, such as Iraq, Syria, Saudi Arabia, Palestine, and Jordan" (Dien 2004, 130).

It was in prisons where most people turned to extremism and terrorism, where members of various groups began labeling everyone other than their "brothers" infidels (Gama'a Islamiya 2002c, 6).[21] According to Gama'a Islamiya accounts, those who began labeling others infidels became like cluster bombs, spreading fanaticism dangerously and accusing everyone of being an infidel (Gama'a Islamiya 2002c, 6).

Change through Debate

As a result of the debates, the Gama'a Islamiya leadership published fifteen books while in prison, officially renouncing violence and giving the reasons for its change of strategy. These debates within the prisons had led to revisions of Gama'a ideology. First, the group assessed its doctrine and actions in a profoundly critical manner. Second, it formulated a new doctrinal and ideological approach, one that made a clear break with the past and provided guidance for the future.

The group transformed because, as al-Zayyat explains, "violence and killings did not bring the desired results."[22] Many criticized the ideological shift, saying the Gama'a members "sold themselves" to the government, to get out of prison. These voices assume a high rationality and pure calculation on the part of Gama'a Islamiya. But was the group really for sale? And if so, what are the implications for potential strategies to buy off radicals? Several circumstances leave room for questioning. The group's members were, by their

own admission, very young and immature when they set off on their violent
path, and minimax cost-benefit calculus did not likely figure into the agenda
of these youngsters' passion for their cause. And if they really were rational
from the outset, why could they not be deterred in the first place? Through
indiscriminate tactics, the group steadily lost popular backing. Moreover,
they did not make any tangible goal a condition for changing their tactics.

That the group was not rational from early on but developed its collective rationality through debate raises an interesting question: how, exactly,
did this change of heart happen? After all, rationality, especially in our
Western culture, is seen as the sine qua non for bargaining. And indeed,
the group itself gives the following reason for the change: "Why we declared in 1997 the peace initiative? Some said we had an agreement. Some
said that it was just a strategy. Some said it was regret. Some said we betrayed Jihad and lost. But it was a new . . . insight into reality. There was no
deal with the state. Many of our leaders took part in debates and declared
peace. . . . It just made no more sense to die" (Gama'a Islamiya 2004, 16).

The group stopped fighting, arguing instead "for an end to the bloodshed
[since] ceasefire is acceptable in Islamic shari'a in the case of weakness" (al-
Zayyat 2004, 75). They asked, "Is it smart to lead war against the whole
world? Was it smart to increase the number of enemies of Islam?" (Gama'a
Islamiya 2004, 19). They came to develop a very rational approach, totaling up what they gained against what they lost, and found that they came
up short (Gama'a Islamiya 2002a). Consequently, they started to advocate
weighing options, giving examples from history and the Quran: "There is
never 100 percent good or bad. One must make a choice. . . . Khalid bin
Walid retreated during a fight. He was called a coward by the others, but
Muhammad called him a hero because he saved 3,000 lives who were to be
lost against 300,000 for nothing" (Gama'a Islamiya 2002a, 13).

Gama'a Islamiya has clearly distanced itself from terrorist tactics. What
is more, it has found a rational approach that is compatible with religion.
It states the down-to-earth pragmatism of its new perspective clearly:
"When weighing interests, always choose the one which can be achieved
in reality and be definite, and not only in theoretical realm and hopes and
dreams" (Gama'a Islamiya 2002a, 26).

The facilitation of communication with and within the group led to
its transformation. After the group's leadership underwent this change of
mind, it could communicate it to the other members through provided
channels of dialogue. The group officially renounced violence, has since
then made several statements on the cease-fire initiative, and has appeared
on TV and radio channels to promote a peaceful approach (to the extent

allowed by the government).[23] Most interestingly, the debates within prison walls resulted in the publication of several books on the group's ideological revisions. In *Initiative for Stopping the Violence,* the group adopts what it calls a "realist vision": "It is wrong to take positions and adopt provisions and opinions without considering the reality. . . . It is obvious that in the fight between Islamic groups and the police, neither one can benefit. The biggest benefactor in the struggle within Egypt are the enemies of Egypt and Islam . . ." (Gama'a Islamiya 2002a, 35).

Apparently, Gama'a Islamiya did not substantially change its cause of confronting the "enemies of Islam." What it changed were the means. Accordingly, al-Zayyat stresses that he "prefer[s] the peaceful da'wa way and that a peaceful strategy does not necessarily imply more lenient goals . . . jihad does not have to be restricted to the armed approach" (al-Zayyat 2004, 75). On the contrary, in its books, the group sees jihad "not only [as] the violence. It is also the time of prayer. It is about making friends, supporting family, contributing to the welfare of society" (Gama'a Islamiya 2002b, 43). Gama'a Islamiya reinterpreted jihad. The transformed concept no longer stands for violent defense. In fact, the group perceives an inherent contradiction between violence and the purpose of Islam. After Gama'a's turnabout, it started arguing against those advocating violent means, saying, for example, that al-Qaeda "misunderstood Jihad" (Gama'a Islamiya 2004, 8).

Whereas terrorists want to force others to accept their demands, values, and way of life, Gama'a Islamiya has come to accept others' demands, values, and ways of life. Their former violent approach isolated them from the population, and now their transformation has put them back in touch with the demands, values, and ways of life of society—in essence, the absence of violence: "Attacking and killing stands against God's wish, and those who kill defenseless individuals will only infuriate God, as it is against Islamic values to commit such crimes" (Gama'a Islamiya 2002a, 92).

Gama'a realized that violent jihad, in trying to replace the primacy of politics, had corrupted the goal. A senior Gama'a member makes the extent of this change even clearer: "We realized that if we were in power we would have to share it anyway. It is like flying an airplane. If you do not communicate with the others, you crash."[24] This senior member, now released from prison, has written his doctoral dissertation on Islam and democracy.

Gama'a Islamiya eventually accepted multipartism. Thus, in 1998 and 1999, it issued two demands to establish a political party. Both times, the government refused. Diaa Rashwan explains: "De facto they tried to have a political party, but it was more a symbolic attempt to confirm that they were serious in their change of mind. When one accepts multipartism, it is part of the transformation into a sociopolitical group. The Gama'a Islamiya transformed, as happened very often in Islamic society. According to such a transformation, multipartism is a part of the political agenda. To ask people to give them their votes and to accept that some people get votes and some not—that is progress."[25]

This transformation is not yet a fait accompli, however. According to Montasser al-Zayyat, Gama'a Islamiya is "still in an inner search stage."[26] What it will find remains to be seen.

Initially, the group was reluctant to engage with the Islamic scholars who offered to speak with them. As al-Zayyat explains, "In the beginning, they had only one opinion."[27] In prison, however, they came into contact with other people and, with them, other views about religion. The group's members had widely varying intellectual backgrounds, and their exposure to other teachings in captivity challenged fixed standpoints.[28] Consequently, the Gama'a Islamiya held deep theological conversations among themselves, reinterpreting religious texts and changing their understanding. Accordingly, says Diaa Rashwan, "They did not know the average school of Islam. They had no time to criticize. [But] the last ten years they had a lot of time to read and compare and also get to know the average schools of Islam, not only jihadi."[29] Similarly, al-Zayyat, who represents his imprisoned "brothers" in the negotiations with the government, says, "They had disputes and arguments from within the group. In prison, they were exposed to other ideas and teachings and began accepting different opinions. It had to do with knowledge and experience."[30]

In its publications, Gama'a Islamiya cites religious texts and Quranic verses, interpreting the ideological shift from a purely religious perspective. The importance of these debates is very much emphasized throughout the books and during interviews. The Egyptian government openly encouraged and facilitated the Gama'a leaders' communications with their followers in prisons throughout the country and abroad.[31] It also allowed the group's leaders to tour the prisons and communicate their new approach to other members. To encourage further debates, Egyptian officials provided the necessary logistics and transported the leaders to prisons throughout the country. The government facilitated Gama'a Islamiya's internal debate by giving access to communication channels, literature, and education, providing exchanges with religious scholars, and allowing the early release of thousands of suspected militants, some of whom had been held for years under the emergency law without being tried or even charged.

Although the debates were sparked by Islamic scholars outside the group, the transformation resulted from arguments within the group. Through these dialogues, Gama'a has developed sympathy for other Muslims affected by violence (for example, by government repression or by the negative impact of violence on the tourism sector), all from the rationality gained through a better comprehension of religion. Thus, its spokesman, al-Zayyat, argues for an end to the bloodshed and points out that "many innocent young people who had not committed any crime were in prison, and that thousands of families were suffering from poverty and other social problems because of the continued detention of their relatives" (al-Zayyat 2004, 75). The group now struggles against the biggest enemy—poverty and economic stagnation—and aims at "building a healthy society to help the interests of our country, our people, the interests of Muslims" (Gama'a Islamiya 2002a).

And perhaps most important, the Gama'a members developed their rationality out of sympathy for one another. Rather than being driven by personal interests, they perceived the senselessness of their fellows' suffering. In one of their books, they summarize this perception: "What we said comes to the following: whatever a Muslim does should be for the good of a group and not only personal" (Gama'a Islamiya 2002a). This sympathy with their fellows shaped their rationality in weighing options and deciding to save rather than slaughter other Muslims, as in the historic example of Khalid bin Whalid, who saved 3,000 from a fight against 300,000. Maybe it is this insight that al-Zayyat refers to in stating, "It had to do with knowledge and experience. They matured, read, and understood the book properly."[32]

Conclusion

The obstacles to the transformation of fundamentalist terrorist groups are many. Gama'a Islamiya's collective irrationality, for example, posed a major challenge because, as Zartman asserts, "revolutionary absolute [terrorists] are nonnegotiable adversaries" (Zartman 2003). Gama'a Islamiya came to understand that violence did not yield any good result. With its extremist approach, the group alienated the population and landed itself behind bars. In captivity, the group weighed gains and losses, and the poor balance eventually led it to conclude that "it made no more sense to die." The members asked themselves what they really had achieved in all those years. The answer was obvious: all they had accomplished was the killing and suffering of more Muslims. The violence had backfired. This new insight became possible only when the group was no longer afraid to face a reality that did not favor it. The escapism into a theoretical realm of hopes and dreams, where the group's actions might seem justified, had nothing to do with what murder and bloodshed were really about. How did Gama'a Islamiya come to perceive the counterproductivity of violence? By getting in touch with its followers' base and reinterpreting the same religion that had been instrumental in sanctioning the killings. The degree of reflection and courage required to undertake such unflinching self-criticism is astonishing, and all the more so for happening during a time of such radicalization on the global Islamist scene.

The group's transformation is a puzzling countertrend for another reason, also: it happened during imprisonment. While it is conceivable that capture and failure could have spurred the change, the reasons that the group itself gives point in another direction. Moreover, torture and hardship in prison usually have quite the opposite result: radicalization. How this transformation could happen is as intriguing and important as it is difficult to answer. The cooperation and concessions by the government surely played a role. But to argue that the group lost everything and transformed merely to grovel its way out of prison is shortsighted and facile. The Gama'a members stress the well-being of their fellows, whether inside or outside the group, over personal gain. To send 3,000 into a fight against 300,000 has nothing to do with holy martyrdom—it is simply unreasonable, irrational. The leaders of the group came to understand this folly, and for this they deserve credit, both individually and collectively. More commonly, we witness leaders sending out others—namely, their own followers—to kill and die in the name of Allah. But the leaders of Gama'a Islamiya realized that retreat in the face of greater strength is quite compatible with religion. It is rational and religious at the same time, because human life is saved. What makes this rationality so difficult to achieve is that no one likes to admit weakness. Weighing costs and benefits is easy if the result is positive; it is a far greater challenge when the outcome is not so cheering. It requires, as Gama'a Islamiya has shown, sympathy with other humans, whose lives are no longer merely an instrument but something of intrinsic value far beyond their mere utility.

As the group's revisions touched "cornerstones of the jihadi legacy," criticism from Islamic hard-liners came hard and fast, blaming Gama'a for selling out the cause, while secularists accused it of merely pretending (el-Hamalawy 2003). The Gama'a members developed their rationality as a result, rather than a condition, of dialogue. They had made it clear that what really changed were their means, so that jihad became not only the violence but also the time of prayer and of making friends. During their terrorist bent, militant jihad had turned into an end in itself, culminating in the Luxor massacre. Then debate illuminated this corruption of the end by the means and engendered a rationality based on differentiating between the two.

The sympathy with others was a result of intense intragroup debates, in which the members focused on the well-being of the group rather than on personal gains. They took the situation of Muslims within and beyond the group into account and clearly distanced themselves from al-Qaeda. Again, it was the leadership that led the group's "inner search." That it was also a result of decades of talking led some to argue that "to convince somebody after fifty-five years to be a democratic group—that is too late."[33] The good news is that the group did renounce violence.

Whereas repression served to radicalize the Gama'a Islamiya members by feeding into the individual desire for revenge, debate opened up the group's leadership to develop a collective rationality. Perceiving the suffering of their followers, the Gama'a leaders realized that fighting for an unachievable end ultimately does no one good. They convinced their followers of the collective rationality of searching for change by peaceful means and thereby aligned individual and collective rationality. Debate was crucial for this process, since keeping in touch with the followers convinced the leaders of the need for change, while listening to the leaders convinced the followers of the new approach. Whereas repression makes violence individually more rational but collectively more irrational, debate can serve to harmonize individual and collective rationality—if it leads the group to adopt peaceful means. Gama'a Islamiya has made this step. Al-Qaeda attempted to discredit the group's revisions—no doubt because it is aware of the impact. It may find itself hoist with its own petard, however, because Islam forbids labeling someone else an infidel—for in the end, labeling others reveals one's own true nature.

Notes

1. *Asharq Alawsat* has obtained a copy of this book, which is regarded as "the last will" of Dr. Ayman al-Zawahiri, excerpts of which are available online (al-Zawahiri 2001).

2. Author interview with Egyptian analyst, Cairo, summer 2006.

3. Author interview with Diaa Rashwan, expert at the Al Ahram Center for political and strategic studies, Cairo, summer 2006.

4. Author interview with Egyptian professor, Cairo, summer 2006.

5. Interview with Egyptian professor, Cairo, summer 2006.

6. Interview with Diaa Rashwan, Cairo, summer 2006. Rashwan is director of the Comparative Politics Unit and editor in chief of the *Directory of World Islamic Movements* of the Al-Ahram Center for Political and Strategic Studies.

7. Interview with Montasser al-Zayyat, Cairo, summer 2006. Al-Zayyat is an Egyptian lawyer defending Islamists. He is also the representative of Gama'a Islamiya's cease-fire initiative.

8. Interview with Middle East analyst, Cairo, summer 2006.

9. This massacre took place in spite of the coincident initiative of peace, because of miscommunications and disagreement between some more radical members and the leadership, which did not approve this attack.

10. Interview with Egyptian newspaper editor, Cairo, summer 2006.

11. Ibid.

12. Omar Abdel Rahman, a blind Egyptian leader of the Gama'a Islamiya, is currently serving a life sentence in a U.S. prison.

13. Interview with Gama'a Islamiya leader, Cairo, summer 2006.

14. Interview with Diaa Rashwan, Cairo, summer 2006. This extremist guidance was not only, or even primarily, Egyptian, as epitomized by Qutb's *Milestones*. Fundamentalists from other countries, such as the Gulf states and Afghanistan, also had a big impact on Gama'a members' thinking.

15. Gama'a Islamiya is considered a terrorist organization by the United States, the EU, and Egypt.

16. Interview with Middle East expert, Cairo, summer 2006.

17. Also, in June 1992, the secular intellectual Faraj Fuda was assassinated, and in October 1994, Nobel Prize winner Naguib Mahfouz was wounded, in attacks by Gama'a Islamiya.

18. Author Interview with Montasser al-Zayyat, Cairo, 2006.

19. See also Hafez 2006.

20. Author interview with senior member of the Gama'a Islamiya, Cairo, summer 2006.

21. One of the many books resulting from the Gama'a's debate and written in prison by its leaders to justify their new, nonviolent approach.

22. Author interview with Montasser al-Zayyat, Cairo, 2006.

23. See, for example, Said 2007.

24. Author interview with senior Gama'a Islamiya member in Cairo, summer 2006.

25. Author interview with Diaa Rashwan, Cairo, 2006.

26. Author interview with Montasser al-Zayyat, Cairo, 2006.

27. Ibid.

28. Ibid.

29. Interview with Diaa Rashwan, Cairo, 2006. "Average school of Islam" refers to moderate streams of Islam.

30. Interview with Montasser al-Zayyat, Cairo, 2006.

31. Al-Zayyat dedicates a significant part of his book to the correspondence that took place between imprisoned members in Egypt and New York.

32. Interview with Montasser al-Zayyat, Cairo, 2006.

33. Author interview with Egyptian analyst, Cairo, summer 2006.

References

Abrahams, Max. 2006. "Why Terrorism Does Not Work." *International Security* 31 (2): 42–78.

Crenshaw, Martha. 1998. "The Logic of Terrorism: Terrorist Behavior as a Product of Strategic Choice." In *Origins of Terrorism: Psychologies, Ideologies, Theologies, States of Mind,* ed. Walter Reich. Washington, DC: Woodrow Wilson Center Press.

Dien, Mawil Izzi. 2004. *Islamic Law: From Historical Foundations to Contemporary Practice.* Notre Dame, IN: University of Notre Dame Press.

Gama'a Islamiya. 2002a. *Initiative for Stopping the Violence (Moubadara Woq'f al-Anf R'ouia Waquiiya Wua Nazra Shariiya)*. Cairo: Islamic Turath.

———. 2002b. *Shedding Light on the Mistakes of Jihad (Taslit al-Addwaa ala ma Waqaa fi al-Jihad min al-Akhtaa)*. Cairo: Islamic Turath.

———. 2002c. *Sin in Excessive Religion (Harma al-Ghouloun Fi al-Din Wua Takfir al-Muslimin)*. Cairo: Islamic Turath.

———. 2004. *Mistakes and Dangerous Consequences of al-Qaeda and Its Strategy (Istratigiya Wua Tafjirat al-Qaeda al-Akhtaa Wua al-Akhtar)*. Cairo: Islamic Turath.

Hafez, Mohammed M. 2003: *Why Muslims Rebel*. London: Lynne Rienner.

———. 2006: "Political Repression and Violent Rebellion in the Muslim World." In *The Making of a Terrorist: Recruitment, Training, and Root Causes*, ed. James J. F. Forest. Vol. 3. London: Praeger Security International.

el-Hamalawy, Hossam. 2003. "Forgive Me, Government, for I Have Sinned." *Islam Online*, Sept. 11. http://islamonline.net access (accessed Dec. 22, 2009).

al-Hashimi, Khaled, and Carolin Goerzig. 2010. "Baseless Jihad." In *Control of Violence: Historical and International Perspectives on Violence in Modern Societies*, ed. Wilhelm Heitmeyer, Hein-Gerhard Haupt, Stefan Malthaner, and Andrea Kirschner. New York: Springer.

Mubarak, Hisham. 1997. "What Does the Gama'a Islamiyya Want?" In *Political Islam*, ed. Joel Beinin and Joe Stork. Berkeley and Los Angeles: University of California Press.

Qutb, Sayyid. 1964. *Milestones*. Cairo: Kazi.

Rashwan, Diaa. 2005. "Remote Targets and Near Ones Too." *Al-Ahram Weekly*, Apr. 28–May 4. http://weekly.ahram.org.eg/2005/740/op44.htm (accessed Oct. 31, 2010).

———. 2008. "Egyptian Islamists and Nonviolence: Views from the Prison Cell." *Arab Insight* 2 (2): 43–52.

Said, Abdel-Moneim. 2007. "Second Thoughts." *Al-Ahram Weekly*, May 24–30. http://weekly.ahram.org.eg/2007/846/op1.htm (accessed Nov. 6, 2010).

Swenson, Elmer. 2005. "Sayyid Qub's *Milestones*." http://gemsofislamism.tripod.com/milestones_qutb.html (accessed Nov. 5, 2010).

Zartman, I. William. 2003. "Negotiating with Terrorists. *International Negotiation* 8 (3): 443–50.

———. 2005. "Need, Creed, and Greed in Intrastate Conflict." In *Rethinking the Economics of War: The Intersection of Need, Creed, and Greed*, ed. I. W. Zartman and C. J. Arnson. Washington, DC: Woodrow Wilson Press; Baltimore, MD: Johns Hopkins University Press.

al-Zawahiri, Ayman. 2001. *Knights under the Prophet's Banner*. Scribd. www.scribd.com/doc/6759609/Knights-Under-the-Prophet-Banner (accessed Oct. 31, 2010).

al-Zayyat, Montasser. 2004. *The Road to Al Qaeda: The Story of Bin Laden's Right-Hand Man*. London: Pluto Press.

8

Tactics in Negotiations between States and Extremists:

The Role of Cease-Fires and Counterterrorist Measures

Kristine Höglund

A re cease-fires and antiterrorist measures effective tools for bringing about negotiations with terrorists? Or do they create obstacles in the search for dialogue? The great bulk of terrorist acts take place within the context of a wider political conflict. Groups such as Basque Homeland and Freedom (ETA), Revolutionary Armed Forces of Colombia (FARC), and the Liberation Tigers of Tamil Eelam (LTTE)—outlawed by the U.S. State Department as terrorist organizations—act within a prolonged and violent terrorist campaign. Their struggles include demands for substantial political or socioeconomic reform. For this reason, an important distinction has been made between negotiations during "practical/tactical" terrorist events such as hostage taking or kidnapping, and "political/strategic" negotiations to end long-standing terrorist campaigns.

This chapter analyzes two tactics that states use to influence extremists and that may influence the opening of negotiations with terrorist groups: (1) mechanisms designed to regulate violence, such as cease-fires or truces, and (2) measures designed to restrict perpetrators, such as banning by making it illegal to be a member of, or provide support to, the group in question. These measures are commonly addressed in the prenegotiation phase. While the government may demand a cease-fire by the terrorists as a condition to negotiation, government-imposed antiterrorist measures can be a hurdle preventing the terrorist group from negotiating with the government. Although cease-fires and antiterrorist measures are closely linked as governments and terrorists engage in negotiation, they have generally been treated as two separate issues related to conflict, and only rarely studied in connection to negotiation. This chapter suggests that the main problem of using tactics to regulate violence, including demands for cease-fires and the banning of armed opposition groups as terrorists, is that these measures deny the opposition group legitimacy and recognition. Since any meaningful negotiation depends on the parties' mutual recognition, these tactics can potentially create obstacles to the inception of negotiation. However, under certain circumstances, measures to regulate violence can also be used as vehicles for building trust and confidence between the government and the terrorists.

The chapter begins with an outline of the theoretical arguments regarding cease-fires and counterterrorist measures providing both incentives and disincentives for negotiations between governments and terrorist groups. Next, the cases are analyzed to probe the dynamics at work in negotiation processes to end long-standing terrorist campaigns within the context of a larger political conflict. Two cases with long-standing terrorist campaigns—Sri Lanka and Northern Ireland—will be discussed at some length. The chapter also examines three other cases of attempted negotiations with groups labeled terrorists—FARC in Colombia, ETA in the Basque conflict, and PLO and Hamas in the Israel-Palestine conflict—to assess the validity of the dynamics uncovered in the Sri Lanka and Northern Ireland cases. For more in-depth discussions of two of these cases, see the chapter on Sri Lanka, by Groeneveld-Savisaar and Vuković, and the chapter on Colombia, by Civico, in this volume. The conclusion provides insights generated from the comparison and points specifically to the precarious relationship between violence-regulating mechanisms and legitimacy.

Obstacles to Negotiations with Terrorists

Negotiations take place when both parties realize that a purely unilateral strategy will not resolve the conflict. However, the start of negotiations may be impeded by conditions pertaining to the relationship between parties (e.g., lack of trust), relationships within the parties (e.g., internal divisions on strategy), and substance or process (e.g., agenda setting). Thus, to overcome some of the key obstacles and for serious negotiations to begin, a period of prenegotiation is often necessary (Saunders 1996; Zartman 1989).

Negotiations with terrorists arise out of the *need to stop violence*. At the same time, the acts of terrorism themselves are a key impediment to negotiations. Governments are reluctant to grant concessions to groups that have committed morally deplorable acts of violence. Initiating negotiations with terrorist groups entails a number of risks. In particular, engaging is likely to be seen as irresponsible and a sign of weakness (Spector 2003, 618–19). Also, governments "must consider how concessions might provoke their own base of support. What may be gained in diminished violence from the challengers may be lost through new violence from the now disaffected members of the establishment" (Sederberg 1995, 309). In this sense, the internal dynamics of the government side might be affected. Rebels, too, may be divided internally on what is termed the "tactical question." The tactical question concerns the difficult issue whether to negotiate or continue the violent tactics.

Moreover, terrorists generally have a difficult time demonstrating credibility, which, in turn, may prevent the government from seeking dialogue (Jönsson 1990; Schelling 1995; Bapat 2006, 226). For this reason, governments frequently demand a cease-fire as a condition for negotiations, to test the terrorists' trustworthiness. The idea is that in the early stages of a negotiation process, a cease-fire can reduce mistrust and cultivate confidence between the parties (Randle 1973, 8; Zartman 1995, 337). A cease-fire can also be used to test whether the terrorist group has control over its cadres or whether spoiler elements will emerge, as Pettyjohn discusses in her chapter.

In many cases, the calling of a cease-fire has been a prerequisite for the start of peace negotiations. Cease-fires, which temporarily regulate military activity, are the most commonly thought-of way to regulate violence before and during negotiations (James Smith 1995; Fortna 2004). There are also other means to provide incentives for terrorists to lay down their arms, such as the provision of amnesties (Hayes 2002). In many peace processes, deliberate efforts have been made to regulate violence by including violence makers in the political process in exchange for their promise to abandon violence. But terrorists may have a difficult time establishing trustworthiness, and the parties may seek other sources of credibility, such as external involvement (Bapat 2006, 214). For this reason, international monitors are often brought in to verify the agreement and to report violations.

Unwillingness of the opponent to accept a cease-fire may also create a dilemma that hinders negotiations (Ikle 1991, 87). Terrorists and other armed groups generally gain a seat at the negotiation table through the power they wield by their willingness to use force (Philipson 2005). This reflects the fact that "[v]iolence is the terrorist's principal mode of operation" (Spector 2003, 616). Thus, pushing parties to lay down their arms too early may have an adverse effect by creating a reluctance to negotiate. Moreover, a cease-fire "removes the dynamic relationship between force and negotiation, and the possibility of last-minute adjustments in power relations" (Zartman 1995, 336–37).

Both individual states and international organizations have taken deliberate *actions short of the use of military force* to tackle terrorist activities. Antiterrorist measures came to the foreground at the international level toward the end of the 1990s, and 9/11 and the "global war on terror" propelled this trend. In 2001, the UN Security Council adopted Resolution 1373, making it mandatory for states to impose financial sanctions against individuals and groups that perpetrate or support activities carried out by groups labeled "terrorist."[1]

Antiterrorist measures can be seen as a type of targeted sanction and are a way of isolating the terrorists (Hayes, Kaminski, and Beres 2003, 463; Cortright and Lopez 2000; Cortright, Lopez, and Gerber 2002; Tostensen and Bull 2002; Wallensteen and Staibano 2005). Although sanctions are often directed against governments, in this chapter "sanctions" refers to actions taken against nonstate groups. Antiterrorist measures and policies adopted by states or organizations can be either of a defensive (deterrence) or proactive (preemption) nature (Crenshaw 2001; Sandler 2005; Bures 2006; Faria 2006). They may include freezing assets, jamming broadcasts, banning travel for individuals or representatives of organization involved in terrorist activities, and criminalizing membership in, or collection of funds for, banned entities. International organizations and individual states have developed lists of proscribed organizations. The logic of these types of sanction is that by raising the costs of pursuing terrorist activities, they will force individuals and groups to abandon terrorism. These measures to counter violence can also encourage terrorists to seek a negotiated settlement with the government.[2]

In practice, however, these measures are not without drawbacks from the point of view of negotiations. First, mutual recognition is necessary for meaningful negotiations to begin (Sederberg 1995, 306). Beyond the suppression of resources that antiterrorist measures may have, labeling a group "terrorist" also denies the outlawed group legitimacy and the possibility of negotiation (Bhaita 2005, 13, Toros 2008). Thus, "isolation or sanctions can, in some circumstances, make an armed group less inclined or able to participate in a peace process" (Ricigliano 2005). Second, bans make it difficult for both domestic and international actors to engage constructively and seek dialogue with proscribed groups (Helgesen 2007). Individuals or organizations that work with the listed groups can easily be labeled "terrorist sympathizers" and can even be breaking the law by being in contact with representatives of the group, even for information or to convince them to enter negotiations (Philipson 2005). Thus, proscription inhibits involvement of international and civil society actors.[3]

Northern Ireland, Sri Lanka, and Beyond

The empirical record of negotiations with terrorist groups shows mixed results on the effect of cease-fires and antiterrorist measures. Some of the dynamics at work are illustrated in the following sections, which draw on insights from five cases. The analysis raises important questions about when and why cease-fires and antiterrorist measures are effective or ineffective tools for bringing an end to terrorist activities and initiating negotiations. The discussion begins with fairly detailed analyses of Northern Ireland and Sri Lanka and then moves on to discuss Colombia, the Basque conflict, and Israel-Palestine.

Northern Ireland

The state-formation conflict in Northern Ireland arose from conflicting ideas on whether the union between Northern Ireland and Great Britain should continue or the province should be part of the Republic of Ireland. In the late 1960s, Northern Ireland saw the emergence and reemergence of militant groups that used terrorist violence to pursue the cause, most prominently the main republican paramilitaries, the Provisional Irish Republican Army (PIRA).[4] Created in 1916, the IRA was active in the struggle against the British, for Irish independence (Coogan 1993; M.L.R. Smith 1995; Taylor 1997; O'Doherty 1998; O'Brien 1999). Sinn Fein, widely seen as the political wing of the IRA, is organized in both the Republic of Ireland and Northern Ireland.

The British government sought to control the activities of Sinn Fein and the IRA by various countermeasures. After violence spread across the self-governing Northern Ireland in 1968–69, British troops were sent in but failed to restore order. In 1971, a policy of internment of suspected terrorists without trial was adopted. The mass arrest of Catholics that followed provoked widespread resentment within the nationalist community. After imposing direct rule on Northern Ireland, the British government attempted a policy of criminalization of political violence to deal with the IRA and other paramilitary groups. Wide powers for the security forces were incorporated into the Northern Ireland (Emergency Provisions) Act of 1973.[5] This criminalization, which also meant a loss of legitimacy for the cause, failed. The withdrawal in 1976 of a "special category" for political prisoners led to dirty protests (in which the inmates refused to leave their cells to wash or use the toilet) and hunger strikes among Republican prisoners (O'Leary and McGarry 1996, 205–06; Dickson 2009).

From 1973, the IRA was a proscribed organization. The Broadcasting Act (1988) made it illegal to broadcast direct statements from outlawed paramilitary groups and their political wings, such as Sinn Fein. These bans led to restrictions on Sinn Fein that made it difficult for moderate parties to enter into dialogue with paramilitaries without themselves being accused of supporting terrorism.

Internationally, the Sinn Fein/IRA was also facing constraints.[6] The IRA relied heavily on the Irish diaspora in the United States for funding the armed struggle, and high-ranking members of the IRA frequently traveled to the United States for propaganda meetings and fund-raising activities. Sinn Fein leader Gerry Adams was denied a visa to enter the United States throughout the 1980s and early 1990s, on the grounds that his political party was supporting IRA terrorist violence. In 1989, the U.S. Defense Intelligence Agency listed the IRA as "one of the fifty-two most notorious terrorist groups in the world" (Sharrock and Devenport 1997, 320).

The U.S. government generally had a noninterventionist policy toward the Northern Ireland questions because of its close relations with the British government. This shifted with the election of President Bill Clinton, who took a more active stance toward the conflict. Though subjected to heavy lobbying from Irish American activists, he denied Gerry Adams a visa on two occasions during 1993. But in late January 1994, Adams was authorized a visa of "limited duration" to enter the United States to address a peace conference. Although the National Security Council and Irish American politicians supported the visa, it went against the wishes of the State Department and the British government. For this reason, Clinton "stood accused of rewarding terrorism" (Dumbrell 2000, 215). But Clinton decided it was time to reach out to Adams, help move the peace process forward, and bring about a cease-fire. In early 1995, Washington lifted the ban on Sinn Fein fund-raising in the United States after Adams publicly promised to move on decommissioning (Dumbrell 2000, 217–18).

The granting of a visa to Adams was important in giving Sinn Fein/IRA long-awaited legitimacy. Although Adams was still banned by the British media, during his visit to the United States he appeared on the media and made headlines all over the world. The decision was very controversial and did not go down well with the British government and the unionist parties in Northern Ireland. But in the end, the granting of legitimacy helped facilitate the subsequent IRA cease-fire and the beginning of negotiations.

A cease-fire was a long-standing demand and a prerequisite from the British government to opening negotiations with the IRA. But although a truce by the IRA in 1975 did not lead to substantial negotiations, the 1994 cease-fire led to negotiations that produced the comprehensive Good Friday Agreement in 1998. In this way, the IRA's moderation preceded moderation by the government. However, the cease-fire opened the way for concessions by the British government (including lifting bans), but due to opposition from the unionist and loyalist camp, several years would pass before the agreement could be struck.

Before the cease-fire, secret channels of communication had been established between the government and Sinn Fein/IRA, although the British government denied it at the time. Moreover, despite being accused of supporting terrorism, the moderate nationalist Social Democratic and Labour Party (SDLP) had secret contacts with Gerry Adams, and a public, historic meeting in 1988.

After the IRA cease-fire in August 1994, there were real hopes that meaningful negotiations would begin. The security situation improved substantially after the loyalist cease-fire. The broadcast ban was lifted on September 16, 1994, shortly after the cease-fire. The next couple of years saw only small moves toward a settlement. The loyalist paramilitaries formally held the cease-fire throughout the negotiation process. The IRA cease-fire broke down in 1996 but was reinstated the next year. A major obstacle was the issue of decommissioning.

The paramilitary cease-fires in 1994 were seen as important shifts toward the start of peace negotiations, but reactions to the republican cease-fire had been diverse. The Irish government received the cease-fires positively and demonstrated its support through public meetings with the republicans. But the British government and, in particular, the unionists were uncertain about the IRA's commitment, since the cease-fire statement had not referred to a "permanent" cessation of the armed struggle. High-ranking government officials did not hold any bilateral talks with Sinn Fein representatives until May 1995.

The British government and the unionists also requested that the IRA decommission its weapons as a "gesture of good faith" (Mac Ginty and Darby 2002, 30; von Tangen Page 1998; Hauswedell and O'Hagan 2001). But the IRA saw turning in its arms as an act of surrender and the government demand as British unwillingness to begin the all-party talks. Over the course of the negotiation process, decommissioning was clearly one of the most contentious issues.

In November 1996, the British and Irish governments presented a twin-track strategy to get to the point where all-party talks could begin.

A visit by President Clinton served as an incentive for the governments to agree on the new strategy. Clinton had earlier refrained from traveling to Northern Ireland, due to the lack of an IRA cease-fire. The new strategy involved establishing an International Body on Arms Decommissioning to report on ways to move the decommissioning issue forward. Former U.S. senator George Mitchell was appointed to chair the commission, and the Irish and British governments planned to start negotiations about twelve weeks after the decommissioning body had begun its work.

The commission had completed its report by the end of January 1996. It was recommended that all-party talks and decommissioning occur simultaneously and that all parties agree to a set of principles before entering into negotiations. The principles included a basic commitment to nonviolence and democracy and became known as the Mitchell principles.

Despite these efforts, patience within the IRA had run out, and the organization's more hard-line elements gained strength at the expense of the moderates. A year and a half after the 1994 cease-fire, in February 2006, the IRA resumed its armed campaign with a bomb explosion in the Docklands area of London. The return to violence left Sinn Fein marginalized in the ensuing peace negotiations. In the meantime, negotiations in an all-party forum began, but Sinn Fein was not allowed into the talks until after the IRA had renewed its cease-fire in July 1997.

The renewed cease-fire did not end the violence entirely. In particular, the killing of loyalist leader Billy Wright in late September 1997 set off a cycle of revenge and counterrevenge killings. Sinn Fein and parties linked to loyalist paramilitary groups were temporarily expelled from the peace talks due to these cease-fire violations. But in early spring of 1998, the negotiations picked up speed, and on April 10, after intense diplomatic efforts, the parties reached a peace agreement. The agreement sketched out new political arrangements for Northern Ireland (Cradden and Collins 1999; Nesbitt 1999; Bew 2000). Still no agreement had been reached on the arms issue, although the parties committed themselves to work for a complete decommissioning.

The cease-fire facilitated the initiation of peace talks, and violence in Northern Ireland decreased substantially (Fay, Morrissey, and Smyth 1998, 17). However, the paramilitaries changed their violence tactics after the cease-fire and the Mitchell principles by, for example, using punishment beatings instead of punishment shootings, so that the violence was not seen as breaching the cease-fire (Mac Ginty and Darby 2002, 89).

The peace agreement was put to a referendum in May 1998, in both Northern Ireland and the Irish Republic. An overwhelming majority (more than 90 percent) of the nationalists supported the peace deal. The unionist community, however, had a more negative outlook on the agreement, and only a slight majority of unionists cast supporting votes. The new provincial assembly was up and running in the year 2000, but the IRA's failure to decommission its weapons hampered its work. Economic sanctions were also used against political parties linked to violence. For instance, the IRA's implication in a serious armed robbery of a bank in Belfast in December 2004 resulted in the removal of financial assistance to Sinn Fein.

The IRA's continued association with violence, in particular in the bank robbery in 2004 and the killing of a Catholic civilian in January 2005, also led the United States to reimpose a ban on Sinn Fein's fund-raising activities. However, since mid-2005, positive developments have taken place. In July 2005, the IRA announced that it "formally ordered an end to the armed struggle" and that all its arms were to be decommissioned. In September of the same year, the arms decommissioning body verified the IRA's last move to put its arms beyond use.

To conclude, in Northern Ireland, issues related to terrorist violence were at the center of the peace process and continued to be a major obstacle in implementing the peace agreement. In the early stages of the conflict, harsh counterterrorist legislation and domestic delegitimization had served to strengthen support for the IRA. Yet during the peace process, the recognition of the IRA internationally (especially by the United States) became an important instrument in bolstering Sinn Fein's legitimacy. Northern Ireland's peace process also highlights the importance of finding the balance of sticks and carrots in the measures to regulate violence. The Mitchell principles were creative in this sense and provided a basis for Sinn Fein's and the IRA's inclusion or exclusion in the peace talks, based on the use or nonuse of violence.

Sri Lanka

The main players in the violent conflict in Sri Lanka have been the Sinhalese-dominated government and the Tamil rebels, the Liberation Tigers of Tamil Eelam, demanding an independent Tamil state in the north and east of the country. The conflict had its genesis in 1983, but there had been recurring spates of violence between the Sinhalese majority and the Tamil minority long before that. The Tamils' grievance has its origin in the discriminatory reforms after independence in 1948, which favored the Sinhalese, after colonial rule had favored the Tamils.[7]

Compared to the conflict in Northern Ireland, Sri Lanka has seen a much larger number of casualties, especially in the last few years of the war. In addition to fighting between the LTTE and government forces in the northern and eastern parts of Sri Lanka, political assassinations and bombings in the capital, Colombo, have been features of the conflict. The LTTE also used suicide bombers as part of the violent struggle and assassinated two leaders who attempted to negotiate with the group: Indian prime minister Rajiv Gandhi and Sri Lankan prime minister Ranasinghe Premadasa. The LTTE also came close to killing president Chandrika Kumaratunga in 1999.

Negotiations to end the conflict between the LTTE and the government began on five separate occasions. The last attempt began after Ranil Wickremesinghe and the United National Party (UNP) won the election in 2001. In February 2002, the parties signed a cease-fire agreement facilitated by Norway. After several rounds of negotiations between the parties, the LTTE left the peace talks in April 2003. Thereafter the peace process stalled, and a massive escalation in late 2005 resulted in a new war, leading to the LTTE's annihilation by the middle of 2009.

Sri Lanka has taken a number of antiterrorist measures. The LTTE was banned as a terrorist group in 1978. The next year, Parliament approved the Prevention of Terrorism Act, which was strongly influenced by British antiterrorist legislation (De Silva 1998, 184–85). But the legislation had the "opposite effect to the one intended, it stiffened the Tamil resistance movement" (Wilson 2001, 124).[8]

In the early stages of the 2002 peace process, deproscription of the LTTE was among the most contentious issues. To achieve recognition and a sense of parity, the LTTE demanded that the government remove the ban before talks could start. For instance, the demand was stated in LTTE leader Prabhakaran's speech at a press conference in April 2002: "The LTTE viewed the deproscription as a visible sign of power asymmetry between the two" (Rudrakumaran 2005). Demands for deproscription aroused strong resistance from the Buddhist clergy and opposition parties (Uyangoda 2003, 3). However, in early September 2002, the government lifted the ban on the LTTE, and later the same month, the first round of talks was held in Thailand.

Internationally, a number of states listed the LTTE as a terrorist organization. India proscribed the group in 1992 after the assassination of former prime minister Rajiv Gandhi. From the end of the 1990s, the Sri Lankan government made deliberate efforts to have the LTTE classified as a terrorist organization. A large diaspora helped finance the armed struggle, and some estimates point to as much as 60 percent of LTTE revenues coming from its international network (both through voluntary donations and through coercion). The United States banned the LTTE in 1999. The UK was a safe haven until February 2001, when the British government outlawed the LTTE. After the attack on the World Trade Center and the

Pentagon in September 2001, the prospects for financing LTTE activities through international sources grew more difficult, and it is reasonable to assume that this affected the LTTE leadership's decision to seek a negotiated settlement instead of continuing the armed struggle. This was indicated in the annual Heroes Day speech, in which Prabhakaran clarified the need to adjust to the changing international context (TamilNet 2002).

Thus, while domestic banning initially bolstered support for the LTTE, changing international norms for how militant groups were countered provided one push factor (although not the only one) for the LTTE to seek negotiations with the government. At the same time, the LTTE refused to enter into negotiations with the government without being legalized and, in this sense, recognized as an equal partner. As in the Northern Ireland case, a combination of push and pull factors in the choice of negotiation tactics appears to be key.

The cease-fire between the government and the LTTE was to be verified and monitored by a Nordic observer mission, the Sri Lanka Monitoring Mission (SLMM).[9] Under the cease-fire, the parties were to retain their military capacity but refrain from offensive actions. A key aim of the cease-fire was to create conditions favorable for peace negotiations.

The cease-fire brought immediate gains in the security situation. For the first time in many years, and within only a few months, freedom of movement of goods and people over the entire island improved. However, cease-fire violations were committed by both parties over the years, with increasing intensity. The information on complaints and cease-fire violations, provided by the SLMM, showed that in the first years of the cease-fire, the vast bulk of the complaints and rulings were against the LTTE. However, after the conflict escalated in 2005, any reference to a cease-fire, by either party, was misleading since both parties violated the agreement regularly. Also, both the government and the LTTE continued to build up their military capacity during the cease-fire (Ganguly 2004, 910–11).

The freedom of movement granted under the cease-fire and deproscription allowed the LTTE to open political offices in government-controlled areas. While this is a necessary step in an eventual transformation of the LTTE into a viable political actor, the newly won freedoms were also used for less benign reasons. For instance, one result was that extortion, intimidation, and forced recruitment expanded beyond the areas of LTTE control.

While the Sri Lankan government unbanned the LTTE ahead of peace talks, the United States and other countries did not lift their "terrorist" designation and ban. This was a way of exerting pressure on the LTTE, but it also undermined the group's willingness to negotiate and, by extension, undermined progress on the peace process. The most blatant example concerns the Washington donor meeting in April 2003. The meeting was a preconference to the Tokyo donor meeting to be held later the same year. But because the United States had proscribed the LTTE as a terrorist organization, representatives from the LTTE could not be invited to the meeting. The choice of location was upsetting to the LTTE and is stated as one of the reasons why it abandoned the negotiations with the government in 2003. The LTTE clearly linked reconstruction efforts and normalization to the establishment of interim institutions that would grant it powers. The LTTE's exclusion from the Washington meeting was, therefore, seen as an indication of the government's unwillingness to establish interim institutions and continue the joint effort for reconstruction (Balasingham 2004). Thus, failure to include the LTTE in these talks undermined the group's confidence in the government and in the peace negotiations.

After the LTTE's withdrawal from the peace talks in 2003, the peace process was characterized by continuing violence and lack of progress in the political arena. The Sri Lankan government's political crisis in April 2004 brought a more hard-line government to power. Shortly before that—to the surprise of both the government and international observers—a splinter group emerged from the LTTE, with heavy internal fighting as a result. Threats, intimidation, and killings between Tamil paramilitaries and within the LTTE outstripped the violence between LTTE and government forces and called into question the value of the cease-fire (Höglund 2005). Several high-profile killings occurred, including the August 2005 assassination of Foreign Minister Lakshman Kadirgamar, allegedly by the LTTE. From December 2005, escalating violence between LTTE and government forces amounted to full-fledged war.

The continuation of such attacks and the lack of progress in the peace process led additional countries to take measures against the LTTE. Canada classified the organization as terrorist in April 2006, and in late May 2006, the EU followed suit after substantial pressure from the Sri Lankan government. Before that, the UK was the only EU member that had outlawed the LTTE. In September 2005, after the assassination of Foreign Minister Kadirgamar, the EU imposed restrictions on LTTE visits to EU countries. The ban seems to have come as a surprise to the LTTE leadership, who had become increasingly isolated. Before the ban, the political wing of the LTTE had received many warnings about developments in that direction but had probably failed to convey this to the leadership. The Nordic members of the EU opposed a full ban because they believed it could affect the functioning of SLMM. This turned out to be the case. When the full ban was imposed in 2006, the LTTE made clear that the

Swedes, Danes, and Finns working for the SLMM were no longer welcome. By September, they had all been forced to leave the mission, with only those monitors from Norway and Iceland remaining. The Sri Lankan army offensive in 2008-09 killed any chance for a peaceful ending to the conflict and destroyed the LTTE, at huge civilian cost.

The Sri Lankan case illustrates how the cease-fire opened up space for serious negotiations. But although a cease-fire was a condition for the government, the LTTE would begin talks only after its deproscription, which points to the importance of mutual recognition and trust building for peace talks to progress. And yet, continuing violence undermined trust and made it difficult for states and international actors (pressured by the Sri Lankan government) not to list the LTTE as a terrorist entity. The proscription marginalized the LTTE and effectively closed the door to a negotiated settlement.

Additional Cases: Colombia, Spain, and Israel-Palestine

How have the same dynamics revealed in Sri Lanka and Northern Ireland played out in other conflicts? To expand the scope of comparison, three further cases merit brief discussion.

Colombia and FARC

In Colombia, the long-standing conflict between the government and the left-wing Revolutionary Armed Forces of Colombia has experienced several incomplete negotiation attempts. The government has pursued different negotiation strategies, both with FARC cease-fires as conditions for talks and with negotiations amid violent confrontation. In many cases, a cease-fire has been the very objective of negotiations. For instance, negotiations between the Betancur administration and FARC produced a cease-fire in 1984. As a result, FARC created a political wing, the Patriotic Union (UP), which took part in democratic politics. But right-wing paramilitary groups with links to the government murdered UP candidates and elected officials. The killings occurred on a large scale over the next couple of years, totaling some 3,000 deaths (Chernick 1999, 176–77). For this reason and others, the cease-fire unraveled after a few years, and FARC resumed the armed struggle.

In the early 1990s, FARC joined other guerrilla groups to develop a common negotiation position. Several meetings were held outside Colombia, again without the condition of a cease-fire. In the talks, the parties got as far as discussing the agenda, but they could not agree on how the cease-fire should be implemented at the local level (Chernick 1999, 181). Due to continued violence by both the guerrillas and the government, negotiations were suspended in 1992.

Similarly, from 1998 to 2002, the Pastrana government sought to negotiate with FARC despite continued confrontation. A large piece of territory was demilitarized and was to be used for meetings between the guerrillas and government officials. In late December 1999 and early January 2000, FARC announced a unilateral cease-fire to help build trust. Its representatives also made a "lessons learned" trip to Europe, to build capacity for negotiations. But the peace process fell apart after FARC hijacked an airplane in which a senator was traveling. The failure to end the conflict led to the growth of paramilitary groups, in particular the United Self-Defense Forces of Colombia (AUC).

FARC has been on the U.S. list of terrorist organizations since 1997 and has also been proscribed as terrorist by the EU. The strong U.S. stance against FARC has not been conducive to peace talks (Tate 2004). President Clinton supported Pastrana's initiative, but after three U.S. citizens were killed in Colombia in 1999, all U.S. contacts with FARC were discontinued. Before the "war on terror," the U.S. focus was on counternarcotics, since FARC has long funded its activities through drug smuggling. In 2000, the Colombian and U.S. governments launched Plan Colombia, which included $1.3 billion in U.S. "emergency aid." In fact, the money was used to support counternarcotics activities. After 2001, the Colombian and U.S. governments used the "war on terror" as a pretext to intensify counternarcotics activities.

After the failed negotiations under Pastrana, and Álvaro Uribe's installation as president in 2002, security became the key priority.[10] No serious attempts to negotiate have been made, although recent years have seen some openings on the issue of prisoner exchange. FARC remains a powerful armed actor due to its revenues from narcotics. But the guerrillas have become increasingly isolated. Their charismatic leader, Marulanda, died in 2008, and several of their hostages escaped, sometimes using clever ruses. The leader's death led to an informal splitting of the movement, with some parts losing their nerve and others turning to harsher terrorist tactics. FARC used to have offices in Mexico City, and strong connections in European leftist circles. The International Crisis Group, in its analysis of FARC's contrasting features, said, "Listed as an international terrorist organization by the U.S. and the E.U., it may be richer than ever, but it is increasingly isolated in Colombia and in the world" (International Crisis Group 2005, 13).

The Colombian case tells us that cease-fires may be necessary to create conditions conducive for peace negotiations. Without a genuine will on both sides to regulate and restrain violence, insecurity may simply be too widespread for parties to push forward with negotiations. International counterterrorism measures, by the United States in particular, have been instrumental in isolating the guerrillas. But this isolation has made it more difficult to reach FARC through dialogue, hampering attempts at reaching a negotiated settlement.

The Basque Conflict and ETA

There have been repeated attempts to negotiate an end to the conflict between the Spanish government and the separatist group Euskadi Ta Askatasuna (ETA). ETA has been struggling for an independent Basque country, encompassing territory in northern Spain and southwestern France. Since the beginning of the conflict, the Spanish government has insisted on a cease-fire before serious talks can begin (Clark 1990). But of the many cease-fires that ETA has declared, few have resulted in any real progress. This is because they have often been of a temporary nature, and ETA has often radicalized its stance after aborted cease-fire attempts. Such was the case following a three-month cease-fire in 1992, which resulted in, instead of talks, an effort to eliminate the ETA leadership.

Major public mobilization against violence resulted in a unilateral and indefinite cease-fire in 1998. But the government refused to hold talks about the demands that ETA had put forward. Eventually, ETA resumed the violent struggle in late 1999. The government accused the separatists of using the cease-fire as a pretext to rearm and regroup. Hopes were revived when ETA announced a "permanent" cease-fire in March 2006, but again serious negotiations were delayed. A bomb attack on the new Barajas Airport in Madrid in December 2006 put an end to the peace process. The attack took place after the ETA had voiced discontent concerning the lack of progress in the talks.

The environment of antiterrorist legislation and counterterrorist measures in which ETA operates has changed dramatically over the years. Under Franco's dictatorship, until 1974, any kind of armed opposition was repressed with scant regard for civilian casualties. In the early years of democracy, antiterrorist measures had the opposite effect of the one intended (Alonso and Reinares 2005, 267). In particular, a counterterrorist paramilitary unit, Grupos Antiterroristas de Liberación (GAL), with links to the government, carried out assassinations of ETA members and civilians loosely connected to the organization, during 1983–87. Disclosure of GAL and its activities strengthened ETA and Basque "radical nationalism" (Mees 2000, 158).

Antiterrorist measures and public pressure in the wake of 9/11 are believed to have hit ETA quite hard (Conversi 2006). Efforts to crack down on ETA included, for example, increased police cooperation within the EU, and the freezing of bank accounts. For a long time, ETA members had been able to seek refuge in France. But after GAL was revealed in the late 1980s, French and Spanish police began working together to combat ETA.

The political activities of the ETA-linked political party Harri Batasuna have been suppressed. Batasuna was outlawed in 2003 for its failure to deplore ETA violence. Newspapers and radio stations have also been closed. The banning of Batasuna was against the wishes of nationalist parties in the Basque parliament. But these actions have weakened ETA and decreased violence (Alonso and Reinares 2005). On March 11, 2004, international terrorism had reached Spain with the Madrid train attacks. The bombings, though initially blamed on ETA, were carried out by Islamist extremists. A problem related to antiterrorist legislation is that ETA prisoners have been dispersed in prisons all over Spain, including in the Canary Islands, far from the Basque areas in the north. This has added new conflict issues and has brought severe criticism from human rights organizations.

Antiterrorist measures, both domestic and international, in the struggle against ETA have contributed to the weakening of the organization but have also added new issues to the negotiation agenda. This case also makes the case that demands for cease-fires can be effective in converting terrorists only if concessions relating to the political conflict are also forthcoming from the other side.

Israel-Palestine: The PLO and Hamas

The long-standing conflict between Israel and Palestine has experienced some of the most intriguing developments regarding negotiations with groups labeled "terrorist." The Palestinian Liberation Organization (PLO) was organized to fight against the existence of Israel and, later, for Palestinian statehood.[11] The PLO put terrorism on the world's agenda, with international hijackings and hostage takings in the 1960s and the 1970s (including the high-profile hostage crisis at the Munich Olympics). Despite such incidents, the PLO had much greater international legitimacy than those groups labeled "terrorist" today, if only because the conflict involves one state's occupation of neighboring territory that does not belong to it (and which, in fact, the United Nations originally set aside as a separate state), whereas the other four cases mentioned here involve terrorism to support breakaway movements internal to one state. For instance, in 1974, the UN General Assembly gave the PLO observer status. During the 1970s and 1980s, more than fifty states recognized the PLO (Donohue 2005, 21).

In negotiation attempts between the Israeli government and the Palestinians, some Arab governments have acted as intermediaries between the PLO and the Israeli government (Kriesberg 2001, 380). In the early 1990s, an internationally mediated peace process, the so-called Madrid process, had begun, but it yielded little substantive progress. Instead, talks began via a secret back channel, facilitated by Norway, producing the Oslo Accords in 1993. The accords had been negotiated against the backdrop of continued armed resistance, and one of the main ends of the deal was to stop the violence. The agreement also provided for the parties' mutual recognition. Israel officially recognized the PLO as the Palestinians' legitimate representative, the Palestinian Authority (self-governing institutions in Gaza and the West Bank) was created, and the PLO accepted the Israeli state.

A key problem with the agreement was that Hamas was not part of the deal (and indeed constituted a common cause that brought Israel and the PLO together). Israel had banned Hamas in 1989 and had imprisoned its leader, Sheikh Ahmed Yassin. Hamas criticized the Oslo Accords and the peace process and continued with suicide bombings and other violent attacks. The Israeli side had recognized that it was a matter of "deal[ing] either with the PLO today, or Hamas tomorrow" (Shikaki 1998, 43). But the peace process and talks about independence were contingent on the Palestinian Authority's ability to crack down on violence against Israel. Israel tried to curb the violence, but much of this effort proved counterproductive. Failure to settle the issues of violence, Israeli settlements in the Palestinian areas, refugees, and Jerusalem resulted in a popular uprising (intifada) in the Palestinian areas in 2000.

The breakdown of the Oslo process resulted in the paradoxical situation in which Hamas, in January 2006, gained democratic legitimacy in the elections to the legislature of the Palestinian Authority. Hamas is designated a terrorist entity by Israel, the EU, Canada, Japan, and the United States, and banned by many other counties. Hamas's aim has been to create an Islamic state in the area that once was Palestine (much of it now within Israeli borders since the division in 1948). Hamas is also an important provider of welfare programs, school funding, health services, and other services, which helps explain its popular attraction in the Palestinian areas.

Although elected to the Palestinian government, Hamas has been subject to economic and diplomatic sanctions from Israel and other Western countries because it does not recognize Israel's right to exist. In May 2006, the United States, Russia, the United Nations, and the EU decided to resume funding, but funds were channeled directly to the Palestinian population, not to the Palestinian Authority. An additional result was the intense rivalry among different Palestinian factions. In 2004, several PLO factions, such as the al-Aqsa Martyrs Brigade, were also designated terrorist organizations by the United States.

Before the election of Hamas to the Palestinian Authority, Hamas had
attempted several cease-fires, which were to serve as test balloons for assessing Israel's willingness to negotiate (Crooke 2005). The cease-fires
yielded few political responses and changed little on the ground. After one
cease-fire ended in August 2003 with bomb attacks on buses in Jerusalem,
more countries, including the EU, outlawed Hamas. While the EU ban
did not influence Hamas much in terms of financing, it further isolated
the organization and pushed it further away from negotiations. In Hamas's
view, the ban "gave the 'green light' to Israel to try to assassinate their leadership" (Crooke 2005).

Conclusions

The comparison of cases of negotiations between governments and armed
opposition groups, with a special eye on the influence of cease-fires and
antiterrorist measures, generates some tentative ideas about how such
measures can impede or help facilitate the initiation of talks between governments and terrorists.

Cease-fires potentially create a number of conditions conducive for
negotiations to end protracted terrorist campaigns. Cease-fires generally
come about in one of three ways: (1) imposed (when it is a condition by
one of the parties, as in the Northern Ireland case), (2) unilateral (when one
of the parties voluntarily offers a cease-fire, as in the case of Hamas), and
(3) bilateral (when both parties agree on a cease-fire, as in the 2002 cease-
fire in Sri Lanka). All three kinds of cease-fire can serve as a test of confidence and be a show of good faith between the terrorists and the government. If a cease-fire improves the situation on the ground, as initially was
the case in both Sri Lanka and Northern Ireland, it can help the government
fend off criticism from those opposed to negotiations with terrorists.

However, a key problem with cease-fires concerns the basic asymmetry between the government and nonstate actors such as terrorist groups.
The government has a legitimate claim to power and, in normal times, a
monopoly on the use of force. To the IRA, LTTE, FARC, ETA, PLO,
and Hamas, one of the few tools they can wield to put pressure on, and
extract concessions from, the government is the use of violence. For this
reason, terrorist groups will be understandably reluctant to abandon the
violence option as negotiations begin. And they will be even more resistant
to demands that they give up their arms before a solution to the conflict
is reached. In some cases, the government side has taken advantage of

cease-fires to crack down even harder on a terrorist group, as in the Basque conflict. In Colombia, right-wing groups took advantage of the cessation of hostilities to kill members of the political party UP, which was an off-spring of FARC, created in the wake of negotiations. Such matters become important especially when a cease-fire is imposed by the government.

The internal dynamics of rebel groups are usually closely linked to these issues and to the question whether to concede to the government require-ment concerning disarmament. In some cases, such as Northern Ireland, conflicts and tensions within a party might even lead to abandonment of the cease-fire. Also, cease-fires may result in the emergence of new forms of violence not regulated in the cease-fire, as seen in both Sri Lanka and Northern Ireland. While negotiating, the parties to a cease-fire have an interest in not being associated with violations of the agreed principles. Thus, cease-fires can be a useful step toward managing or resolving a con-flict, although they can be expected to be temporary and breakable until the final agreement is reached.

The analysis of antiterrorist measures, short of the use of force, by do-mestic and international actors also yields some interesting insights. Dra-conian counterterrorist legislation was introduced in both Sri Lanka and Northern Ireland to deal with the LTTE and the IRA respectively. How-ever, these measures had the counterproductive effect of strengthening sympathies for the terrorists. Similar developments have also come about in the Basque conflict. It remains an open question whether the ban on Batasuna helps explain the decrease in ETA's violent activity or merely prevents dialogue. It is a tricky question for policymakers, since political activity can be misused for militant mobilization (Höglund 2008).

The experience in Sri Lanka is that bans have not been able to alter mat-ters on the ground, although the changing international climate, particu-larly after 9/11, may have cut some of the LTTE's revenues from abroad. On the other hand, removing a group from a terrorist list can provide a positive incentive by granting legitimacy, as a reward and encouragement for moves toward negotiation (see also Toros 2008). In Sri Lanka, unban-ning the LTTE was a condition for the organization to initiate talks with the government. Similarly, in Northern Ireland, the U.S. entry visa granted to Gerry Adams was an important impetus to convince the IRA of the benefits of a cease-fire. Moreover, criminalization and bans isolate a terror-ist group and can prevent the strengthening of moderate strands within it, which might otherwise provide a platform for negotiations. The exclusion of the LTTE from the Washington donor meeting had a negative effect by increasing the LTTE's sense of marginalization, eventually resulting in its withdrawal from the talks. On the other hand, the legalization of a terrorist group can facilitate the development of a political track by allowing the group to open political offices and carry out political activities. Of course, a crucial distinction between the LTTE and the IRA is that the IRA has had a strong political counterpart in Sinn Fein, which has been able to develop a political strategy and has exerted pressures on the IRA to lay down its arms. The existence of a political wing may be the condition that allows cease-fires and counterterrorism measures to take hold.

How are counterterrorist measures such as bans and criminalization linked to measures through which violence between governments and terrorists is regulated? This chapter suggests that both these kinds of tactics relate to issues of legitimacy. A government's demands for a cease-fire, as well as its designating a group a terrorist organization, enables the government to demonstrate the illegitimacy of the group's activities. Since meaningful negotiations require the parties' basic mutual recognition, issues of legitimacy must be dealt with in the prenegotiation phase. Talking both implies and requires mutual recognition, and recognition is the first step toward productive talks.

Notes

1. Security Council Resolution 1373 built on the 1999 Convention for the Suppression of the Financing of Terrorism. The Security Council also established the Counter Terrorism Committee (CTC)—a committee with unusually strong financial and political support—to monitor compliance and help countries implement the resolution. For a critical view on the EU lists, see Guild 2008.

2. David Cortright and George A. Lopez distinguish between a "punishment" and a "bargaining" model of sanctions (Cortright and Lopez 2000; Cortright, Lopez, and Gerber 2002).

3. As a parallel example, indictments of war criminals by the International Criminal Tribunal for the former Yugoslavia have made constructive engagement with some actors in the Balkans more difficult.

4. "Unionists" commonly refers to those who maintain that Northern Ireland should remain in the United Kingdom of Great Britain and Northern Ireland (UK). Loyalists are those in favor of Northern Ireland's remaining in the UK and who use violence to pursue that goal. A majority of unionist and loyalists are Protestants, who make up about 60 percent of the population in Northern Ireland. Nationalists share an Irish national identity and contend that Northern Ireland should be united with the Republic of Ireland. Republicans are those who have been willing to use violence in the struggle for unification with the Republic of Ireland. Nationalists and republicans are mainly Catholic.

5. Other acts: S.20(1), Prevention of Terrorism (Temporary Provision) Act 1989; S.1(2), Terrorism Act.

6. The Irish government, also, has put various restrictions on the IRA. The broadcast ban was lifted in January 1994, giving Sinn Fein access to Irish media.

7. Around 74 percent of the population in Sri Lanka are Sinhalese, while the Tamils constitute approximately 18 percent. Muslims, identified as ethnically distinct group, make up around 7 percent.

8. See also Manoharan 2006.

9. For more on the cease-fire, the violence, and the SLMM, see Höglund 2005.

10. However, Uribe initiated talks with the AUC after a unilaterally declared cease-fire in December 2002. After 9/11, the AUC had gone on the U.S. terrorist list. The negotiations resulted in the demobilization of more than 30,000 paramilitaries under the legal framework Justice and Peace Law. The law has been viewed as extremely controversial because it gives too many concessions to those responsible for grave human rights abuses.

11. PLO was an umbrella organization. Its largest faction is Fatah.

References

Alonso, Rogelio, and Fernando Reinares. 2005. "Terrorism, Human Rights and Law Enforcement in Spain." *Terrorism and Political Violence* 17 (1): 265–78.

Balasingham, Anton. 2004. *War and Peace: Armed Struggle and Peace Efforts of the Liberation Tigers.* London: Fairmax.

Bapat, Navin A. 2006. "State Bargaining with Transnational Terrorist Groups." *International Studies Quarterly* 50 (1): 213–29.

Bew, Paul. 2000. "The Belfast Agreement of 1998: From Ethnic Democracy to a Multicultural Consociational Settlement?" In Cox, Guelke, and Stephen 2000.

Bhaita, Michael V. 2005. "Fighting Words: Naming Terrorists, Bandits, Rebels and Other Violent Actors." *Third World Quarterly* 26 (1): 5–22.

Bures, Oldrich. 2006. "EU Counterterrorism Policy: A Paper Tiger?" *Terrorism and Political Violence* 18 (1): 57–78.

Chernick, Marc. 1999. "Negotiating Peace amid Multiple Forms of Violence: The Protracted Search for a Settlement to the Armed Conflicts in Colombia." In *Comparative Peace Processes in Latin America,* ed. C. J. Arnson. Washington, DC: Woodrow Wilson Center Press.

Clark, Robert P. 1990. "Negotiating with Insurgents: Obstacles to Peace in the Basque Country." *Terrorism and Political Violence* 2 (4): 489–507.

Conversi, Daniele. 2006. "Why Do Peace Processes Collapse? The Basque Conflict and the Three-Spoilers Perspective." In *Challenges to Peacebuilding: Managing Spoilers during Conflict Resolution,* ed. Edward Newman and Oliver Richmond. New York: United Nations University Press.

Coogan, Tim Pat. 1993. *The IRA.* London: HarperCollins.

Cortright, David, and George Lopez. 2000. *The Sanctions Decade: Assessing UN Strategies in the 1990s.* Boulder, CO: Lynne Rienner.

Cortright, David, George Lopez, and Linda Gerber. 2002. *Sanctions and the Search for Security: Challenges to UN Action.* Boulder, CO: Lynne Rienner.

Cox, Michael, Adrian Guelke, and Fiona Stephen, eds. 2000. *A Farewell to Arms? From "Long War" to Long Peace in Northern Ireland.* Manchester, UK: Manchester University Press.

Cradden, Terry, and Neil Collins. 1999. "The Northern Ireland Peace Agreement." In *Political Issues in Ireland Today,* ed. Neil Collins. Manchester, UK: Manchester University Press.

Crenshaw, Martha. 2001. "Counterterrorism Policy and the Political Process." *Studies in Conflict and Terrorism* 24 (5): 329–37.

Crooke, Alastair. 2005. "In Search of Respect at the Table: Hamas Ceasefires 2001–03." In Ricigliano 2005.

De Silva, K. M. 1998. *Reaping the Whirlwind: Ethnic Conflict, Ethnic Politics in Sri Lanka.* New Delhi: Penguin.

Dickson, Bruce. 2009. "Counter-Insurgency and Human Rights in Northern Ireland." *Journal of Strategic Studies* 32 (3): 475–93.

Donohue, Laura K. 2005. "Terrorism and Counter-Terrorism Discourse." In *Global Anti-Terrorism Law and Policy,* ed. V. V. Ramraj, Michael Hor, and Kent Roach. Cambridge: Cambridge University Press.

Dumbrell, John. 2000. "Hope and History: The US and Peace in Northern Ireland." In Cox, Guelke, and Stephen 2000.

Faria, Joao Ricardo. 2006. "Terrorist Innovation and Anti-Terrorist Policies." *Terrorism and Political Violence* 18 (11): 47–56.

Fay, Marie Therese, Mike Morrissey, and Marie Smyth. 1998. *Mapping Troubles-Related Deaths in Northern Ireland 1969–1998.* 2nd ed. Derry/Londonderry: INCORE.

Fortna, Virginia Page. 2004. *Peace Time: Cease-Fire Agreements and the Durability of Peace.* Princeton, NJ: Princeton University Press.

Ganguly, Rajat. 2004. "Sri Lanka's Ethnic Conflict: At a Crossroad between Peace and War." *Third World Quarterly* 25 (5): 903–18.

Guild, Elspeth. 2008. "The Uses and Abuses of Counter-Terrorism Policies in Europe: The Case of the 'Terrorist Lists.'" *Journal of Common Market Studies* 46 (1): 173–93.

Hauswedell, Corinna, and Liam O'Hagan. 2001. "Demilitarisation in Northern Ireland: The Role of 'Decommissioning' and 'Normalisation of Security' in the Peace Process." Paper read at Ethnic Studies Network Conference, Derry/Londonderry, June 27–30.

Hayes, Richard E. 2002. "Negotiations with Terrorists." In *International Negotiation: Analysis, Approaches, Issues,* ed. Victor A. Kremenyuk. San Francisco: Jossey-Bass.

Hayes, Richard E., Stacey R. Kaminski, and Steven M. Beres. 2003. "Negotiating the Non-Negotiable: Dealing with Absolutist Terrorists." *International Negotiation* 8 (3): 451–67.

Helgesen, Vidar. 2007. "How Peace Diplomacy Lost Post 9/11: What Implications Are There for Norway?" *Oslo Files on Security and Defence,* no. 3.

Höglund, Kristine. 2005. "Violence and the Peace Process in Sri Lanka." *Civil Wars* 7 (2).

———. 2008. "Violence in War-to-Democracy Transitions." In *War-to-Democracy Transitions: Dilemmas of Peacebuilding,* ed. Anna Jarstad and Timothy Sisk. Cambridge, UK: Cambridge University Press.

Ikle, Fred Charles. 1991. *Every War Must End*. Rev. ed. New York: Columbia University Press.

International Crisis Group. 2005. "War and Drugs in Colombia." Crisis Group Latin America Report. no. 11, Jan. 27.

Jönsson, Christer. 1990. *Communication in International Bargaining*. London: Pinter.

Kriesberg, Louis. 2001. "Mediation and the Transformation of the Israeli-Palestinian Conflict." *Journal of Peace Research* 38 (3): 373–92.

Mac Ginty, Roger, and John Darby. 2002. *Guns and Government: The Management of the Northern Ireland Peace Process*. Basingstoke, UK: Palgrave Macmillan.

Manoharan, N. 2006. "Counterterrorism Legislation in Sri Lanka: Evaluating Efficacy." East-West Center, Policy Studies 28. www.eastwestcenter.org/file admin/stored/pdfs/PS028.pdf (accessed Nov. 12, 2010).

Mees, Ludger. 2000. "The Basque Peace Process, Nationalism and Political Violence." In *The Management of Peace Processes*, ed. John Darby and Roger Mac Ginty. Basingstoke, UK: Macmillan.

Nesbitt, Dermot. 1999. "An Assessment of the Belfast Agreement." In *Striking a Balance: The Northern Ireland Peace Process*, ed. Clem McCartney. London: Conciliation Resources.

O'Brien, Brendan. 1999. *The Long War: The IRA and Sinn Féin*. Dublin: O'Brien Press.

O'Doherty, Malachi. 1998. *The Trouble with Guns: The Republican Strategy and the Provisional IRA*. Belfast: Blackstaff.

O'Leary, Brendan, and John McGarry. 1996. *The Politics of Antagonism*. 2nd ed. London: Athlone.

Philipson, Liz. 2005. "Engaging Armed Groups: The Challenge of Asymmetries." In Ricigliano 2005.

Randle, Robert F. 1973. *The Origins of Peace: A Study of Peacemaking and the Structure of Peace Settlements*. New York: Free Press.

Ricigliano, Robert, ed. 2005. *Choosing to Engage: Armed Groups and Peace Processes*. London: Conciliation Resources.

Rudrakumaran, Visuvanathan. 2005. "Asymmetries in the Peace Process: The Liberation Tigers of Tamil Eelam." In Ricigliano 2005.

Sandler, Todd. 2005. "Collective versus Unilateral Responses to Terrorism." *Public Choice* 124: 75–93.

Saunders, Harold H. 1996. "Prenegotiation and Circumnegotiation: Arenas of the Multilevel Peace Process." In *Managing Global Chaos: Sources of and Responses to International Conflict*, ed. C. A. Crocker, F. O. Hampson, and P. R. Aall. Washington, DC: United States Institute of Peace Press.

Schelling, Thomas C. 1995. *The Strategy of Conflict*. 2nd ed. Cambridge, MA: Harvard University Press.

Sederberg, Peter C. 1995. "Conciliation as Counter-Terrorist Strategy." *Journal of Peace Research* 32 (3): 295–312.

Sharrock, David, and Mark Devenport. 1997. *Man of War, Man of Peace? The Unauthorised Biography of Gerry Adams.* Basingstoke, UK: Macmillan.

Shikaki, Khalil. 1998. "Peace Now or Hamas Later." *Foreign Affairs* 77 (4): 29–43.

Smith, James D. 1995. *Stopping Wars: Defining the Obstacles to Cease-Fire.* Boulder, CO: Westview Press.

Smith, M. L. R. 1995. *Fighting for Ireland: The Military Strategy of the Irish Republican Movement.* London: Routledge.

Spector, Bertram I. 2003. "Negotiating with Villains Revisited: Research Note." *International Negotiation* 8 (3): 613–21.

TamilNet. 2002. "LTTE Leader Calls for Autonomy and Self-Government for Tamil Homeland." Nov. 27. www.tamilnet.com/art.html?catid=13&artid=7902 (accessed Nov. 8, 2010).

Tate, Winifred. 2004. "No Room for Peace? United States' Policy in Colombia." In *Alternatives to War: Colombia's Peace Processes,* ed. Mauricio García Durán. London: Conciliation Resources.

Taylor, Peter. 1997. *Provos: The IRA and Sinn Fein.* London: Bloomsbury.

Toros, Harmonie. 2008. "'We Don't Negotiate with Terrorists!' Legitimacy and Complexity in Terrorist Conflicts." *Security Dialogue* 39 (4): 407–26.

Tostensen, Arne, and Beate Bull. 2002. "Are Smart Sanctions Feasible?" *World Politics* 54 (April): 373–403.

Uyangoda, Jayadeva. 2003. "Sri Lanka: 'A Pragmatic' Peace Agenda." In *Sri Lanka's Peace Process: Critical Perspectives,* ed. Jayadeva Uyangoda and Morina Perera. Colombo: Social Scientists Association of Sri Lanka.

von Tangen Page, Michael. 1998. "Arms Decommissioning and the Northern Ireland Peace Agreement." *Security Dialogue* 29 (4): 409–20.

Wallensteen, Peter, and Carina Staibano, eds. 2005. *International Sanctions: Between Words and Wars in the Global System.* London: Frank Cass.

Wilson, A. Jeyaratnam. 2001. *Sri Lankan Tamil Nationalism.* New Delhi: Penguin.

Zartman, I. William. 1989. "Prenegotiation: Phases and Functions." *International Journal* 44 (2): 237–53.

———, ed. 1995. *Elusive Peace: Negotiating an End to Civil War.* Washington, DC: Brookings Institution Press.

9

Eluding Peace?

Negotiating with Colombia's ELN

Aldo Civico

This chapter focuses on Colombia's Ejército de Liberación Nacional (ELN), or National Liberation Army, which has been involved in intermittent negotiations with the government for more than twenty years. More deeply, the chapter examines an extremist organization's attitude toward negotiation, and how and why this attitude has changed over time.

Since its inception in the 1960s and until the mid-1980s, the ELN was firmly opposed to any form of dialogue with the Colombian government. Influenced by its definition of revolution and by the idea of taking and subverting power, it did not conceive of the possibility of compromise and negotiation, even opposing citizen participation in elections. For the ELN, the transformation of the conflict had to happen not through dialogue or negotiations, but as a result of revolutionary violence overturning the bourgeois state. The goal was not transformation but substitution through destruction.

If this was the basic premise of the ELN's struggle, when, and why, did it start talking about peace? And in what terms? How did it frame a discourse of negotiation, and how did its discourse about peace change over time? What did the ELN *mean* by "peace," and how was it to be achieved? Was negotiation part of its overall war strategy, or was there also a shift toward a peace strategy? And how did the state respond to the shifts within the ELN?

This chapter aims at understanding how a terrorist organization and a state defined themselves through negotiations and how the negotiations shaped their perceptions of each other. A deeper understanding of these shifts helps us better understand the knowledge accumulated in the dialogue attempts with the ELN, the character of the ELN today (and its current attitude toward peace negotiations), and how a more nuanced strategy for a new scenario with this insurgent group might be imagined.

An examination of the ELN's experience in negotiations is useful beyond simply broadening our understanding of this particular organization. Using it as a case study allows us to ask bigger questions about other conflicts as seemingly intractable as the one in Colombia. What are the root causes of the Colombian conflict, and how did these causes change over time? And why, despite many efforts from a variety of players, was it never possible to reach a lasting agreement? The intractability of the Colombian conflict underscores the importance not only of short- and medium-term efforts but also of holistic, long-term thinking if peace is to emerge. Such an endeavor will necessarily require thinking about negotiation and peace processes between a state and a political organization termed "terrorist."

This present chapter is based on the knowledge, understanding, and insights gained about the ELN since 2003, when I first had the opportunity to interview Francisco Galán, then the group's spokesperson, in the high-security prison of Itagüí. During 2005–07, as a researcher at the Center for International Conflict Resolution at Columbia University, I was able to observe the dynamics of the latest attempts at an accord between the ELN and the Colombian government. In addition to my conversations with Francisco Galán and the civil guarantors of the so-called Casa de Paz, in July 2007 I had an insightful interview in Cuba with Pablo Beltrán, a member of the ELN Central Command and, at the time, the organization's chief negotiator.

This chapter briefly presents the historical context of the ELN's beginnings in the 1960s. It then focuses on the 1980s, a period of considerable structural change within the ELN, when the group was adamantly opposed to any dialogue with the state, while other terrorist groups, such as the Fuerzas Armadas Revolucionarias de Colombia, or Revolutionary Armed Forces of Colombia (FARC), were involved in such negotiations. This is the time when the ELN elaborated the concept of *poder popular* (popular power), shaping the organization's strategy and its perception of its role in the history of Colombia. In the 1990s, during the end of Virgilio Barco's presidency and the beginning of the César Gaviria administration, important shifts happened in the ELN's discourse, which began to include talk about a political solution to its conflict with the government. This trend gathered strength during the presidency of Andrés Pastrana, when the ELN integrated direct negotiations into its strategy and searched for a negotiated solution to the conflict. The last part of the chapter analyzes the efforts at ELN-government dialogue during the two presidential terms of Álvaro Uribe Vélez.

The Beginnings

Colombian politics in the period immediately following World War II was dominated by sectarian violence between factions of the Conservative and Liberal parties, Colombia's two traditional political groups. This era, 1946–58, was called simply *la violencia*. Its early days were marked by the April 9, 1948, assassination of Jorge Eliécer Gaitán, an astute and charismatic leader of the Liberal Party, who had skillfully interpreted the grievances of a disenfranchised majority, who rallied around him. As a presidential candidate, Gaitán proposed a reformist program asking for redistribution of wealth and increased political participation. The Colombian oligarchy, marked by strong internal cohesion, was terrified of the town squares filled with angry blue-collar workers mobilized by Gaitán. The oligarchs felt threatened by his success in building a united front of the people (Sánchez and Meertens 2001; Bergquist, Sánchez, and Peñaranda 1992; Pecaut 2001).

Gaitán's death sparked a wave of sectarian violence reaching the remotest corners of the country. The division was so deep, the Liberal Party withdrew from the presidential election campaign of 1949, resulting in the election of Conservative Laureano Gómez. Gómez established a regime of terror and legitimized the formation, in the provinces, of local paramilitary groups called "*chulavitas*." Facing the impossibility of civil resistance against the state-sanctioned terror and violence, Liberal guerrillas arose in many parts of the country, especially in the former settlement areas of Sumapaz and the south of Tolima, Llanos Orientales, Magdalena Medio, Alto Sinú, and Alto San Jorge (on the border between the departments of Córdoba and Antioquia).

In 1953, General Gustavo Rojas Pinilla assumed power in a devastated country. Leaving behind the discourse of war and terror, the general promoted a language of forgiveness and national reconciliation. He offered a unilateral cease-fire, which was soon reciprocated by the guerrillas, and an unconditional and general amnesty. His motto was "the fatherland above the parties." The era of General Rojas Pinilla finished with the establishment of the Frente Nacional, or "National Front," an arrangement whereby the Conservative and the Liberal parties took turns governing the country.

While the agreement put an end to the civil war, the unintended consequence was the exclusive occupation of the entire political space by the two traditional parties, leaving little room for alternative democratic political participation (Roldán 2002). As a result, low-intensity conflict continued. In the resistance of some peasant armed groups—a remnant of the liberal guerrillas of the 1950s—the government saw the possibility of a serious Communist threat, and so, at the beginning of the 1960s, it implemented Plan Lazo, a counterinsurgency strategy designed with the advice of the United States. This was followed by the battle of Marquetalia, whose insurgent survivors, a few years later, founded the FARC, a guerrilla group that felt excluded from the political process and so conducted revolutionary violence against the state.

During this period, the triumph of Fidel Castro in Cuba produced a wave of expectations and illusions across Latin America's political left. Many social movements arose, and among them, in 1962, a group of young men went to Cuba, where they received military training and planned to bring the revolution of Castro and Che Guevara to Colombia. One of these young men was Fabio Vásquez, who, once back in Colombia, assumed leadership of the group, which eventually became the ELN, officially founded in the municipality of San Vicente de Chucurí on July 4, 1964. The group had decided that the Department of Santander, in northeastern Colombia—characterized by a long history of civic resistance and opposition—was the ideal place to ignite the revolution. And in fact, in 1929, the department had been one of the scenes of the so-called Bolshevik insurrection, when artisans and peasants launched simultaneous attacks in many different parts of the country, most notably in San Vicente de Chucurí, future cradle of the ELN. This event demonstrated the readiness of artisans, peasants, and workers to use violence as a strategy to knock down the resistance of their political adversaries. The state responded with brutal repression, thus reinforcing the perception that the state manifests itself only through coercion. While the state interpreted the insurrection as a mere security problem that force could resolve, the political left in Colombia affirmed that only socioeconomic and political reforms could address the root causes of that rebellion. These two different perceptions still find an echo today in the differing discourses of the Colombian government and the ELN.

Inspired, like other insurgent groups of the Andean region, by Regis Debray's book *Revolution in the Revolution,* the ELN in its first phase aimed at radical social transformation, to be achieved through confrontation and violent struggle with the state. Very soon the ELN adopted a discourse of national liberation (thus distancing itself from classical Marxist discourse). In the "Manifest of Samacota," the ELN declared its intent to "make Colombia a dignified fatherland for all honest Colombians!"

The 1970s were a decade of profound crisis for the ELN, which almost disappeared. Those years were marked by the rigorous offensive of the Colombian army, guided by the doctrine of national security of that time in Latin America and aimed against the internal enemy: Communism. Like other national governments in the region, the Colombian government had stepped up its repression of social movements, unions, and armed insurgency. After a major military success, an expansion of the guerrilla war from its area of origin to the departments of Bolívar and Antioquia, and the increasing support of peasants, the ELN suffered a major military defeat by the Colombian army in northeastern Antioquia, in the municipality of Anorí, in mid-September 1973.

It took the intelligence and strategic work of its new political commander, Manuel Pérez, a former Catholic priest from Spain, to give the ELN a new organization and a new vision. In just a few years, it became one of the most influential guerrilla groups in Colombia. Its new vision was grounded in the idea of a fight against the imperialistic phase of capitalism and the bourgeois state, using the Vietnam resistance as its model. An armed struggle would bring about a revolutionary social force.

The ELN aimed at the "guerrillarization" of the social struggle, anticipated by civic and peasant mobilizations and strengthened by political propaganda. It was around this time that the Domingo Laín front came about in Arauca Department, bordering Venezuela—a sign of the ELN's increasing regionalization and its integration within niches of popular support. The overall strategy of *poder popular* provides an important insight in the ELN definition of revolution and power. Unlike other armed groups, the ELN never envisioned itself as the sole, or even main, force overthrowing the state. It saw itself as nourishing and supporting the rise of a popular force that would eventually generate a popular revolution producing the transformation.

The concept of power within the ELN becomes more evident with a focus on its modus operandi. Drawing from the experience of other insurgencies in Latin America, such as in El Salvador, the ELN considered itself a parallel power, coexisting side by side with the local state authorities. For instance, it did not remove mayors or try to install its own in the municipalities of its territories. Rather, the ELN preferred to be in conversation with mayors and made them accountable on public spending. As Francisco Galán explained in an interview, the ELN saw itself as the "guardian of resources dedicated to the common good of the community." Acting as the mouthpiece of the peasants and workers to local authorities, it would negotiate, for example, the installation of a first-aid post, the construction of a road, or an agreement on the kind of security to be provided by a police station. In other words, the ELN operated as a power alongside the official power, with the aim of influencing it. The practice was never to substitute one power for another, because the overthrow would be the result of a transformation propelled by a vast popular revolution, with the ELN in merely a supporting role.

In an internal document of the early 1980s, the ELN defines its war fronts as basic structures that guide and support social movements, both politically and militarily, in their struggle against the bourgeois power. It talks about the need to guide the masses toward a political and military struggle within the system: "[The front has] to lead and to promote all aspects of class struggles; to prepare and develop the war, to organize the production and other social activities from a war mentality and willingness to become power" (Medina Gallego 2008, 558).

This definition also suggests that for the ELN, the political dimension took precedence over military action, which was only in support of the political. The command of an ELN front rested not in the military but in the political leadership. This is why the best metaphor for the ELN is not an army but an armed political party, an armed union, or, as Galán puts it, "an armed church."

The 1980s: The Attempt to Unite the Guerrilla Front

When Belisario Betancourt, a populist leader with conservative roots, became president (1982–86), he intended to implement a political agenda that would address what he called the "subjective" and "objective" causes of the conflict, and would bring about significant reforms to open up the political system. Part of his strategy was to include civil society in the dialogues with the guerrilla groups. His efforts led to the cease-fire agreement of La Uribe (1984) with the FARC (Pecaut 2008). But overall, the Betancourt administration's attempts failed because of lack of political support and because of significant resistance from the armed forces. This resistance reached its height when members of the urban guerrilla group M-19 occupied the Palace of Justice, and the Colombian army responded with a use of force that, after twenty-eight hours of combat, left eleven judges of the Supreme Court dead. About the same time, the leaders and candidates of the Unión Patriótica, a political party created with the hope of encouraging the FARC to shift from violence to politics, were systematically assassinated, leading to further mistrust between the guerrilla groups and the government (Dudley 2004).

[handwritten margin note: Require the ELN to hold democratic elect.]

The peace efforts of those years failed also because the guerrilla groups used the negotiations as a breathing space and to strengthen their political and military capability. During this time, the ELN held an intransigent position opposing any form of dialogue and criticizing those groups that entered into negotiations with the government. It also opposed the formation of the Unión Patriótica, because the ELN historically opposed participation in the electoral process. In fact, while it promoted its activity as political, it was always outside and opposing the traditional and institutional ways. Creating a party or participating in electoral politics was tantamount to agreeing with the political regime in place. The ELN was committed to creating an alternative not from within the current political regime but from without. In those years, it concentrated its efforts on strengthening the unity of the revolutionary movement. The effort to unify the guerrilla front produced the so-called Trilateral, including the ELN, the Partido Revolucionario de los Trabajadores (PRT), and the Revolutionary Integration Movement-Free Fatherland, or MIR-Patria Libre. This alliance was created in opposition to the dialogue between the FARC and the Colombian government. The ELN had the impression that the country was in a prerevolutionary phase, since the so-called popular sectors were particularly active in organizing protests and strikes—thus, there was a combination of both social protest and armed struggle.

Other groups joined the unification effort, and on May 25, 1985, during the "Summit of Unity," a meeting of several guerrilla organizations, the participants—M-19, the Popular Liberation Army (EPL), ELN, PRT, and the Frente Ricardo Franco—created the National Guerrilla Coordination. The FARC was not a part of this unity because of its talks with the government. In its first public document, in 1985, the new umbrella organization wrote, "The way towards unity has not been an easy one, especially when there are clear ideological and political differences between the organizations that form the Coordinadora Nacional Guerrillera. . . . We point out the importance and legitimacy of the armed struggle and we coordinate guerrilla warfare with other forms of struggle. Moreover, we work to give to the Colombian revolution a unified Army and, aware about this need, we commit to achieve this objective" (Vargas Velásquez 2006, 251).

This alliance, like others that followed, was not an agreement to overcome violence and find a negotiated solution to the conflict, nor was it an alliance to express a common political platform—it was a military alliance to strengthen the effectiveness of the armed struggle. In the same fashion, in June 1987, the ELN and the MIR-Patria Libre, an insurgency, formed the Unión Camilista-ELN (UC-ELN), another important alliance intended to advance the formation of a popular, democratic, and revolutionary

[handwritten: FARC / Negotiations among Guerilla Org.]

government. Milton Hernández, a member of the ELN Central Command, writing about the history of the ELN, underscored that these alliances were considered an "important progress in developing our revolutionary struggle" (Vargas Velásquez 2006, 251).

Despite disagreements between the FARC and the National Guerrilla Coordination, it was clear to all that the guerrilla movement would not be a united front unless the FARC joined. During the summer of 1987, leaders of the M-19 reached out to FARC leaders, and after a meeting in Sumapaz, more cordial relations were restored. In September 1987, the UC-ELN, the Comando Quintín Lame, EPL, M-19, and FARC signed a document marking the formation of the Simón Bolívar Guerrilla Coordination. The inclusion of the FARC signified a more complete and potentially more powerful alliance. Again, the aim was not political but purely military. These alliances mirrored the intention of the insurgency to move from guerrilla warfare to conventional warfare against the Colombian army.

Caracas and Tlaxcala

During 1989–90, three presidential candidates—Luis Carlos Galán Sarmiento of the Liberal Party (August 1989), Carlos Pizarro Leongómez of the Alianza Democrática M-19 (1990), and Bernardo Jaramillo, leader of the Unión Patriótica (1990)—were killed in Colombia by a murky alliance of drug lords, paramilitaries, corrupt politicians, and state agents. In 1990, César Gaviria of the Liberal Party was elected president (1990–94). His aim was to promote a Constituent Assembly. The promulgation of a new constitution represented for Gaviria an important step toward peace, allowing former combatants, especially those of the M-19, to enter the political process. Some guerrilla groups, such as the Comando Quintín Lame and the PRT, disarmed and demobilized. The formula for the negotiations implemented by Gaviria resembled that used by President Virgilio Barco (1986–90) for the demobilization of the M-19, which had split from the Coordination: a unilateral cease-fire and an agreement contemplating the demobilization and political reintegration of former combatants at the end of the process.

While initially talking peace, President Gaviria also upheld and intensified the military offensive against the insurgency. The most significant and dramatic moment of this time was marked by the army's bombardment of the FARC headquarters, the so-called Casa Verde, on December 9, 1990, during the election for the Constituent Assembly. In response, the Coordination intensified its military actions and occupied the Venezuelan embassy. This action led to the intense three-day meeting at Cravo Norte in Arauca, which led to various dialogues in Caracas, which the parties viewed with some optimism.

The dialogues in Caracas started on June 3, 1991, in a building of the Simón Bolívar University, on the outskirts of the capital. The ELN issued a statement saying it was open to discussing the possibility of a cease-fire, but Francisco Galán, its mouthpiece, had also clarified that the ELN would not renounce military action during the talks. Difficulties between the two delegations emerged early in the dialogue. The government wanted to give priority to a cease-fire negotiation, while some members of the Coordination were mostly interested in negotiating their participation in the Constituent Assembly. This discordant note of disparate agendas would be a constant feature of the talks, with the government emphasizing military and security concerns while the ELN focused on political reforms and the root causes of the conflict.

The government proposed a cease-fire involving both domestic and international monitoring, and the concentration of guerrilla forces in specific areas of the country to enable effective monitoring of the cease-fire. The Coordination refused. This is of particular interest, given that a similar proposal would again disrupt government-ELN negotiations in 2008. In Venezuela, one of the leaders most opposed to the proposed areas of concentration was Francisco Galán. When the ELN killed a liberal politician and former president of the Senate, Aurelio Iragorri Hormaza, the government unilaterally interrupted the dialogue in Caracas.

The process resumed five months later in Tlaxcala, Mexico, on March 10, 1992. The Coordination issued a document to discuss the root causes of the conflict: the effects of neoliberal policies, the exploitation of the country's natural resources, corruption in the public administration, the militarization of national life, and the lack of respect for human rights. A mutually agreed-upon agenda for a peace strategy emerged from the dialogue, contemplating the items proposed by the Coordination. But when talks resumed, the government unilaterally modified the previously agreed agenda, causing the official suspension of the process. In a joint statement, the parties declared their readiness to resume talks in October 1992, but later statements by President Gaviria declaring total war against the insurgency closed the possibility of a political solution to the armed conflict.

Despite their failures, the dialogues in Caracas and Tlaxcala are important in indicating the ELN's shift toward moderation. With that experience, the ELN and the Coordination acknowledged the possibility of a political and negotiated solution to the Colombian conflict. In a letter to Congress on January 25, 1992, the Coordination emphasized that the dialogues in Venezuela and Mexico had produced an agenda for peace. Moreover, for the first time, the insurgency proposed regional dialogues for peace, with the participation of local and regional authorities and political and social organizations, in order to incorporate public opinion in shaping the vision and goals for each department and the nation as a whole. This wide participation would be the ELN's persistent refrain in every proposal and interaction with the government.

The ELN and the Political Solution

For the ELN, Caracas and Tlaxcala marked a further shift toward the possibility of a negotiation with the Colombian government. This was a major change, influenced by several factors. For one, the ELN had learned from a former Vietnamese general that during the Vietnam War, even in the thick of military confrontation, a communication channel between the parties in conflict had stayed open. And Fidel Castro played a role when he sent both the ELN and the FARC a message that the time for armed struggle in Latin America was over and that it was necessary to negotiate.[1] Cuba also became the neutral site for talks between the ELN and the Colombian government during the Pastrana and the Uribe administrations. But in both Caracas and Tlaxcala, the various members of the Coordination had arrived with their own agendas and with no common position, which became a major impediment to the talks. More important, the end of the Cold War meant the end of opposed global ideological blocs. The talks in Venezuela and Mexico were the ELN's first experience engaging in a dialogue with the Colombian government, and ever since, it has considered talking to the enemy a real possibility. Talks have integrated the ELN's overall strategy and complemented, not replaced, its use of violence. Talks became an added element to the same strategy—another means to reach the same goal.

As early as 1987, an internal ELN document had mentioned that addressing the long-standing grievances with the government required an "open space . . . to look for a political solution to the civil war and to the specific manifestations of the conflict" (Medina Gallego 2008, 456). It is worth noting, however, that the proposed political solution was conceived not as a product of a peace process with the Colombian government but as a solution produced outside existing state institutions, by a *parallel and alternative* government, created in opposition to the power of the state.

The idea of a political solution was further developed in the 1990s and geared toward finding a solution to the root causes of the Colombian conflict. During the government of Ernesto Samper, the ELN considered the possibility not of a comprehensive peace process but of negotiations to implement the Geneva protocols and thus free the civilian population from the hardships of war. This initiative was spurred by the massacre of Tatueyó, in which Ricardo Franco, a FARC commander, killed 160 of his own people, whom he suspected of working for Colombian military intelligence. A senior M-19 commander, Álvaro Fayed, disturbed by this development, visited Manuel Pérez, head of the ELN Central Command, and strongly asserted that a commander has no power of life or death over his subalterns. Fayed spoke about the need to humanize war, and the ELN listened. It began to study international humanitarian law and how to implement it in the context of the Colombian armed conflict.

As a result, rather than follow M-19 and other guerrilla groups in entering a formal peace process with the Colombian government, the ELN conceived the possibility of partial negotiations, focused on specific issues of international humanitarian law. From a prison cell in Bogotá, Francisco Galán and ELN commander Felipe Torres became an important interface between the government and the ELN Central Command, but the attempts failed when a minister of the government, Fernando Botero, created the Convivir, a private paramilitary security agency, in the southern town of Popayán, in Cauca Department. The ELN perceived this as a show of bad faith by the government and an increasing risk of an ongoing dirty war.

A National Convention

The 1996 disclosure that cocaine money had partially financed Ernesto Samper's presidential campaign provoked a major scandal and a deep crisis in Colombian political life. In response, the ELN launched the idea of a National Convention. It described the purpose of this new body in an internal document: "The National Convention will provide the guidelines that will allow us to overcome the crisis of our country.... The Convention will elaborate the basis for a political agreement for social reforms and transformation; the democratization of the State and of society" (ELN 1996).

This represented another major shift in the ELN's direction. For the first time, the group emphasized participation and the need for consensus, and the National Convention became a pillar of its discourse for a political solution to the conflict.

But the idea of a National Convention did not signify a desire to *negotiate with* the government. The ELN's overarching aim was still to create an alternative power and an alternative form of government. Thus, the National Convention must be understood as the ELN's willingness to engage in dialogue with Colombian society *but not with the government*. The ELN saw a negotiated solution as the product of a dialogue between itself and society, with the insurgency an essential part. Through this dialogue, an alternative power would eventually emerge with the needed solutions to the conflict's long-standing grievances, and this power would eventually substitute for, and overthrow, the bourgeois state.

The Pastrana Years

Andrés Pastrana (1998–2002) comfortably won the presidential election in a runoff against Horacio Serpa. His promise to pursue peace and dialogue with the insurgency had gained him the sympathy of the Fuerzas Armadas Revolucionarias de Colombia-Ejército Popular, the FARC-EP. Once Pastrana was sworn in, arrangements were made to start talks. The longing for peace at the time was also expressed by a lively civil society. On October 26, 1997, in a referendum, over ten million Colombians voted for respect for international humanitarian law and for a negotiated solution to the armed conflict in Colombia. Moreover, in a meeting facilitated by the Colombian and German Conferences of Catholic Bishops, civil society leaders met in December that year with an ELN mouthpiece in Mainz, Germany, and produced the agreement of July 15, 1998. This was another important expression of the ELN's willingness to engage in dialogue with Colombian society but not with the government.

Though not properly a peace accord, the agreement represented a consensus on five key points: humanization of the war; control of abuses by the parties in conflict; respect for the Ottawa Convention regarding the use of land mines; the primary importance of civil society's participation in peace processes; and a possible national convention, defined as a space for resolution of social and political disagreements, negotiation, and national reconciliation. Although the ELN remained firm in its opposition to disarmament and demobilization, interestingly, it recognized and admitted that a solution could emerge from dialogue. This was quite a reversal from its intransigent position of the 1980s, when it opposed and condemned any attempt at dialogue.

A series of talks between the Colombian government and the ELN started in October 1998. It was the first time that the ELN unilaterally agreed to enter into direct negotiation with the government. This was a sea change. The talks experienced a first interruption when the government denied the ELN a demilitarized area (like the one it granted to the FARC in Caguán) in the Sur de Bolívar zone. Social movements supported by paramilitary organizations propelled opposition to establishing this area. The talks resumed thanks to a civic initiative, the Comisión de Facilitación

Civil. Dialogues with the ELN continued between Caracas (where the ELN had an office of representation) and Sur de Bolívar, and finally in Havana, Cuba.

Ultimately, the talks failed. The faltering of the peace process with the FARC had negative repercussions on negotiations with the ELN as well, and on March 31, 2002, President Pastrana announced the formal breakdown of talks with the ELN—a decision that took many involved in the talks (including the ELN negotiators) by surprise. The ELN accused the government of calling off the talks unilaterally. The lack of progress on a cease-fire was probably the main reason President Pastrana called off the talks. According to Peace Commissioner Camilo Gómez, the ELN was under pressure from the FARC not to sign an agreement with the government. Moreover, the ELN had accumulated long experience in guerrilla warfare and armed resistance, but none in negotiation and in formulating solutions to the conflict. This imbalance of skills and experience had a negative impact on recent attempted negotiations and may also in the future.

At the same time, the government maintained that negotiation of a cease-fire was essential to establish trust between the parties, and it demanded the de facto disarmament and demobilization of the insurgency as a condition for a cease-fire and a subsequent peace process.

One further aspect is noteworthy: during the Pastrana administration, the Colombian government, consenting to a request by the ELN, allowed members of the international community to be present as observers. Though not acting formally as facilitators or mediators, the governments of Spain, France, Switzerland, Cuba, and Venezuela were invited as external observers. The presence of foreign representatives from this time forward in the Colombian government's negotiations with armed groups is a benefit stemming directly from the peace process attempts with the ELN.

Negotiations during the Uribe Administration   *First*

Hopes for talks between the ELN and the Colombian government resumed in the fall of 2005. After a frustrated attempt at direct talks, led by the Mexican government during 2004–05, informal talks began between ELN spokesman Francisco Galán and emissaries of the Colombian government, in the high-security prison of Itagüí, near Medellín. The participants hoped to identify the conditions necessary to revive negotiations.

On June 9, 2005, at the outset of his reelection campaign, President Álvaro Uribe uttered statements that caught the attention of the ELN Central Command and paved the road for new talks. "To the ELN," said Uribe, "I want to give all the chances for peace. . . . If the ELN accepts a cessation of hostilities, the government accepts not to advance military operations against it, as long as the cease-fire is upheld. . . . The ELN does not have to demobilize; neither does it need to disarm. What is needed is a cessation of hostilities. Demobilization and disarmament are points of arrival" (El Tiempo 2005). The government ratified the president's words in a document later sent to Francisco Galán.

In response, after overcoming deep skepticism expressed in many documents over the summer, the ELN Central Command proposed an exploratory dialogue between the ELN and civil society and began to envision a possible summit with the Colombian government in a foreign country. In another document, it also identified the principal obstacles that it believed had hindered a negotiated solution to the armed conflict: (1) the government's denial of social, economic, and political causes at the root of the conflict; (2) the government's presumption that peace is a matter concerning the insurgency and the government, and not a right and a duty for all Colombians; (3) the government's denial of the deep humanitarian crisis produced by the conflict; (4) the government's denial of the very existence of an armed conflict; and (5) the government's failed negotiation with paramilitary groups (ELN 2008).

In September 2005, the Colombian government granted house arrest to Francisco Galán in the Casa de Paz (House of Peace) in the hills surrounding Medellín. This was a space conceived by a group of civil society leaders where society could elaborate and present proposals for a future peace process with the ELN. Civil society's participation in a peace process had always been an emphasis of this guerrilla organization. The ambitious aim of Casa de Paz was to include civil society in supporting the peace process and offering solutions—in other words, as a peace lobby from below.

After three months of meetings at Casa de Paz, talks between the Colombian government and ELN delegations began in Havana, Cuba, during December 16–21, 2005. This was the first of eight rounds of talks.

Over a period of almost two years, the negotiation produced a total of eighteen documents. The parties reached their first major milestone at the end of the fourth round of talks, in October 2006. They agreed that a framework agreement should contemplate participation by civil society and the international community and create an environment conducive to peace (cessation of hostilities and humanization of the conflict). Further, they mutually recognized the goodwill of both negotiating parties and agreed to establish formal negotiations. The exploratory phase was thus completed, and the process entered its second phase.

In the spring of 2007, tensions between the two parties grew, and the sixth round of the Havana talks began in April under a thick cloud of pessimism and acrimony. Spain, Norway, and Switzerland had been designated to attend the talks as foreign observers, but the Colombian government, concerned that the ELN had manipulated their participation to raise international awareness and delay decision making, suspended all international participation. From April to August 2007, owing to the firm position of President Uribe's government, no facilitators assisted the parties in their negotiation. In New York, at a meeting with the UN Department for Public Affairs, Colombian vice president Francisco Santos declined the United Nations' offer to facilitate the negotiation. The Colombian government's long-standing tradition of avoiding third-party mediation or facilitation has been an ongoing obstacle to resolving the conflict. Indeed, with the fighting seemingly intractable, the parties' mutual distrust has grown until both are cynical about the possibility of reaching a negotiated solution. The presence of an external mediator or facilitator would help create a minimal level of trust for the parties to agree on an agenda and move forward.

Despite the initial tensions, during May and June the parties managed to make substantial progress and draft the framework agreement. Indeed, during recess in early June, meetings at Casa de Paz were colored by optimism. Members of the ELN negotiating team were comfortable that between June and July a cease-fire would be signed. The parties admitted that much more progress was needed on how to monitor the cease-fire, but the ELN was confident that a solution could be worked out, and acknowledged that never in the history of negotiations between the ELN and the Colombian government had so much progress occurred. Statements made by the parties before convening again in Havana justified this optimism. Colombia's high commissioner for peace, Luis Carlos Restrepo, declared, "This round of talks will be very productive and will provide very positive news to the country" (Restrepo 2007).

The Framework Agreement

The sound and comprehensive character of the draft framework agreement reflected the hard work and dedication of the parties. In the agreement, the ELN pledged to suspend every kind of military action, including those against the civilian population. It further committed to suspend its attacks on the infrastructure of the country, while the government agreed to halt any offensive activity against the guerrilla group. Moreover, the ELN committed to stop its practice of kidnapping, to free the hostages it already held, and to engage with the government in demining programs. Both parties further agreed on the importance of including civil society in a peace process. The means of both terrorism and counterterrorism were suspended.

Despite the optimism surrounding the framework agreement, in July the talks ran into a new crisis, which has since deepened. On June 28, FARC announced that eleven regional parliamentarians of the Valle del Cauca Department, kidnapped in 2002, had been killed. Outraged Colombians took to the street, calling for the guerrillas to stop kidnapping and to free their hostages. Almost five million people participated in the marches throughout Colombia. This massive outcry may have made it politically more difficult for Uribe's government to negotiate with the ELN. At any rate, around that time, High Commissioner Restrepo made his demands to the ELN much more radical and inflexible, and hopes for signing a framework agreement faded away.

In July 2007, the government, reversing President Uribe's 2005 assurance that all he demanded from the ELN was a cease-fire agreement, asked the ELN to publicly declare its firm commitment to disarm and demobilize. In an interview, Restrepo affirmed, "The government requests that the members of the ELN concentrate in delimited areas of the national territory and that they be identified, so that we can do an adequate verification [of the cease-fire]" (Nuevo Arcoiris 2007a). He went on to say that the ELN must make an "immediate decision" not to be a clandestine organization anymore and further declared that the Colombian state, not a neutral third party, would be responsible for monitoring the cease-fire. Furthermore, he suggested that the ELN should convene a congress to decide whether to enter the democratic process (Nuevo Arcoiris 2007a). The Colombian government was demanding, de facto, that the ELN not only sign a cease-fire as a first step toward a larger and more comprehensive peace process but also (paralleling the process followed with the United Self-Defense Organization of Colombia paramilitaries) commit to surrender and disarm. It was as if the British government had forced the IRA, as a prerequisite to signing the Good Friday Agreement, to concentrate itself in a delimited area of Ireland, identify its members, and commit from the start to decommissioning its weapons. (This was a possibility that Senator George Mitchell, acting as a facilitator in the talks in Northern Ireland, had excluded.)

The ELN vigorously rejected the Uribe government's proposal, describing it, if accepted, as suicidal. At the negotiating table, the ELN declared that it was ready "neither to demobilize, nor to disarm, nor to concentrate in response to the government's needs" (ELN 2007).

At the same time, the ELN showed no readiness to unilaterally free its hostages, indicating a poor ability to read the mood of the country, which, over the past ten years, had grown weary of guerrilla violence and harassments. Also, evidence provided by the Colombian government showed an increasing involvement of some ELN war fronts in the production and trade of cocaine. In different areas of the country, but especially in the department of Nariño, ELN fronts had established alliances with drug cartels such as the Rastrojos.

Was the ELN really committed to a peace process? In its congress of July 2006, it reaffirmed the need to deepen its resistance against the oligarchy. Was the ELN really searching for a political solution to the conflict, as it claimed? The inflexibility of both parties, and their mutual distrust, strained the atmosphere of the negotiation, which, after a moment of hope, had reached an impasse.

In August 2007, several attempts were made to reanimate the process. The ELN's chief negotiator, Pablo Beltrán, wrote a letter to the newly elected president of the Colombian Senate, Nancy Patricia Gutiérrez, a member of President Uribe's coalition. In her inaugural speech, she gently pressed the government to pursue a cease-fire agreement with the ELN. The speech met with the support of a group of leading congressional Democrats from the United States, who encouraged any attempt to find a negotiated solution to the armed conflict. The letter to the president of the Senate was signed by Representatives James McGovern, Ike Skelton, Tom Lantos, and Eliot Engel. The letter was acknowledged by ELN chief negotiator Pablo Beltrán, who, in a letter to an international symposium on cease-fires, wrote that "in the hands of the elites of the U.S. and Colombia lies the key that will allow not to perpetuate the conflict, but to open the path towards a political solution of the conflict." Beltran went on to emphasize that "it is of most importance that sectors of U.S. society support the peace and reconciliation efforts in Colombia" (El Tiempo 2007).

On August 14, the National Peace Council (NPC) was summoned to discuss the peace process and the status of the framework agreement.[2] The same day, the newspaper El Tiempo organized an international seminar on cease-fires, where the cases of Northern Ireland and the Philippines were presented in depth.[3] At the end of that day, both President Uribe and High Commissioner Restrepo made statements hinting at greater flexibility by the government. Senator Gutiérrez affirmed that the intense lobbying for a renewed peace process had achieved its hoped-for effect.

When talks resumed in Cuba on August 20, a delegation of the NPC was invited to listen to the presentations of the two negotiation teams. However, when the two sides met again face-to-face in the solitude of the Cuban diplomatic compound of El Laguito, mistrust, frustration, and resentments resurfaced, leading to a negative outcome of the round. High Commissioner Restrepo left Cuba without setting a new date for follow-up talks. It was at this point that the president of Venezuela, Hugo Chávez, appeared on the stage.

Get them to
request a 3rd Party

The Mediation Efforts of Hugo Chávez

Until August 2007, Venezuelan president Hugo Chávez had maintained a neutral stance toward the Colombian conflict and its parties and had not sought to play any specific role. Meanwhile, President Uribe faced mounting pressure of public opinion that demanded a humanitarian agreement for the liberation of the FARC's hostages. Thus, Uribe, despite his reluctance to seek any agreement with the FARC, invited Chávez to facilitate negotiations with the FARC and the ELN.

When Presidents Uribe and Chávez met in Hato Grande, near Bogotá, on August 31, 2007, relations between the two countries were at its best. Despite their ideological differences, not only did the two heads of state seem to share empathy and trust, but the two countries had reached important agreements on a gas pipeline from the Colombian region of La Guajira to the Venezuelan city of Maracaibo. Moreover, the possibility of an additional pipeline, through Colombia to Panama, was also under consideration.

Initially, President Chávez proved effective. In the first weeks of his mediation efforts, he was able to open channels of communication with both the FARC and the ELN, and top leaders from the two insurgent groups traveled to Caracas and met with him and his emissaries. Chávez's quirks and idiosyncrasies had always caused concern among analysts and observers, but after the first few weeks, skepticism gave way to hope and even a degree of optimism. The sense was that the Venezuelan president would be able to achieve results with both guerrilla groups.

Though with far less publicity and media attention than the FARC facilitation was getting, President Chávez was also making progress in his talks with the ELN Central Command. After talks had reached a dead end in August, the ELN went through two months of in-depth internal consultation to evaluate the process and plan the road ahead. It now saw President Chávez's intercession as a unique opportunity to breathe life into a moribund process and to advance the group's demands. In the eyes of the ELN, the president of Venezuela represented that trusted and credible third party that had been missing since the peace process with the Uribe government began in the fall of 2005. The ELN was confident that Chávez would listen to its claims, and trusted his ability to facilitate a cease-fire agreement that was fair.

To highlight the importance of the moment, the commandant of the ELN, Nicolás Rodríguez Bautista, alias Gabino, left the security of Central Command headquarters in the mountains for Caracas, to meet with President Chávez. Gabino was accompanied by the organization's number two, hard-liner Antonio García. The ELN delegation met with President Chávez in the presidential palace in Miraflores on November 15, 2007.

President Uribe's high commissioner for peace, Restrepo, was also present. In an interview with Colombian analyst León Valencia, Commandant Gabino declared that the ELN was ready to sign a framework agreement with the Uribe government.[4] "There is a different kind of atmosphere in Latin America," Gabino declared, "and I am enthusiastic about the possibility to sign a dignified peace. This is why I took the risk to come [to Caracas]." Gabino added that to sign an agreement with Uribe, whom the ELN considered the most genuine representative of the oligarchy they had been fighting against, would give even more authority and credibility to the agreement (Valencia 2007).[5]

Despite some progress, Chávez's mediation efforts were soon clouded by his bold and colorful public statements, which became more and more problematic for the Colombian government. President Uribe grew increasingly uncomfortable with Chávez's handling of the negotiations.

It was President Chávez himself who provided his Colombian counterpart with the pretext to fire him. On November 21, Chávez broke protocol and spoke directly over the phone with the Colombian military command. In response, President Uribe abruptly called off Chávez's role as a go-between, and that same night, a mouthpiece for Uribe declared on national television that the breach had led to the decision to terminate President Chávez's role as mediator.

President Chávez was outraged, and relations between the two countries plummeted into a perilous downward spiral. Chávez called the Colombian president a "liar" and a "coward," while President Uribe, referring to Chávez, declared, "We need a mediation against terrorism and not legitimizers of terrorists" (Nuevo Arcoiris 2007b). On January 21, 2008, President Chávez declared that neither the FARC nor the ELN was a terrorist group, and invited President Uribe and foreign governments to recognize both groups as "insurgent organizations." Furthermore, he accused the Colombian government of looking for war. Uribe's sudden decision, though mainly directed at Chávez's handling of negotiations with the FARC, also had an impact on negotiations with the ELN, which resented the unilateral termination of the Venezuelan president's role. As a result, a new round of talks with the Colombian government, set to begin in Cuba on December 15, 2007, was called off (Nuevo Arcoiris 2007b).

Since President Uribe terminated President Chávez's role as mediator, there has been no exchange between the Colombian government and the ELN Central Command. In December 2007, the government sent the Central Command a new proposal to resume talks, but to date it has not received a reply. On the contrary, the ELN has intensified its belligerent attitude.

The Colombian government's military successes against the FARC throughout 2008 and 2009 make it difficult to imagine a scenario for negotiation with the ELN in the near term. Besides current power dynamics, there remains an ideological obstacle to the resumption of talks: the two parties' differing, even polarized, perspectives on the negotiation and its objectives.

Capitalizing on Colombians' broadly felt frustrations over the fiasco in the FARC peace process during the Pastrana administration, President Álvaro Uribe had won his first election, in 2001, with a landslide victory on the promise to defeat the guerrillas militarily. The sense of security that he was able to convey to his fellow citizens through his "democratic security" policy ensured his triumphant reelection in 2006. Although he agreed to engage in negotiations with the paramilitaries in 2003, Uribe always resisted committing to direct talks with the guerrillas and opted instead for the use of force. When he opened the opportunity for talks with the ELN in 2005, his campaign for reelection had just begun, and he needed to consolidate and broaden the scope of his democratic security policy. But for President Uribe's government, a negotiation is considered a tool for a forced termination to the conflict. It is not a space to explore solutions and transformations but, rather, a strategy to subjugate rebels and force them to bend to the will of the state and its indisputable legitimacy.

Since 1996, negotiations have been part of the ELN's strategy to advance the structural transformation of the country, removing the root causes of the armed conflict. For the ELN, a peace process is the locus from which to generate a broad and deep consensus, not only between the government and the insurgents but also within all of Colombian society. It is this broad, still very vague and undefined scope that makes the ELN's position at the negotiating table weak. The ELN would certainly benefit if it could bring well-formulated and detailed demands to the table. If the group remains vague in its objectives, its more intransigent wing will look more determined and therefore gain greater internal consensus. This type of consensus is currently pushing the ELN further away from the negotiating table.

The ELN Today

The chief reason that the latest negotiation attempt lost steam is that the ELN never made the decision to abandon war. Until an insurgency reaches this determination, a productive peace process will be difficult, perhaps even impossible. On this major point, debate within the organization is still tumultuous and divisive. While the ELN leaders are agreed on the necessity of talks, they do not yet agree on the necessity to abandon war. Moreover, the government and the ELN have never shared a common vision and definition of peace. Francisco Galán wrote, "The parties failed to envision what the ultimate goal of the process should have been . . . For the ELN, it meant an opportunity for an incremental change of the state's structures, while, for the government, it meant the opportunity to subject the ELN to justice" (Galán 2009). Other factors that brought the negotiations to a halt were lack of trust between the parties, the absence of clear mechanisms for society to participate, the government's exclusion of international observers, the government's demands that ELN members identify themselves during the cease-fire and concentrate themselves in specific areas, and the lack of a written agreement concerning Venezuelan president Chávez's role as facilitator. Francisco Galán wrote, "The abrupt suspension of the [Chávez's] facilitation of the dialogue with the ELN, as well as of the liberation of FARC hostages, undermined the insurgency's trust in the process and made them abandon the negotiation table" (Galán 2009).

The failure to reach an agreement pushed the ELN to more radical forms of armed resistance, strengthening its capability and logistics and consolidating its activity and outreach in its territories. In addition, it radicalized its ideological discourse with an effort to rediscover and update the classics of guerrilla warfare, develop the Bolivarian philosophy, maintain a discourse of class struggle, and reassert the permanent legitimacy of its founding documents. In an online publication in 2009, the ELN declared, "We reaffirm our commitment to continue our revolutionary struggle from our insurgent perspective, to prepare our forces to resist and to fight the war-oriented assault of the current government" (ELN 2009). It is important to note the agreement reached at the end of 2009 between the FARC and the ELN to stop their ongoing military confrontations with each other in different areas of the country.

On the political front, the ELN has continued the conversation with local governments as well as with social and political organizations present in major urban centers. Interviews with demobilized ELN members confirm also that the group is maintaining contacts with the Venezuelan government. But the ELN has not yet managed to establish meaningful conversations on a national level or formulate viable proposals for resolving the armed conflict. This is partly a result of the halt in the latest negotiation. But another factor is Francisco Galán's decision, after serving for more then a decade as the ELN's spokesman and its bridge to the Colombian government and major civil society organizations, to leave the ELN ranks and declare his opposition to war and violence.

The most worrisome development is probably the ELN's increasing involvement, in some parts of the country, with drug trafficking. Though the Central Command has maintained its official opposition to any alliance with drug cartels, the ELN is, in fact, increasing its narco penetration, especially in the departments of Nariño, Cauca, and Chocó, where it provides security for coca plantations, laboratories, and routes. The ELN justifies its drug trafficking, citing the need to resist military pressure from the Colombian army, the lesser stigma associated with drug trafficking than with kidnapping, and the fact that cocaine money has already heavily penetrated the nation's economy and government.

Conclusion: Why Negotiate with the ELN, and How?

"If there is no negotiation, the violence attractors will radicalize and give life to new dynamics of the conflict," Francisco Galán explained in an interview. A negotiation could avoid a deepening alliance between the ELN and the FARC to wage a more effective armed resistance, and an attendant increase in drug trafficking, crime, and new expressions of violence on the borders with Venezuela and Ecuador. Moreover, a peace negotiation would increase urban security and deepen democracy. A negotiation could be seen as the consolidation of President Uribe's democratic security policy. It would also improve relations with neighboring countries, especially Venezuela and Ecuador. Today a peace process in Colombia needs to mirror a geopolitics of peace and the normalization of today's tense relationships among countries of the region.

A peace process will also have to tackle the issue of drug trafficking, which has become a central component of the conflict. The drug trade, especially in the peripheral regions, is the primary generator and perpetuator of the social and armed conflict in Colombia. Whereas a political negotiation with drug cartels is not viable, a negotiation for the submission to justice (as Italy did successfully in its fight against the Sicilian Mafia) might be an important contribution to reduce drug trafficking, dismantle important logistical structures, and loosen the ties between traditional insurgency and more recent forms of organized crime. Without a combined effort to resolve the armed conflict and reduce the influence of drug cartels, the likelihood of guerrilla fronts becoming organized crime cells is significant. This would keep the stage set for the perpetuation of violence.

One lesson learned from the history of peace processes in Colombia is that an insurgency's willingness to negotiate does not signify its resolve to engage in a peace process. As we saw with the ELN, often a negotiation represented a tactical opportunity for the insurgency to strengthen its political profile, reach out to civil society organizations and foreign governments, and reorganize militarily. But it did not reflect any shift toward renouncing violence.

No peace process will be productive and successful until the insurgency reaches the internal decision to abandon violence. Only then will talks be conducive to resolving the conflict. Today in Colombia, the conflict's ripeness for resolution will be measured by the insurgency's express understanding that the time for armed struggle is over. A strategy today needs, above all, to convince the ELN that the time for armed struggle is long past and that violence does not transform Colombia's injustices and inequities but only adds to them. The ELN still has not reached this conclusion. Therefore, the message to the ELN guerrilla should be an invitation to abandon the armed struggle in Colombia and elsewhere on the continent, look for a negotiated political solution, and abandon the opportunistic alliance with drug trafficking.

Moreover, because of the history and the nature of the ELN, the departments can play a major role in a peace process. A negotiation effort should stand on two pillars: on a national level, negotiating a political and judicial solution; on a regional level, putting together different agendas to address such issues as local economic development, land rights, transparent and democratic governance, and so on. It is not possible to resolve an armed struggle unless alternative solutions emerge that will make peace much more convenient and beneficial than violence.

To create an environment conducive to a peace process, the prenegotiation phase will be at least as important as the negotiation itself. Talks with the ELN cannot be the product of improvisation and should not wait for the insurgent group to abandon violence and initiate a negotiation. Rather, such a predisposition should be encouraged and nourished from outside. This can be done through back channels and quiet diplomacy. The cases of Northern Ireland and Israel hold important lessons on the use of intelligence agents to further a peace process. The use of secret back channels could generate within the ELN a change in perception about the current reality in the country and the international scenario and encourage the moment of ripeness. Using secure, direct, and quiet channels of communication, conversations should be promoted both with the members of the Central Command and with local ELN war fronts.

A few actors are well suited for peace lobbying. The Catholic Church, through its local bishops, can play a major role in opening communication channels and establishing trust. Also, ELN members who are inmates in various prisons across Colombia can play a very important role as well. The experience of Francisco Galán and Felipe Torres shows that prisons are important venues for exploring and elaborating ideas, analyzing issues, and testing solutions. Inmates can become a valuable conduit between the leadership of an insurgency and the government. Talks can also be established between the inmates and vital sectors of society. The experience not only in Colombia but also in Northern Ireland and South Africa offers lessons learned about the role that prisoners can play in envisioning and creating conditions for a peace process.

As Georgetown political scientist Marc Chernick states, the history of peace in Colombia is a history of missed opportunities (Chernick 2008). But the past is not just a summary of failures, for each failed attempt contains lessons that can be put to good use in engineering a productive process with a sound legal framework as opposed to simply improvising on the fly. There is no military solution to Colombia's stubborn, decades-long conflict. The only possible solution is a negotiation that makes legitimate, good-faith steps to address, resolve, and transform the long-standing grievances that have marked that country's destiny.

Notes

The research was made possible by a grant from the government of Norway. I am also thankful for the assistance of Saruy Camilo Tolosa Bello in conducting archival research on the ELN.

1. Castro conveyed this message to the FARC during the negotiation in El Caguán, during the Pastrana administration. He reiterated this message more recently, in August 2010, when he met in Havana with Colombian senator Piedad Córdoba.

2. The NPC, created by law in 1998, is made up of representatives of the three branches of government, along with oversight and monitoring bodies, churches, trade union confederations, business associations, universities, and organizations representing small farmers, ethnic minorities, retired members of the security forces, women, peace activists, human rights defenders, and victims of forced displacement.

3. The Center for International Conflict Resolution at Columbia University, the Project on Justice in Times of Transition, and the Bogotá-based think tank Nuevo Arcoiris also promoted and organized the seminar.

4. León Valencia is the president of the think tank Nuevo Arcoiris. Himself a former member of the ELN Central Command, he demobilized with his faction in 1994, under President César Gaviria.

5. Valencia (who met Gabino on November 20) clarified in a conversation with me that Gabino was speaking about a cease-fire, not a peace agreement.

References

Bergquist, Charles, Gonzalo Sánchez, and Ricardo Peñaranda, eds. 1992. *Violence in Colombia*. Wilmington, DE: Rowman and Littlefield.

Chernick, Marc. 2008. *Acuerdo posible: Solución negociada al conflict colombiano armado.* Bogotá: Ediciones Aurora.

Dudley, Steven. 2004. *Walking Ghosts: Murder and Guerrilla Politics in Colombia.* New York: Routledge.

ELN. 1996. "III Congreso." Unpublished internal document.

———. 2007. Comunicado de prensa. *Voces de Colombia,* July 24. www.eln-voces. com (accessed Oct. 30, 2007).

———. 2008. "Superemos los obstáculos." www.eln-voces.com (accessed Dec. 31, 2008).

———. 2009. "Comunicado ELN." www.eln-voces.com (accessed Nov. 10, 2009).

El Tiempo. 2005. "Uribe saludó a reinsertados." *El Tiempo,* June 10.

———. 2007. "Impulso a acuerdo con el ELN." *El Tiempo,* Aug. 15.

Galán, Francisco. 2009. "Columna de pacho." *El Colombiano* (Medellín), July 17.

Medina Gallego, Carlos. 2008. "ELN. Notas para una historia política." Unpublished manuscript, Universidad Nacional, Bogotá.

Nuevo Arcoiris. 2007a. "Políticas públicas de paz. Compilado de prensa." Internal document, Corporación Nuevo Arcoiris, Bogotá, June.

———. 2007b. "Políticas públicas de paz. Compilado de prensa." Internal document, Corporación Nuevo Arcoiris, Bogotá, Dec. 15.

Pecaut, Daniel. 2001. *Orden y violencia.* Cali, Colombia: Norma.

———. 2008. *Las FARC: ¿Una guerrilla sin fin o sin fines?* Bogotá: Lignes de Repéres.

Restrepo, Luis Carlos. 2007. "Comunicado Alto Comisionado por la Paz." Alto Comisionado por la Paz, Bogotá.

Roldán, Mary. 2002. *Blood and Fire: La Violencia in Antioquia, Colombia, 1946–1953.* Durham, NC: Duke University Press.

Sánchez, Gonzalo, and Donny Meertens. 2001. *Bandits, Peasants, and Politics: The Case of "La Violencia" in Colombia.* Trans. Alan Hynds. Austin, TX: University of Texas Press.

Valencia, León. 2007. "Queremos firmar la paz con Uribe: 'Gabino.'" *El Tiempo,* Dec. 8, 2007.

Vargas Velásquez, Alejo. 2006. *Guerra o solución negociada. ELN: Origen, evolución y procesos de paz.* Bogotá: Intermedio Editores.

Part III

Conclusion

Conclusion
When and How
to Engage

I. William Zartman and Guy Olivier Faure

The record shows that states and extremists do engage, even though not always successfully. Even with engagement, the attendant obstacles and risks often prolong and overcome the effort. The initial reaction between states and terrorist organizations is one of confrontation and isolation. Perhaps early engagement would have been more effective both in handling the issue or grievance and in preventing terrorism. This is the realm of normal politics, and it accounts for innumerable cases of terrorism that have *not* occurred (Zartman 2003). States should indeed be responsive to rising problems, felt injustices, and potential grievances, and when they are, the normal political process works. But such foresighted preemptive action is not always practiced and indeed not always possible. Demands are often unacceptable, remedies impossible, and opponents unreasonable opportunists, driven millennialists, or ambitious revolutionaries. So the second phase, after the normal politics have failed, is a time of confrontation in an effort to overcome the challenge. Both sides are in to win, to make the other side give in.

The outcome at any point is victory/defeat, continued escalating confrontation, or stalemate of one of two sorts: either a mutually hurting stalemate or an S^5 (soft, stable, self-serving stalemate). In the absence of victory, the contending parties have to consider negotiation. But when? The parties themselves are unlikely to think on their own of negotiation; they are caught up in winning, locked in conflict, bedeviled by demonizing, unable to think of alternative ways out. It is axiomatic that parties caught in a conflict need help to get out of it. They are too enmeshed in the conflict itself, too committed to their course of action, too convinced by their own rhetoric and beliefs, too engaged before their followers, to give much careful attention to the possibility and advisability of engaging and negotiating with the adversary. So the question of when to engage confronts would-be mediators as strongly as—and probably earlier than—it faces the antagonists in a terrorist conflict. Thus, the relevant question becomes, what are the defining conditions when the parties to a terrorist conflict, or another state interested in mediating it, consider negotiation and engagement appropriate policy options, and how should the policy option be pursued?

Some Answers

Most simply, states engage when they have to, when the isolation policy is failing and the failure is painful to the state. A failing policy can be sustained as long as the failure does not have negative consequences. This simple basis for understanding a policy change is open to much greater refinement and interpretation by policymakers and public analysts alike. It is less decisive as a basis for change when applied to conflicts with terrorist political organizations than when applied to conflicts with states, because of terrorists' heavy reliance on commitment and indoctrination (Zartman 1995). Failure is less evident when purpose is imbued with rightness and righteousness and the cause has a distant—even otherworldly—horizon.

The preceding chapters have provided further refinements to this guideline. Groeneveld-Savisaar and Vuković give a very direct answer, based on interests: mediating states engage in terrorist conflicts when the conflict area is one in which they have strong interests. And when they do, their engagement requires firm deployment of carrots and sticks to win the antagonists away from their course of confrontation. The same reasoning applies to the state that is actually in the conflict: if the conflict is outside the state's area of interest, it is a mosquito bite, worth only balm and fly swats in response, but not the enticements and deterrents needed to bring the opponent to effective engagement. Engagement, as much as confrontation, requires the expenditure of power to make the conciliatory policy worthwhile to the terrorists. The chapter's reasoning then joins good insights from other work on mediation, indicating that biased mediators are helpful when they work to deliver the party they are biased toward, and that a sense of equality between the parties is necessary for engagement to be pursued effectively.

Pettyjohn brings out a different analytical variable: moderation. The mediating state (in this case, the United States) will engage with the terrorist organization when (1) there is no moderate alternative to deal with and (2) the organization shows signs of moderating. Again, the same reasoning applies to the state in the conflict and, by extension, to the terrorist organization. Engagement is designed to produce moderation and will not be undertaken if moderation is already available elsewhere or if the extremists have not shown an ability to moderate. This means that the terrorists will be expected to show some engagement tendencies of their own before the state will take the step. The terrorist organization's steps are expected to be internal—rhetoric, soundings, hostage release, schisms, and so on—whereas the state's first move would be interactive, or external. Terrorists may also moderate by coming together around a common, moderate platform with moderate groups behind the same cause. Or they may, as Pettyjohn suggests, find themselves engaged in processes—cease-fires, electoral competition, parliamentary processes, marginal negotiations, informal conferences—whose mechanics and spirit gradually force moderation on them. Again, the hanging question is, how much moderation does it take to be productively involved in a moderating relationship such as engagement? The balance sheet indicates the difficulty of launching engagement.

Zartman and Alfredson found a number of different explanatory variables, beginning with the necessity imposed by a hurting stalemate or by the state's need for an agreement that only the terrorists could provide—two sides of the same coin (Zartman and Alfredson 2010). Again, this presupposes that the terrorist organization is also ready to negotiate, either because it occupies the other side of the mutually hurting stalemate or because it sees that it can get something in exchange for acceding to the state's need for an agreement. In both cases, gains were seen to be available through engagement: in the first, gains through the reduction of losses; in the second, outright gains. In both cases, these gains must be weighed against another measure: opportunity gains, or gains to be achieved by *not* engaging (i.e., chances of winning or of not losing what one had to pay to get an agreement). Another variable was the pressure from mediators, persuasive because it convincingly promised a better outcome, because the mediator used tough persuasion, or because not to listen to the mediator would be costly to the party's relationship with the mediator. These reasons echo implications of Groeneveld-Savisaar and Vukovic's argument for firm engagement by the mediator to end a terrorist conflict.

These findings can be totaled for some sharper, though preliminary, generalizations. Not surprisingly, states reach out to terrorist organizations when they must, as participants or as mediators—when the conflict matters to them or hurts them enough, when they need the terrorists' agreement to achieve their goals, and when the previous policy of indifference or active isolation has proved unsuccessful in ending the terror. But the states must also feel some reassurance that their gesture will be productive and that a change in policy stance is actually possible. To gain this assurance, they need to continue active involvement in the conflict as they add incentives to their offers of contact without totally abandoning their previous pressure, even if that pressure is only a threat to return to isolation and confrontation. States also need to feel that enough moderating dynamics are present within the terrorist organization to signal a change of direction and produce a continuation of internal change. All these elements are judgment calls, but this is what policy is made of (Zartman 2005, 2010).

More Questions

Even if the signs on the surface are sharp, the ground underneath is squooshy. Beneath these conclusions lie problematic soft spots in conducting the process of engagement—questions that include initiating and concluding the process, handling the participants, evaluating their readiness, and balancing the tactics. Precise guidelines to understanding and action can go only so far before running into uncertainties, judgment calls, and contradictions. Discussion of each of the following contradictions will conclude with a proposition and its exception, as a summary of knowledge and a challenge to application. An effort to face and even overcome such contradictions is as important for practice and policy as it is for analysis and understanding.

The soft areas begin with the distinction between talking and negotiating: states should talk, even if they don't negotiate, with terrorists, although talking and negotiating overlap. The second distinction is between ends and means: negotiations can seek to pull opponents away from the use of violence (means) even if not from their causes and beliefs (ends), though in fact it is the ends that are used to justify the means. Third, one cannot negotiate with total absolute terrorists, but negotiations are required in order to turn total absolutes into negotiable types. Fourth, similarly, moderation is both a condition and a process for engagement and negotiation, but how much moderation is needed before negotiation can begin or can be attained as a result? And finally, parties are always horizontal coalitions held together by purpose and legitimacy, but how can moderate factions be enticed into negotiations without losing the unity and legitimacy of the whole?

Initiating the Process: Talking versus Negotiating

It is important to develop all contacts possible with all types of terrorists and terrorist supporters. In hostage situations, negotiation is what terrorists want. They seek contact, and much of the actual negotiation process is devoted to maintaining it, establishing stable relations with the terrorist, and bringing him to the negotiations he seeks (Faure and Zartman 2010).[1] But in dealing with terrorist organizations, negotiation is not what the terrorists want. For that very reason, talking is crucial—to find out information, sow doubts, crystalize goals, develop interlocutors, and set up a negotiating situation.

Talking and negotiation are both part of engagement, but talking is not negotiating. It can be carried out at lower levels, it does not involve legitimizing and recognition, and it seeks merely exchange (or extraction) of information. Talking in its larger context, as opposed to a policy of isolating, is the first step of engagement (Sayigh 2008). One element of engagement is the changing of images, ideas, and even goals, as well as exchanging views about them. Exchanging is the path to changing, on both sides. So, officially, from a state's policy perspective, the distinction between talking and negotiating is sound, although analytically, from the negotiation point of view, the line between the two is blurred. In other words, much of negotiating involves talking (engagement); talking does not necessarily involve negotiation but is only the likely prelude to it.

Talking and negotiating are a process, not an event. The initiation of either should be taken not as a total policy revision but rather as an investigation of possibilities and intentions, and an attempt to sound out and attract the other side into flexibility and moderation. It is not by public statements that one knows whether the opposing party is an absolute or a contingent terrorist—that is, nonnegotiable or negotiable—and, if an absolute, whether total or conditional (Zartman 2003). In the process of sounding out possibilities of talking and negotiating, one does not begin with a prominent, authoritative figure, as Lambert emphasizes (see also Combalbert 2010). Intermediaries are necessary as a first step toward communication—and often even as the last step of negotiation, behind the public view of strident statements, as Groeneveld-Savisaar/Vuković and Pettyjohn show.

The importance of talking emerged in both studies of the terrorists' life cycle, in leading to negotiation, and also in de-escalating the tendency to terrorism, through engagement in early and later phases without any specific negotiating. Indeed, talking not only can prepare for negotiation but can also be the surrogate for negotiating, making specific deals unnecessary. Talk was the basis of preventive and corrective policies carried out in London and Cairo, as Lambert and Goerzig have shown, pulling past and future terrorists away from their extreme methods and showing that their ends did not require—indeed, prohibited—these methods. The other case studies show the importance of talking to find out aims and entice negotiations, even if the ensuing negotiations should break down in the end. Talks preceded the sporadic negotiations in Colombia by years, and indeed, more such talks might have prevented the shifts in attitude that occurred on both sides and led to negotiation collapse, as Civico describes. Similarly, the absence of adequate talks before negotiations can be seen at the root of the collapse of the Sri Lanka negotiations, analyzed by Groeneveld-Savisaar and Vuković. Norway started talking with Sri Lankans in 1999, and negotiations opened in 2002 but broke down the next year over waffling positions on the issue of federalism versus independence (Lilja 2010, 101). Seven years of talks took place before real engagement and negotiation began in El Salvador in the 1980s (De Soto 1999). A decade of talks in South Africa on the Namibian question in the late 1970s and 1980s preceded the decision to engage in 1986, followed by another year of talks before actual negotiations began, ending in an agreement in 1988 (Sisk 1995; Zartman 1995). Talking is a necessary, lengthy phase before obstacles can be cleared, the prenegotiation process completed, and negotiations begun (Stein 1989).

> *Proposition 1: Talks and other contacts are a prime means of engaging terrorists—separate from, but a condition to, negotiations.*

> *Proposition 1a: However, while talking is inherent in negotiation, negotiation is not necessarily inherent in talking.*

Concluding the Process: Ends versus Means

Do not negotiate belief systems, but rather seek to de-escalate means from violence to politics. This distinction is crucial to understanding negotiating possibilities with terrorists, and harder to discern, either conceptually or tactically, than the talk/negotiate gray area. What is important for reducing terrorism is to break the link between ends and means, whether or not the ends are downgraded. The extremists need to be shown that their ends are not worth the means deployed, because the means are not successful in attaining the ends. States should engage and negotiate not *because of* terrorist violence but *to end* terrorist violence.

Yet ends do justify means (as in many other instances, despite the mantra to the contrary), so the terrorist, convinced that his ends require or at least condone terror, has to be converted to a contrary conviction, as Lambert, Civico, and Goerzig explore in different ways, showing how a group can keep the faith but express it in nonviolent ways. Thus, a simple agreement to abstain from violence is shaky as long as it does not rest on further agreement that the ends do not require violence—and that requires getting into the belief system. Thereafter, the two sides can focus on terms of trade, composed of elements more important to the receiving than to the giving party, and leaving aside for the moment those conflicted elements that are important to both (Homans 1961; Feste 2010).

The dilemma is best handled by sequencing. Negotiations with extremists need first to be focused on downgrading the means, convincing the extremist to give up violence as a way to attain the ends. The negotiator must emphasize the negative relation, that "the armed struggle is not reaching its aim"—in the words of the ELN and Gama'a Islamiya spokesmen, that terrorist means are counterproductive to attaining the goals—and that only when the extremist agrees to change the means can discussion of the ends begin. The state must make a similar even if not equivalent effort, as Höglund discusses and Civico illustrates; a cease-fire must be two sided, but further disarmament efforts can come only later on in the negotiations. To achieve a change in means, the negotiator must also offer alternative means, such as autonomy or electoral participation, as the FARC came to achieve in the mid-1980s in Colombia and as the PLO achieved in the mid-1990s in Palestine (Pruitt 1997; Eisenstadt and García 1995). Thereafter, in the new situation, the ends can also be downgraded over time, although an immediate, explicit statement of that intent would heighten terrorists' wariness of downgrading even the means. Israel could not understand the gradual downgrading of ends by the PLO and Hamas, just as Colombia could not understand the same process by the ELN.

But even with sequencing, things are not clear-cut. As with any other negotiations involving the movement of conflict from violent to political means, terrorist violence is not likely to be turned off as if by a spigot, as negotiators in Sri Lanka and Colombia found out. Operating cells may be far from central command and control, geographically or organizationally; a little testing along the margins may be practiced; and central command may well want to remind the engaging and negotiating state (and vice versa) that violence is still possible if sincere negotiations are not engaged (Zartman 2006, 2010). It has been established in nonterrorist conflicts and also in Höglund's chapter that a solid cease-fire is not likely to occur until the end of the negotiations, not near the beginning (Mahieu 2007). Similarly, it has been shown that when sporadic violence continues into negotiations, parties who break off the negotiations are primarily those reluctant to negotiate at all and that are looking for an excuse to break off (Höglund and Zartman 2006). As with moderation, ending the terrorist means is a process before it is a condition.

Islamic parties in Morocco, Jordan, and Algeria, for example, have been admitted into the political system upon renunciation of violence, although it is still unclear whether they have also renounced the goal of an Islamic state. Hezbollah and Hamas, on the other hand, were admitted into the political system in Lebanon and Palestine, presumably on the basis of the same renunciation, and yet their unchanged goals continue to be used to justify their unchanged means. Note that what separates the two groups of cases is that in the first, there is someone to "hold" the system (the monarchy, the army), admit participants into it, and control their participation and their promise, whereas in the second, no such higher authority exists to control admissions and behavior. On the other hand, the cease-fire and end to terrorism as well as military action in Sri Lanka was only a tactical ploy for both government and terrorists, and both used it to rearm.

The question of qualified admission into the political system is especially relevant to the matter of negotiations with the Taliban, which have been mooted since 2008 and tentatively attempted more recently (Tellis 2009; Dorronsoro 2010). If simple persuasion concerning the inappropriateness of violence is not effective, negotiations to end violence require a payment in return. Bringing the extremist organization into the political system has two conditions: that the extremists be ultimately engageable (see the discussion of "moderation," below) and that the state be strong enough to stand as a viable partner. Anything less than both is a surrender to the extremists. If the extremist organization—the nationalist terrorist organization (NTO) discussed by Pettyjohn—seeks autonomy or another form of self-government for a region of an established state, as in the case discussed by Groenevelt-Savisaar and Vuković, its nature is more easily acceptable and the state needs to assure its own overarching sovereignty in exchange for its respect for the regional desire for self-rule. If the organization seeks to enter the political arena as a party facing the electorate, as in the case discussed by Civico, presumably it can take its chances among the other parties, although cases such as Algeria in 1990 show that the political system must be robust enough to face the challenge—the second condition. But if the organization seeks to replace or share power with the government as part of the negotiated deal, the conditions are crucial. Probably neither is fulfilled in contemporary Afghanistan, for example, where the Taliban's attachment to its aims (and past record in charge of the state) appears clear and where the state suffers from weakness and illegitimacy.

On occasion, talks and negotiations can be used to address the terrorists' goals directly. Sowing appropriate doubts about the ends can work backward to downgrade the means. The use of Islamic authorities, for example, to show that indiscriminate violence is un-Islamic serves at least to break the link between ends and means and even weakens some of the ends, as both Goerzig and Lambert explore, showing how Islam does not condone terrorism. Convincing political Islamists, Tamil or Acehnese separatists,

Colombian radicals, or Irish republicans that inclusion in the daily practice of politics, in legislation and election, is a more appropriate and achievable goal than takeover of the state is a basic step in removing the threat of terror. This approach is not one for negotiation in a sole encounter but rather a long-term strategy involving many other approaches besides negotiation.

Yet there is another hand. As noted, terrorism and extremism are generally warning signs—canaries in the mine—of real problems and felt grievances that need to be addressed. As already noted, a resolute pursuit of the Middle East peace process at the end of 2001 would have been a warranted action consistent with U.S. past policy and present values, despite its unlikely effect on al-Qaeda. As the Civico chapter has shown, a government agreement to address the real problems of Colombian society would have been helpful to the attempts to end violence and terrorism. It is not "giving in" to terrorism to consider its underlying causes.

> *Proposition 2: Negotiation should focus first on removing terror as a means to a goal, and leave changes in the extremists' ends and goals to the subsequent phase of engagement.*

> *Proposition 2a: However, where ends are within the negotiator's reach, an agreement in a terrorist conflict is more stable if the ends justifying the terrorist act are addressed directly.*

Handling the Parties: Absolutes versus Contingents

"Absolutes" is an analytical category, not a fixed condition (Hayes, Kaminski, and Beres 2003; Zartman 2003). The fuller characterization might be, "Absolutes are beyond negotiation as long as they remain absolute." The challenge, therefore, is to shake them loose from their absolute characteristics. Unlike contingents, absolutes have no political agenda for negotiation (any more than do many governments). Their belief system prohibits and excludes negotiation. Also, they are usually physically beyond contact and communication. Even when talk is initiated, it serves as an occasion to repeat systemic beliefs and reinforce fixed positions. The state is the evil enemy, negotiation is selling out, and there is nothing to talk about. These characteristics constitute the barriers that have to be penetrated if negotiation is to take place. This also means that they should not go unchallenged.

Lowering these barriers to talking and negotiating is often a long-term job for education in multiple forms, but a major ingredient in a positive strategy is to make quite plain that dropping violence will be rewarded. More than any other single factor, the absence of this ingredient explains the failure of the Colombian and Sri Lankan negotiations, as analyzed by Civico and by Groeneveld-Savisaar and Vuković. Behavior and beliefs are altered by effective present constraints and future inducements—a two-handed policy. Concessions and compensations do not have to be offered on a platter, as conditions, before negotiations begin, but the parties can indicate indirectly that movement on the other side could be rewarded by corresponding inducements. Contingent inducements can be offered as trial balloons to penetrate the absolute refusal of absolutes and wean them away from terror as a means to their ends. It must be made plain, however, that inducements are not bought by terror but will be the basis of discussions once violence is dropped. The point is to indicate that beyond the change in methods lies the possibility of talking about goals.

Present constraints involve the terrorists' inability to attain their goals. Terrorism is defined by the UN Security Council as violent acts designed to create a state of terror in the general public, and by the U.S. government as politically motivated violence against noncombatant targets to influence an audience (UNSC 2001; U.S. Code 2001). The current struggle is not between the West and al-Qaeda (which is beyond negotiation) for each other's agreement but between the two sides for the support of the world Muslim population. Terrorists, like revolutionaries, are fish supported by public waters, acting to destroy the state's public support and gather their own. The state needs to be engaged in the mirror-image struggle, seeking to defend its own public support but also to undermine the public support—drain the public waters—behind the terrorists. When the absolutes see their public support waning, they tend to question the solidity of their own strategies and beliefs (Cronin 2008, 2009). Indeed, terrorist acts themselves may serve to undercut the support of the very public they seek to win over (or at least intimidate) (della Porta 2009). As well as being an insight into the strategic situation of terrorists, this is also an admonition to terrorism-fighting states to keep their own act clean and their values unsullied, that is, "Don't let them make us into them."

Nonetheless, isolation may be an effective tactic, under specific conditions. If there is a competing but moderate group that can be rewarded and strengthened by showing progress toward a similar goal, isolation of the terrorist extremes may prove successful as support turns to the successful moderates, as Pettyjohn has argued. Moderate Islamists in Algeria and Morocco have been rewarded with a place in the political system and—in Algeria—even in the government, draining support from the radical party and the smaller remnant groups. And yet al-Qaeda in the Islamic Maghrib (AQIM) reemerged in 2007-08, challenging the weak government but not gaining popular support. Isolating the terrorists and favoring the moderates has been an Israeli and Western strategy toward Hamas and Fatah in Palestine—with failed results because of the absence of inducements that

Israel is willing to offer. Shift of support cannot be expected to be total, and so the calculation of weight between the moderates and the spoilers has to be made carefully and sustained over time. Many times, insufficient support is produced over time, and the moderates are overcome again by the unrepentant terrorists.

Proposition 3: "Absolute terrorist" is an analytical category from which the terrorists may be made to emerge through present constraints and future inducements.

Proposition 3a: However, a two-handed policy confrontation along with engagement is also conceivable, only on the condition that the hard hand offer strong inducements to the terrorists to change their policy.

Evaluating Moderation: Process versus Condition

Moderation is the condition for negotiation with terrorists. They must demonstrate a willingness to temper their behavior, change their means, and open their attitudes to productive discussions. Until such evidence of moderation is forthcoming, little progress can be made in negotiation, and, indeed, actual negotiation cannot begin, almost by definition.

But moderation is also a process, a polysemic concept that is both fixed, as a hurdle, and moving, as an action to jump the hurdle. The challenge is posed in determining how much of the process is needed to achieve the condition, and how dynamic an interpretation of the condition can be sustained. Moderation is a process that takes place in imperceptible stages, with terrorists checking, explicitly or implicitly, at each step to make sure they are moving in a satisfactory direction, responding to implacable constraints and receiving satisfactory rewards for their movement. Such movement—the process—can never be counted as irreversible; the Colombian ELN and the Sri Lankan LTTE made distinct moves toward moderation and then pulled back, and even terrorists in the nationalist movements in Algeria and Macedonia slipped back into their tactics after independence when they felt that their independence dividend was not what they expected.

Moderation as a condition must be considered dynamically, even though its continuation is not assured. Movement through early phases may well produce further movement on its own if properly induced and rewarded, and failure to respond to the early phases of the moderation process may cut the process short. Thus, negotiators will often be in the position of perceiving some movement toward moderation but having to bet on its continuation to fulfill the condition. The IRA agreed to "stand down" but not disband, to not use its arms but not to decommission, leaving its negotiating partners unsure how much moderation had occurred or whether the condition had been met, until finally full acceptance was reached fully five years after the Good Friday Agreement.

There is no rule stating when the process has cleared the hurdle or whether it has enough forward momentum to carry it on to complete moderation. There is not even a conceptual formulation of the process that permits a firm analysis. It remains up to the mediators or the state (or the moderating terrorists on the other side) to make the best evaluation and take their chances. It also remains up to the state to block the success of the terrorist means, leaving the door open to alternative means to the terrorists' ends. But it also remains up to the attracting party to continue its inducements and rewards enough to pull the other side solidly into the moderation outcome—without, however, selling out to the other side. That combination is called a two-handed strategy. Obviously, the uncertainty is great and the risk enormous.

Proposition 4: For effective negotiations to take place, moderation as a process needs to overcome moderation as a condition.

Proposition 4a: However, moderation as a process needs to be evaluated as it proceeds, to judge whether it contains the momentum necessary to qualify for continued inducements and, eventually, reach the stage of a condition.

Balancing the Tactics: Division versus Unity

No negotiating team is unified and homogeneous. Much theoretical discussion of negotiation assumes the contrary, usually in order to be able to make conceptual analyses, theoretical models, and generalized statements (Zeuthen 1968; Nash 1950; Rubenstein 1981). In fact, the dynamics within the sides and parties are usually as dramatic as those between parties (Anstey, Meerts, and Zartman 2010; Cunningham, Bakke, and Seymour 2010; Staniland 2010; Woldemariam 2010; Lilja 2010). Negotiations between the state and terrorists are adrift in this gray area, too. On one hand, both sides maintain the assumption of unity, and inside stories often confirm how centralized control is strongly asserted, as within the LTTE, the PLO, and Colombia's M-19 (Lilja 2010; Asencio and Asencio 1982). Dissenters are repressed, excluded, or eliminated. On the other hand, any progress toward negotiation with terrorists, particularly in strategic/political situations, depends on getting to some of the members of the other side and gradually winning them over, not to the state's opposing point of view but to the idea of negotiating at all. Moderation comes in pieces as well as in phases.

Negotiation is pact making. The party on one side makes a pact with a party on the other side to establish some sort of relationship and work together to maintain it. Neither party represents its whole side, but in the best cases the outliers simply fade away before the fait accompli. Both parties are linked by the agreement, with an obligation to each other and to themselves. In the first part, by their signature they pledge to honor and support each other in upholding the agreement and in selling it at home. Even before the agreement is signed, progress toward it depends on an implicitly repeated sense of requitement—the notion that concessions will be reciprocated and the process of moderation rewarded. In the second part, they pledge to themselves to represent the interests of their entire side and to convert or marginalize any other parts or parties of their own side that are left out of the agreement. In a telling example noted by both Pettyjohn and Höglund in their chapters, representatives from the Israeli Labor government and the PLO negotiated and signed an agreement made in Oslo in October 1993, to the exclusion of Hamas, making a pact designed to meet their own needs and interests, although neither party was able to deliver its side despite the implication that it would do so. The Colombian government and the moderate faction of FARC designed an agreement in the mid-1980s to engage the terrorists in national politics as the Unión Patriótica, and they would have won some elections had their candidates not been assassinated by right-wing militias. The militant wing of FARC drew its conclusions. The UN mediator brought together the various parties of Afghanistan in a *loya jirga* (national assembly) in Bonn in 2001 to set up a new state after the NATO invasion, to the exclusion of the Taliban and Pakistan. In Rwanda, the Arusha Agreement of 1993 was a pact between an unstable government and the Tutsi Rwandese Patriotic Front, to the exclusion of the genocidal Coalition for the Defense of the Republic, which thereafter spoiled the agreement. Earlier, the nationalist movements of Tunisia (the Neo Destour) and Algeria (the National Liberation Front), both labeled terrorists, negotiated with France to the exclusion of other nationalist organizations (the *fellagha* and the Algerian National Movement respectively), which the agreeing parties then colluded to eliminate.

Thus, negotiation over terrorism implies finding a moderate party on each side, making a deal and a pact between them, and then closing ranks and restoring unity on each side to carry out the deal. This is a major challenge in dealings between the state and political terrorist organizations. Negotiating tactics involve identifying and communicating with the moderate faction, engaging it and then negotiating with it, and then working discreetly with it to marginalize or co-opt outliers and spoilers not in the pact. On one hand, as in any situation, negotiation must not be conducted only with the most moderate fringe, with which agreement is easiest but which cannot carry its side; it must be a process of agreement between the major factions of both sides. On the other hand, it is unlikely that the whole side will be engaged in significant negotiations. In between, the negotiator must calculate a pact with a sufficiently moderate or moderatable part of the spectrum on the other side—often neither extreme but, rather, the middle of the side—that leaves an insignificant part of the side isolated as a spoiler. Of course, the state may simply negotiate a split with the extremists, co-opting one faction and defeating the rest, as Sri Lanka did with the LTTE and as may be a strategy in Afghanistan. There is no mathematical formula to help identify weights and positions in the spectrum, but the criteria for a successful negotiation and stable agreement are clear.[2]

> *Proposition 5: Negotiators begin by identifying and engaging central but moderatable parties among terrorists and then splitting their ranks to make a pact calculated to engage the majority of each side.*

> *Proposition 5a: However, faced with terrorists (and often governments) who maintain purpose and legitimacy by opposing engagement, negotiators must then close ranks of legitimacy again around a new policy of negotiation.*

Conclusion: Improving the Process

There is no theory of negotiating over terrorism. Such negotiations simply lie on the fragile, delicate edge of the possible and exemplify the most tentative aspects of the general negotiation process. Negotiations over terrorism are merely an extreme case of any negotiating situation. The decision to negotiate is uncertain, the opening positions are far apart, there is no zone of possible agreement between them, and the conflict is so conceived that there is no mutually hurting stalemate or sense of a way out. And terms of trade, joint sense of justice, and consensus on the nature of the problem and its solution—all elements in a formula for agreement—are absent. Yet these are the challenges that the negotiating process must overcome if it is to reach a successful outcome, whether merely an agreeing formula, a managing formula, or a resolving formula. Engagement is a slow process; it takes time to overcome suspicion and commitment on the other side and to weather the rebuffs that are bound to meet it at first. Awareness of these elements enables a better analysis of the conflict situations and a more successful venture into the difficult terrain of engagement.

There is no doubt that the overall strategy should be two-handed: carrots and sticks, fighting terrorism and offering terrorists a way out. To get to actual negotiations, the state must keep both hands active, protecting its population and combating terrorism to make it impossible as a means of achieving its goals, and at the same time offering credible inducements to pull terrorists away from their methods and way of thinking. The terrorists already use one hand, the violent one, and so would be well advised to extend the other as well.

There are lessons from this for both sides. On one of the two hands, opportunities do not look good unless the present course is blocked; therefore, the basis of an effective policy is a vigorous interdiction of terrorist acts. There is no condoning violent acts against innocent civilians, or acts designed "to create a state of terror" in the general public, to quote one of the definitions. At the same time, it is worth pointing out that terrorism fits into the notion of the nation-state and democratic governance. We hold that government represents the people and that policy emanates from the people, who are the source of its legitimacy. Therefore, the people as much as the government are combatants—and the ultimate policymakers. Of course, to attack and terrorize them only exacerbates their obduracy—a strategic mistake by the terrorists. And in that case—to close the circle of reasoning—government is all the more obliged to protect its legitimizing people from terrorist attack.

On the other hand, terrorists, like any other negotiating partner, must be bought off their current course by inducements, either to lower their ends or to change the means by which they seek to attain them. Loathsome though the terrorists or their methods may be, if one is to draw them away from their tactics and change their ways, they must be given something in exchange. Also, even though "root causes" are a long way from being the source of terrorism and so are not material for negotiations, it is wise to pay attention to contextual and structural conditions that lie behind the terrorists' response and make it understandable even though not condonable.

Clearly, it is better to engage whenever possible. Engagement is not a reward; it is a cheaper way of attaining one's goals, for both sides. Of course, states have to declare a nonnegotiation policy lest they invite blackmail; terrorists do not have this problem. Some terrorists, as repeated many times above, are absolutes who, in their current state of mind, are not open to negotiation. It is the state's challenge to move them to contingency and, if they are immovable, to isolate and defeat them. The chapters in this volume have focused on questions of when, how, and why. Hopefully, they have been useful in opening opportunities for reducing both extremism and its underlying grievances.

Notes

1. In references to terrorists, the masculine pronoun is used here simply because, in almost all cases, the principal terrorists and their colleagues are male (even though there are sometimes a few females in the group).

2. None of the increasing number of studies—largely quantitative—of agreement durability take this seemingly obvious element into account.

References

Anstey, March, Paul Meerts, and I. William Zartman. 2010. *To Block the Slippery Slope: Reducing Identity Conflicts and Preventing Genocide.* Oxford: Oxford University Press.

Asencio, Diego, and Nancy Asencio. 1982. *Our Man Is Inside.* Boston: Little, Brown.

Combalbert, Laurent. 2010. "Guidelines for Negotiating with Terrorists." In *Negotiating with Terrorists,* ed. Guy Olivier Faure and I. William Zartman. New York: Routledge.

Cronin, Audrey Kurth. 2008. *How Terrorism Ends: Understanding the Decline and Demise of Terrorist Campaigns.* Princeton, NJ: Princeton University Press.

———. 2009. "How Terrorist Campaigns End." In *Leaving Terrorism Behind: Individual and Collective Disengagement,* ed. Tore Bjørgo and John Horgan. London: Routledge.

Cunningham, Kathleen, Kristin Bakke, and Lee Seymour. 2010. "Shirts Today, Skins Tomorrow: The Effects of Fragmentation on Civil War Processes and Outcomes." Paper presented at the annual convention of the International Studies Association, New Orleans, Feb.

De Soto, Alvaro 1999. "Ending Violent Conflict in El Salvador." In *Herding Cats,* ed. Chester Crocker, Fen Osler Hampson, and Pamela Aall. Washington, DC: United States Institute of Peace Press.

della Porta, Donatella. 2009. "Leaving Underground Organizations: A Sociological Analysis of the Italian Case." In *Leaving Terrorism Behind: Individual and Collective Disengagement,* ed. Tore Bjørgo and John Horgan. London: Routledge.

Dorronsoro, Gilles. 2010. "Afghanistan: Searching for Political Agreement." Carnegie Endowment for International Peace, Apr. http://carnegieendowment.org/files/searching_polit_agreement.pdf (accessed Oct. 31, 2010).

Eisenstadt, Todd, and Daniel García. 1995. "Colombia: Negotiations in a Shifting Pattern of Insurgency." In *Elusive Peace: Negotiating an End to Civil Wars,* ed. I. William Zartman. Washington, DC: Brookings Institution Press.

Faure, Guy Olivier, and I. William Zartman, eds. 2010. *Negotiating with Terrorists.* London: Routledge.

Feste, Karen. 2010. *Terminate Terrorism: Framing, Gaming, and Negotiating Conflicts.* Boulder, CO: Paradigm.

Hayes, Richard, Stacey Kaminski, and Steven Beres. 2003. "Negotiating the Non-Negotiable: Dealing with Absolutist Terrorists." *International Negotiation* 8 (3): 451–67.

Höglund, Kristine, and I. William Zartman. 2006. "Violence by the State: Official Spoilers and Their Allies." In *Violence and Reconstruction*, ed. John Darby. Notre Dame, IN: Notre Dame University Press.

Homans, Charles. 1961. *Social Behavior: Its Elementary Forms.* New York: Harcourt, Brace and World.

Lilja, Jannie. 2010. "Disaggregating Dissent: The Challenges of Intra-Party Consolidation in Civil War and Peace Negotiations." PhD diss., Univ. of Uppsala.

Mahieu, Sylvie. 2007. "The Best Timing for a Ceasefire." *International Negotiation* 12 (2): 207–28.

Nash, John. 1950. "The Bargaining Problem." *Econometrica* 18 (2): 155–62.

Pruitt, Dean G., ed. 1997. "The Oslo Negotiations." Special issue, *International Negotiations* 2 (2).

Rubenstein, Ariel. 1981. "Perfect Equilibrium in a Bargaining Model." *Econometrica* 50 (1): 97–110.

Sayigh, Yazid. 2008. "Negotiation and Peace Processes." In *Perspectives on Radicalisation and Political Violence*, ed. Peter Neuman. Papers from the First International Conference on Radicalisation and Political Violence, London, Jan. 17–18.

Sisk, Timothy. 1995. *Democratization in South Africa.* Princeton, NJ: Princeton University Press.

Staniland, Paul. 2010. "Insurgent Fratricide, Ethnic Defection, and the Rise of Proto-State Paramilitaries." Forthcoming.

Stein, Janice Gross, ed. 1989. *Getting to the Table.* Baltimore, MD: Johns Hopkins University Press.

Tellis, Ashley. 2009. "Reconciling with the Taliban? Toward an Alternative Grand Strategy in Afghanistan." Carnegie Endowment for International Peace, Apr. http://carnegieendowment.org/files/reconciling_with_taliban.pdf (accessed Oct. 31, 2010).

UNSC. 2001. Resolution 1373, *Threats to International Peace and Security Caused by Terrorist Acts.* http://daccess-dds-ny.un.org/doc/UNDOC/GEN/N01/557/43/PDF/N0155743.pdf?OpenElement (accessed Oct. 27, 2010).

U.S. Code. 2001. *Definition of Terrorism under U.S. Law.* Title 22, US Code, §2656f(d). http://terrorism.about.com/od/whatisterroris1/ss/DefineTerrorism_5.htm (accessed Oct. 31, 2010).

Woldemariam, Michael. 2010. "Why Rebels Collide." PhD diss., Princeton Univ.

Zartman, I. William, ed. 1995. *Elusive Peace: Negotiating an End to Civil Wars.* Washington, DC: Brookings Institution Press.

————, ed. 2003. "Negotiating with Terrorists." Special issue, *International Negotiation* 8, no. 3.

————. 2005. *Cowardly Lions: Missed Opportunities to Prevent Deadly Conflict and State Collapse.* Boulder, CO: Lynne Rienner.

————. 2006. "Negotiating Internal, Ethnic and Identity Conflicts in a Globalized World." *International Negotiation* 11 (2): 253–72.

————. 2010. *Preventing Identity Conflicts Leading to Genocide and Mass Killings.* New York: International Peace Institute.

Zartman, I. William, and Tanya Alfredson. 2010. "Negotiating with Terrorists and the Tactical Question." In *Coping with Terrorism,* ed. Rafael Reuveny and William Thompson. Albany, NY: SUNY Press.

Zeuthen, Frederik. 1968. *Problems of Monopoly and Economic Warfare.* 2nd ed. London: Routledge and Kegan Paul.

About the Contributors

Aldo Civico is assistant professor in the Department of Sociology and Anthropology at Rutgers University and codirector of the Center for the Study of Genocide, Conflict Resolution, and Human Rights. He also directed the Center for International Conflict Resolution at Columbia University. During 2005–08, he facilitated talks between the Colombian government and the ELN guerrilla organization. In the 1990s, he was a senior policy adviser to the mayor of Palermo, Italy, and participated in the anti-Mafia social movement. He wrote *Las guerras de doble cero* (Bogotá: Intermedio, 2009) and "Portrait of a Paramiliary," in *Engaged Observers* (Rutgers University Press, 1997).

Moty Cristal, CEO of Nest Consulting, is an expert negotiator and crisis manager. He served in 1994–2001 in various official positions on negotiation teams with Israel's Arab neighbors. A retired lieutenant colonel with extensive operational experience, he lectures worldwide on crisis negotiation and complex crisis management. He teaches negotiations, international negotiations, and crisis management at Tel Aviv University and the Interdisciplinary Center in Herzelia and is a visiting scholar in leading negotiation institutions. He graduated from Bar-Ilan Law School and Harvard Kennedy School of Government and is completing his PhD at the London School of Economics.

William A. Donohue is Distinguished Professor of Communication at Michigan State University. His research interests include language and international dispute resolution, hostage negotiation, and divorce mediation. Dr. Donohue is a past president of the International Association for Conflict Management and is on the editorial boards of *Negotiation and Conflict Management Research,* the *Journal of Conflict Resolution,* and several other journals in the field of communication.

Guy Olivier Faure teaches and does research on international negotiation, conflict resolution, and strategic thinking and action. He is on the steering committee of PIN/Clingendael, a program linking 5,000 people involved in international negotiation. He has written, cowritten, or edited 16 books and over 100 articles. Recent publications include *How People Negotiate* (Kluwer Academic); *Negotiating with Terrorists: Strategy, Tactics, and Politics* (Routledge) and *Escalation and Negotiation* (Cambridge University Press), both with I. William Zartman; and *Culture and Negotiation* (Sage), with Jeffrey Rubin. His works have been published in twelve languages.

Carolin Goerzig is a postdoctoral fellow at the EUISS, within the framework of the Transatlantic Post-Doc Fellowship for International Relations and Security (TAPIR) program. Her University of Munich doctoral work on negotiating with terrorists has led her to complete field research in Colombia, Egypt, Syria, and Turkey. She has been a visiting researcher at the London School of Economics, a participant in the Young Scientists Summer Programme of the International Institute of Applied Systems Analysis in Austria, and a Marie Curie Fellow at the Department for Peace and Conflict Research at Uppsala University.

Maria Groeneveld-Savisaar is a PhD candidate at the University of Tartu, the Institute of Government and Politics. She received a BA in Political Science at the University of Tartu and an MA in International Relations and European Studies from the Central European University. In 2006–08, she worked as a political officer with the European Commission Delegation in Sri Lanka. In 2009, she was a visiting PhD candidate at Leiden University's Institute of Political Science. Her research focuses on military and political resistance in small states.

Kristine Höglund is associate professor in the Department of Peace and Conflict Research, Uppsala University, Sweden. Her research has covered issues such as the dilemmas of democratization in countries emerging from violent conflict, the causes and consequences of electoral violence, the importance of trust in peace negotiation processes, and the role of international actors in dealing with crises in war-torn societies. She is the author of *Peace Negotiations in the Shadow of Violence* (Martinus Nijhoff, 2008) and is currently coediting *Understanding Peace Research: Methods and Challenges* (Routledge, forthcoming 2011).

Maha Khan, a native of Pakistan, has seven years of experience conducting social policy research in Pakistan, East and West Africa, the UK, and the

United States. Her research has focused on social and gender inclusion and on violent extremism. She holds a master's degree in international relations and international economics, with a focus on conflict management, from the Johns Hopkins University School of Advanced International Studies (SAIS).

Robert Lambert is codirector of the European Muslim Research Centre (EMRC) at the University of Exeter and a lecturer at the Centre for the Study of Terrorism and Political Violence (CSTPV) at the University of St. Andrews. In January 2010, he was awarded a PhD for a research dissertation analyzing the legitimacy and effectiveness of police partnerships with Muslim community groups in London. In 2008, Lambert was made a member of the Order of the British Empire by HM The Queen in acknowledgment of his thirty-one years' service with the Metropolitan Police Service in London.

Camille Pecastaing is an assistant professor in the School of Advanced International Studies (SAIS) at the Johns Hopkins University. He leads the Behavioral Sociology Project at SAIS and participates in the Johns Hopkins Evolution, Cognition, and Culture Project. He researches and writes on the Muslim world, social and cultural evolution, identity systems, coalitional aggression, ethnic conflict, and terrorism.

Stacie L. Pettyjohn is an associate political scientist at the RAND Corporation. She was previously a TAPIR Fellow at the RAND Corporation, a Peace Scholar at the United States Institute of Peace, and a Research Fellow at the Brookings Institution. Her research has focused on U.S. foreign policy, terrorism, and deradicalization. She has published articles in *Security Studies* and *International Negotiation*.

Siniša Vuković is a PhD candidate at Leiden University's Institute of Political Science. He received a BA in Political Science and International Relations at the Sapienza University of Rome and an MA in International Relations and Diplomacy from Leiden University and Netherlands Institute of International Relations "Clingendael." His research focuses on comparative analysis of multiparty mediation processes. He has conducted research at the International Institute of Applied Systems Analysis (Laxenburg) as PIN's YSSP candidate and was a visiting research associate in the Conflict Management Program at Johns Hopkins University's School of Advanced International Studies.

I. William Zartman is the Jacob Blaustein Professor Emeritus at the School of Advanced International Studies (SAIS) of The Johns Hopkins University in Washington, and member of the Steering Committee of the Processes of International Negotiation (PIN) Program at Clingendael. His doctorate is from Yale (1956) and his honorary doctorate from Louvain (1997), and he received a lifetime achievement award from the International Association for Conflict Management. He is author of a number of books, including *Negotiation and Conflict Management*, The *Practical Negotiator, Ripe for Resolution* and *Cowardly Lions*. He is also president of the Tangier American Legation Institute for Moroccan Studies (TALIM), and was founding president of the American Institute for Maghrib Studies and past President of the Middle East Studies Association.

Index

United States
Institute of Peace Press

Since its inception, the United States Institute of Peace Press has published over 150 books on the prevention, management, and peaceful resolution of international conflicts—among them such venerable titles as Raymond Cohen's *Negotiating Across Cultures*; John Paul Lederach's *Building Peace*; *Leashing the Dogs of War* by Chester A. Crocker, Fen Osler Hampson, and Pamela Aall; and *American Negotiating Behavior* by Richard H. Solomon and Nigel Quinney. All our books arise from research and fieldwork sponsored by the Institute's many programs. In keeping with the best traditions of scholarly publishing, each volume undergoes both thorough internal review and blind peer review by external subject experts to ensure that the research, scholarship, and conclusions are balanced, relevant, and sound. With the Institute's move to its new headquarters on the National Mall in Washington, D.C., the Press is committed to extending the reach of the Institute's work by continuing to publish significant and sustainable works for practitioners, scholars, diplomats, and students.

Valerie Norville
Director

About the
United States Institute of Peace

The United States Institute of Peace is an independent, nonpartisan institution established and funded by Congress. The Institute provides analysis, training, and tools to help prevent, manage, and end violent international conflicts, promote stability, and professionalize the field of peacebuilding.

Chairman of the Board: J. Robinson West
Vice Chairman: George E. Moose
President: Richard H. Solomon
Executive Vice President: Tara Sonenshine
Chief Financial Officer: Michael Graham

Board of Directors